MAKING **REFUGE**

GLOBAL
INSECURITIES

A series edited by
Catherine Besteman and
Daniel M. Goldstein

MAKING
REFUGE

SOMALI BANTU REFUGEES
AND LEWISTON, MAINE

Catherine Besteman

DUKE UNIVERSITY PRESS   DURHAM AND LONDON   2016

Printed in the United States of America on acid-free paper ∞
Designed by Heather Hensley
Typeset in Minion Pro by Westchester Publishing Services

Library of Congress Cataloging-in-Publication Data
Besteman, Catherine Lowe, author.
Making refuge : Somali Bantu refugees and Lewiston, Maine /
Catherine Besteman.
pages cm—(Global insecurities)
Includes bibliographical references and index.
ISBN 978-0-8223-6027-8 (hardcover : alk. paper)
ISBN 978-0-8223-6044-5 (pbk. : alk. paper)
ISBN 978-0-8223-7472-5 (e-book)
1. Somalis—Cultural assimilation—Maine—Lewiston.
2. Somali diaspora.
3. Lewiston (Me.)—Ethnic relations.
I. Title. II. Series: Global insecurities.
E184.S67B47 2016
305.893'54074182—dc23 2015026280

Cover art: Lewiston, 2008. Photograph by Caroline Turnbull.

The writer and scholar A. C. Johnson insisted that the idea of community should include strangers. He said that interconnectedness is what takes place between the community and the stranger. One not only becomes a person through one's community but also through the stranger. To avoid the disasters of the past, Johnson said, the figure of the stranger ought to be continually reinvented, and it is the specific task of the intellectual in a society to be an advocate for the stranger—to insist on responsibility for the stranger as constitutive of collectivity itself.

—ANTJIE KROG, *Begging to Be Black*

CONTENTS

TERMS AND ABBREVIATIONS

adoon	Derogatory word for slave
Bartire	Subclan of the Darood clan family
clan	Kinship unit of Somali society
CPHV	Center for the Prevention of Hate Violence, based in Portland, now closed
Dadaab	Refugee camp in Kenya
Dagahalley	Part of Dadaab refugee camp
Darood	One of Somalia's five major clan-families
DHHS	Department of Health and Human Services
EBCO	Ethnic-based community organization
ELL	English language learner (used instead of English as a second language)
GA	General Assistance
Hawiye	One of Somalia's five major clan-families
Ifo	Part of Dadaab refugee camp
jareer	Literally, hard hair; racialized term that preceded the creation of the name Somali Bantu
jileec	Soft; used to describe non-jareer Somalis
Kakuma	Refugee camp in northern Kenya to which Somali Bantus accepted for U.S. resettlement were moved when conditions in Dadaab became too dangerous for them

Maay Maay	One of the two official languages of Somalia
Mushunguli	Ethnic group and language of minorities from lower Jubba Valley who are descendants of enslaved Ziguas brought to Somalia
NGO	Nongovernmental organization
ooji	Derogatory word for slave
ORR	Office of Refugee Resettlement, in the U.S. State Department
Rahanweyn	One of Somalia's five major clan-families
SBYAM	Somali Bantu Youth Association of Maine
TANF	Temporary Assistance to Needy Families
UNHCR	United Nations High Commissioner for Refugees
VOLAG	Voluntary agency, of which eleven are federally funded to resettle refugees

TIMELINE OF EVENTS

1991	Collapse of Siad Barre's government.
1991–93	Violence against civilians peaks in Jubba Valley region and villagers from Banta flee.
1992	Launch of Operation Restore Hope, a multinational humanitarian military intervention, followed in 1993 by UNOSOM, a U.S.-led UN-backed intervention.
1993	Black Hawk Down incident in Mogadishu and conclusion of UNOSOM.
1995	Some refugees in Dadaab return to Jubba Valley but many flee again for Kenyan refugee camps because violence is still pervasive.
1994–97	Somali Bantu refugees in Dadaab attempt to negotiate resettlement in Tanzania and Mozambique.
1999	United States agrees to accept 12,000 Somali Bantus for resettlement as "persecuted minorities."
2001	Reverification in Dadaab of Somali Bantu names on Mozambique list for U.S. P2 resettlement.
	Somali refugees already resettled in United States begin moving to Lewiston.
	Lewiston and Portland jointly receive an Unanticipated Arrivals grant (2001–5) from U.S. Office of Refugee Resettlement.

2002	Reverified Somali Bantus in Dadaab trucked to Kakuma.
	Mayor Raymond writes the Letter to Lewiston's Somali community.
	World Church of the Creator rallies to support Lewiston's right to bar entry for immigrants.
	Many and One Rally at Bates College opposes the Letter and the World Church of the Creator rally.
2004	Catholic Charities VOLAG agrees to provide services to refugees in Lewiston through the Unanticipated Arrivals grant.
	Somali Bantus begin arriving in United States.
2005	Somali Bantu families in United States begin relocating to Lewiston.
	Trinity Jubilee creates after-school homework help program targeting children from refugee families.
2006	Catherine and Jorge reconnect with old friends in Lewiston.
	U.S. Department of Justice mandates creation of ELL program in Lewiston public schools.
	Somali Bantu community association EBCO created.
2007	Somali Bantu EBCO wages campaign for self-representation and translation with social services providers.
	Mayor Gilbert elected.
2008	Maine Department of Health and Human Services assigns a supervisor the responsibility for overseeing refugees' benefits.
	Somali Bantu Youth Association of Maine created.
2009	International Clinic closed.
	Beth is hired by a local NGO to work on child development with ten refugee families.
	Local agency in charge of million-dollar federal empowerment zone grant denies all grant applications from refugee-based community groups but then reverses the denials and offers grant-writing workshops along with funding.
	Community collaborative subcommittee on parental concerns is disbanded after confrontational meeting between parents and school administrators.

Lewiston High School graduates the first four Somali Bantu students.

Museum LA *Rivers of Immigration* exhibit opens.

Local newspaper publishes article alleging Somali gang attacks in downtown Lewiston.

2010   Police department opens downtown substation with community resource officers.

Grief counselor allowed to offer a ten-week after-school program with ten boys from refugee camps who lost a family member.

Memo circulated to teachers and social services providers warning about Somali GANGS.

SBYAM oral history project with Somali Bantu teenagers and elders.

Advice for America conference.

First arrests of Somali Bantu youths.

SBYAM begins meetings between refugee parents, social services workers, and police about parental concerns.

2011   Robert Macdonald elected mayor.

2013   Robert Macdonald reelected mayor.

ACKNOWLEDGMENTS

Many thanks, first and foremost, for the friendship of and collaborative work with many refugee friends in Lewiston, Syracuse, Hartford, and elsewhere who so strongly encouraged this book project and who offered so much time, trust, and faith in me to ensure its completion. Unbounded gratitude to Rilwan Osman, Muhidin Libah, Abdulkadir Osman, Iman Osman, Asha Iman, Jimcoy Salat, Amina Caliyow, Ambiya Bulo, Jama Mohamed, Abdirisak Malin, Mohamed Farah, Abdi Maalin, Ibrahim Bashir, Bashir Osman, Nur Libah, Robiye Nur, Abdullahi Nur, Sahara Mahamed, Shobow Saban, Abdi Abdi, Ibrahim Abdulle, Mohamed Negeye, Abikar Gedi Gale, Haji Adan, Abdulkadir Matan, Rahima Deekow, Mohamed Deekow, Fatuma Mohamed, Ali Shangole, Omar Hussein Mayange, Hamadi Osman Mahamba, Abdullahi Mokema Mohina, Mberwa Sadik, Fatuma Hussein, Ismail Ahmed, Sahal Nur, Gure Ahmed.

For teaching me about social services and immigration policy in Maine and for sharing their work in Lewiston, thank you to Anne Kemper, Kim Wettlaufer, Julia Sleeper, Marc Robitaille, Craig Johnson, Bill Rousseau, Tom Murphy, Gillian Bourassa, Ellen Alcorn, Sherry Russell, Eileen Manglass, Gena Wilson, Alice Haines, Casey Nguyen, Qamar Bashir, Luke Nya, Arabella Perez, Mary Lafontaine, Pedro Rojas, Ben Chin, Catherine Yomoah, David Maclean, Holly Stover, Huda Daud, Inza Ouattara, Jeanne Hutchins, Lisa Sockabasin, Ron Taglienti, Noel Bonham, Danny Danforth, Rachel Degroseilleurs, Beth Stickney, Elizabeth Eames, Gus Leblanc, Pamela Ericson, Shayna Malyata, Roger Jack, Patricia MacKinnon, Caroline Sample, Cheryl Hamilton, Phil Nadeau, Larry Gilbert, Steve Wessler, Nancy Mullin, Susan Martin, Sue Charron, Leon Levesque, and others who will remain anonymous.

Many colleagues read part or all of the manuscript and kindly alerted me to oversights, weaknesses, and slippages. I am indebted to Daniel Goldstein, David Gordon, Rilwan Osman, Muhudin Libah, David Friedenreich, Mary Beth Mills, Heath Cabot, Winifred Tate, Chandra Bhimull, Ushari Mohamed, David Strohl, Britt Halvorson, Marnie Thompson, Erica Iverson, Dan Van Lehman, Sarah Shields, and two anonymous reviewers. Thanks as well to colleagues who talked through this project and associated papers with me, especially Janelle Taylor, Roger Sanjek, and Andrew Altschul. Remaining inaccuracies are, of course, my responsibility.

Chapter 1 is a revised version of "A Refugee Odyssey: A Story of Globalization and Somali Bantu Refugees," *Anthropology Now* 1, no. 2 (2009): 96–108.

For fellowships, residencies, and support during writing, I thank Eileen Gilooley and the Heyman Center of Columbia University, American Council of Learned Societies, the John Simon Guggenheim Memorial Foundation, Bellagio Center of the Rockefeller Foundation, John Torpey and the CUNY Graduate Center, Colby College, Maine Humanities Council, Suzanne Cusick, and the Princess. (And for the 1980s fieldwork and archival work I acknowledge with gratitude Sigma Xi, School of Advanced Research, National Endowment for the Humanities, American Philosophical Society, Wenner Gren Foundation, and the Land Tenure Center at the University of Wisconsin.)

Thanks to audiences at Colby College, Bates College, Bowdoin College, Tufts, Harvard, Columbia, CUNY Graduate Center, University of Washington, University of California at Berkeley, American University, University of Tennessee, St. Mary's, Bellagio Center, University of Colorado, School of Advanced Research, University of California–Irvine, Syracuse University, and Middlebury College, whose comments and questions prompted rethinking, revising, clarifying, or tossing out bad ideas altogether.

My family has been intimately involved in this book project in a multitude of ways. The love and support from the Besteman/Lauderbaugh/Pike/Wagenheim crowd is extraordinary. Jorge Acero, Gabriela Acero, and Darien Acero, who live in my heart, make this work possible.

Introduction

Somalia, 1988

As Ibrahim and I walked back to the small village of Banta on a narrow foot-path through fields tall with corn, a low growl silenced our chatter about the weather and the possibility of rain. We instantly fell silent and slowly turned to see an adult male lion stepping out of the corn onto the path about a dozen feet behind us, assessing us with what we hoped was little interest. We froze, panicked, understanding the real possibility of attack and the futility of attempting to run away. After looking us over, the lion tossed his head and crossed the path into another cornfield, disappearing from view but leaving us trembling with our hearts in our throats. Shocked, we exchanged astonished glances and quietly agreed to move as quickly as possible without running toward the village. Ten minutes later we came upon a village farmer in her field and breathlessly described to her our adventure. Her kids ran ahead with the news and by the time we reached the village our neighbors were gathering to hear all about our encounter with the lion. Xassan, the government-appointed head of the village and the patriarch of the family compound where I lived, was distinctly displeased and demanded that I stay within the confines of the village until the lion had left the area. We learned that the lion had already killed a camel and damaged several farms before our late afternoon face-to-face meeting. Our assault by a lion would have been a major headache for him.

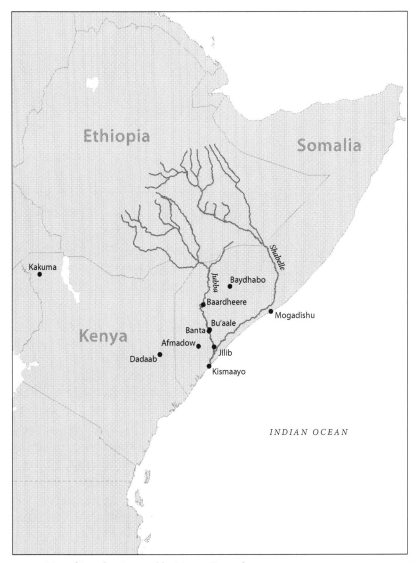

MAP 1 Map of Somalia. Prepared by Manny Gimond.

Everyone recognized that my year-long presence in his village caused him enough stress without having to explain to the government how he had allowed the resident foreign anthropologist and her field assistant to be mauled by a lion.

That evening, our neighbors Caliyow Isaaq, Cali Osman, and Cabdulle Cabdi came by to hear our story. Abdiya, who sometimes cooked our evening corn porridge when we were out all day, offered her comments on our adven-

FIGURE I.1 Banta, 1988. Photograph by Catherine Besteman.

ture. Within a few days the lion moved out of the area and I was once again allowed to roam through the farmlands and bush areas outside the village. Often my neighbors' children, who normally spent their days playing in the village and helping their parents in the fields, tagged along. Since the village had no school, the kids led fairly unstructured lives and put their time to good use making up games and songs, and poking holes through the walls of my mud hut to see what I was doing inside.

With my photographer husband, Jorge Acero, I lived in Banta, on the banks of the Jubba River in southern Somalia, as an anthropologist in 1987–88 and later published two books about life there.[1] The books relied heavily on what I learned from village elders: my friends Caliyow Isaaq, Cali Osman, Sheikh Axmed Nur, and those even older like the great historian Idow Roble and the delightful storyteller and poet Daliya. When my husband and I left Banta in 1988 to return to the United States, we promised we would revisit Banta in the years ahead to see how the children had grown, to find out who had married whom, and to meet the new children and grandchildren. We never had the chance because within three years the village was consumed by civil war.

Lewiston, Maine, 2010

Just over twenty years later, I attended an emergency meeting in a small dingy conference room in an ugly building in downtown Lewiston, Maine, to discuss claims in the local newspaper that violent gangs had formed in the city's downtown and public housing neighborhoods. Sitting around the table were a Lewiston police officer, several social workers, and my old neighbors from Banta, whose children were those accused of forming the gangs. Abdiya, who married Idow Roble's son and now has seven kids, sat on my right. Caliyow Isaaq's daughter Aliyah, who now has four sons, was on my left. Daliya's daughter, a mother of five, was next to Abdiya, and Abdiya's sister-in-law, mother of seven, was next to her. Other parents from villages near Banta were on the other side of the table. Cali Osman's son Idris, the community youth leader, had organized the meeting.[2]

The parents, distressed, were at the edge of their understanding about what was happening to their children. Their frustrations with navigating American society, their awareness that their children were stigmatized in Lewiston, and their fears about the impact on their children of the grotesque aspects of American culture filled the room. Sitting there, I couldn't help but reflect on the strange and unexpected journey that had brought Banta's war survivors to Lewiston, turned subsistence farmers into accused gang members, and unexpectedly reconnected Banta's refugees with their former ethnographer twenty years after they lost contact.

In January 1991, as Somalia's president-dictator Siad Barre fled the capital in a tank to escape from advancing oppositional militias, villagers in Banta did not realize that the collapse of the Somali government would bring murder, rape, starvation, kidnapping, and torture to their village. They did not realize that within a year they would be fleeing for their lives across hundreds of miles of desert to Kenya. They did not realize that, after enduring a decade and half in refugee camps, some of them would end up trying to rebuild their lives in the United States. The war arrived in Banta in the form of weapons acquired by some and used against others, of small bands of armed militias entering the village and demanding food, abducting youths, and raping and forcing girls into involuntary "marriages." The war made farming risky and food production insecure because of the possibility of attack in distant fields. It collapsed family coherence as militia members carted off daughters, killed fathers in front of their children, and raped mothers. It brought destruction to closely knit communities, extended family networks, subsistence farming based in generations of deep environmental knowledge, and a social order based on family, faith, and coresidence.

How do people whose entire way of life has been destroyed and who witnessed horrible abuses against loved ones construct a new future? How do people who have survived the ravages of war and displacement rebuild their lives in a new country when their world has totally changed? That is the story of this book.

Banta, 1980s

Since its collapse into civil war in 1991, Somalia has become the poster child for every bad keyword in the contemporary political lexicon: failed state, tribalism, mission creep, civil war, warlordism, Islamic fundamentalism, terrorism, refugees, piracy. From the 1990s through the second decade of the twenty-first century, Somalia has regularly appeared in the news as the worst humanitarian crisis in the world. The 1993 Black Hawk Down debacle, when eighteen U.S. troops were killed in a street fight in downtown Mogadishu by supporters of the warlord they were seeking, was a defining moment in shaping a more cautious future for American military intervention in complex political, military, and humanitarian emergencies. A decade and a half later, Somalia still capped the list of humanitarian disasters. Veteran political scientist Kenneth Menkhaus noted that during 2007–8 Somalia was the most dangerous area in the world for humanitarian workers, while Human Rights Watch identified Somalia as the "most ignored tragedy in the world." In 2008 and again in 2009, *Foreign Policy* magazine declared Somalia "The #1 Failed State" in its Failed States Index, a label echoed in a 2009 *New Yorker* article on Somalia called "The Most Failed State." Two decades after the collapse of Somalia's government, the advocacy group Refugees International and the Center for Strategic and International Studies continued to call Somalia "the worst humanitarian disaster in the world," and journalist James Fergusson labeled Somalia "the world's most dangerous place."[3] Out of a very competitive field of collapsed states, civil wars, refugee crises, and centers of terrorism, Somalia has topped everyone's list of humanitarian disasters since its civil war began in 1991.

Just a few years before Somalia's collapse, Jorge Acero and I arrived in Banta to begin our year of residence while I conducted the fieldwork that I hoped would result in my dissertation and PhD in anthropology. We were recently married and Jorge had agreed to come with me to rural Somalia for a year so long as we could squeeze in a side trip to Mt. Kilimanjaro and the Seychelles. Deal. We took up residence in two small mud huts included in the ring of small mud huts that formed the family compound of Xassan Isaaq, the head of the village. Our compound included Xassan's two wives, their three sons and a baby daughter, one daughter-in-law, and a granddaughter. Occasionally another daughter or grandchild or two would move into the compound for a few weeks or months as well. Because Xassan was the village head, he made it clear that we were living in his compound so he could monitor who had access to our dwelling and attempt to ensure our safety. It was a busy compound, as much village business took place in our courtyard and people regularly streamed in

FIGURE I.2 Xassan's compound, Banta, 1987. Photograph by Jorge Acero.

and out to discuss their troubles, feuds, and gossip. The village committee of elders held their meetings in the courtyard, and the rare visiting government official was received there. While living in Xassan's compound enabled him to monitor my activities, it also ensured I stayed current with village events.

Village life adhered to the rhythm of the seasons, farming, and religious practice. Banta's five hundred residents lived in an assortment of small round and rectangular huts made of grass and mud. Separated into two neighborhoods by a central grassy field where kids played, the village overlooked the Jubba River, high and swift in the rainy season and low and muddy in the dry season. The river provided water for drinking, cooking, and bathing, and its annual floods fertilized the small farming fields, although flood season also brought the dangers of wandering crocodiles and hippos. As is typical in many African farming villages, extended families shared living spaces, food, cooking, child care, work, and the few material possessions owned by each family. Women hauled water from the river, made charcoal from branches gathered from the bush to fuel the fire for cooking pots, and wove the beautiful palm mats that adorned most huts. Men and women farmed their small plots by hand, built their homes from local materials, and bartered their produce for meat and milk with nomadic livestock herders. Healers made medicinal treatments from local flora, and men carved the wooden vessels villagers used for drinking and storing water, used alongside the ubiquitous brightly colored plastic jerry cans imported from China. Small children wore shorts or T-shirts or loose frocks; adults had one or two outfits that they wore to shreds. Every household had a few short-handled hoes, the primary piece of farming equipment used by villagers, as well as a few cooking and eating utensils. Everyone subsisted on what they grew on their small farms, which produced a modest and sometimes insufficient diet of cornmeal porridge, corn kernels fried in sesame oil, corn kernels boiled with beans and served with oil and sugar, cornmeal biscuits baked in underground ovens, wild greens and volunteer cherry tomatoes sautéed in oil, and bartered camel and cow milk as well as the occasional roasted camel, cow, chicken, or goat meat consumed at feasts and ritual events.

As the resident anthropologist and photographer, Jorge and I did our best to adapt to local life, conforming to village norms, eating a steady diet of corn prepared in a variety of ways, drinking and bathing in the water hauled from the muddy Jubba River, and cultivating our own tiny garden. Every week we would drive into Bu'aale, the local town and provincial capital, for provisions like oil, sugar, pasta, rice, and coffee, usually bringing along a car full of villagers doing the same thing. Everywhere we went, small gangs of kids followed us, since we were the only local oddities and undoubtedly offered comic appeal with our novelty and awkwardness. Whereas the villagers' lives followed the demands of subsistence farming, ours followed the requirements of anthropological inquiry. Jorge documented village life through his camera lens, gaining minor celebrity status as the area's sole photographer and producing a large collection of formal portraits, taken at the request of villagers, in addition to hundreds of photographs of village life. I spent my days walking the farmlands to map land use patterns, interviewing elders to chronicle local history of the Jubba Valley, and chatting with neighbors to grasp local customs and social relations.

A primary goal of anthropological fieldwork is to gain an understanding of how those being studied make sense of their world. My year in Banta taught me a great deal about how a small community dependent on subsistence farming engages their environment and relies on networks of mutual care and support to weather the droughts and celebrate the times of plenty, how people marginalized by poverty, history, and identity navigate the power hierarchies that constrain their lives, and how people who live at the edge of material destitution find much to value, celebrate, love, and enjoy in their daily lives. I learned about the power of kinship, the joy of religious belief and practice, and the humiliation of racism. Most presciently, however, I learned how people manage in a social and physical environment defined by profound insecurity.

During my stay, a brutal climate and total dependence on seasonal rains for cultivation made food production, and thus nutrition, insecure; a system

FIGURE I.3 Handwoven mats at Sheikh Axmed Nur's compound for Xawo's wedding, 1988. Photograph by Jorge Acero.

FIGURE I.4 Pastoralist girl bartering milk, Banta, 1987. Photograph by Jorge Acero.

FIGURE I.5 The anthropologist in her kitchen, Banta, 1987. Photograph by Jorge Acero.

FIGURE I.6 Jorge Acero taking portraits in Banta, 1987. Photograph by Catherine Besteman.

of medical care dependent on local traditional healers and prayer made childbirth and recovery from everyday illnesses like malaria, gastrointestinal troubles, and respiratory diseases insecure; a predatory military and urban elite made self-sufficiency insecure; and the perilous creatures with whom villagers shared their landscape—hippos, crocodiles, lions, pythons—made mundane tasks like drawing water, bathing, weeding, and walking to the distant farms insecure. But these insecurities did not emerge from the barrel of a gun. The invasion of the village by armed militiamen in 1991 destroyed the fine balance of self-reliance and reciprocity that had long sustained village life.

Jorge and I were living in New Mexico when Somalia fell apart. As I was finishing my doctoral dissertation about life in the Jubba Valley, we watched from afar in 1990–91 as the government collapsed in the face of growing opposition and armed militias claimed control over large swaths of territory throughout the country. Our only personal source of news about Banta's fate came in letters from the few international humanitarian workers who remained in the area during the first few months of the war. The final letter we received before the relief workers evacuated reported that almost all the children under the age of five in Banta had died from starvation, and that our field assistant Ibrahim had been shot trying to reach the relief center, which had promised to evacuate him. He had not arrived at the relief center by the time the final relief workers left. After we lost our last local contact, we followed the reports from 1992 to 1994 by human rights groups on the patterns of genocidal violence in Jubba Valley villages by militias and the flight of tens of thousands of survivors across the border into Kenya.

Unable to track what was happening in Banta and uncertain about how to translate my intimate knowledge of life in the valley into anything useful in the face of war's wrenching violence, I wrote furiously for a decade, pouring my knowledge into publications about the structures of inequality and racism that made the Jubba Valley villagers particularly vulnerable in the war for territorial control that followed the collapse of the government.[4] I could not imagine how I might reconnect with the survivors from Banta. Searching the huge refugee camps for people I knew seemed voyeuristic and pointless, as I had no ability to offer meaningful assistance or support. Writing became my form of activism and engagement, although it remained unclear whether anyone cared or how my accounts might benefit those fleeing for their lives.

In early 2001, after I had published my research on Somalia, taken up a teaching position at Colby College in Maine, and temporarily relocated to South Africa to begin a new research project on reconciliation and postapartheid transformation, a researcher and former UN staffer named Dan Van Lehman contacted me with the information that the United States had decided to accept 12,000 Somali Bantus for resettlement. Since my publications had been useful in making the case for their resettlement, he asked if I would consult on a background report he and his colleague Omar Eno were writing to educate the American refugee resettlement agencies that would be managing the resettlement process.[5] I was initially mystified by the name "Somali Bantu" until Dan explained that this was the new name for the former farmers from the Jubba Valley, created in the refugee camp for the process of managing their resettlement process. This was stunning news, as I belatedly learned that after a decade in refugee camps, Jubba Valley farmers who had fled the war were coming to the United States under a brand new name! After returning to Maine in 2004, I provided consultancy services for several different resettlement agencies across the country, hoping that these connections might help me locate survivors from Banta, but to no avail.

Lewiston, Maine, 2006

Every year for Martin Luther King Day, Bates College in Lewiston, Maine, just an hour from where I live, organizes panel presentations and other events on diversity for the broader community. In anticipation of the 2006 MLK celebration, Bates College anthropologist Elizabeth Eames phoned to ask if I would join a panel of Lewiston's newest immigrants, Somali Bantu refugees who were just starting to arrive in town, augmenting the large population of Somali refugees who had begun moving to Lewiston in 2001. My role on the panel would be to provide a bit of historical information about Somalia's civil war, after which several of the newly arrived refugees would share parts of their stories. I eagerly agreed, hoping the new arrivals might bring news of villagers from Banta, although a familiar feeling of bitterness complicated my anticipation of the panel. I knew from the human rights reports about the horrors committed by Somali militias against Jubba Valley farmers and suspected it was extremely unlikely that I would ever again encounter anyone I knew from the middle valley, where Banta was located. The reports from the resettlement agencies that contacted me in 2004–5 for background information about the Jubba Valley suggested that the majority of the 12,000 Somali Bantu refugees accepted for resettlement came from the lower Jubba Valley, so I assumed few refugees from the middle valley, where Banta was located, would be among them. While I wished to offer what I could to Somali Bantus now living in the United States, I expected a familiar pang of resentment that the people I had known would not be among them.

On MLK Day I arrived early at Bates and went to the designated classroom to wait for the appointed time, thinking over my commentary and steeling myself to remain in control of my emotions. Danny Danforth from the Bates

Anthropology Department found me sitting there alone and invited me out to the building's large atrium, where the other panelists were assembled. I introduced myself to the four men and asked one—Sadiq, who had the best English—where he was from in Somalia. "Bu'aale," he answered, to my astonishment. Bu'aale, a dozen kilometers away from Banta and the regional capital of the middle Jubba Valley, was the destination for our weekly shopping trip for extra provisions during our stay in Banta. "Do you know Banta?" I asked. "Of course!" he responded. "I used to live in Banta." Another of the panelists excitedly said, "You know Banta? I'm from Banta! I lived there my entire life!" I explained that I knew Banta because I had once lived there too, in the late 1980s. The men scrutinized me dubiously and said, "We don't know you, but we knew Katrine and Horay and we are waiting to find them." "But I'm Katrine!" I exclaimed. Words came tumbling out as we clarified who we were. The men had been teenagers when we lived in Banta: Jorge and I had helped the mother of one of the men, who was ill during our stay. The man from Bu'aale had been part of that small group of boys who used to follow us around town when we did our shopping. They protested that I looked so much older—I now wear glasses! They had never seen my hair, which had always been covered with a headscarf in Banta. And, distressingly, they pointedly noted how much weight I had gained. Within minutes it was time for our panel presentation.

The presentation passed in a daze. I introduced some Somali history and the history of U.S.-Somali relations, and then each panelist spoke briefly about his experiences during the war. The stories were horrible, of attacks by militias and raiders, who separated the women and girls from the men in order to assault them; of families being separated as they ran through the bush to escape from attacks; of parents, siblings, children being murdered before their eyes for no reason; of the long, terrifying trek to the Kenyan border. The packed room was captivated as each man told his harrowing tale and spoke of the challenges of establishing a sustainable life in the United States with limited English language and literacy skills. Driving home, I was almost numb. It seemed cosmic that refugees from Banta should end up an hour away from me, in central Maine.

The phone calls began the next day. Abkow, the panelist from Banta, and Sadiq, the man from Bu'aale, told me about all the other families from Banta now relocating to Lewiston. Cali Osman's wife Isha had recently arrived in Lewiston with her youngest son, Idris, and several other children. When they heard the news that Jorge and I were also living in Maine, Isha said, "I knew we would find Katrine!" Abdulkadir, who had worked for me in Banta as a field researcher, was in Lewiston with his wife and children. Everyone was asking about the baby I was carrying when I left Banta in 1988. They had heard rumors that it was a girl called Faduma Banta. "Bring her to Lewiston!" Isha commanded through Sadiq. "I want to see that child!"

The coincidence of this reunion brought me back into a new relationship with the people from Banta, 7,000 miles and twenty years away from where we first met, and led to the work toward this book. Over the past decade I have traversed the United States reconnecting with Banta villagers and others from the middle Jubba Valley in their new homes in Hartford, Syracuse, Seattle, and Portland, Oregon. In Lewiston I have spent countless hours with Sadiq, Isha, and especially her son Idris, Abdulkadir, and others, learning about what happened to them in Banta during the war and in the camps after they fled. I have been reminded of Somali cultural practices like extraordinarily democratic community gatherings where people get to talk for as long as they want about whatever is most important to them, and everyone listens with respect—one dimension among many of a profound orientation toward communal life that is under siege in a country known for individualism. I have witnessed countless struggles over the transformation of communal practices and values: the bewilderment of parents bringing up children American Style in a context of extreme consumerism, the concerns over transforming gender roles as women gain independence from male control and men's understanding of their roles begins to falter, the new identity associations that result from being black in America, and the shifting of authority from elders to youths because of the latter's vastly superior English language and literacy competency.

My research has also made me a witness to the struggles and efforts of many non-Somali people in Lewiston who now orient their lives toward working with refugees, including doctors, social services workers, and teachers, as well as community police officers who, in the words of one of their leaders, strive to "police from the heart." Their belief that the future of refugees in Lewiston is the future of Lewiston contrasts with the stolid insistence by some in positions of power that they will not change their institutions to accommodate refugees because of their view that refugees must follow a path of conformity and assimilation. My research reveals that assimilation is not a one-sided affair, however, and that the refugees in Lewiston are changing all aspects of the city for everyone.

"The Armpit of Maine"

Lewiston, Maine, seems like an unlikely destination for African refugees. A postindustrial city, economically ravaged by the closure of mills that a century ago drew tens of thousands of French Canadians to the area for work, Lewiston has a recent history of population loss and economic depression. People leave Lewiston rather than move there. Yet, beginning in 2001, thousands of Somali refugees looking for safety, a low cost of living, financial support, and a way to re-create community support structures chose to move to Lewiston of their own accord, dramatically transforming the city over the next decade. Their arrival provoked furious debates about the cost of poor immigrants to Lewiston's precarious economy and the impact of cultural and racial difference on the city's proud Franco-American identity. Before the 2001 arrival of Somalis, Lewiston was 96 percent white and "the most Franco city in the U.S."[6] By the end of the decade, Somalis had become about 15 percent of the population, and the changes they brought to the city were everywhere in evidence, from the school hallways to the city's main street.

Lewiston was totally unprepared for the influx of Somali refugees since city leaders had never indicated to anyone that the city wanted to become a resettlement site for new immigrants. But after arriving in the United States, refugees are as free as anyone else to move where they wish. When Somali refugees decided to move to Lewiston, arriving weekly between 2001 and 2006, their presence provoked massive controversy about economic security, charity, moral responsibility, difference, and the boundaries of community, debates fueled in intensity by the bright lights of major media coverage about the apparent incongruity of Africans in Maine. That Lewiston should become home to thousands of Somali refugees struck many observers as incredible and astonishing, bringing the spotlight of national and international media attention to a city unused to being the object of interest. Journalists from major news magazines such as the *Economist*, *Newsweek*, the *New Yorker*, and *Mother Jones*, as well as from leading newspapers, TV news programs, and National Public Radio programs, regularly showed up in Lewiston to see the social experiment for themselves.

The city of about 35,000 is an old mill town built largely by Catholic French Canadians who came to work low-paid, physically demanding jobs in the textile and shoe mills over a century ago. Settling into an ethnic enclave of tenement buildings that now form the core of Lewiston's downtown, the French Canadian immigrants held the lowest-paid jobs, occupied the lowest economic strata, and experienced persistent economic insecurity, discrimination, and exclusion from the local hospitals and schools that were dominated by the city's more prosperous Protestant population.[7] Since the late 1880s, Lewiston has been burdened by hostile and denigrating attitudes toward its mill-working citizenry because of its relative poverty and the perceived ethnic insularity of its Catholic Franco-American population. When the late twentieth-century wave of deindustrialization closed the mills, Lewiston started losing its youth to more prosperous places, and few immigrants chose Lewiston as their new home, leading to decades of population loss (a 15 percent drop between 1970 and 2000),[8] a rise in apartment vacancies, a flat-lining of the economy, and the identification of Lewiston's downtown area as the poorest census tract in Maine, with a poverty rate of 46 percent.[9] Prior to 2000, the city held the dubious distinction of having the lowest family and per capita income in the state. The arrival of thousands of refugees beginning in 2001 thus could be viewed as an assault on an already struggling city or as a force of renewal.

Despite the city's waning fortunes, the people who lived there continued to share a stubborn, tough pride about their community and its hardscrabble history. During his tenure as the first Franco-American governor of Maine, Paul LePage often recounted his hard childhood as a boy living on the streets of downtown Lewiston to escape his abusive mill-worker father, whose drunken rages became regular assaults on his wife and eighteen children. In LePage's account, his survival depended on the kindness of Lewiston's prostitutes, strippers, tavern keepers, and others living on the edge, reinforcing the image of Lewiston as a place of rough living, marginal lives, and a dysfunctional Franco-American underclass while at the same time offering a model of Franco-American assimilation and upward mobility through determination and hard work. A teacher in Lewiston who doesn't live there shared her view, which I also heard from many others, that downtown Lewiston has always been a place of poverty, insularity, and expectations of failure, suspicious of outsiders, anti-intellectual, and resistant to ideas coming from the outside, a pattern reinforced generation after generation and becoming the city's stereotype. Describing the experiences of her Somali junior high students who come to school with tales of drunken fights, domestic assaults, and middle-of-the-night police raids in the downtown apartments of their non-Somali neighbors, she worries that the historic cycle of downtown violence and failure will also engulf them. The principal of a downtown elementary school tells me that Lewiston's downtown has always had a terrible reputation for "groups involved with drugs, having fights, in the news. It's always the downtown. Those 'downtown families' have always been in the media as an image of disgrace and deviance." The schoolteacher wonders if the arrival of a large Somali population might be the wedge that breaks the cycle, or if the newcomers will be absorbed by old patterns of poverty, insularity, and failure.

Lewiston's strip malls tell the contemporary economic story of the city, anchored by Save-A-Lot, Chapter 11 Buy-Back Store, Dollar Tree, Dollar Store, Family Dollar, Big Lots, Big Bargains, and the Goodwill Store. Next to the Save-A-Lot mall at the crest of the hill overlooking the downtown, the view of the city is dominated by the huge cathedral, rising above the multitude of houses like a gray anchor. A river weaves around downtown, giving the panorama a serene New England feel. Continuing down the hill toward downtown, one passes the Italian Bakery on the left and Maillot's Sausage Factory on the right, incongruously stuck between the school bus yard and a new mosque. Lewiston's downtown tenements begin after you pass Head Start and the Tri-County Mental Health building, evoking historic visions of industrial workers crowded into derelict four- and five-story walk-ups. Rows upon rows of tenements are squeezed together, with listing front porches and yards holding assorted broken toys, frayed and dirty blankets, and garbage. Every few blocks one or two tenements are boarded up as uninhabitable because of high lead levels or massive disrepair, and vacant lots bear evidence of tenements burned to the ground in recent arson attacks. In the morning or early afternoon, streams of kids walking to or from school hold up traffic, sometimes walking alongside adults heading to Adult Education, which shares the building with the downtown neighborhood's elementary school.

The large park in the middle of the downtown neighborhood offers basketball courts where lots of Somali and non-Somali kids play, a skate park where no Somali kids play, and large grassy areas where groups of moms and kids or men lounge in the warmer months. Trinity Jubilee, the downtown soup kitchen, food pantry, help center, and day shelter, sits at one corner of the park, its muddy courtyard filled with men and women smoking and hanging out because they have no place else to be. Some of the city's most derelict housing neighbors Trinity, with filthy windows, broken front doors, perilously dipping porches. The city's police station borders another side of the park, ensuring a constant police presence in the densely settled neighborhood. In addition to the two large public housing projects on the outskirts of the city, Hillview and Tall Pines, the downtown neighborhood has the highest concentration in the city of immigrant refugees and is the place where the newest refugees usually settle while waiting for an opening in the nicer outlying housing projects.

After I began to spend several days a week in Lewiston following the MLK reunion to reconnect with old friends from Banta and begin the research for this book, acquaintances elsewhere in Maine offered a number of pithy descriptions of my new field site, the city colloquially called "the armpit of Maine" by people who don't live there. One incredulous colleague, shaking her head at my plan to undertake a long-term study in Lewiston, warned, "Lewiston is a snakepit." Holding his hands together in a tight ball, another colleague reminded me, "Lewiston is like this. It's always been this totally closed place, where people don't want anything to do with outsiders. They want to *keep people out*. It's a place with a strong Franco history, very insular, self-isolating. They don't want anything to do with the rest of the world. It's like a little world

FIGURE I.7 Downtown Lewiston, 2008. Photograph by Caroline Turnbull.

unto itself." Friends offered condolences that I had to spend so much time there. But for Somali and Somali Bantu refugees looking to create a new community in an affordable place unmolested by the crime they experienced in the large city public housing projects where they first landed after arriving in the United States, Lewiston seemed to offer what they wanted.

By 2010, Lewiston's main downtown street, Lisbon Street, offered a striking portrait of a city in the midst of transformation. Entering downtown, one passes the Adult Bookstore, ironically located directly across from the police station, and then a clothing store for outdoorsmen before reaching the first of the business blocks, beginning with Smart Interpreters, which offers English-Somali language translation services, followed by the Safari Coffee Shop and the African Immigrants Association office. The Mogadishu Store, the Barawaka Store, and a dozen more Somali-owned stores take up the next few blocks, their entrances and sidewalks always filled with men chatting in Somali. My favorite store, Aliyow's, carries products available in many of the nearly two dozen Somali-owned shops: coffee with ginger, samosas, spices, fabrics, colognes, halaal meat, and lots of packaged foods labeled in Arabic. Across from Aliyow's, one of the Somali cafés does a bustling business, scenting the street with roasting vegetables and spices. Interspersed between the Somali stores are older stores and offices: lawyers' offices, the Lewiston-Auburn

FIGURE I.8 Lisbon Street, Lewiston, 2014. Photograph by Jorge Acero.

arts collaborative, (former) U.S. congressman Mike Michaud's office, a pawn shop, a Subway shop, Doucette Insurance, Twin Variety, New Beginnings Youth Outreach office, and Labor Ready training center. A large empty lot breaks up the blocks of shops, adjoining a tall skinny building that houses all sorts of community organizations and lawyers' offices, including the Somali Bantu community association.

The corner in front of the public library, across from the vacant lot, is filled every afternoon with boisterous high school kids—mostly girls in hijab sparkling with sequins and bright colors—making their way to their after-school homework help sessions. The library is always full of people, as it is one of the only places in town that intentionally embraced Somali newcomers with afternoon programming and a Somali-speaking outreach coordinator. All along Lisbon Street women in sandals, long dresses, henna tattoos, and headscarves stroll along calling out to each other, chatting or snapping at the men gathered in front of every Somali store.

At the far end of the street, past the Indian restaurant, the bank, the district court, more lawyers' offices, and several empty storefronts, is the fanciest restaurant in town, next to the Somali mosque. White lawyers in business suits pass Somali girls in hijab and white teenagers in tattered clothes and multiple piercings, while bank workers in sensible pumps and raincoats walk alongside men in sarongs or floor-length garments on their way to the mosque. There are always lots of vans of Somali shoppers maneuvering the narrow street to reach their destinations. Lisbon Street feels like the active main street of a small city, with everyone going about their business in the midst of conversations and playing kids, like any town anywhere in America.

Reunions

After the MLK panel reunion, I asked Abkow and Sadiq if the Banta families living in Lewiston would like to see some of the slides and photographs Jorge had taken during our year in Banta. Our collection of photographs included hundreds of elegantly posed formal portraits, many in black and white, that the villagers had requested of themselves during our stay, but also hundreds of candid shots of villagers farming, cooking, playing, building homes and furniture, getting married, celebrating, shelling, pounding and grinding corn and sesame, and more. We had scores of photos of other midvalley villages, shots of the river and farm fields in different seasons and of local flora and fauna, and images of the local pastoralists who migrated through the bush outside Banta, bringing into the village their milk to trade for corn or their animals to access the river. We also had tape recordings of the wedding music for the marriage of Caliyow Isaaq's son to Sheikh Axmed Nur's daughter, as well as recordings of Cali Osman reciting poetry and playing his flute.

Abkow and Sadiq responded that the Banta families in Lewiston wanted to arrange the slide show as soon as possible. After Anne Kemper, the coordinator of the Adult Learning Center in Lewiston, offered the large gymnasium in Lewiston's Multipurpose Center for the gathering, a date was chosen and announcements went out to the Somali Bantu population in Lewiston. Jorge and I spent every evening for the next two weeks reviewing our slides from Banta to compile our show, remembering names, places, family networks, and the mundane rhythms of daily life in a small farming village. As the day of the event approached, I became increasingly nervous about what emotions the photographs might provoke. Would people become overwhelmed by seeing what they had lost? Or would the photographs provide joyful remembrance of happy moments and loved ones no longer alive? What if seeing the photographs provoked trauma and people broke down during the event? We were uncertain about how to plan for such a possibility.

I phoned Abkow and Sadiq with my concerns, but they responded that everyone wanted to see the photographs, even though some of those featured might be dead, stressing that the photographs of their past lives would not add any more trauma to what people had already endured. Rather, everyone was eager to see the photographs and to remember their lives before the war. As we prepared our slide show, our anxiety mounted as we wondered whether we would be able to remember everyone accurately, whether people might come whom we were not expecting, whether there would be rage, tears, despair. I no longer had any aptitude in the Somali language and was chagrined and embarrassed that I could no longer speak to people I used to communicate with. On the day before the event, I finally unearthed my census data from Banta and typed up the names of everyone by household who was living there in 1987–88. The evening was devoted to making large display posters of the census, along with mounted prints of black-and-white portraits of Banta residents.

On the day of the event, over a hundred people streamed into the gymnasium. As people arrived and we found mutual recognition in each other's aged faces, it was a shock to realize how short everyone was; in my memories they were all tall and strong and dignified. When I embraced Isha, her head barely reached my chest. She immediately asked to see the child I was carrying in Banta, now a nearly adult eighteen-year-old, whom she hugged hard and long. I couldn't keep my eyes dry. Isha was with a large group of children and grandchildren, depending on her youngest son, Idris, for translation. He was four when we lived in Banta and I remember him as a quiet, shy child, but standing before me was an obviously bright, thoughtful, competent young man speaking excellent English. An older man arrived, catching my eye over the crowd—Axmed Baraki, who was married to Binti, one of my first friends in Banta. Our poster included a photograph of Binti and their son; both are now dead. The nephew of Sheikh Axmed Nur arrived, and I showed him the elegant black-and-white portrait of his uncle. The nephew gave us the news that Sheikh Axmed Nur was still living in the refugee camp in Kenya, hoping that his family reunification application would one day allow him to join his children in the United States.

The son of our neighbor and dear friend Cabdulle Cabdi was one of the first through the door. Iman was just a baby when we lived in Banta and had no memory of his parents, who died when he was a toddler. Nor did he remember his dead grandfather, caught in a stately pose by Jorge's camera. Iman examined their photos, searching for his likeness in their faces.

FIGURE I.9 Sheikh Axmed Nur, Banta, 1988. Photograph by Jorge Acero.

Daliya's daughter arrived and burst into tears upon discovering our portrait of her dead mother sifting corn. Everyone started naming those captured in the portraits: Ganuun is dead. Although Caliyow Isaaq is dead, his only surviving wife, Jimcoy, is in Maine. One of his other wives, Amina, is dead, but their daughter Binti, caught on camera as a delightfully happy baby, now lives in the United States. Matan Garad is dead but his son Abdulkadir, who as a teenager worked as my field assistant collecting harvest information and measuring farms, now lives in Lewiston as a married father of eight. Khalar! Our old friend Khalar is still alive but living in extreme poverty outside Banta. As the names from the census were read aloud for those who could not read, people started calling out their fates. People continued arriving as the tape of wedding music played in the background, and someone informed us that the wedding couple, Mohammed and Xawo, now lived in Hartford. Because so many women were weeping openly as they listened, I asked if we should turn off the music. No! they protested, insisting they wanted to hear it to enjoy the memory of marriage rituals in the village.

FIGURE I.10 Iman Osman as a baby in his mother's arms in Banta, 1987. Photograph by Jorge Acero.

FIGURE I.11 Iman Osman as a teenager in Lewiston, 2008. Photograph by Elizabeth Milliken.

FIGURE I.12 Daliya sifting corn, Banta, 1988. Photograph by Jorge Acero.

FIGURE I.13 Amina Cabdulle and Binti Caliyow Isaaq, Banta, 1988. Photograph by Jorge Acero.

FIGURE I.14 Abdulkadir Matan Garad with his niece and nephew, Banta, 1988. Photograph by Jorge Acero.

FIGURE I.15 Abdulkadir Matan Garad in his Lewiston apartment with some of his children, looking at a copy of the photograph in figure I.14, 2009. Photograph by Catherine Besteman.

FIGURE I.16 Mohamed Caliyow Isaaq and Xawo Sheikh Axmed Nur, Hartford, 2009.
Photograph by Catherine Besteman.

Finally it was time to begin the slide show and the audience quieted, en-
grossed, as they struggled to make sense of the photographs and the faces
frozen as they were eighteen years before. I recalled when we first offered
photographs as gifts during our stay in Banta and discovered that people had
no idea what they were seeing; making sense of the small images was challenging to many who were unaccustomed to likenesses of any kind. Jorge reminded me that people were often disturbed by photographs that didn't show
the entire body or that had funny angles that distorted people's bodies, such as
a photograph—which we thought was beautiful—of Iman's cousin, our young
neighbor Marian, weaving a mat, that everyone derided as making her look
like an ant because of the angle.

As people got used to what they were seeing, they asked to repeat the
entire show a second time, this time calling out names to identify those appearing on the screen. The photograph of Abshirow, stylishly dressed in his
velvet jacket, standing with his wife Muslimo and baby son, evoked shrieks:
"Look how dressed up he looks, standing in front of his *mundul* [round
house made of mud and grass]," someone yelled out. Abshirow and his family were resettled in Texas, but, like many other survivors from Banta, later
moved to Lewiston. A photograph of Axmed Baraki, now elderly and seated

FIGURE I.17 Marian Cabdi Dhaqane, Banta, 1988. Photograph by Jorge Acero.

in the audience, provoked cries of delight. In the photograph he appears young and very strong, wearing shorts and a large wrap on his head while working with a group of men to construct a frame for the room of a new mundul. Axmed Baraki himself got far more excited about a photograph of one of his farms, calling out the name of its location. Several women exclaimed with satisfaction at the beauty of the nicely tilled farms that appeared in several photographs.

We followed the second showing of the slides with a tape of Cali Osman's poetry recitation and flute performance, which everyone asked to hear a second time, and then a third time. Then everyone wanted to watch the entire slide show again, identifying still more people, including Sahara Mahamed, now living in Lewiston but unable to attend because she was about to give birth. Forthright and confident as a young girl, she stands in the photo as if she owns the world. I asked about her parents, who were good people and friends. The answer, of course, was that they were dead.

The photographs of young children guarding fields of sesame against the predations of birds and monkeys elicited lots of comments, as did the photographs of people in the unsteady village canoe crossing the Jubba River. The third time through the slide show, people recognized the images of religious and ritual activities, commenting in excitement on their old festivals. Slides of hoes, machetes, and other long-lost farm tools evoked lots of chatter.

FIGURE I.18 Iman's brother guarding stacks of sesame on his father's farm, Banta, 1988. Photograph by Jorge Acero.

As the festivities wound down, everyone asked for copies of photos and CDs of the music. Sadiq and Abkow remained to help clean up after people dispersed, sharing more information about what actually happened in Banta and beginning the long process of recounting Banta's history since our departure. We learned that several of those who appeared in the photographs had become perpetrators of violence during the war—killing, kidnapping, and ransoming. Over the next two years, as I reconnected with Banta's survivors in Lewiston, Syracuse, and Hartford, I pieced together the story of what happened in Banta, recounted in the following three chapters.

My first visit to a Somali Bantu home in Lewiston occurred a few weeks after the Bates MLK panel, when Jorge and I went to visit Sahara, who as a young girl had stood guard over me as I wrote my field notes each evening, shooing away other villagers who might disturb my concentration, and who now, as a married mother, had given birth to her sixth child the day after the slide show. Sahara's downtown tenement building was a creaky old four-story walk-up, listing slightly to the right. We climbed to the top floor up the narrow twisting stairs through thick dust, cigarette butts, and garbage to a door with "Sahara Mahamed" scrawled in pencil. Inside, the apartment was transformed from grimy Lewiston tenement to lively Somali space. Colorful woven plastic mats covered the floor, brightly patterned nylon drapes flowed along the walls from ceiling to floor, and bunches of plastic flowers dangled from the corners. A cascade of plastic flowers woven into a garland hung to the floor from a ceiling hook in the middle of the room, making a gay centerpiece. The aesthetic was a modernist rendering of the beautifully colored woven palm frond mats that used to grace the walls, beds, and floors of Banta's small huts, a new style that has since become very familiar to me. Sahara's six children assembled to meet us: six-year-old twins Xassan and Xussein, born in Dagahallay (in Dadaab) refugee camp, Gamana and Khadija, born in Kakuma refugee camp, giggly toddler Yasmin, born in Georgia, and the tiny newborn Lewiston native Sahel, sleeping in the center of a bare mattress. In addition to the single mattress, an old TV on a small side table completed the room's furnishings. An adjoining bedroom held another single mattress atop more floor mats. As we talked, the kids rolled around on the mattresses and the mats—lacking toys or books, there seemed to be little else for them to do but watch TV and wrestle. Jorge and I exchanged a look of concern, sharing a mutual reaction to the reality of seven people in a one-bedroom apartment with a long trek down four flights of stairs to get to the street. Sahara had recently relocated to Lewiston from Atlanta, where debts had overwhelmed the struggling family shortly after their arrival in the United States. Her husband remained in Georgia to pay off the bills before joining his family. As I was to learn, Sahara's apartment was just like the apartments of most newly resettled Somali Bantus: hardly any furniture other than an old donated mattress or two; life lived on the floor, where everyone ate, slept, played, and talked; all windows and walls covered with bright curtains; and lots of bright plastic flowers everywhere. A phone and an old donated VCR completed the standard furnishings in most homes.

When her tenement building burned down a few months after our visit, another large refugee family from Banta took Sahara's family into their small two-bedroom apartment while she waited for a new apartment to become available. Such strong community support structures remained firmly in place despite the repeated ruptures experienced by refugees in the resettlement process, making visible the kinds of communitarian practices typical of the refugee community that many of Lewiston's poorer residents lacked. Indeed, seven years later, when arson destroyed several tenement buildings downtown and left two hundred people homeless, all the Somali Bantu families found housing with friends and relatives while their non-Somali neighbors had to move into public facilities or short-term hotel rooms provided by the city until they could find somewhere else to go. To re-create their structures of mutual support was precisely why Somali Bantu refugees chose to leave their sites of initial resettlement throughout the United States to live together again in Maine.

The Argument of the Book

Drawing on oral history interviews with war survivors from the Jubba Valley; published reports about the Kenyan refugee camps; seven years of advocacy work, collaborative projects, and ethnographic fieldwork in the United States; and extensive engagement with social services providers and others in Lewiston, this book develops an understanding of the lives of resettled refugees that contradicts some of the most consistent claims in the media about refugees and their resettlement. One is the assumption that refugees are apolitical, docile, dependent recipients who benefit enormously from humanitarian intervention. Another is the claim that immigrants to America share a common trajectory of assimilation.

Policies involving immigrants and refugees will be one of the most pressing issues of the twenty-first century. Although the language of emergency used by the United Nations High Commissioner on Refugees (UNHCR) defines refugees as a crisis situation rather than the norm,[10] those who have lived in refugee camps for generations know differently. In numbers that currently exceed fifteen million, refugees are staying in camps for longer periods of time than ever before, and many live in camps that have existed for decades.[11] Grandparents are raising grandchildren in camps where they themselves grew up. Refugees appear to have become a permanent part of the contemporary global landscape, the state of exception that has become normal. "They are at the heart of the definition of the world order and the debates it raises."[12]

Containing and constraining the mobility of refugees, who as border crossers are dangerous and mistrusted by the states that take them in as well as by the states that try to keep them out, is a major global enterprise, as manifested in the construction of massive refugee camps where humanitarians house and care for those displaced by war or disaster. Because, despite all evidence to the contrary, refugee camps are envisioned as temporary solutions to short-term crises, less than 1 percent of those who live in them are referred for resettlement to a third country. What is supposed to happen to the rest? As Zygmunt Bauman and many others argue, refugees are a product of our current world order; their numbers are not going to diminish; and their persistent presence is a reality the world must confront.[13] The vast number of refugees, especially those who have lived for decades in "temporary" camps, begs the question: what kind of world do we want to live in? Is a safe, secure world one in which millions of people are stashed in temporary refugee camps for a lifetime?

With a focus on their experiences as recounted to me by Somali Bantu refugees, part I asks what humanitarianism feels like to those who are its objects. What expectations and burdens accompany the extension of aid in the form of refugee camps and resettlement opportunities? We will see how humanitarianism in the form of refugee camps feels constraining and debilitating to refugees who are working to retain agency over their lives and how refugees learn to navigate within and push back against the constraints on their freedom imposed by humanitarians and the states whose interests they represent.

Anthropologists recognize that memories play tricks, that current experiences reshape recollections of past events, and that stories are told with an eye to their possible future significance. Refugees, in particular, learn to tell stories about their experiences in particular ways because of the requirements imposed on them by refugee camp administrators, as I discuss in chapter 3. While I have no way to verify the particulars of the stories I retell here, the version of events recounted in the first three chapters reflects the things I heard over and over again as I crossed the country to reconnect with Banta's survivors. Chapter 1 begins in 1988, our final year of residence in the village, sweeps back to the early twentieth century, and then follows the events precipitated by the arrival of armed militias in Banta in 1991. Chapters 2 and 3 follow my old neighbors as they fled the Jubba Valley for Kenyan refugee camps, where they lived for the next decade and a half.

Part II of the book takes up the question of what happens when refugees move in next door; when dependent objects of humanitarian charity become neighbors with rights. U.S. media and the UNHCR promoted the U.S. offer of refuge through resettlement to Somali Bantu refugees as a purely humanitarian act to rescue a displaced, persecuted minority group from an uncertain future. But what does the offer of refuge actually mean? How is refuge envisioned and actually enacted? What happens when a town that did not invite refugees finds itself unwittingly becoming their place of refuge? Part II reviews the competing and contradictory responses by Lewiston's residents to the unexpected arrival of thousands of refugees, exploring the debates about economic responsibility, moral responsibility, security, and community that immigration provokes.

Part III takes up the question of immigrant integration. The favored melting pot image of America acknowledges the country as a nation of immigrants, but the "land of opportunity" in the popular national narrative rests on the assumption that immigrants assimilate to mainstream American culture as they follow the trajectory of upward mobility blazed by previous generations of immigrants. But what does integration actually mean? Even though the idea of the melting pot has long captured the national imagination, the iconic image of the current era is perhaps more one of crashes and clashes, manifest in fears about immigrants and the differences they bring. Samuel Huntington's article "The Clash of Civilizations" and his book *Who*

Are We?, Robert Kaplan's article "The Coming Anarchy," the film *Crash*, and many other popular narratives warn of the dangers of culture clashes, violence, and destruction precipitated by immigration.[14] Those fearful of insecurities introduced by immigration argue that clashing and crashing is what happens when integration fails and such fears animate reactionary measures such as laws making English the official language. When immigrants are black and Muslim in addition to non–English speaking, what is integration to the Euro-American white mainstream supposed to look like?

This book contains crashes and clashes: Somali Bantu villages are crashed and destroyed by Somali militias; Somali Bantus and I crash into each other after twenty years; Somalis and Somali Bantus crash Maine and clash with Mainers. But much more interesting than the clashes and crashes are the stories that are left out of such narratives: the seepages, mutual transformations, and slow border crossings of all kinds (linguistic, cultural, ideological, philosophical, cultural) that accompany human mobility. While Lewiston's story has its share of racists and xenophobes, a far more accurate portrait of the experience and impact of migration captures how refugee immigrants and locals negotiate coresidence, creating arenas of care, solidarity, collaboration, and mutuality as people from very different backgrounds work out ways to live together, create community, and envision a collective future. This process is not without struggle, of course, but integration works both ways: immigrants adapt to their new society but their neighbors also adapt to the new ways of being-in-the-world that immigrants bring. This books shows how and why.

PART I Refugees

Becoming Refugees

In a world of globalization disengagement from
Africa's violence is no longer an option.
—Paul Richards, *Fighting for the Rain Forest*

In 1988, Cali Osman lived behind our dwelling in Banta in a row of neat mud houses with his three wives, ten children, divorced sister, several nephews, and elderly widowed aunt. Caliyow Isaaq and his large family—three wives, twelve children—lived across the path from our compound; his wife Amina (pictured in the introduction, fig. I.13) was a frequent guest in our house. Sheikh Axmed Nur (pictured in the introduction, fig. I.9) lived across the village from us with his two wives and six children. Although each family lived at the barest subsistence level, surviving on what they grew on their farms and sold for a few hundred dollars each year, each was considered wealthy in family and by reputation. Cali Osman was a nationally recognized poet in a country where poetry is revered, viewed by his community as an intelligent and wise elder often sought for his mediation and oratory skills.[1] We spent many happy evenings tucked into a circle with other villagers listening to his poetry as a bonfire roared. Caliyow Isaaq was a master carpenter and head chef for the village feasts, often called on for his surgical abilities as well. Sheikh Axmed Nur, a powerful healer and religious leader, was known far and wide

FIGURE 1.1 Cali Osman making furniture, Banta, 1987. Photograph by Jorge Acero.

for his curing skills and the ability to communicate with the spiritual domain. As my mentors in village life in 1987–88, these men and their families spent countless hours with me, so the survivors from these families were among the first people from Banta with whom I sought to reconnect. Recounting the experiences of these three families reveals how war arrived in Banta, how the farmers became refugees, and how Somalia's civil war is a global story.

From their photographs, one could imagine Cali Osman, Caliyow Isaaq, and Sheikh Axmed Nur as peasant-everymen living at the very edges of the world: remote, isolated Banta was hundreds of miles from any paved roads, inaccessible for half the year during the rainy season, and lacking in electricity, running water, and any electronic form of communication with the outside world except Caliyow Isaaq's battery-powered radio. The women in their families typically owned one dress each; their children worked in the fields since there was no local school. It might seem logical to conclude that families like these in a village like Banta lived more or less off the global grid—unaffected by global events, by larger political and economic currents sweeping the globe.

FIGURE 1.2 Rainy season travel in the Jubba Valley, 1988. Photograph by Jorge Acero.

In fact, quite the opposite is true. As many anthropological accounts demonstrate, people in villages like Banta are profoundly affected by global processes and decisions made by elite world leaders. The roots of the conflict that tore apart Banta stretch back to the Indian Ocean slave trade (which was stimulated, in part, by the transatlantic slave trade), weave through the colonial era with the imposition of European domination that reshaped African borders and identities, were nurtured through the political alignments demanded by global superpowers during the Cold War, shifted again with the imposition of "development" initiatives by the world's wealthier countries to remake the world's poorer countries through capitalist interventions, and exploded with the fall of the Berlin Wall. The stories of what happened during the war to the families of Cali Osman, Caliyow Isaaq, and Sheikh Axmed Nur are simultaneously global and local; their fates were shaped at the intersection of global and local politics.

Race and Ancestry

In contexts of civil war, violence often absorbs and makes harmfully meaningful historically shaped ethnic, racial, kin-based, or religious differences.[2] The same is true in Somalia, where race and ancestry became vital identity markers when Somalia's civil war spread to the Jubba Valley. Our story begins a century ago, when the parents of Cali Osman and Sheikh Axmed Nur were born in the upper Shabelle Valley, located in the border region where Ethiopia and Somalia now meet, a geographical area contested by the Somalis who lived there, Ethiopians, Italian and British colonial militaries, and anticolonial Somali dervish militias.[3] The families of Cali Osman and Sheikh Axmed Nur were members of one of Somalia's ethnic minority groups who came under the authority of one of Somalia's prominent clans. Their ancestors probably preceded the arrival of Somali speakers in the region centuries ago; linguists and historians suggest that after Somali speakers moved into the Horn, autochthonous groups like those along the upper Shabelle converted to Islam and adopted one of the Somali languages, accepting a client status in relation to the more recently arrived Somali pastoralist clans.

The constant violence and conflict created by the international political actors trying to carve out colonies both under and independent of European control at the turn of the twentieth century produced a flow of refugees out of the upper Shabelle region, which included the parents of both Cali Osman and Sheikh Axmed Nur. As members of a Somali-speaking ethnic minority group, both families migrated into the Jubba River valley, where other ethnic minorities already lived, to settle in a farming village on the banks of the river.

Detailed oral histories and early colonial documents describe how the Jubba Valley had been settled by people whose parents and grandparents had been slaves in Somalia. A robust Indian Ocean slave trade operated in the nineteenth century, bringing tens of thousands of slaves from the east coast of Africa up to Somalia, where they were put to work on Somali-owned plantations stretching south along the coast from Mogadishu. The plantations produced food for the Somali plantation owners but also for trade to the Arabian Peninsula and beyond.[4] Slaves who eventually escaped or were manumitted, like Caliyow Isaaq's grandparents, fled into southern Somalia's Jubba River valley to form independent farming villages, where they were later joined by refugees from the violence along the upper Shabelle, including the families of Cali Osman and Sheikh Axmed Nur.

By the mid-twentieth century, slavery had officially ended under British and Italian colonization, and population movements had settled into a pattern: free farmers of slave or non-Somali ancestry lived in small sedentary villages along the river, and Somali pastoralists maintained a nomadic lifestyle on the plains stretching to either side of the river valley. Everyone in southern Somalia knew the status differences that separated those living in Jubba Valley farming villages from everyone else because of their stigmatized slave (or non-Somali) ancestry, linguistically recorded in the derogatory terms used to identify them, such as *ooji* and *adoon*.[5] Riverine farmers were considered more "African," in contrast to the purported Arabic ancestry of ethnic Somalis, a difference recognized in the widespread use of mutually exclusive

FIGURE 1.3 Somali pastoralists migrating outside Banta, 1988. Photograph by Jorge Acero.

physical terms to define the two groups: *jareer*, which means "hard hair," described those of slave or non-Somali ancestry, and *jileec*, which means "soft," described those identified as ethnic Somalis.[6] Although many Jubba Valley farmers shared languages, religion, and many cultural practices with other Somalis, a ban on intermarriage between the two groups maintained the former's inferior status, as did Italian colonial labor policies that targeted farmers, but not pastoralists, for forced labor requirements.

During my stay in Banta, I carefully documented the ways in which local residents mediated and managed the tensions provoked by Somali understandings of hierarchy and inequality that prized those of jileec status and subjugated those identified as jareer. Despite their non-Somali ancestry, everyone in Banta claimed membership in a Somali clan, either on the basis of the clan identity of the person who had originally enslaved their ancestors, or through an ancestor's later adoption into a clan for protection and identity within Somali society. Scholars describe Somali kinship as a segmentary lineage structure, in which every Somali is a member of one of five major clan families (Darood, Dir, Isaaq, Rahanweyn, and Hawiye), each of which encompasses large groups of lineages in a cascading set of lineage-based kinship groups determined patrilineally.[7] Every Somali claims membership in a particular lineage of a particular clan, and can identify his or her relationship to every other Somali through tracing his or her connections through the overarching kinship system. The lineage and clan structure provided the basis for social and political life, including knowing one's enemies and allies when conflict occurred.[8]

Banta included families who claimed membership in three of Somalia's five major clans (Darood, Rahanweyn, and Hawiye), although the connections between families of different clan membership far outweighed the distinctions among them.[9] In Banta, people married and shared friendships across clan lines, and when compensation had to be paid for a crime committed by a villager against someone from outside the village, all of Banta's families contributed rather than just the offender's clan relatives. In short, lineage and clan membership was far more important for claiming membership within broader Somali society than it was for structuring life within the village.

The jareer villagers in Banta used their membership in Somali clans to negotiate their relationships with the jileec Somali pastoralists who lived on the plains stretching away from the riverbanks: the Darood to the west and the Rahanweyn and Hawiye to the east. Because of their social status above those farmers identified as jareer, Somali (jileec) pastoralists who entered Jubba Valley villages seeking water or food felt entitled to assault, harass, and intimidate local farmers with relative impunity. My field notes are filled with stories about pastoralists grazing their animals on farmers' ripening crops and assaulting those who attempted to defend their fields against invading hungry cows. My Banta neighbors usually explained this abuse as the behavior of particularly aggressive Somali individuals rather than as an expression of collective discrimination by pastoralist (jileec) Somalis against minority (jareer) farmers, and they attempted time and again to use the language of clan to seek compensation and mediation for their injuries.

While the majority of Banta villagers claimed to be affiliated with jileec Somali clans who lived to the east of the Jubba River valley, several Banta families maintained close ties with jileec Somali pastoralist families of the Darood clan, whose territory stretched to the west of the Jubba Valley. Xassan, the head of the village in whose compound I lived, had a close relationship with a Darood pastoralist family because his wife, Hamara, claimed Darood clan membership. Hamara's father, Bilaal, was a locally powerful elder from Kakole, a village near Banta also on the west bank of the Jubba River, which was almost entirely populated by his extended family, all of whom claimed Darood clan membership.[10] During my year in Banta I spent dozens of hours interviewing Bilaal about local history, including the history of slavery that his family shared with most villagers in the Jubba Valley. His grandfather, captured in Tanzania for enslavement in Somalia, had assumed Darood clan identity after gaining his freedom, and his offspring continued to claim that identity, seeking solidarity with the Darood pastoralists who lived in the bush to the west of Banta and Kakole.

In addition to the kinship and trading ties that many village families maintained with pastoralists living in the bush outside Banta, several former pastoralist Darood families had settled in Banta after losing their livestock to drought and disease, maintaining a neighborly but guarded relationship with other villagers. Maxamed Gedi, his brother Said, Xussein, and other Darood arrivals joined the village after receiving land grants from village elders. Although the male Darood village residents were recognized as rather severe and hostile personalities, they never caused any outright trouble within the village during my stay.

Despite the villagers' efforts to claim a foothold in Somalia's system of clans, I soon learned that the Darood pastoralist families with whom they traded in the bush outside Banta did not share their perception of membership in Somali society. After witnessing numerous instances of abuse by pastoralists against villagers, followed by mediation by clan and village elders to determine compensation, I began interviewing Darood pastoralist leaders from the bush surrounding Banta about their perception of shared clan allegiances with the villagers. In our interviews, they scoffed at the efforts of middle valley farmers to seek membership in Somali kin groups. One local Darood leader explained that the Jubba Valley farmers could never be treated as equal lineage members and avoided reenslavement by his clan only because of national laws against slavery. Siad Barre had in fact outlawed the entire clan system in Somalia, making clan- and slave-based hierarchies and distinctions illegal. Although it is hard to describe the dictator as a protector of human rights, the Somali Darood clan leaders living outside of Banta insisted that Barre's antislavery laws were the only thing keeping them from reenslaving Jubba Valley farmers.

So in 1987–88, a détente based on a mutually recognized inequality between jareer and jileec residents characterized life in the middle valley. While status differences gave jileec pastoralists the upper hand in compensation negotiations when they harmed villagers, shared clan membership between some pastoralist and farmer families provided a language to seek mediation and compensation, even if it was usually paltry and begrudging. Within the village, jileec former pastoralists of the Darood clan held no special power because they were so clearly in the minority and received land for farming only through the good graces of the jareer village elders. Banta farmers held allegiances to both their village and their clans; having never been forced to choose sides, they could maintain an imagined balance of clan and village associations that allowed them to navigate the status differences between jileec and jareer as best they could. No one in Banta realized how murderously meaningful the status hierarchy separating jareer from jileec would become.

The Cold War Comes to the Jubba Valley

When independence from colonial control arrived in 1960, the parents of Cali Osman, Caliyow Isaaq, and Sheikh Axmed Nur had survived the forced labor campaigns of the Italian colonizers in the Jubba Valley as well as the British-Italian skirmishes that passed control over the Jubba Valley back and forth between the British and the Italians until independence in 1960. The colonial-era conflict in the upper Shabelle region had come to an unquiet conclusion in the mid-twentieth century when international powers ultimately settled on a border between Somalia and Ethiopia that granted to Ethiopia a large chunk of Somali-inhabited territory. Somalis were understandably outraged, and a discourse of irredentism—a desire to reunite within one nation-state all the territory occupied by Somali speakers—pervaded nationalist Somali rhetoric after independence in 1960.

Siad Barre came to power as Somalia's president in a coup in 1969, advocating a political platform he called scientific socialism. He initially allied himself with the Soviet Union, from whom he received weaponry, military assistance, and economic support. Seeking to fulfill his irredentist goals, Barre launched an attack against Ethiopia in 1977 to reclaim the Somali-inhabited territory ceded to Ethiopia decades earlier. But when the Soviet Union chose to back Ethiopia, their other client in the Horn of Africa, Siad Barre expelled the Soviets from Somalia and turned to the United States for patronage, offering access to Somalia for military bases in return for massive foreign aid. In the context of Cold War geopolitics, the United States saw Somalia as a strategic prize because of its location on the Indian Ocean and its proximity to the Persian Gulf. During the 1980s, the United States made Somalia its second largest recipient of foreign aid in Africa, granting Barre hundreds upon hundreds of millions of dollars in military and economic aid. Analysts estimate that Barre received over a billion dollars in foreign aid from international sources during the 1980s, an astounding figure for a lightly populated, arid country with few natural resources.[11]

Barre put the money to good use, employing the familiar pattern of patrimonial politics to consolidate power in the hands of his closest relatives and trusted advisors, particularly those of the Darood clan living in the south. Barre skillfully manipulated the clan system to privilege some clans at the expense of others, leading commentators like British anthropologist I. M. Lewis to conclude that Somalia's civil war represented a victory of clan politics over state building. Other observers, including me, emphasized how the wealth flowing into Somalia from foreign aid enabled the growth of an elite, urban-based class of politicians and businessmen with close government connections. Class-based inequality had arrived in Somalia, joining hierarchies of race and ancestry created previously through the slave trade and migration.[12]

However one understands the manipulations of Barre's rule, several things are clear: his alliances with the United States (and formerly the Soviet Union) weaponized the country and maintained his regime; he used massive state resources gained from foreign aid to bolster his bases of support, primarily in the south, against northern clans and communities that protested against their exclusion from his largesse; and his practice of patrimonial politics enabled urban-based political and business elites from Mogadishu to use the instruments of the state to enrich themselves at the expense of their fellow citizens.

What did foreign aid and the patrimonialism it funded mean for Cali Osman, Caliyow Isaaq, and Sheikh Axmed Nur, living in Banta in the distant Jubba Valley? Despite the massive amount of aid flowing into the country under Barre's dictatorship, villages like Banta received no benefits from it. There were no schools, medical facilities, infrastructure, roads, policing, or state support structures. The only way that Banta experienced the foreign aid flowing into the country was that foreign and multilateral development agencies involved in shaping Somalia's postsocialist economy identified the Jubba Valley as ripe for capitalist transformation. The World Bank planned to build the second largest dam in all of Africa on the upper Jubba Valley; the U.S. Agency for International Development (USAID) and European development agencies planned to build paved roads and commercial irrigation projects throughout the valley, and USAID planned and funded a land reform program to privatize all land ownership. In 1988, when I scrutinized the official land registry for Banta in the Ministry of Agriculture, I discovered that all the land in Banta had been legally claimed by businessmen and politicians from Mogadishu who had never lived there, but who were waiting to exercise their new ownership rights until the foreign development agencies completed their projects.[13] One evening after this discovery, as I sat with Banta villagers around a bonfire discussing their future, Cali Osman predicted they would all end up as landless, impoverished wage laborers on commercial plantations owned by wealthy urban businessmen. We never imagined a worse fate was in store for them. The takeover by city overlords might have dismantled the delicate, if unequal, balance between jareer and jileec residents in the Jubba Valley in a way that was harmful to both groups if the war hadn't changed everything.

Civil War

Just after our departure from Somalia the Berlin Wall fell, and the reverberations of this globally momentous event reached all the way to Banta. The dictator Siad Barre—ally of the United States, kept in power largely by U.S. aid—suddenly became a pariah in the new global order, in which alliances and enemies were no longer defined by the "free" world versus the communist world. In the new world order that emerged after the fall of the Berlin Wall, people like Siad Barre were expendable to the United States, and Barre was very quickly redefined in speeches in the U.S. Congress as a human rights abuser. Although Barre's government had regularly imprisoned and tortured its dissenters, the regime's heinous actions became important to U.S. politicians only after communism collapsed and it was difficult to justify U.S. support for such a dictator any longer. As insurgencies against Barre's totalitarian rule mounted within Somalia, Barre struggled to maintain control by bombing and strafing villages in the north in retaliation for insurrection by northern-based political opponents. The United States dramatically cut aid to Somalia in 1990, and within a year Barre's government collapsed under pressure from armed antigovernment groups that had joined forces to oust him.

Although life under Siad Barre had not been easy for Jubba Valley farmers, what happened after his government collapsed was horrific.[14] Fleeing Mogadishu for Kenya in 1991, Barre and his militia came through the Jubba Valley, pursued by opposing militias chasing him out of the country. As his supporters made their way up the valley, they distributed weapons and military vehicles to his Darood clan allies, the Somali pastoralists who inhabited the plains to the west of the valley, admonishing them to maintain control of the valley and not cede it to the incoming Hawiye militias who were pursuing him from the east. These livestock herders–turned–militiamen began a cross-river campaign to push back the incoming militias arriving from the east. The unarmed farming villages got caught in the crossfire, to their profound devastation.[15]

In the confusing weeks following Siad Barre's flight up the valley, Bu'aale was one of the first towns in the middle valley to experience deadly violence when a Darood militiaman opened fire in the marketplace, killing three farmers he suspected of trying to buy weapons.[16] Darood pastoralists-turned-militia began turning their guns against local farmers in order to assert control over the valley, killing those who resisted. About a dozen men of Duqiyo, a small village between Banta and Bu'aale, disobeyed an order issued by a militiaman not to leave the village; for punishment they were marched to a large mango tree, tied to its base, and shot to death. They had been trying to sneak into Bu'aale for provisions. Their bodies were left to rot, spied upon by small children from Bu'aale who came to investigate. Refugees from Duqiyo and Bu'aale began arriving in Banta, looking for security with their relatives.

But within Banta, families from the Darood clan that had settled in the village as farmers, including Maxamed Gedi, his brother Said, Xussein, and a few others, had obtained guns from their relatives in the bush and used them to take over Banta. They compiled a list of the names of everyone in the village and began to police everyone's movements in and out of the village, trying to assert demographic control and to hinder possible interactions with Hawiye militias. Calling themselves a "committee," Maxamed Gedi and his group kept accounts of the villagers' crop production, requiring each family to report to the committee on their farm's production and claiming a portion of everyone's harvest as a residential tax, which they redistributed to their pastoralist Darood clan relatives in the bush. Some of their relatives from the bush even moved into the village to join them, living off the work of the unarmed farmers.

Kidnapping and ransom, the fund-raising method used by criminals throughout the world, became their primary strategy for obtaining food. Initially they targeted the new arrivals seeking refuge in Banta after fleeing violence in other communities. Maxamed Gedi and his contingent would imprison newcomers until their village relatives paid their "entry tax." Sadiq, who fled to Banta from Bu'aale after witnessing the massacred Duqiyo men, remembers such abductions as a rite of passage, even joking that they were like immigration control. But Maxamed Gedi and the others soon turned on their long-time neighbors, beating them up, imprisoning them, and then demanding a ransom from their families as a tool of control and humiliation, particularly against the village elders.

Sitting on the floor mats in her tiny Lewiston apartment while her grandchildren listened with rapt attention, Cali Osman's wife Isha recounted the Darood men's stranglehold on the village, describing how Maxamed Gedi captured her son, Ciise, tied him to a tree, and beat him until she and Cali Osman ransomed him with their harvest, thus imperiling their other children's food security for the season. Her enduring fury and rage were apparent as she described the escalating assaults by the Darood men against their Banta neighbors.

"Were you surprised your neighbors could turn on you like that?" I asked.

"I was surprised!" she responded, emphatically. Echoing the ethic that dominated village life during my stay in Banta, Sadiq added, "Before the war we all lived together. We helped each other. If there was a funeral or a wedding, we all worked together and helped each other. So it was really surprising that this could happen."

FIGURE 1.4 Ciise Cali Osman, Banta, 1988. Photograph by Jorge Acero.

FIGURE 1.5 Isha Iman, wife of Cali Osman and mother of Ciise, in center looking over her shoulder at the camera, Banta, 1988. Photograph by Jorge Acero.

With trepidation, I asked about our old friend and mentor Bilaal, the Darood-affiliated elder of Kakole and great historian, father to Hamara, in whose compound we lived during our stay. Isha became animated with disgust. "They were the worst! He was with them! He took over! He was one of the Darood who carried weapons and attacked and violated everyone. His family was the cause of the biggest problems. His son killed at least a hundred people. His Banta wife fled to Kakole, and they all participated in the attacking and looting of the other surrounding villages. It was like they wanted to take over and control everything and everybody." She described how Bilaal and his sons used their weapons to control the neighboring villages, assisting the pastoralist Darood occupiers in their rapacious demands for food. Isha concluded her appalling tale about Bilaal's collusion with the occupiers, shaking her head: "He had totally changed."

Weapons enabled militiamen to make claims on women. Armed Darood militiamen demanded marriages with village women of their choice, including women who were already married. The dissolution of social bonds forged through marriage rituals, which are always accompanied by exchanges of gifts and food between the couple's families, struck a blow at the very basis of village life. Bilaal's militia forced his Banta granddaughters (the daughters of my former landlords) to divorce their husbands and move in with Darood militiamen. One refused and fled the village for refuge in Kenya with her husband. "Those with guns could do whatever they wanted—they demanded whatever they wanted," Isha remembered. Maxamed Gedi and Saïd appropriated their neighbors' belongings at gunpoint, including Caliyow Isaaq's radio and the jacket Jorge had given him as a parting gift. Moving on from simply demanding food, they began taking clothes, raping women, and terrorizing the village.

The burden of handing over their harvest as a "tax" or as ransom meant constant and increasing hunger. "Every farmer supported three extra people!" Sadiq explained as he emphasized the toll on Banta farmers of supporting the armed pastoralist invaders and their relatives. Those with weapons not only demanded the lion's share of the harvest but also required the farmers to transport their harvest into the bush to the families of the occupying militia. Caliyow Isaaq's brother was ordered to carry the goods for two families, but as it was too much for him, he took one load, intending to return for the second. In fury, the man whose goods would be the second load shot him in the legs for his failure to cart the entire burden at once. Axmed Baraki recounted how the armed occupiers used villagers as target practice, mimicking one occupier who, he claimed, had said, as he took aim at a farmer-turned-porter, "Let's see if I can shoot him from this far away."

After initially focusing on new arrivals in Banta, Maxamed Gedi and his gang turned their attention to the village elders in order to disempower them, particularly Sheikh Axmed Nur in retaliation for his refusal to hand over his precious bow and arrow to the militia committee. One of his sons, Cabdullahi, recounted his family's story as we sat surrounded by photographs from Banta in Sadiq's Lewiston apartment. Cabdullahi was visiting Lewiston for a wedding from his new home in Syracuse, but before heading to the wedding feast we sat for several hours remembering prewar life in the village and talking about what had happened to his family during the war. As his stories about the war unfolded, his cell phone rang constantly with calls from his relatives from Lewiston, Hartford, Springfield, and even Kenya, who wanted to add their memories to our conversation. Studying the photographs and the 1988 census I had created of Banta residents, his eyes brimmed with tears. "All those people," he said, shaking his head. "So many dead."

His was the first family in Banta to experience murder. After Sheikh Axmed Nur's son Kahiye failed to return from his farm one day, a group of elders, including Sheikh Axmed Nur, Cali Osman, and Caliyow Isaaq, went searching for him, accompanied by militia members Maxamed Gedi and Said. After three days of searching, his body was finally located hidden in the bush, with three bullet holes in his neck and upper back. Caliyow Isaaq extracted a bullet, matched to an AK-47, the make of gun used by Maxamed Gedi and his cohort. Cali Osman's eldest daughter, Rabaca, overcame her fear and reported that she had seen Kahiye pass by her on the day he disappeared as she was collecting firewood, followed by Maxamed Gedi and Said. Shortly thereafter three shots rang out. Upon hearing this news, Caliyow Isaaq flew at Maxamed Gedi in such a rage that his children, in fear for his life, had to forcibly restrain him. Maxamed Gedi denied the ensuing accusation of murder, retaliating against the elders by arresting them and their sons for ransom. Over the next few months, Maxamed Gedi and his gang repeatedly abducted, tied up, and beat the elders and their adult sons, demanding payments of money, sesame oil, and corn for their release. Sheikh Axmed Nur's second son, Ahmadey, was told he was the next target for assassination, but with only two bullets this time. He immediately fled the area. The turn toward assassination signaled a transformation in life; the transition from demanding food to killing neighbors marked a point of no return.

A brief respite arrived when the Hawiye militia from the east side of the Jubba River valley managed to push the war front across the valley and take control of the west bank of the Jubba, occupying Banta. The Darood occupiers retreated to the west, and Cali Osman composed a poem savagely mocking their behavior and praising the incoming Hawiye occupiers. But their relief was short lived as the Darood militias managed to push back the Hawiye offensive, returning to retake Banta with enormous fury over the humiliating and widely repeated poem. In Somalia, poetry has long held tremendous political power, used as a weapon of war, broadcast over the radio and shared through recitations in camel camps and farming villages at night. Although the returning militia raided the village to kill Cali Osman, they only succeeded in killing two other village farmers while Cali Osman and his family escaped, spending the next several months living on the run in the bush. Cali Osman's sons remember how they stole into villages at night to get food to augment their dependence on wild foods they could scavenge and how the family members arranged themselves across the treetops at night to sleep in order to escape militia patrols. In one funny story, Cali Osman's son Cabdulkadir recounted a night he passed hiding in a warthog hole, desperately trying not to disturb the resident warthog. Cabdulkadir recalled how fear and constant movement exhausted the family, forcing Cali Osman to negotiate with the Darood occupiers to rewrite his poem in their honor, which they accepted in return for allowing him to return to Banta. Cabdulkadir and Idris believe he agreed to this compromise in order to plan his escape to Kenya along the route that began in Banta.

The family returned to an utterly polarized village. The Darood militia had successfully enlisted several non-Darood village men as their foot soldiers, including our old friend Adan, a village elder who claimed an affiliation to a clan not shared with any other villagers. Initially Adan had attempted to play the role of negotiator between the occupying Darood militia and the other villagers. In my conversations with Banta's survivors in the United States, we puzzled for hours over the behavior of prominent former Banta elders like Adan, my landlord Xassan, and other village men who assisted the occupying militia, finally concluding that they must have felt they had little choice; they were also threatened by those with guns. While they did not participate in any killings or beatings, their negotiations between the occupiers and their Banta neighbors rarely helped the latter. Over time, Adan's mediation efforts shifted toward collusion with the militia as he began reporting on the villagers' movements and harvests, assisting the Darood occupiers in determining whom to kidnap and for how much. Eventually his compound, right next to the compound of Sheikh Axmed Nur, became a storehouse of weapons for the Darood and part of their Banta militia base for attacking other villages. He even threw out his daughter's husband and allowed a Darood militiaman to marry her and take control of her former husband's home, clothing, and farms. "Can

FIGURE 1.6 The road to Kenya from Banta, 1988. Photograph by Catherine Besteman.

you imagine?" Sadiq asked incredulously. "The new husband walked around wearing the first husband's clothes!"

Becoming Refugees

Shortly after their return from life on the run, Cali Osman's family joined together with Caliyow Isaaq's family in a group of about two hundred people to flee the village in a daring midnight escape. Amazingly, they managed to keep their plans a total secret from everyone else, to ensure the militia members could not block their departure or kill them for their disobedience. Sadiq recalls, "We woke up one morning and all those people were gone!" The militiamen were furious—they had just lost an army of food producers.

The trek to Kenya through hundreds of miles of desert was challenging, and one of Cali Osman's wives died of starvation along the way. The journey, while grueling, benefited from the help of Somali pastoralists near the Kenyan border who, along with the International Committee of the Red Cross (ICRC), offered assistance and support to the fleeing refugees. Identifying the refugees as starving farmers with nothing left to steal, the mosques broadcast messages asking people to refrain from attacking them. The local pastoralists benefited from the presence of the ICRC, which was operating in the area to support fleeing civilians, and understood that it was to their advantage to offer support for the refugees.

Arriving at the Kenyan border, Isha recalls, "We all just fell down and couldn't get up." They were met by UNHCR workers who transported them to the refugee camp at Dadaab. In a cruel twist of fate, many in their group immediately fell terribly ill and died by the score from prolonged diarrhea, including two of Caliyow Isaaq's three wives, Faduma and Amina, along with three of Amina's daughters. Caliyow Isaaq himself died soon thereafter. Out of the sixteen members of Caliyow Isaaq's family who survived the trek from Somalia, seven died from diarrhea and vomiting shortly after arriving at the camp. Caliyow Isaaq's only surviving wife, Jimcoy, and eldest son, Mohamed (who married Sheikh Axmed Nur's daughter Xawo), took over the responsibility of caring for all six of the children left orphaned.

A few weeks after the flight of Cali Osman and Caliyow Isaaq's group, Sheikh Axmed Nur led another secret midnight escape of a large group of about one hundred from Banta to the Kenyan border. This group included Sadiq and Maliya, a married daughter of Cali Osman and Isha. They set out late at night, separating into two groups when some of the members wanted to rest, but Darood militiamen caught the resting group after pursuing them through the bush. The militiamen poured out all their water and confiscated their food and other belongings in an effort to force them to return to Banta. Maliya managed to escape the attack and ran ahead to alert the traveling group, which included Sheikh Axmed Nur, a central target of the pursuing militiamen, to forge ahead. The second group decided to continue as well, even though they knew this choice would mean death for many. Maliya made it to the refugee camp, where she also succumbed to the deadly diarrheal disease, becoming the first of Cali Osman's children to die.

The families of Cali Osman, Caliyow Isaaq, and Sheikh Axmed Nur were among the tens of thousands of famers from the Jubba Valley streaming toward the Kenyan border in 1992. As the fighting between various armed militia groups raged back and forth across the Jubba Valley, militias targeted valley farmers because they lacked protection—none of their jileec Somali clan allies came to their defense—and as farmers they were food producers and thus were attacked for their food reserves by hungry but non-food-producing militias. Tens of thousands of farmers were killed throughout the valley in 1991–92 defending their food reserves. Human rights organizations like Amnesty International, Human Rights Watch, and Africa Watch reported the appalling levels of violence directed against Jubba Valley villagers in the first years of the war. As Cali Osman, Caliyow Isaaq, and Sheikh Axmed Nur were escaping with their families from Banta, an Oxfam official called the valley "one big graveyard."[17]

The refugee camps offered little relief. The three families had lost many members and friends to starvation during the long trek from Banta and to

FIGURE 1.7 Maliya Cali Osman, Banta, 1988. Photograph by Jorge Acero.

the diarrhea that overcame them so soon after their arrival in the camps. The abuse at the hands of Somalis they experienced in Banta persisted in the camps, where jareer Somalis were constantly harassed, assaulted, and insulted. For women the situation was extreme: in one of our conversations about the camps, Isha closed her eyes, remembering: "The rapes. So many rapes." In our conversations over the years, many of my Banta friends mentioned the daily rapes, a horrific aspect of camp life repeatedly noted in reports by humanitarian and human rights agencies.

After several years in the refugee camps, news came of a UN and U.S. peace-keeping mission in Somalia, and the UNHCR, who ran the refugee camps, facilitated the repatriation of Somali Bantus to Somalia.[18] Cali Osman was eager to return. His sons remember his frustration at his enforced dependence and subjugation in the camps and his decision that he would rather die in his own village than live on handouts as a refugee. Remembering the threats against his surviving sons, Sheikh Axmed Nur chose to remain in the camps until he felt more certain about the prospects for peace.

FIGURE 1.8 Ambiya Cali Osman, center, and friends, Banta, 1988. Photograph by Jorge Acero.

Cali Osman's entire family except for the eldest children, son Ciise and daughter Rabaca, returned to the village in 1995, but discovered that "it was worse than ever," according to Isha. A few days after their return, their fifteen-year-old daughter, Ambiya, was stolen by a Darood man—Xussein's brother—who pointed a gun at Isha and forced her daughter away with him to another village. "I couldn't protect my daughter," Isha lamented, her face crumpling as she recounted her helplessness.

The much-publicized international peacekeeping mission had the contradictory effect of enhancing violence in the valley rather than reducing it, as different militias jockeyed to consolidate their control over territory. As those with weapons became increasingly murderous against villagers, Cali Osman's family debated whether they should risk another flight through the desert to Kenya when Isha announced her intention to flee once again. After losing Ambiya at gunpoint, it was the only way she believed she could protect her remaining children. Her chance came when a Darood woman drawing water from the river in the center of Banta was attacked by a crocodile. In the ensuing hysteria, the woman's armed relatives demanded that all the village men and boys run into the river to save her. Isha grabbed her youngest sons and fled the village. Remembering that moment, Isha's son Idris recounted how Maxamed Gedi ran after Isha, shooting at her, "But she was faster!" Another son hid in the bushes, while Cali Osman was forced to

FIGURE 1.9 Cali Osman on the banks of the Jubba River, Banta, 1988. Photograph by Jorge Acero.

enter the river with the other village men. Isha and her youngest children united with the son who hid in the bushes, and made it all the way back to Kenya, although this trip was far worse than the previous journey because no nongovernmental organizations or pastoralists offered assistance this time. Idris shuddered as he recalled the murky, urine-filled cattle ponds that offered rare and brief respite from their terrible thirst on the brutal three-week trek. This time they were refused entry at the border, in contravention to international protocol, but after several days of hiding at the border they managed to sneak across and walk all the way back to Dagahalley, one of the refugee camps at Dadaab.

Although Isha had lost two of her children, she had managed to save five, including her orphaned nephew whom she was raising as her son. But she soon learned that she had lost her husband as well: Cali Osman did not make it out of Banta. His family never saw him again. Refugees arriving at the camps brought them the news that he had perished.

Somalia's Civil War Is a Global Story

Civil war is always a global story. It is a story of how political divisions that become weaponized through engagements with global forces convert the nuanced differences characteristic of local life into deadly antagonisms. It is a story about how war, fostered by transnational networks, arms suppliers, external funding support, and global geopolitical connections, colonizes local inequalities and makes them murderous. It is a story about how status differences that neighbors manage and endure as part of daily life can become lethal in the context of uncertainty and violence. War arrived in Banta because a foreign-supported dictator used his access to U.S. and European foreign aid, granted because of Cold War interests, to arm local pastoralists, who then turned the weapons against their marginalized and stigmatized farmer-neighbors to acquire food, enslave labor, steal women, and claim rights to land made valuable through the expectation that international donors would return to resume their massive development projects. Somalia's civil war is indeed complicated, but the support of the U.S. government for a merciless dictator who armed his country and fostered discord among his citizens is a reminder that while the ultimate responsibility for war and peace lies with local people, behind every story of civil war is a story of connections and influences that span the globe.

Somalia's civil war is also a story about how terrible things have to be for farmers to abandon their land. Cali Osman, Caliyow Isaaq, and Sheikh Axmed Nur farmed the same plots their parents had farmed, harvesting enough to be able to marry several wives and support many children and grandchildren. Each man had earned a strong local reputation for prowess in valued skills—poetry and music, carpentry, healing and religion—in addition to wisdom, yet the men decided, together with their wives, to abandon their homes and risk a brutal journey with their children and grandchildren through the desert to Kenya, a flight that cost each family beloved members and that ultimately resulted in the dispersal of survivors between Somalia, Kenyan refugee camps, and throughout the United States.

Finally, Somalia's civil war is a story of the contemporary responsibilities and forms of mutuality wrought by the hierarchical historical engagements of the slave trade, colonization, and foreign aid. The connections and confrontations among the international actors who built, shaped, or profited from slavery, colonialism, Cold War patronage, and wartime intervention provoke contemporary questions about the relationships between Somali slave descendants and their pastoralist neighbors and between all Somalis and their former colonizers and Cold War patrons. If disengagement from Africa's violence is no longer an option in a globalized world, as Paul Richards argues in this chapter's epigraph, that is because Africa's violence is produced through its global entanglements. If localized violence has global origins, how is responsibility for the consequences of violence to be managed?

Writing about the refusal of French intellectuals to engage moral postcolonial questions of identity and difference because of their unwillingness to acknowledge the deep and profoundly complex connections of colonialism, Achille Mbembe cautions that, through slavery and colonialism, "the inhabitants of the earth were juxtaposed or brought together in a unity that is both emblematic and problematic. We are thus compelled, through these events, to pursue the question of all possible conditions of an authentic human encounter. . . . This encounter must begin through reciprocal disorientation."[19] "Reciprocal disorientation" is a scholarly phrase, perhaps, but an apt description of the decades following the flight of Somalis and Somali Bantus from Somalia to Kenya to Lewiston, as they reunited under very different circumstances in places of refuge, and as their dislocations brought them into close and intimate encounters with the American citizens whose taxes helped to fund American Cold War patronage, development schemes, and military interventions that destabilized their homeland. The following chapters follow them on their journey.

CHAPTER 2

The Humanitarian Condition

Physical movement is the natural, normal given of
human social life; what is abnormal, changeable,
and historically constructed is the idea that human
societies need to construct political borders and
institutions that define and constrain spatial mobility
in particular, regularized ways, such that immobility
becomes the norm.
—Noel Salazar and Alan Smart, "Anthropological
Takes on '(Im)Mobility'"

After their second flight from Somalia to Kenya, Isha and her remaining children rejoined the survivors from Caliyow Isaaq's family and Sheikh Axmed
Nur's family in the Dadaab refugee camps, where they became "official refugees," a legal category that exists in the contemporary world to manage and
contain people out of place. Before returning to their story in chapter 3, here
we examine what it means to be a refugee in the contemporary world.

Refugees are distinguished from other diasporic, mobile, transnational,
and displaced people by law and by policy. A specific set of international and
national laws defines the category of refugee, and a specific set of policies
directs the administration and legal movement of people who are formally

recognized as belonging to this legally defined category. To many Americans, the figure of the refugee is one of pathos: a person stripped of an identity, a country, and a culture, dependent upon the largesse of humanitarian agencies and the wealthy donor countries that fund them for sustenance and care. Anthropologist Michel Agier describes the refugee as living "at the outer limits of life—physical, social, political and economic—almost dropping out of the common space that should naturally connect all human beings."[1] The refugee's life, he says, is "a form of *no longer being* in the world, for a certain time or forever."[2] Philosophical and social science scholarship on refugees locates their exclusion from the international order of state structures as the basis for their liminal status, an apolitical existence theorized most influentially by Giorgio Agamben as the quintessential example of "bare life." Agamben argues that the origin of state power rests on the ancient Roman category of *homo sacer*, the figure whose expulsion from political life makes clear the political structures of belonging. Agamben's description of homo sacer—the person stripped of community, belonging, sociality, and identity, and reduced to bare life—offered a striking and useful image for a generation of scholars writing about contemporary refugees.[3]

While such an image departs from the actual experiences of many refugees in ways I explore later, the conceptual reduction of refugees to icons of bare humanity serves several purposes in the contemporary world. In a series of groundbreaking publications, anthropologist Liisa Malkki demonstrated how the treatment of refugees as people out of place affirms the legitimacy of an international order of nation-states in which everyone must belong somewhere.[4] Because their forced border crossing renders refugees effectively stateless and thus threatening to territorial sovereignty, the world's political powers define them as people who must be contained and managed, a problem to be solved by international institutions whose function it is to maintain the global order of nation-states.[5] The result is the creation of an "international refugee regime" consisting of an interconnected set of humanitarian institutions, policies, protocols, and practices that direct the management of people who, through forced displacement across an international border, are no longer nationally rooted as citizens.[6]

The image of refugees as bare humanity stripped of an identity and a home provokes concerns about moral responsibility for their care, a task often understood as based on an ethic of a shared humanity and undertaken by the humanitarian institutions that support the international refugee regime.[7] About half of the world's refugees are cared for, administered, and contained in refugee camps—the central node in the refugee regime—until they can return home or are accepted for resettlement in another country. As places that both sustain and constrain people out of place, refugee camps enact the tension between repression and compassion, as anthropologist Didier Fassin has noted, based in a moral economy "oscillating between sentiments of sympathy on the one hand and concern for order on the other hand, between a politics of pity and policies of control."[8] Refugee camps provide food and rudimentary shelter, as well as basic health care and sometimes education, but deny residents the right to self-determination, mobility, economic activity outside the camp, and participation in democratic decision making or self-governance. To the contrary, the humanitarian institutions that manage refugee camps desire their charges to remain passive, silent, apolitical, grateful, and dependent, while in turn benefiting from the representation of refugees as hapless victims because such an image is useful for attracting the charitable support of donors.[9] Refugees carry an iconography of destitution that inspires moral questions about the relationship between shared humanity and charity, an imagery unprovoked by other kinds of immigrants (such as tourists and guest workers). Thus refugees are a particularly compelling and confounding object of humanitarianism: they are simultaneously threatening and pitied, feared and revered as figures of base humanity, subject to judgments about their legitimacy as innocent victims and their worthiness for humanitarian charity and rescue.

The story of how Somali Bantus living in Kenyan refugee camps navigated the international refugee regime to gain resettlement in the United States demonstrates the limitations and condescending assumptions built into the portrayal of refugees as passive recipients of charity who have lost their place in the world. While the decision by the United States to accept almost 12,000 Somali Bantus for resettlement was heralded as a triumph of the humanitarian ethic of rescue and care by the UNHCR, the U.S. government, and the American media, in their own accounts Somali Bantus claim to be authors of their fate and creative strategists of their life trajectory. Their story challenges presumptions that African refugees in refugee camps are highly dependent on humanitarian largesse and "lacking a capacity for enterprise."[10] But, as we shall see, their ability to craft a path toward resettlement required careful navigation of the multiple, competing, and overlapping tensions of refugee identity. This chapter reviews the assessment by the U.S. government and UNHCR of Somali Bantus as worthy humanitarian subjects. Chapter 3 juxtaposes the image of Somali Bantus as dependent victims promoted by UNHCR and the United States with the version of their "rescue" told by my Somali Bantu interlocutors.[11] The contradictions in these accounts raise uncomfortable and difficult questions about the nature of humanitarianism and the role allotted to refugees in tales of global humanitarianism.

The International Refugee Regime

Contemporary scholarship on the history of the refugee as a figure of pathos, fear, or rescue identifies the post–World War II demographic upheaval in Europe as the foundational moment for the emergence of an interlinked international bureaucratic apparatus for identifying and controlling refugees. Although sociologist Saskia Sassen suggests that prior to the twentieth century, population movements within Europe followed a pattern defined primarily by labor migration and the term "refugee" only referred to French Huguenots who fled France after the revocation of the Edict of Nantes in 1685, historian Peter Gatrell traces the massive population movements in Europe that accompanied war and conflict between European empires prior to World War I.[12] Small nongovernmental organizations (NGOs) and humanitarian organizations addressed the needs of certain European refugee groups prior to World War I, but the large-scale movement of people in Europe did not immediately precipitate an international crisis because so many Europeans found new homes in America. Between 1881 and 1930, 27.6 million people, mostly from Europe, arrived in the United States.[13] America's liberal immigration policy until the early twentieth century offered free entry to anyone in good health, an open-door policy that narrowed only with the Chinese Exclusion Act of 1882, making Chinese the first ethnic group subject to immigration restrictions in the United States.[14]

"World War I marks the beginning of a period when the modern European state and its politico-military project create the setting for massive refugee movements on a scale hitherto not seen," writes Sassen.[15] European states were consolidating nationalist identities during this era, exchanging populations in a bid for nationalist homogeneity and pushing out those viewed as undesirable or not belonging, especially Jews.[16] Hannah Arendt famously labeled those forced from their homes by totalitarian movements during this era, most especially Jews, "the scum of the earth," arguing that "they were received as the scum of the earth everywhere" because of the power of totalitarian movements to disintegrate the concept of inalienable human rights everywhere.[17] The corresponding growth in anti-Semitism in the United States meant barriers to entry for Jews in the years leading up to and during World War II.[18] Engaged in its own process of national consolidation around a particular identity based on a specific construction of whiteness, the U.S. government implemented increased restrictions on immigration in the 1920s that privileged northern and western Europeans through an assignment of quotas by national origin for immigrant admissions, precipitating an even greater crisis in Europe as eastern and southern Europeans faced new barriers against their admission to the United States.[19] These barriers meant that many Jews attempting to escape Europe during World War II were refused admission.

Post–World War II Europe was a landscape of displaced people; millions of Europeans had been uprooted from their homes and had no place to go. President Truman committed to the creation of the International Refugee Organization in 1946 to manage the situation of Europe's displaced population, precipitating a political battle in the United States about the country's responsibility to assist and offer entry to Europe's displaced people.[20] While the initial focus of refugee relief organizations operating in Europe was repatriation, growing Cold War concerns shifted attention to protecting and resettling rather than repatriating people fleeing communism. Despite the anti-Semitism and anti-immigrant sentiment that characterized American views of refugees during and after World War II, the United States accepted about 350,000 refugees from 1945 to 1950.[21] Scholars suggest guilt about the Holocaust and the efforts of the American Jewish lobby confronted American anti-Semitism and concerns about Jewish links to political subversives, eventually tipping the American refugee debate in favor of a more welcoming policy for those fleeing communist countries, including Jews.[22]

The creation of the UNHCR in 1949–50 replaced the International Refugee Organization and was followed by the 1951 Convention Relating to the Status of Refugees, an attempt to codify a definition of and protections for refugees. Signatories to the 1951 convention could limit the definition of a refugee to people in Europe, thus excluding groups like Palestinians who were displaced in the 1948 war.[23] The United States initially refused to contribute funds to the UNHCR or to sign the convention because it did not want to be held accountable for helping refugees,[24] although it did ultimately sign the 1967 Protocol Relating to the Status of Refugees, which expanded the protocol for refugees to the global arena and which became the basis for refugee admittance policy in the United States until 1980. The familiar language of the convention defines a refugee as a person who, "owing to well-founded fear of being persecuted for reasons of race, religion, nationality, membership of a particular social group or political opinion, is outside the country of his nationality and is unable or, owing to such fear, is unwilling to avail himself of the protection of that country; or who, not having a nationality and being outside the country of his former habitual residence as a result of such events, is unable or, owing to such fear, is unwilling to return to it." A key feature of the convention and protocol was the principle of nonrefoulement, an agreement that refugees could not be forced to return to the places they had fled in order to escape persecution.

The creation of these instruments for managing people forced to flee their home countries left in place a profound contradiction that continues to this day to constrain the ability for self-determination of people escaping persecution. The mandate of the UNHCR was simply to offer protection to people who had fled their home countries (in accordance with the convention definition) through granting a formal designation of refugee status, which protects those so labeled from being forcibly returned to the place from which they fled. It is an administrative designation, intended to categorize and identify people out of place and to offer refugees protection in a way that would minimize their presence as a problem for states. (The preamble to the convention makes this last point clearly in "expressing the wish that all States, recognizing the social and humanitarian nature of the problem of refugees, will do everything within their power to prevent this problem from becoming a cause of tension between States.") At its inception, the UNHCR provided no logistical support to refugees; this was the purview of other NGOs, which had taken over the management of refugee populations in Europe after World War II from the Allied military forces.[25] Only gradually did the UNHCR mandate grow to include responsibility for setting up and managing refugee camps.

Refugee camps exist because the principle of nonrefoulement is not matched by a legal right to asylum for those officially designated as refugees; refugees cannot be forced to return to their home countries, but no other county is obligated to take them in.[26] Camps, as warehouses for those in refugee limbo, thus exist to care for, contain, and monitor people designated as refugees and to ensure that they do not attempt to settle or assimilate into other countries outside of legal channels for immigration. The emergence of the international refugee regime after World War II is thus most fundamentally about protecting the global system of national sovereignty by containing and monitoring people out of place because they have fled across an international border. It is not about supporting the rights of refugees to self-determination. Emphasizing this point, anthropologist Shahram Khosravi, who himself lived in refugee camps after fleeing Iran, wryly observes, "Refugee camps constitute the most significant characteristic of the modern nation-state."[27]

It is worth noting that the creation of the international refugee regime as a form of protection for national sovereignty accompanied decolonization and the postcolonial consolidation of newly independent countries firmly within the nation-state model. Thus, at the very moment that former colonies were transitioning to independence, former colonizers were working to ensure the hegemony of an international structure to control population movement, enforce the nation-state as the only form of internationally recognized political belonging, and make certain that they could retain supreme authority over who crossed their borders. Like the "murderous humanitarianism" that colonial powers employed in the age of colonialism, the contemporary international refugee regime can be recognized as a postcolonial continuation of colonial policies of containing, boundary making, and control.[28] Historian Peter Gatrell notes that by the turn of the twenty-first century, over half the world's refugees were located in Africa, where anticolonial struggles, Cold War proxy wars, and struggles over control of resources produced massive refugee flows following the end of colonial rule. "The experiences of countless refugees in the African continent have been bound up with the refugee camp," he writes, arguing that the bureaucratic approach to containment and control by humanitarian institutions that is the hallmark of the contemporary international refugee regime emerged in postcolonial African refugee camps.[29]

Following Malkki's ethnographic and theoretical work on the emergence of the international refugee regime to manage people dangerously out of place, more recent ethnographic research on refugee camps offers a sharply critical view of their purpose and role in the contemporary world and the treatment of those who live there. Critics argue that the international refugee regime exists to protect the wealthier countries in the global north, which fund the humanitarian agencies that manage the camps, from the movement of people in the global south, where the majority of refugees originate and the majority of refugee camps are located.[30] As of 2012, four-fifths of the world's refugees live in poorer countries in the global south, with Pakistan, Democratic Republic of the Congo, and Kenya hosting the most refugees per gross domestic product. Although scholars argue that the movement of refugees across borders in the global south is often linked to political and economic practices of wealthier, powerful countries in the global north (such as Cold War–era support for abusive leaders, structural adjustment policies mandated by donor governments that enabled land alienation from poor farmers, support for multinational corporations that use violence against local populations, or conflicts fueled by the extraction of resources valued by the global north), governments in the global north desire what geographer Jennifer Hyndman calls "strategies of containment": practices that humanitarian agencies utilize to keep refugees away from the borders of donor nations in the north and close to the borders of the countries in the global south from which they have fled.[31] Critical scholars thus argue that the international refugee regime and its humanitarian practices are based on a fundamental inequality that grants power to the global north (and the staff employed by humanitarian agencies funded by a few countries in the global north) over people in the global south who are fleeing persecution, war, or disaster.[32]

Currently, the overwhelming orientation of the international refugee regime is to warehouse and repatriate refugees rather than to enable permanent resettlement outside the refugee camp in another country. Rising neoliberal concerns in donor countries in the 1980s about welfare dependency resulted in an emphasis on repatriation rather than third-country resettlement, producing a new context where, according to law professor and former deputy high commissioner of UNHCR T. Alexander Aleinikoff, "refugee law has become immigration law, emphasizing protection of borders rather than protection of persons."[33] For the past two decades, the UNHCR has requested resettlement for only about 1 percent of the total number of refugees administered in UNHCR refugee camps, while the number of refugees living in such camps for over ten years continues to grow.

Although initially envisioned as a temporary measure to protect and contain people who have fled their home countries, refugee camps now appear to be a permanent fixture of the global landscape. Like those at Dadaab, many camps house people whose families have lived in them for three generations. Yet the humanitarian management of refugee camps continues to rely on the logic of camps controlled by humanitarian agencies as temporary responses to crises, rather than permanent residential locations where residents participate in governance, have free mobility, and have universal opportunities for education and economic activity. Despite their longevity and size, refugee camps do not appear on maps, are not factored into population statistics of host countries, and are treated as zones of exclusion within rather than as part of the countries in which they are located. This fallacy is a collective form of denial and fantasy that only serves the interests of countries who do not wish to allow refugees to cross their borders.

Describing the international refuge regime in such harsh terms challenges the conventional and popular perception of humanitarianism as motivated by a charitable impulse to help people in need on the basis of a sense of a shared humanity. Certainly, many who choose to work for the humanitarian agencies that manage refugee camps do so from an altruistic ethic of mutual humanity and genuine care and bring an enormous personal commitment and ideology of hope to their jobs. The point is not that they are confused or misinformed; it is, rather, that the broader system is set up to maintain inequality, disempower refugees, and protect the borders of the global north, in addition to providing care for displaced people while global powers determine where they will be allowed to go. As political scientist Jenny Edkins says, "The role of humanitarian intervention can be seen as a tightening of a global structure of authority and control."[34]

Somali Refugees, Dadaab

When Somalis began arriving in large numbers in Kenya after 1991, the Kenyan government provided land for refugee camps but, at the insistence of UNHCR, ceded to it responsibility for camp management, which, in turn, subcontracted to other NGOs for services in the camps (such as CARE, Medécins Sans Frontières, and others).[35] The UNHCR holds sole authority for recognizing and registering refugees (although this task was also subcontracted to other NGOs under the management of UNHCR). New arrivals are interviewed in order to distinguish between "legitimate" refugees, who are granted admission to the camp and ration cards for food, and "fakers," who are denied ration cards and the right to live in the camp. Camp policy forbids Somali refugees with ration cards from leaving the camp boundaries to travel or engage in economic activities outside the camps and requires their participation in regular head-count exercises within the camps designed to ensure control over the distribution of ration cards. Originally built in 1991–92 to house 90,000 refugees, by 2012 Dadaab was home to over 460,000 refugees, including some who had been there since its inception.

Anthropologists and other scholars working in refugee camps describe them as "space(s) of exception" that offer "a unique setting for the arbitrary exercise of power" where refugees, as recipients of charity, have no rights or legal claims, and "everything is possible for the people in control."[36] Ethnographers describe the refugee camps at Dadaab as a zone of "supreme power" wielded by UNHCR and other humanitarian agencies whose staff actively reduce resident refugees to life in its barest form.[37] Detailed, on-the-ground ethnographic studies of the Dadaab camps provide ample evidence of these claims, documenting the ways in which camp policies and practices disempower refugees, who are often treated with contempt and condescension and denied any voice in democratic decision-making processes. Camp administrators offered researchers explicitly antidemocratic explanations about their resistance to refugee participation in the governance of the camp.[38] Jennifer Hyndman, who worked in the Dadaab camps in the 1990s, describes her shock at the neocolonial hierarchy of camp life, where expatriate administrators lived separately from the camp in an exclusive, well-guarded compound where they were served by poorly or uncompensated refugees, while local staff lived on-site in small dwellings and had unchecked authority. She describes the specter of foreign camp administrators carrying out head counts in ways that camp residents resisted, and how the power hierarchy between them allowed the former to label the latter (namely the Sudanese and Somali resident refugees who objected to the administration and management of such forms of ordering and labeling) as uncooperative and difficult. Based on her two years of research in the Dadaab camps in 1999–2001, anthropologist Cindy Horst reported that camp management was characterized by corruption, a lack of accountability, and a condescending view of refugee aid as charity that allowed camp staff to distribute ration cards and other services in an authoritative, demeaning way.[39]

Refugee studies scholars and activists Guglielmo Verdirame and Barbara Harrell-Bond conducted a detailed review in 1997 of the conditions of UNHCR refugee camps in Kenya and Uganda, and their published exposé offers a devastating portrait of UNHCR management of the Kenyan refugee camps that housed Somalis, charging UNHCR and its subcontractors with allowing discrimination against Somali Bantus, exploiting refugee employees by paying them minimal incentives rather than salaries, withholding food as a form of control, engaging in humiliating, degrading practices toward refugees by treating them as potential liars and cheats, utilizing various strategies to keep refugees from being able to get ration cards in order to minimize the number of people with refugee status, withholding information about asylum applications and procedures to which refugees are legally entitled, and denying any right of appeal for administrative decisions about refugee status or asylum applications.[40] Echoing Philip Gourevitch's charge in his *New Yorker* article about the humanitarian industry that "humanitarians . . . enjoy total impunity," Verdirame and Harrell-Bond conclude that "camps are spaces that are virtually *beyond the rule of law* and in which the life of refugees ends up being governed by a highly oppressive blend of rules laid down by the humanitarian agencies and the customary practices of the various refugee communities" (such as Somali racism against Somali Bantus).[41]

Scholars' complaints about the management of the Dadaab camps were not just about administrative corruption, authoritarianism, and condescension but also took note of the extreme insecurity that pervaded the camps. Banditry, assault, and rape occurred frequently both inside the camp and outside the perimeter of the camp where refugees had to travel to get water or firewood or to move between the camps that made up Dadaab. Jeff Crisp's 1999 report on Dadaab's rampant insecurity acknowledges a few policies introduced by UNHCR in an attempt to better protect the people living there, but Cindy Horst's 2006 ethnography concludes, "The Dadaab camps do not naturally provide economic and physical security to the refugees who live there. On the contrary, the camp organization itself serves to exacerbate feelings of uncertainty and insecurity."[42]

Somali Bantu friends now living in Lewiston, Syracuse, and Hartford hold profoundly unhappy memories of life in the Dadaab camps. Some, like Sheikh Axmed Nur's son, could not find words to describe life there. Abshirow, whose photograph in the velvet dinner jacket so delighted the slide show audience, told me, simply, "It was so horrible that it is undiscussable. No one should have to be in such a place." My former research assistant Abdulkadir described how he lived on the perimeter of the camp with his wife and children for years after they were denied the right to live inside before finally being granted refugee status because a BBC report exposed the appalling living conditions of Abdulkadir's family and others, who lived in makeshift dwellings made of tree branches, dependent on begging food from camp residents. Many of the memories people shared mentioned the sexual abuse of women, the almost arbitrary decision-making power of camp administrators, and their ill treatment as ethnic minorities by their fellow Somali refugees.

The racism experienced by jareer minorities in Somalia persisted in the camps. Isha's son Iman recalled the taunts of "adoon!" from jileec camp residents he endured every week when he visited the camp market, his family obligation as the youngest child. The first Somali Bantu man to graduate from high school in the camp recalls arriving at school one day to find his desk defaced by graffiti in black marker with the phrase "JAREER but smart." The teacher told the culprit to clean it up, which he did with a razor, permanently destroying the desk surface. The young jareer men who determined to use their time in the camp to study, like Sadiq, recall their fury at how they were treated by their fellow Somalis, who barred them from the paying camp jobs controlled by Somali camp staff, mocked them in public, and belittled their academic accomplishments. Somali Bantus in the United States say that while UNHCR and its contracted agencies administered the camp, the few Somali staff employed by the agencies acted as gatekeepers for the limited number of paying jobs available to qualified refugees. Revealing a small arena of refugee control, one Somali Bantu told me, "The whites [running the camps] just worked their jobs. They just make their money but they don't know anything. They hired whomever their Somali employees said to hire." When one Somali Bantu friend received the highest score on a qualifying exam for a paying camp position to register deaths, Somali applicants who scored lower told the authorities he would be killed if he was awarded the job. Although the authorities offered the position to him at his own risk, he declined it. Researchers and Somali Bantus alike describe how racism against Somali Bantus continued unabated in the Dadaab camps.

U.S. Resettlement

Although warehousing and repatriating refugees remains the priority for UNHCR and its primary funders, UNHCR will facilitate resettlement applications for selected groups and individuals.[43] Countries can choose to accept refugees for resettlement according to whatever principles they wish, and thus the history of refugee resettlement in the United States has been closely tied to U.S. political interests. From 1945 to the mid-1980s, the United States accepted more than 2 million refugees, over 90 percent of whom came from communist countries because the U.S. government used the offer of refuge, through presidential parole power, as a political tool against communism.[44] Those accepted included 40,000 Hungarians after the 1956 Soviet invasion, nearly 800,000 Cubans after the Cuban revolution, 100,000 Soviet Jews in the 1970s, and, after the fall of Saigon, 1.5 million Vietnamese and Cambodians.[45] Refugees fleeing authoritarian regimes supported by the United States during this era, such as those of several Central American countries, were rarely admitted through official channels.

The large number of Indochinese and Soviet Jewish refugees admitted into the United States from 1975 to 1979 precipitated a restructuring of American refugee admittance policy, resulting in the 1979 creation of the Office of the U.S. Coordinator of Refugee Affairs and the passage of the Refugee Act of 1980. The act replaced the presidential ad hoc practice for admitting refugees with a baseline quota for refugees, initially set at 50,000 per year, and gave Congress a role in identifying refugees for admittance. Most significantly, the act extended the definition of a refugee beyond someone fleeing from communism and laid out a formal system for greater coordination among the UNHCR, State Department, Department of Justice, and the court system for deciding which refugees to accept.

While many refugee activists heralded the 1980 Refugee Act as a victory for humanitarianism because refugee admissions were no longer to be exclusively tied to American political interests, a combination of factors soured American enthusiasm for admitting refugees after the passage of the act.[46] Hundreds of thousands of Cubans, Haitians, and Indochinese arrived in 1980, their numbers augmented by other immigrants from many countries, and American host communities were uncertain about and increasingly unwilling to commit to supporting more new arrivals.[47] Concurrent with the passage of the act, when President Reagan assumed office in 1980 he dropped the number of refugee admissions from 234,000 in 1980 to 173,000 in 1981, to 70,000 in 1985–86. The concerns about welfare dependency that characterized political rhetoric during the early 1980s extended to include refugees as well, stoking the anti-immigrant/antirefugee sentiments that remain powerful today.

During the heyday of U.S. refugee resettlement (1945–80), hardly any of those admitted were African (in 1980, Africans constituted less than 2 percent of admitted refugees[48]), a pattern that continued into the 1990s as overall refugee admissions continued to shrink while refugee flows in Africa grew. By the late 1990s, members of the Congressional Black Caucus, some of whom participated in NGO-hosted trips to African refugee camps during the 1990s, stepped up their lobbying efforts to raise the ceiling on African refugees accepted for resettlement.[49] In the 1970s the caucus had protested the virtual open-door policy offered to Cubans while hundreds of thousands of Haitians were deported, suggesting a racist refugee policy was in effect. In the 1990s, when caucus members protested the generous admittance policy for those fleeing the Balkan wars while keeping the door closed for Africans, the U.S. government responded to this embarrassing criticism by asking the UNHCR to identify a discrete group of Africans who might qualify for resettlement.[50]

The UNHCR identified two African groups as resettlement priorities: the Sudanese "Lost Boys" and the "Somali Bantus," describing both as extremely vulnerable groups who could not be returned to their home countries. In 1999 the United States offered both groups P2 status, a resettlement designation given only to groups "of special humanitarian concern."[51] As plans got underway to bring the Somali Bantus to the United States, the resettlement program announcements in UNHCR publications and the American media introduced them as a "persecuted minority" with a history of slavery who had no other place to go. Somali Bantus seemed to offer a perfect profile of innocent victims whose history resonated with American shame about slavery and pride about the civil rights era, a point noted in an issue of UNHCR's *Refugees* magazine devoted to the Somali Bantu resettlement program in advance of their arrival in the United States: "Ironically, their existence had many parallels with former slaves in America's deep south until that country's 1960's civil rights movement changed history."[52]

The Somali Bantu issue of *Refugees* described their history of ill treatment and subjugation in Somalia, their persecution during the war, and their lack of resettlement alternatives: "For a decade the U.N. refugee agency tried to find a new country for approximately 12,000 so-called Somali Bantu, a group whose ancestors were seized by Arab slavers from their ancestral homelands, who continued to be widely discriminated against and victimized in their 'new' home in Somalia prior to the war and who vowed they would not return to that country even if peace is restored."[53] The magazine described failed

UNHCR efforts to resettle the Somali Bantus in their "ancestral homeland" in Tanzania in 1993 and Mozambique in 1997, efforts thwarted by the budget constraints of those governments. According to the magazine, the rejections left the Bantus dispirited and without hope, until news arrived of the U.S. offer to accept the group, initiating "a breathtaking journey from a semi-slave past to a future of unlimited freedom and choice."[54]

Refugee activists heralded the announcement of the Somali Bantu resettlement program as a triumph for humanitarianism. In her review of the decision-making process to offer P2 resettlement to the two African groups, legal scholar Heidi Boas argues that the resettlement offer demonstrated that the power of interest groups and the ethic of humanitarianism had at last become more significant than foreign policy objectives in the decision about who would receive refuge in the United States.[55] Boas suggests that a humanitarian ethic, rather than national self-interest, must have motivated the resettlement offer because the Somali Bantus brought no relevant skills, education, resources, family ties, or international significance to the United States and would need "round the clock help in navigating through a culture so different from their own" after their arrival.[56] Lamenting this same conclusion, the Center for Immigration Studies, a partisan anti-immigrant organization, criticized the offer of refuge to Somali Bantus as indicative of a shift from foreign policy and national interest to a "global human rights agenda" as the guiding force of U.S. refugee resettlement.[57]

Affirming the humanitarian theme, news reports across the United States promoted an image of American benevolence in choosing the Somali Bantus for resettlement. Newspaper accounts described the Somali Bantus as utter victims in desperate need of rescue: the *New York Times* described the Bantus as living at the very bottom of the bottom of the barrel in Dadaab, while the Somali Bantu issue of *Refugees* described them as submissive, intimidated, and charmingly naive and a UNHCR source told the *Washington Post*, "The Somali Bantus are the closest thing you will find to a people who are stateless."[58] News reports described their mistreatment and extreme discrimination by Somalis, emphasizing their darker complexion as compared to ethnic Somalis, a theme repeated in other reports as well despite its inaccuracy.[59] Descriptions such as "Africa's lost tribe" (*New York Times*) and "among the most persecuted people on earth" (*National Geographic*) highlighted the group's vulnerability and history of exploitation as descendants of slaves.[60] The news article titles affirm the humanitarian impulse: "Somali Bantu, Trapped in Kenya, Seek a Home" (*New York Times*); "US Opens Arms to Bantu Somalis" (*Christian Science Monitor*); "Following Freedom's Trail" (*Newsweek*).[61]

Because of their illiteracy, lack of education, rural background, and history of persecution, Somali Bantus were widely described as particularly needy and unprepared for modern life. News accounts revealed acute fascination with a primitive-meets-modern theme, demonstrated in the repeated contrast between Somali Bantu prewar life and the life that awaited them in the United States. "Most have never seen a light switch or telephone, or even a building that wasn't made of mud," reported *Newsweek*. *Refugees* magazine explained, "They are sturdy farmworkers with few other skills, who have never turned on an electric light switch, used a flush toilet, crossed a busy street, ridden in a car or on an elevator, seen snow or experienced air conditioning." The *New York Times* described them as "almost completely untouched by modern life. . . . They measure time by watching the sun rise and fall over their green fields and mud huts."[62]

A Horatio Alger undercurrent accompanied their characterization as contemporary primitives. The Somali Bantu issue of *Refugees* called them "a lucky few" and a *New York Times* article lauded the United States as "A Place of Miracles" for the refugees, while the Center for Immigration Studies complained that Somali Bantu refugees won "the jackpot" with the "dazzling" opportunity to come to America.[63] While celebrating the "dazzling" opportunity afforded by the resettlement plan, news accounts and policy documents nevertheless predicted that, because of their backwardness and lack of exposure to modern technology, the transition to life in the United States would be difficult and challenging for resettled Somali Bantus. Reporting on the plans to prepare Somali Bantus for their journey to the United States, *Refugees* magazine said they would receive a crash course in cultural orientation and basic survival skills for adapting to American life, although the *Newsweek* article cautioned, "What happens next is surprisingly unclear. . . . Some relief officials worry that the government isn't doing enough to ready the Bantus for life in America, and that those who are unable to find jobs will wind up trading one kind of poverty for another." The article ends with a quote from a Somali Bantu man: "'I hear the government lets you keep a cow wherever you want in America,' he says with obvious pleasure. 'I need a cow, because I need fresh milk.'" The reporter concludes, "Imagine his surprise."[64]

Security Is the Top Concern

Despite the abundant accolades celebrating the humanitarian basis for the Somali Bantu resettlement program, security protocol remained the top concern in its management. Assuaging any doubts about the legitimacy of Somali Bantu refugees as worthy recipients of humanitarian charity in the post-9/11 age of suspicion, U.S. news reports confirmed that upon their arrival, Somali

Bantus would be "one of the most heavily screened groups of prospective immigrants to the US."[65]

In Kenya's refugee camps, UNHCR (and its subcontractors) have absolute authority over which cases are referred and then approved for resettlement, an assessment of legitimacy determined through interviews by administrative and contracted staff. As the number of refugees seeking resettlement has grown while the desire of potential host countries to accept refugees for resettlement has shrunk, the UNHCR interview process has become saturated with suspicion and an orientation toward rejecting resettlement applications. Verdirame and Harrell-Bond reported that according to an authority in Dadaab at the time of their study in 1997, the UNHCR had denied 75 percent of the resettlement applications of refugees living there.

After the 1999 U.S. State Department announcement of the Somali Bantu resettlement plan,[66] interviews to confirm the legitimate claim to refugee status and persecution of Somali Bantus living in Dadaab got under way. Even though Somali Bantus were given a P2 group designation for resettlement, refugee resettlement protocol still required validation of every single person included in the group resettlement plan. Somali Bantu applicants had to pass a series of tests to be accepted as part of the resettlement program, after which they were transferred to another refugee camp in northern Kenya, Kakuma, for further processing. To the consternation of refugee activists and humanitarians in the United States, as well as the refugees themselves, the process ended up taking five years because of repeated delays prompted by security concerns.

The repeated post-9/11 suspensions of the Somali Bantu resettlement process provoked angry denunciations of the U.S. government's commitment to humanitarianism by refugee activists who argued that the case for resettlement for this group had already been made and that the refugees selected for resettlement had already been verified and confirmed. Bill Frelick, director of policy for the U.S. Committee on Refugees, argues that U.S. refugee resettlement post-9/11 dramatically shifted away from the humanitarian ethic that was supposed to guide the offer of resettlement following the 1980 Refugee Act to a new "security model" in which "refugees often came to be regarded with deep suspicion, sometimes seen as being terrorists themselves or as being the sea in which the terrorist fish could hide and swim. Fear of terrorism often exacerbated preexisting xenophobic and racist tendencies."[67] Whereas during the Cold War years refugees were viewed as heroic, freedom loving, and politically valuable, Frelick says post-9/11 refugees are suspected of colluding with terrorists: "Under the security paradigm, refugees are devalued to the point where providing asylum or intervening to provide source-country solutions are trumped by the desire to keep terrorists out."[68] In his February 12, 2002, testimony to the Senate Judiciary Immigration Subcommittee about the post-9/11 suspension of refugee resettlement, Frelick expressed his frustration: "I will hasten to add that very few of the groups that I would mention would be ones that would [be] unfamiliar to the State Department. We have been in discussions with them for years on some of these groups, Somali Bantu in Kenya, for example, or the Baku Armenians in Moscow, and I'd have to say that the response has often been bureaucratic, passive, and at times downright uncaring and cynical."[69]

In the same Senate hearing, Leonard Glickman of the Hebrew Immigrant Aid Society added that the State Department had appeared to be reforming the resettlement process, then said,

> It sort of ground to a halt this end of the summer, this past fall, and nothing has happened, and I think one of the most startling examples of that is the Somali Bantu. I mean, it was clearly identified as a group that were in need of resettlement, in need of the protection of the United States. Everybody was on the same page, including PRM [U.S. State Department Bureau of Population, Refugees, and Migration], that this was a group that—and UNHCR, that this was a group that needed our services, and not a single Somali Bantu has arrived in the United States. It's outrageous.[70]

Defending the resettlement policy and reminding the activists that Somali Bantu resettlement depends on U.S. generosity, Gene Dewey, the newly minted director of PRM, cautioned the Senate subcommittee, "Perhaps only in America are the people and its leaders capable of waging a major military campaign while keeping the imperatives of humanity both in assistance and refugee admissions at the top of the national agenda."[71] In fact, refugee admissions were not a priority that year, when the United States filled far less than half of the 70,000 slots designated for refugees. Despite the fact that the Somali Bantu had already been accepted and screened for resettlement, they were given none of the 2002 slots and only 803 of the 70,000 slots in 2003.[72]

A U.S. State Department document with the subtitle "Case Study of Processing Complexity and Unforeseen Delays" confirms that security concerns caused the repeated delays in the Somali Bantu resettlement process.[73] The first planned visit to Kakuma refugee camp by Department of Homeland Security officers for reverification was canceled because of ongoing post-9/11 fears of insecurity for U.S. personnel in the camp, and then processing was further delayed by a corruption scandal involving camp staff and administrators who were accused of selling slots in the Somali Bantu resettlement program to Somalis. About the repeated delays, the State Department report explained, with no hint of irony, "This lag necessitated a new round of security and medical clearances, because such clearances are good only for a limited period." New security concerns, and then flooding, further delayed the review of new cases until 2004, by which time the processing of most Somali Bantu had taken five years.[74]

The penultimate step in the resettlement process was a final interview in Nairobi, after which Somali Bantus either boarded a plane to the United States or were rejected and sent back to Kakuma refugee camp with no right to appeal their rejection. By the time a person reached the interview in Nairobi, he or she had already been verified by UNHCR staff as a member of the Somali Bantu "persecuted minority group," reverified by a special UNHCR reverification team in 2001, rescreened by the International Office of Migration for the transfer to Kakuma refugee camp, cleared by U.S. Department of Homeland Security staff in Kakuma for the trip to Nairobi, and approved by an FBI background check and a health screening, becoming the most heavily screened immigrants in American history.

Conclusion

The humanitarian lens focuses on refugees as innocent victims of political struggles not of their making, reduced to bare humanity, dependent on charity. During the Cold War, the American offer of refuge was a political act wrapped in a discourse of moral responsibility for those fleeing communism, including Southeast Asians abandoned by the U.S. withdrawal from Vietnam. As the Cold War drew to a close, refugee activists hoped an apolitical form of charitable humanitarianism would replace the old political calculus, identifying the offer of refuge to Sudanese Lost Boys and Somali Bantus as an indication of such an orientation.

As the number of refugees continues to grow, and as security concerns pervade the U.S. refugee resettlement process, refugee activists and scholars debate the criteria that should be used for determining resettlement priorities. Some, like anthropologist David Haines, criticize the withering American commitment to accepting refugees, betraying what he chidingly calls an "on-the-run morality," a concern shared by many scholars arguing for an expansion in American refugee admissions.[75] Other writers attempt to define a new ethics of resettlement humanitarianism in a world complicated by mobility of all kinds, seeking to draw clear lines between those eligible for resettlement because they are fleeing physical persecution and those ineligible because they are fleeing starvation resulting from economic policies or disasters that have destroyed their livelihoods.[76] Those who advocate for the rights of people to move in search of safety or a better life for any reason at all reject such a distinction, while noting that those most at risk for starvation after an economic or environmental disaster are usually those most marginalized by their governments.[77] Anthropologists studying shifting trends of asylum in Europe ascertain the rise of a new moral discourse reshaping resettlement bureaucracy, suspecting a new hierarchy of suffering and rescue is taking shape that prioritizes the ill as most worthy of asylum, while barriers to other asylum applications continue to grow.[78]

Imagining refugees as problems to be solved because they are people temporarily out of place whose liminality threatens international order, whose dependence requires charitable support, and whose lack of citizenship means they lack political rights and claims obscures the fact that refugees are always going to be active political agents intricately connected to and engaged in international affairs. Anthropological studies that critically deconstruct humanitarian practice reveal its basis as a technology of power wielded by powerful sovereign nations against the mobile, reliant on inaccurate assumptions, images, and moral discourses. As mobility increases because of the forces of modernization and globalization, and as new generations continue to come of age in refugee camps, it seems clear that the mobility associated with seeking refuge is no longer an aberration to be reconciled with international order, but rather may be *remaking* international order. Sociologist Zygmunt Bauman calls refugees "the waste of globalization," but they are also icons of globalization. Humanitarianism, as a technology for managing people out of place, thus loses its discursive luster as charity based on compassion and becomes recognized, instead, as a political act of control and domination.[79]

Somali Bantus appeared to fit the image of the perfect refugee, described in UNHCR publications and American news reports as apolitical victims living in a premodern state of feudal serfdom. Yet, as the previous and next chapters show, this image is a fabrication, crafted out of the image of innocent victimhood required by the international refugee regime and the savvy political foresight of the Somali Bantus themselves. Despite the *New York Times'* claim that the Somali Bantus are "almost completely untouched by modern life," their history is shaped by forces associated with modernity. Colonial battles and the slave trade brought their ancestors to the Jubba Valley early in the past century, after which the history of U.S. and European involvement in Somalia helped to define their valley as an object of international development interest, to support and fund a land reform program that would disenfranchise the farmers living there, to maintain as a Cold War ally a regime that engaged in significant human rights abuses and held little popular support, to support the massive weaponization of the country, and then to topple that regime. Theirs is a story of entanglements with very modern phenomena, and their liminality as refugees in Kenya is tied to the particular history of Somalia's engagements with its foreign donors.

In chapter 3 we turn to the story Somali Bantus tell of their journey to America. This story is far, far more complicated than a simple tale of humanitarian generosity extended to helpless, dependent victims.

Becoming Somali Bantus

The misplaced assumption that high dependency
ratios in camps or among self-settled refugees
deprived them of a capacity for enterprise is belied
by the historical evidence, although this is not to
overlook the fact that refugees might emphasize
their vulnerability for tactical reasons, such as to
improve access to resources.... Refugee life in camps
has, so to say, never stood still.
—Peter Gatrell, *The Making of the Modern Refugee*

Describing what happened when the armed Somalis took over Banta, my former field assistant Garad explained, "Before the fighting started I thought I
was Somali, but after the Somalis pushed us aside I understood I was different.
Before that all I knew was I was Somali, same culture, same religion, but when
they took over Banta and ordered everyone around and called us adoon I realized I was different. After we escaped to Kenya was the time we understood
we had another name, Somali Bantu."

Even though middle Jubba residents had been loath to speak about their
experiences of abuse during my residency in Banta, at the Bates MLK Day panel
the panelists departed dramatically from their previous script, speaking

passionately about the significance of the Somali Bantu identity and how this identity as a racially stigmatized minority targeted them for abuse and exploitation in Somalia and in the camps. They described how their history of enslavement and minority status led to their marginalization, poverty, illiteracy, lack of education, and assaults they regularly experienced guarding their fields against encroaching pastoralists in prewar Somalia, as well as the rapes, theft, and humiliation that characterized their lives in the refugee camps. Although their unequal status was patently obvious during my year in Banta, and although I had written extensively on the jileec-jareer prewar hierarchy, I had never heard any Jubba Valley farmers talk so publicly like this before the war. To the contrary, as noted in chapter 1, whenever Somali pastoralists assaulted or abused villagers the matter was handled through clan mediators, who attributed any violence to individual malevolent personalities, while middle valley villagers resisted the idea that they shared an overarching identity around which they could unite. But in their 2006 MLK Day panel presentation, each speaker claimed a deeply felt sense of historic injustice on the basis of this group identity, making it clear that a new overarching identity based in the collective experience of racism had emerged from the violence of Somalia's war and the farmers' experiences in the Kenyan refugee camps. The emergence of Somali Bantu identity is a remarkable story of how cultural creativity, bureaucratic mandates, and social entrepreneurship combined to produce a new identity out of ethnic ambiguity and injustice.

Not only had the Somali Bantus found a collective voice with which to articulate their historical grievances, they also claimed an active role in negotiating a future free from injustice. As I visited friends from Banta in their new homes in Lewiston, Hartford, and Syracuse, I realized that their version of their resettlement story departed considerably from the popular story of their utter victimization and rescue by UNHCR and the U.S. media recounted in chapter 2. In place of describing themselves as apolitical, dependent, premodern victims, Somali Bantus in the United States recall their leaders as architects of their group resettlement who actively pursued resettlement options, crafting an identity that met with UNHCR approval, partnering with UNHCR staff to delineate who could participate in the resettlement program, and introducing the various criteria for evaluating the legitimacy of Somali Bantu applicants. Their story is one in which they created an essentialized identity in collaboration with UNHCR's need for clear definitions to determine refugee legitimacy and worthiness. In the process, they embraced the Somali Bantu label as personally meaningful, claimed precolonial tribal and linguistic associations that were required of Somali Bantu identity, crafted a narrative of suffering that matched UNHCR's desire for victimization, and reconfigured families to conform to U.S. family forms. In their version, which is nevertheless replete with instances of failure and compromise, they were the planners, strategists, and actors, and UNHCR was a reluctant but powerful collaborator.

Refugee camp administrators see like a state, so to speak.[1] They count, name, categorize, ration, assign ID cards, and require stable identities, stable camp residence, and respect for borders. Refugees behave like (many) citizens, evading state surveillance, strategizing to maximize their opportunities, negotiating relationships to access resources, moving for better opportunities, superimposing their models of kinship on top of official (camp) models of kinship, shifting their identity registers to match the context, and agitating for civil rights. These are all forms of refugee agency, even if they often get identified as noncompliance or fraud by humanitarian agencies and are ignored in the scholarly and popular focus on bare life and disempowerment.

Departing from the focus on the international refugee regime as a technology of power, this chapter flips the lens to view humanitarianism from the vantage point of refugees, who figure out how to navigate top-down bureaucratic structures of decision making in ways beneficial to them.[2] This chapter contributes to a new focus on refugee agency in the scholarship on humanitarianism, a focus that explores how refugees find and create spaces for action, collaborate with activists to elude and challenge structures of control, and articulate an alternative politics of identity and self-determination beyond their identity as exemplars of bare life. Attending to the political strategies pursued by refugees requires a multilayered approach that takes into account how refugees conjoin local currents, such as cultural discourses and regional politics, to what is happening globally as diasporic refugee and global activist networks articulate new forms of political subjectivity.[3] Adopting this perspective, this chapter tries to see like a refugee.

The "Weird Name Bantu"

In his discussion of Somali Bantu ethnicity, political scientist Kenneth Menkhaus observed that the rapid creation of Somali Bantu identity after 1991 is particularly remarkable "because the community possesses almost none of the features typically associated with a cohesive ethnic group."[4] Prior to the onset of Somalia's civil war, the Jubba Valley villagers who carried the jareer label did not speak a common dialect, share a common kinship system, or even subscribe to a common history. Many villagers in the lower Jubba River valley continued to identify with their preenslavement East African ethnicities such as Yao and Makua. One group who lived in the lower Jubba Valley, the Mushunguli, still spoke Zigua over a century after their Zigua ancestors from Tanzania had arrived as slaves in Somalia. In contrast, farmers in the middle valley claimed no relationship with their ancestors' pre-Somali ethnicities. Jareer members of Somali clans in the interriverine area felt strong affiliations with their Somali clan identity, not their connections to other jareer. Scholars and Somali Bantus agree that prior to the civil war, those identified as jareer perceived no common identity and no one used the term "Somali Bantu."

Italian colonial authorities may have been the first to use the term "Bantu" to describe villagers in the Jubba Valley. As with colonial regimes elsewhere in Africa, Italian colonial authorities treated the Jubba Valley villagers as free labor for colonial projects. Beginning in 1935, the Italian colonial government required all Jubba villages to send a quota of men and women to work on colonial plantations on a rotating basis, a practice bitterly remembered during my stay in Banta by elderly villagers as the *kolonya* and the *teen*. The colonial authorities used the term "Bantu" to distinguish the riverine farmers (encompassing the range of ethnic identities then recognized in the valley, such as "Shabelle, Shidle, Makanne, Eyle, Elay Baydabo, Shanbara, Zigula, Gosha, Mushunguli"[5]) whose labor could be commandeered for colonial projects, from the pastoralist (jileec) Somalis, who were not required to provide free labor. Colonial authorities eager to claim the labor of riverine farmers thus reinforced the jareer-jileec distinction by introducing administrative categories to clearly distinguish between farmers as jareer-Bantu, who were subject to coerced labor campaigns, and the pastoralists as jileec–ethnic Somalis, who were not.[6] Recounting the multiple abuses suffered by his father's generation during the era of Italian colonialism, one elder from Banta now living in Lewiston reflected, "The Italians were only colonizing the jareer, not the Somalis."

But while the jareer-jileec distinction clarified status in social encounters and identified those subject to colonial labor expropriation, it did not create an overarching ethnic identity among those recognized as jareer, nor did it introduce the word "Bantu" into popular Somali discourse. For most of the twentieth century, riverine identities remained diverse, localized, and, in many regions, as in Banta, negotiated in relation to surrounding Somali pastoralist groups. Although everyone knew that many of the ancestors of valley farmers were slaves, during my stay in Banta, middle valley farmers were unwilling to speak of themselves as holding a unified group identity on this basis. As the great Banta historian Iidow Roble had told me during the first of our many interviews in 1987 about valley history, "Everyone here is descended from slaves, but no one talks about it."

The term "Bantu" reappeared after 1991 during the civil war when foreign humanitarian workers struggling to ensure the delivery of emergency food rations to riverine farmers adopted it as a catchall term for the farming populations along the Jubba and Shabelle Rivers targeted by Somali militias.[7]

Menkhaus, who worked with the UN peacekeeping effort in the early years of the civil war, notes that Western relief workers were appalled at the indifference of Somalis to the plight of the jareer because the relief workers did not immediately understand that the Somalis did not consider the jareer part of their society. "This point is critical," Menkhaus writes, "because it suggests that the virtual holocaust visited upon low-status groups such as the jareer in 1991 and 1992 was not just a tragic result of warlords and young gunmen run amok; it was also the result of conscious decisions by clan elders and militia leaders over who lived and who died, an 'allocation of pain' which reflected the ethics and logic of the existing social order in crisis, and which betrayed the fact that low status members of the clan simply did not matter enough to live."[8] Menkhaus explains that humanitarian workers revived the use of the term "Bantu" to describe the jareer populations who were suffering so much during the early years of the war. When the media picked up on the term in 1992, "In the eyes of the external world, if not yet inside Somalia, a new ethnic category was taking shape."[9]

The widespread violence against jareer Somalis in 1991–92 precipitated a growing political consciousness among jareer people that began to grow within Somalia and the refugee camps in Kenya over the next few years. Somali Bantus now living in the United States recall that a UNOSOM (United Nations Operation in Somalia) officer from southern Africa stationed in Mogadishu with the UN peacekeeping force from 1992 to 1995 encouraged the use of the term "Bantu" to describe jareer Somalis.[10] When Somali minorities complained to him about their treatment by other Somalis, he reportedly suggested that they should self-identify as Bantu. The few educated Bantu started using the term "Bantu," and Somali Bantu activist Omar Eno recalls that the term quickly gained currency with educated minority political elites who founded the Somali African MUKI political organization to represent minority interests on the national scene.[11] Omar Eno and his brother Mohamed, both academics, became outspoken advocates of the rights of Somalia's jareer minorities, persistently campaigning for recognition and international support.

Their flight across the Kenyan border into the refugee camps in 1992–93 brought together jareer from across southern Somalia and across Somali clan affiliations for the first time.[12] One elder in Lewiston explained,

> In earlier times, jareer in Baay [interriverine] and Kalafo [Ethiopia] areas didn't ever have the chance to encounter each other. . . . Baay jareer and the Gosha [Jubba Valley] jareer lived too far away to intermarry, but once they encountered each other in the camps it is no problem for them to marry. But they cannot marry Somalis because the Somalis considered themselves

superior and called them adoon. They would tell their daughters and sons that jareer were inferior, with a nose as big as a heel, idiots, and if they married one no one would cry for them when they died.

Jareer Somalis quickly learned they would be on the bottom of camp hierarchy. Somalis within the camps who had access to funds from remittances or camp administration jobs hired jareer Somalis, who lacked such connections, as the camp's manual laborers to work as porters, to dig and clean latrines, to gather wood (a perilous occupation due to attacks and rapes), and as domestic servants and builders. In my interviews with Somali Bantus about their memories of Dadaab, I repeatedly heard, "You'll never find a Somali man digging a latrine!" One Somali Bantu refugee in Lewiston related his memories of assaults suffered by so many Somali Bantus in the refugee camps:

> The land [in the camps] was for the Somalis and they controlled everything. They sexually abused the women and beat brutally the men because they claimed control of the land, and if they caught Somali Bantus gathering wood they attacked. The Kenyan government believed the land was for Somalis, so no one policed it. They had permission from the government to do what they were doing. The men's job was to gather building materials, women's to gather firewood. They paid Somalis to get access to the wood for building. The women wouldn't negotiate—if they got caught they'd start running. The men would negotiate. They'd take money with them and if they got caught they'd try to negotiate payment. The women would go in groups and if they got caught they'd all start running and whoever was grabbed would get sexually assaulted. They'd keep her hostage, beat and rape her, and then let her go and her community would take her to the hospital to tend to her injuries and to the police to file a report. It happened weekly. We had no way to protect the women. Women have much worse memories than men.

Furthermore, as noted in chapter 2, Somalis were put in charge of the few key positions in the camp staff structure available to refugees, which ensured that access to paid jobs within the camps remained limited to Somalis and was not extended to jareer camp residents, thus further enabling the ongoing hierarchy of jileec and jareer Somalis. Somali Bantu elders living in the United States told me that as jareer Somalis began to grasp how their experiences of subjugation in Somalia and in the camps extended across all Somali clans, their leaders began articulating a common experience of subjugation based on their separate ancestry and history of discrimination by Somalis. The leaders of one of the most organized jareer minority groups in the camps, the Mushunguli, were among the first to advance a request to resettle on the basis of their ancestral and linguistic connections in Tanzania, which is where the ancestors of the Mushunguli originated before being sold into slavery in Somalia.

One of the oldest Somali Bantu leaders in the United States, a Hartford resident I'll call Abdulle, described to me how in 1992 the Mushunguli leaders decided that every block in the refugee camps where Mushunguli lived should elect a leader who would represent the minority residents of the block. The leaders met to discuss their options, deciding to appeal to Tanzania on the basis of ancestral connections, which had been sustained through the movement of people traveling back and forth between the lower Jubba and Tanzania in earlier years. The Mushunguli leaders sent representatives from the camps to Tanzania to pursue the possibility of an official resettlement program there and asked UNHCR to invite an official Tanzanian delegation to the camps to meet the refugees, who were asked to perform traditional dances to prove their cultural connections. Dan Van Lehman, the UN field officer in Dagahalley (one of the Dadaab camps) who had witnessed their exploitation in the camps and supported their efforts to seek a resettlement solution for themselves, remembers the Mushunguli leaders as "the drivers of the process."[13] Van Lehman learned about the minority community after witnessing an altercation in Dagahalley camp one morning in early 1992 at the water pump when an ethnic Somali woman attempted to bar a Mushunguli woman from accessing water. When he intervened, Van Lehman was startled to discover the Mushunguli woman spoke Swahili and Zigua. Because of his fluency in Swahili he was able to forge relationships with the Mushunguli leaders who spoke Swahili, including the Mushunguli leader in the Dadaab camps, Mberwa Haji. He learned of their marginalization in Somalia and in the camps, and, furious that such racism persisted in the camp he was running, determined to assist their efforts to find a resettlement solution. Van Lehman explained to me that he and the Mushunguli leaders decided to use the term "Mushunguli"

> to encompass all native Zigua and all native Maay Maay–speaking Bantu as long as they were the descendants of people originally from Tanzania, Malawi, Mozambique, and Kenya. . . . The slave ancestry of the Mushunguli seemed to put them at a distinct social and security disadvantage compared to the other Bantu from farther up the Jubba River and even those from the Shabelle River Valley. The Mushunguli refugees had already began [sic] migrating "illegally" to Tanzania when their leaders approached me for help. I recognized [that] the slave ancestry of the Mushunguli, possibly for the first time in their history, could possibly be used to their

advantage by appealing to the Tanzanian, Mozambican, and international diplomatic communities to do the right thing to help these descendants of slavery finally gain their human and civil rights through intra-African resettlement. . . . The Mushunguli—loosely defined as the descendants of the East African slave trade who either retained their ancestral language, culture, or both—recognized the potential of their historical story and organized themselves according to their East African ethnic group.[14]

When the delegation from Tanzania arrived in Dadaab in response to the invitation from the Mushunguli leaders and Van Lehman, they recognized and affirmed the historic ties between Mushungulis from Somali and Zeguas in Tanzania. Ultimately, however, the Tanzanian government decided the country could not afford to accept more refugees for permanent resettlement, a decision Van Lehman blames on UNHCR ineptitude and unwillingness to support the refugees' initiative. Van Lehman claims that even though several donor nations indicated their desire to contribute funds to support the resettlement process, the UNHCR response was "brutally diplomatic" and slow. He told me, "The Tanzanians were willing to welcome the Mushunguli, but the UNHCR dragged its feet on guaranteeing financial and diplomatic support. The Tanzanians only rescinded their offer after Rwanda blew up."[15]

Despite Tanzania's refusal to officially accept Mushunguli refugees, Mushunguli and other jareer refugees started an "underground railroad" to Tanzania, through which Van Lehman estimates about 5,000–10,000 refugees relocated to Tanzania, some to Mkuyo refugee camp and others into the general population.[16] Van Lehman, Mberwa Haji, and other Mushunguli leaders continued to discuss other possible African resettlement sites, deciding in 1994 that Mozambique might be a good fit, a possibility Van Lehman pursued when he left the UN that year to return to graduate school at Cornell. His master's thesis analyzed the failed Tanzanian resettlement effort, argued that the UN was hobbled by an institutional and cultural bias toward European and U.S. resettlement based on an incorrect assumption that African countries are bureaucratically incapable of managing refugee resettlement, and developed a plan for how to successfully engineer an inter-African refugee resettlement program.[17]

In 1996 Van Lehman returned to East Africa in a series of jobs with CARE that he thought might help him pursue a plan for Mushunguli resettlement in Mozambique. The Mushunguli elders performed cultural dances for Van Lehman's video camera, which he used to make their case to Mozambican politicians and UNHCR officials in Maputo, returning to Dadaab in 1996 to keep the Mushunguli informed about his efforts on their behalf. After a debate in the Mozambican Parliament, a delegation was sent to Dadaab to interview the Mushunguli leaders.

Abdulle remembers the delegation from Mozambique arriving in the refugee camps to meet with the Mushunguli leaders, once again asking for a performance of cultural dances "to see if [they] were authentic." In preparation for their visit, the Mushunguli leaders from each of Dadaab's three camps laboriously compiled handwritten lists of jareer refugees who would qualify for resettlement in Mozambique on the basis of ancestral ethnic connections, although many jareer did not sign up because they feared relocating to a non-Muslim country, were suspicious of the resettlement plan, were away from the camps during the time period when the lists were being created, or because they weren't entirely sure they qualified under the Mushunguli ethnic label. Sheikh Ahmed Nur refused to sign up for resettlement in Mozambique because, according to his children who eventually resettled in the United States, he was uncertain whether the list would be used to benefit those who signed up and he held out hope that he could return to his farms in Somalia. His adult children disagreed and put their names on the list. Isha, Cali Osman's wife, also refused to sign up for resettlement because she was wary of relocating to a non-Muslim country, but her daughter Rabaca stole Isha's identity documents one day while she was away from her house and registered Isha along with Isha's other children, whom Rabaca believed would have an opportunity for education only if they left the camps. Caliyow Isaaq's surviving family members all added their names to the list. The final set of handwritten lists included about 10,000 names.

In 1998, Mozambique responded that as a poor country struggling with the aftermath of devastating floods and a long, brutal civil war, they could not accept refugees. The Mushunguli leaders felt deflated and Van Lehman was furious with UNHCR for refusing to offer greater assistance. After years of work on the Tanzanian and Mozambican resettlement efforts, Van Lehman says he finally realized "the UN just didn't want to do it" because of its biased view that only Europe and America are appropriate locations for third-country refugee resettlement. But the years of active attempts at resettlement by the Mushungulis and Van Lehman, in addition to the lobbying by Eno and other educated Bantus for the recognition of Somali minorities by the international community, raised their profile for UNHCR administrators, who responded by designating the Mushunguli as a vulnerable population in need of a resettlement solution. They had made themselves visible as a group with a coherent ethnic identity and a history of exploitation, and they fit the profile sought by the United States in response to the Congressional Black Caucus's charge of racist resettlement priorities.

Although Van Lehman recalls that he and the Mushunguli leaders decided to use Mushunguli rather than Bantu or jareer as the basis for inclusion on the 1997 list because they thought the latter terms would be too broad, jareer leaders were beginning to articulate a shared identity that included more than those who claimed the more specific Mushunguli identity associated with farmers from only the lower Jubba Valley. Jareer leaders from throughout the Jubba Valley viewed the resettlement effort on the basis of minority status as relevant to them as well because of their shared jareer status, and thus many non-Mushunguli minorities also signed up for possible resettlement in Mozambique. That the term "Mushunguli" initially became an umbrella ethnic term was not as significant as the emerging recognition by jareer Somalis that they had experienced similar patterns of discrimination and violence specifically because of their jareer identities, patterns that continued to dominate their lives in the camps through hierarchies in access to camp jobs, cultural broker positions, food rations, remittances, and the experience of constant, everyday acts of racism. The efforts of the Mushunguli leaders and Van Lehman led to the eventual acceptance of "the weird name Bantu," as one elder in Lewiston amusingly put it, by most jareer Somalis in the camps.[18]

Recalling the impact of the Mushunguli leadership in the refugee camps to enlist other jareer Somalis in their efforts to find a third-country resettlement, Sadiq explained:

> Mushungulis were the ones convincing us to use the term. They spoke the language of Tanzania and northern Malawi so they were having this nice connection. They would go back and forth and convince us what to do next. They didn't want to go back to Somalia because they were killed the most. They were not integrated with the Somali tribes [clans] like we were [e.g., jareer from the middle Jubba Valley] and were brutally killed because of it. They tried to convince us not to return. They did a lot of work to convince us. Sometimes they brought someone who lived in Tanzania and had lived in Somalia a long time ago to convince us. Somalis also tried to convince us that Tanzania and Mozambique would enslave us. But we didn't believe them.

Alongside the efforts of Mushunguli leaders to generate a broader consciousness among jareer Somalis in the camps, non-Mushunguli jareer leaders prompted by the political efforts of Mushunguli leaders also pursued connections among jareer refugees. During our conversation in his Hartford home, Abdulle showed me an elaborate, hand-drawn map he created in 1993–94 in the refugee camp in order to document the shared experiences of jareer all over southern Somalia. From painstaking research involving hundreds of interviews in which he asked jareer Somalis to name their village and the next villages to the north and south as far as they had traveled, he drew a color-coded map depicting the location of every jareer village in the Jubba Valley from which refugees fled to Kenya. He drew another color-coded map of the entire country to show the location of other jareer communities as well as the origins of the militia groups who attacked them, so he could show other jareer "where those who killed us came from." These maps provided his fellow jareer refugees with a visual image of their collectivity and helped them understand their shared victimization as jareer under attack from Somalis from throughout the country.[19] He believes his map was important for consolidating a group identity among jareer refugees, and indeed I heard about the influence of his map from numerous Somali Bantus in other U.S. cities. A major incident in 1998 further confirmed the distinction between Somalis and Somali minorities in Dadaab. Because of their suspicions of rampant ration card fraud, camp administrators mandated that all resident refugees had to surrender their ration cards and be issued new ones, an exercise rejected by Somali refugee leaders, who demanded a boycott of the process. But when Somali Bantu refugees refused to comply with the boycott and lined up to be reverified, Somalis attacked them and in the ensuing violence, which lasted for three days, the camp was shut down. Several Somali Bantus were killed and scores wounded. Many Somali Bantus told me that this event solidified any remaining uncertainty about Somali Bantu identity among jareer camp residents. As a Somali Bantu man in Seattle explained, "If you fought with the Somali Bantus and tried to reregister, you were a Somali Bantu. If you didn't, you were a Somali Somali."

While the elders claim their leadership produced a broad understanding of a shared identity among Somalia's diverse jareer population, young adult Somali Bantus in Lewiston, Hartford, and Syracuse lay their own claim to the Somali Bantu label, recalling that they learned the term from their Kenyan teachers and security guards in the refugee camps who told them they looked Bantu, like other Kenyans, rather than Somali. Their school textbooks taught them about the Bantu migrations and the distinction between Bantus, Cushites, and Nilotes, offering a connection to Bantus elsewhere in Africa and to their teachers that made the label appealing to jareer teenagers, who experienced camp life as profoundly racist. Abdirisak remembers the taunts of his Somali schoolmates about his participation in school: "Wow, the world has changed. Now you can see ooji wearing a uniform, going to school!" Sadiq, one of the first young jareer Somalis to pass the high school entrance exam in the camps, remembers a fellow Somali student pointing to him in order to mock other Somali students who failed the high school entrance exam, saying,

FIGURE 3.1 Abdulle, Catherine Besteman, and Haji Adan pointing to the middle Jubba region on Ibrahim's hand-drawn map. Photographer unknown.

"Even monkeys can pass the exam to go to high school!" Their success in the camp schools emboldened young Somali Bantus, for whom the Bantu label offered a positive self-identity that allied them with their Kenyan teachers. I heard from numerous young adult Somali Bantus that their generation introduced the term "Somali Bantu" to their elders, who adopted it as an English-friendly moniker for jareer people. The U.S. government adopted the term "Somali Bantu" in the announcement of the special resettlement program.

When the U.S. government decided to grant Somali Bantus P2 status, a 1999 State Department cable sent to all African diplomatic posts announcing the decision to accept the Somali Bantu included a point of clarification: "Note on nomenclature: This group is sometimes loosely referred to as 'Mushunguli.' However, that name is sometimes used more restrictively for a single subgroup of the larger group 'Somali Bantu,' which is the term employed here. It must be stressed that not all Somali Bantu are part of the P-2 designation, but only those whose names are on the lists provided to the department by UNHCR."[20]

The list provided by UNHCR was the 1997 list compiled for the failed Mozambique resettlement. Since the final list of those to be included for P2 resettlement identified Somali Bantu rather than only Mushunguli as the target population and since several years had passed since the creation of the original list, the authorities faced the significant challenge of reverifying who qualified. Following the announcement of the U.S. resettlement program, Van Lehman recalls, "All of a sudden, everyone was a Somali Bantu," and Somalis as well as Somali Bantus not initially included on the list began jockeying and strategizing to be included. The result was confusion and ambiguity on the part of the administrators (all non-Somali) who were charged with reverifying the names on the list although they had no clear idea about who actually qualified.

Self-Essentializing, the "Anticorruption Committee," and Family Restructuring

Somali Bantus recall the reverification procedures as a test of wits as much as of legitimacy. As word of the U.S. resettlement program spread throughout the camps, refugees whose names were on the Mozambique list had to find a way to prove that they still belonged, jareer refugees whose names did not appear on the list had to convince the interviewers that they should belong, and non-jareer Somali refugees who wished to claim a spot tried to reinvent themselves as Somali Bantus. Although the interview and screening procedures were controlled by foreign staff and ethnic Somalis employed by international organizations and later by U.S. immigration authorities with Somali translators, Somali Bantus nevertheless attempted to assert control over whatever aspects of the screening process they could access. Because of the slippage between the terms "Mushunguli" and "Somali Bantu," the jareer leaders attempted to control the definition of Somali Bantu to ensure those with historically legitimate claims to jareer identity would be included while excluding those they defined as ethnic Somalis.

A special reverification team was brought in by UNHCR, headed by a man named Andrew Hopkins, to review each claim, a process that initially rejected 10,000 new claimants. Of those remaining, the team interviewed 14,000 individuals, rejecting another 2,000 as illegitimate. The initial reverification review concluded in December 2001, but because the Dadaab refugee camps were deemed too dangerous for U.S. personnel to visit for the final screening due to heightened post-9/11 security concerns, in 2002 the agencies involved in the resettlement process decided to truck all 11,860 reverified Somali Bantu over 900 miles to the distant Kakuma refugee camp in the northwestern corner of Kenya at a cost of U.S. $2.7 million, a task managed by the International Office of Migration (IOM). In a wry aside describing the experiences of Somali Bantus in this process, the *Economist* commented, "They have been through a lot—persecution in their homeland, civil war, a decade languishing in refugee camps, and the tragi-comic experience of being trucked across Kenya to meet American officials who dared not visit them."[21]

Somali Bantus recount how their leadership worked closely with the UNHCR reverification team to ferret out fakers: Somalis masquerading as Somali Bantus by changing their names or physical appearance or claiming kinship connection with someone on the 1997 list, efforts sometimes facilitated by complicit or corrupt Somali interpreters, or even by Somali Bantus who desperately needed the money they could gain by selling a spot in their family to a non–Somali Bantu. Somali Bantu leaders offered a list of stereotypical physical features to guide the non-Somali reverification staff in how to recognize and distinguish Somali Bantus, including markers like hard curly hair, broad flat noses, and short muscular bodies.

Ethnographic descriptions of the asylum interview process across a range of settings—refugee camps, UNHCR offices, U.S. Department of Homeland Security (or the former Immigration and Naturalization Service), U.K. Home Office, French National Court of Asylum—reveal a set of confrontational interview strategies used by refugee admissions interviewers intended to trip up applicants by repeatedly asking confusing questions about chronology in order to find inconsistencies.[22] Ethnographic accounts report that interviewers presume applicants are not telling the truth and demand from them a coherent life story rooted in "a place, a culture, a language, and a religion";[23] that interviewers focus on questions about language, ethnicity, identity, indigeneity, and culture that often make no sense to applicants; and that interviewers expect applicants to use particular terms and discourses to describe their victimization (such as genocide, rape, etc.) that may not be familiar to applicants or may not be the words they would use to describe what happened to them and their families.[24]

These practices characterized the Somali Bantu reverification process as well, where jareer Somalis quickly learned that they had to adhere to a very narrow set of criteria to claim an identity as a legitimate Somali Bantu. In addition to the physical criteria noted above, a confluence of tribal, linguistic, and geographic markers emerged during the reverification process as definitive indications of legitimate Somali Bantu identity. All applicants had to claim to speak either Mushunguli or the Jubba Valley regional dialect of Maay Maay, and all had to claim membership in one of the five East African tribes from which the enslaved ancestors of the jareer Somalis who had settled in the lower Jubba Valley originated, even though jareer Somalis from elsewhere no longer recognized these ancestral associations. (As one former Banta resident now living in Lewiston cheerfully told me, "Now we are all Yao and Makua!") Finally, because their collective status as a persecuted minority group was the basis for preferential treatment for Somali Bantus, Somali Bantu applicants understood that a narrative of victimization was a required part of the interview process. Somali Bantus learned to narrate personal stories of abuse and attack by Somali militias, and were asked to repeat these stories for verification at different points in the resettlement interview process. "We all have our story," one man told me, as he recounted his version of the personal trauma narrative he was asked to recite for each interview during the resettlement process, "even if the things we had to describe aren't exactly what happened." In a conversation with a friend from Banta about the resettlement process, he said, "My mother was killed. My father died. I was left alone." "Really?" I asked, upset to hear this news. "No!" he responded, realizing I had missed his point. "That's what I had to tell the interviewers. That's not what really happened."

In their study of the emergence of trauma as a trope of contemporary life, Fassin and Rechtman observe, "Trauma offers a language in which to speak of the wounds of the past—of slavery, colonization, or apartheid. Claimed by the protagonists themselves, trauma becomes once again an argument in struggles for recognition of the plurality of memory—even if this violates historical reality."[25] Condensing a general experience of marginalization into a personal narrative of individual trauma is a strategy used by asylum seekers everywhere to conform to the requirements for personal victimization desired by resettlement authorities. As the Somali Bantu experience shows, such shapeshifting of facts is not illegitimate, for everyone applying for resettlement suffered numerous losses of various kinds—of immediate or extended family members, of homes and land, of a way of life, of security—whether or not they themselves experienced intimate forms of violence against their persons.

By working with the UNHCR representatives to develop a set of criteria for determining Somali Bantu legitimacy, Somali Bantu leaders helped craft a coherent identity of ethnic uniformity where none had existed before. The mirage of uniformity came at a high price for those whose physical features or narratives did not conform closely enough to the model adopted by the foreign staff of interviewers, however. Many Somali Bantus in Lewiston remember the pencil test, for example, used to distinguish between those with "hard hair" and those with "soft hair," although many legitimate jareer failed the test and were rejected.[26] Sadiq recalls the anxiety he felt after being asked to walk across the interview room, since the interviewers were told that the gait of Somali Bantus differed from that of ethnic Somalis. Other Somali Bantus recall interviewers scrutinizing the shape and size of their noses and hands, since Somali Bantu noses are supposed to be flat and broad and their hands short and thick.[27]

Although the reverification process in Dadaab for boarding the buses to Kakuma was, by all accounts, messy, confusing, and complicated by the ignorance of foreign interviewers, the ambivalent role of Somali interpreters, and the efforts of ethnic Somalis to find a way to be included, Somali Bantus claimed it gave their leaders another opportunity to assert some control over who got to continue in the resettlement program. I heard about the Somali Bantu anticorruption committee that developed an elaborate system of dots and stars to identify fakers on the UNHCR registration lists for those reverified for the bus trip to Kakuma, which would allow Somali Bantu leaders to identify interlopers as they lined up to board the buses. Recalling how some Somalis attempted to pass as Somali Bantus by rubbing dirt in their hair to make it "harder" and dressing in shabby clothing, the Somali Bantus working with Andrew Hopkins's verification team pointed out the "infiltrators," who would be pulled out of the line at the last minute to ensure that those who identified them would not suffer retribution in the camps.

Although the decision to relocate the final stages of the Somali Bantu resettlement program to Kakuma was intended to minimize opportunities for infiltration by ethnic Somalis and to protect Somali Bantus from the persistent efforts by Somalis to claim resettlement spots through threatening or bribing Somali Bantus into accepting non–Somali Bantus as family members, in Kakuma the Somali Bantu community itself was riven by accusations that some of its leaders were selling resettlement slots to ethnic Somalis and that some people were identifying others as fakers in retribution for personal vendettas.[28] After Dan Van Lehman learned in 2001 of the U.S. resettlement plan for Somali Bantus, he visited Kakuma with activist Omar Eno in 2002 after hearing about the accusations of fraud, eventually exposing the corruption in an international scandal that shook up the administering agencies and resulted in the firing of staff and the hiring of more Somali Bantu staff and interpreters. Van Lehman recalls,

> The Heads of the US government, the UNHCR, and the IOM dealing with the Somali Bantu in Kenya—usually all having little or no knowledge of Somalia, the Somali Bantu, or even any African language, ran the registration process. These heads, mostly foreigners, depended on the translation and guidance of more literate and educated dominant clan Somalis. To say the least, it was a BIG mess with lots of corruption and even a UNHCR scandal with European and African UNHCR staff caught for taking bribes from the Somali Somalis who were trying to get to the USA as Bantu refugees. We think that anywhere from 5–15% of all Bantu resettled, especially early on, were not Somali Bantu.[29]

Accusations of corruption resulted in more stringent criteria in the next stage of reverification, during which several of my Banta friends were rejected. When Isha's daughter Rabaca appeared for her final verification interview in

Kakuma with her husband of twenty years, the American interviewer scruti-nized their physical features and announced that he did not believe Rabaca's husband was really a Somali Bantu. He applied the pencil test, which Rabaca passed but her husband failed (the pencil stuck in her hair, but moved more easily through his hair). While she was accepted for resettlement, the inter-viewer rejected her husband and seven children, giving her the choice of con-tinuing in the asylum process alone or remaining with her husband and kids in the camp and giving up the opportunity for resettlement. She gave it up.

Isha's oldest son, Ciise—the son who had been one of the first kidnapped in Banta—was also rejected, along with his family. The interviewer studied his face and decided he was not a real Somali Bantu, rejecting him on the spot. Isha faced the horrible choice of continuing the resettlement process with her youngest kids and leaving behind her two oldest children, or consigning all her children to life in a refugee camp. At the urging of her children, she ulti-mately chose to continue the process.

Sadiq's story had a better ending. At the conclusion of their final reverifica-tion interview in Kakuma, the interviewer asked Sadiq's small daughter, "Do you like video games?" His daughter had no idea. She'd never heard of them. Through this question, Sadiq learned they were accepted for resettlement in the United States.

In addition to creating and conforming to a coherent ethnic identity and repeating a narrative of personal victimization, Somali Bantu refugees also learned how to reshape their families to match American kinship criteria. The fact that so many households had different members than when they had first signed up for resettlement in 1997 created a dilemma in the reverification pro-cess. Although once identified as a bona fide refugee and awarded a ration card, refugees are supposed to remain inside the confines of the camp and not engage in economic activity across its boundaries, in fact refugee camps are dynamic places and refugees can be highly mobile; they move between the camp and outside towns looking for economic opportunities; they move (illicitly) back and forth across borders to get news from home or to visit family members in other countries; they move between households as people marry, divorce, foster, and adopt. Households expand as new refugees arrive in the camps. Probably most of the households on the 1997 list had changed a great deal by the time of the reverification process in 2001, and everyone was scrambling to present a portrait of the household that conformed to the expectations of the interviewers.

In the calculus of resettlement, the American standard of economic depen-dents defines who can count as part of a family. Juvenile children ages seventeen and under are considered economic dependents and parents can thus include them in their family unit for resettlement. Children eighteen and older, even if unmarried, even if living in the same household, are not economic dependents and thus must be considered separately. Siblings and cousins occupy the same relational category for Somali Bantus, but not for American interviewers, for whom one's children are one's economic dependents but one's nieces and nephews are not. After they grasped the family model being used to manage the resettlement process, refugee families figured out ways to turn extended families into nuclear families while trying to avoid having to lop off those family members who could not fit into the new model.

For example, one friend who signed up for resettlement in 1997 later took in a girl who was not on the 1997 list for resettlement because she had no family and no one had signed her up. My friend presented her at the resettlement interview as a new, still juvenile, daughter-in-law. This came as a surprise to my friend's sixteen-year-old son who, during the interview, suddenly became a husband. It was the only way to include the girl in the family resettlement, or she would have been left behind. Additionally, my friend was raising several orphaned nephews as her own children in conformity with the Somali understanding of kinship. My friend, all her children, and the new daughter-in-law were all reverified.

In addition to turning nieces, nephews, and orphans into one's children, families also turned their children into orphans to enhance their chances for resettlement. A friend's eldest son, Jamal, was unmarried but over the age of eighteen, and since young men in that demographic category are often treated with particular suspicion by American interviewers, the family reconfigured itself to improve his story in the resettlement interview. Some of Jamal's adult siblings had already been rejected for resettlement although his parents had been accepted, so the family decided to present Jamal with one of his young cousins as a family unit of orphaned brothers in which eighteen-year-old Jamal was the caretaker for his sixteen-year-old cousin. Everyone traded names to make this presentation of the family unit work, and they were approved.

In similar and creative ways, families successfully and unsuccessfully strategized to turn cousins into siblings, nieces and nephews into children, orphans into family members, and family members into orphans in order to present family structures that were legible and desirable to American interviewers while also being as inclusive as possible. Polygynous households faced a particular challenge. Since polygynous marriages are forbidden in the United States, all polygynous households accepted during the reverification interview were dissolved. Polygynously married men had to choose one wife with whom to be resettled, leaving their other wives to resettle separately as single-parent households in an enforced separation that was often a great hardship for cowives who depended on each other for support and for children who were separated from their father and siblings. Abdiya was settled separately from her husband and cowife, becoming a single mother of five juvenile children. Her eldest, beloved son, Abdullahi, was rejected.

The married children of Sheikh Axmed Nur and Caliyow Isaaq, Xawo and Mohamed, also passed all the reverification tests for resettlement. They had taken into their family all of Mohamed's half siblings when Mohamed's father Caliyow Isaaq and two of Caliyow's three wives died from the diarrheal disease, thus presenting themselves for reverification as a nuclear family of two parents and six children. Since Sheikh Axmed Nur had never signed up for resettlement, he remained in Dadaab refugee camp after Xawo and Mohamed and all their dependents were taken to Kakuma. Wanting to see their daughter one last time before her departure for America, Sheik Axmed Nur and Habiba, Xawo's mother, traveled three days by bus to Kakuma, arriving just hours after Xawo and her family boarded a bus to Nairobi to begin her journey to the United States. They never had the chance for a farewell.

After years of waiting in Kakuma, those who had passed all the reverification tests were subject to yet one more final screening in Nairobi before being allowed to board the airplane for the United States. If they failed their screening in Nairobi, they were sent back to Kakuma and prohibited from appealing the decision or reapplying. If they passed, they had to sign a promise to pay back the cost of their airfare and then boarded the plane.

Many Somali Bantus describe the final predeparture Nairobi interview as the most terrifying moment in their long journey of interviews and background checks. Knowing that they were on the cusp of departure, and that any small mistake would cost them their opportunity to resettle, Somali Bantu families carefully took note of the errors that had destroyed the resettlement chances of those ahead of them. In contrast to the earlier stages of the resettlement process, I heard no stories of Somali Bantu control or effective intervention in the final verification screening in Nairobi, in which interviewers seemed to have absolute authority over the fates of the applicants. Abdirisak's parents were rejected because the translator misunderstood the term used by the husband for his wife, translating their relationship as clan based rather than a marriage. Because of this one translation error, they were rejected from the resettlement process and returned to the camps. Another family was split after the interviewer questioned the family members separately about their breakfast that morning. While the mother said she had rice with camel meat, her teenage sons reported rice with goat meat. The interviewer decided that the children were not actual family members and gave the mother the choice of boarding the plane for the United States with only her four younger children or returning with her teenage sons to Kakuma with no chance to appeal their rejection. The mother chose to board the plane with her four other children and leave her two teenage sons behind, hoping to be able to apply for family reunification for her sons after arriving in the United States.[30] A news report from the *Los Angeles Times* tells of a fourteen-year-old boy returned alone to Kakuma after his responses to interview questions in Nairobi differed from those of his family members, who were allowed to board the plane: "Hussein is one of scores of Somali Bantu refugees who say their dreams of relocating to the United States were shattered when immigration officials broke up their families, sending some to America and others back to Kakuma. Husbands have been separated from wives, children from parents, brothers from sisters." The article reports that because of new interview procedures introduced in August 2004, between August and October 2004, 305 of 5,407 applicants interviewed in Nairobi were sent back to Kakuma. In 103 cases, the rest of the family decided to continue to the United States, but in 96 cases they decided to give up the opportunity for resettlement and returned to Kakuma with no right of appeal.[31]

A friend from Banta was luckier. He knew many families had been sent back to Kakuma after failing their Nairobi interview because different family members had given different answers to questions, or because the interviewer decided they were lying about their family composition. Since the 1997 registration and the 2001 reverification, he had added to his family an orphaned relative who was not on the original list. For the final interview, he claimed the relative as his wife's brother and their juvenile dependent. Because the relative was a new addition to the roster, the interviewer compared every feature—the shape of his eyes, nose, ears with my friend's wife, who cried throughout the interview, distraught with worry, saying, "He is my brother! He is my brother!" My friend had instructed his kids to stay completely silent during the interview. Two days after their interview, they learned they had passed and would be leaving that night, after promising to repay the $3,200 cost of their airfare. When I asked why he was willing to put his family and his dreams of education at risk for a relative who was not an actual brother in the American sense, my friend shrugged and responded, "My relative's family was dead and he had been left alone. When he got to the camps he lived with us. He became part of our family. There was no way we could leave him."

Conclusion

What is remarkable about this account is the insistence by my Somali Bantu interlocutors on their involvement in almost every step of the resettlement process. As I argued in chapter 2, the Eurocentric discourse of humanitarianism imagines refugees as people who through their territorial displacement and violent loss are stripped of agency, reduced to a bare life of simple survival and dependence on charitable intervention. The figure of the refugee simultaneously carries the stigma of destitute humanity, a person out of place, and an implication of moral responsibility. The offer of refuge is thus imagined as a reprieve to their state of bare survival: an act of humanitarian charity and a gift of renewed life so they can (re)attain a qualified life—but only if they are judged to be truly worthy.

From the vantage point of refugees, however, the space of refuge is clearly a landscape of mistrust, suspicion, and militaristic control. Ethnographic accounts reveal that almost no one involved in the management of refugee camps actually sees camp space as a pacific refuge or believes the refugees housed there are uniformly apolitical innocent victims. Refugee camp administrators do not see refugees as destitute victims, as evidenced by their efforts to contain refugee political agency, constrain refugee mobility, reject refugee efforts toward democratic camp decision making, and exert rigid control over the interview process for determining resettlement candidates. Resettlement administrators do not see refugees as innocent victims, but rather understand refugees to be strategic and manipulative, as evidenced by the insistence on stringent reverification practices and resettlement officers' suspicions of refugee fraud. Host country citizens who live outside refugee camps do not see their neighbors living inside the camps as suffering victims stripped of agency, but rather often see them as competitors (for resources, money), as consumers (for small businesses), as political threats, and as warriors. A more thoroughly grounded ethnographic portrait of those who continue to subscribe to the refugee-as-hapless-victim image, which I imagine is limited to certain European and American publics, would help reveal how this image is used to bolster a global humanitarian regime dependent on charitable funding from those publics.[32]

The evidence suggests that the bulk of those who know, engage with, and control refugees do not see refugees as hapless, pathetic people reduced to bare survival, but rather fully understand refugees to be agents who use mobility, narrative, competition, voice, and tactics to construct strategic subjectivities in their places of refuge, whether in refugee camps, cities where they live illegally, or third-country resettlement sites. Hosts, administrators, and refugees simultaneously view refugees as strategists, competitors, entrepreneurs, mobile agents, possible frauds, and perpetrators of violence, in addition to victims, dependents, and charity recipients. The tension between, on the one hand, the suspicion of refugees as political and economic agents who strategize and conspire, and, on the other, the humanitarian discourse that defines the granting of refuge as moral responsibility and charity means the space of refuge is contested, tense, and a site of struggle. Refugees in this space work out ways to be active agents in constructing their lives while simultaneously adhering to a regime of rules, policies, and attitudes that expect them to behave like docile, grateful subjects.

The story of how jareer became Somali Bantus is a case in point. The argument here is not that the creation of Somali Bantu identity was a fraudulent process, but rather that it was a necessary process within the demands of the international refugee regime, a bureaucratic apparatus that insists on a particular narrative of trauma and persecution told in terms of essentialized identities in which culture, race, and place are inextricably linked. Not everyone who was resettled as a Somali Bantu suffered to the same extent, but the Somali Bantu label gave a name to their suffering of historical injustices as a group. It coalesced under one label a history of slavery, colonization, and apartheid; it provided a language for group recognition of a shared past of discrimination and degradation. The particulars—whether one really identified as Yao or Makua, whether one really spoke Mushunguli or Maay Maay, whether one really witnessed one's father being killed or mother being raped—seemed less significant than the historical fact of subjugation and the certainty of future persecution in Somalia. Those who chose to self-identify as Somali Bantus were given certain parameters to work within and, wishing to take charge of fashioning their future, used them to craft identities, life narratives, and family structures to find a home within a global system that mandates membership in a state, somewhere.

One of anthropology's signature strengths is its ability to recognize and demonstrate human creativity and agency continually to make new social worlds in even the most extraordinarily dehumanizing circumstances. Refugees see their lives as constrained, of course, but also see themselves as creatively exercising their capacity to remake their world anew, to strategize, manipulate, redefine, and engage with the categories and boundaries drawn around them. Nuancing Agamben's portrait of the utterly excluded, Somali Bantu refugees actively worked the systems that excluded them to find a spot defined by them in the international order. They did so by creating an identity that would gain traction, lobbying for resettlement in countries they selected, cultivating support from relief agency staff, playing the category for resettlement made available to them, taking on new family configurations, and accepting as their own generalized stories of suffering.

As resettled refugees in the United States, Somali Bantus are offered the possibility of citizenship (although only after many hurdles), but they continue to play with and redefine their political and social identities in ways that transcend and even repudiate the nation-state model of citizenship and belonging.

One might accept a new identity as Mohamed, child of Nassir and Fatuma, legal resident of the United States, while simultaneously holding an identity as Axmed, child of Jamal and Nurta, residents of a refugee camp. Unlike undocumented immigrants, they hold a legal identity, but, in a way, it is a doppelgänger identity because so many have transformed their personal narrative in conformity with the requirements for refugee identity. Such transformations do not mean their new identities are not real; rather, they are simultaneous and coexistent with their pre-resettlement identity. All resettled refugees I know share this social and political condition of identity doubles. (Many years after their resettlement, when my Somali Bantu friends began gaining U.S. citizenship, one of the first things many did before obtaining a passport was to change their names back to their pre-resettlement names. Birthdates were impossible to change, even though the birthday of every single adult I know is recorded as January 1, reflecting the uncreative efficiency of resettlement interviewers charged with filling out paperwork for people who do not record their birthdates. I heard how the universal January 1 birthday presents problems with authorities who become suspicious when they see that the same birthday is recorded on everyone's driver's license. "It's embarrassing!" one man tells me.)

The story of Somali Bantu resettlement thus has three concurrent themes: humanitarian rescue as narrated by UNHCR, NGOs, the media, and the U.S. government; cruelty and humiliation, as evidenced by the experiences of families broken apart by the resettlement process, accusatory interview styles, and the insistence that indigent refugees cover the cost of their airfare to the United States, ensuring they arrive in their new home already deeply in debt; and refugee bravery, courage, tireless self-advocacy, and tactical manipulation of a system of exclusionary and constraining rules. All are true. Which we tell depends on our agenda: the first offers self-congratulations and benefits donors but positions refugees in ways that are condescending and belittling. The second offers an indictment of the entire process, calling for policy reforms and systemic overhaul, but also overlooks the role refugees themselves play in working the system to their advantage. The third applauds as a success the story of refugee initiative and self-help but downplays the enormous barriers to their self-determination put in place by a system almost totally stacked against them.

Although almost 12,000 Somali Bantus were eventually resettled in the United States, almost every family who came was forced to leave behind someone precious: a child, a spouse, a parent, a sibling. Upon arrival, most families immediately filed P3 family reunification requests for their family members left behind. Isha's son Idris filed for his sister Rabaca and her family and his brother Ciise and his family. Xawo and her brother filed for their parents, Sheikh Axmed Nur and Habiba. Abdiya filed for her son Abdullahi. But soon thereafter the U.S. State Department decided that Somali family reunification appeals were too fraudulent for the system to manage and suspended the program, even for family members who could demonstrate conclusively their relationship through expensive DNA tests or the testimony and photographs of an anthropologist.

One afternoon in 2008 as I sat with several refugees from Banta discussing the P3 applications, Sadiq's phone rang. It was news from Kakuma: Sheikh Axmed Nur's wife Habiba had died that morning. A couple years later, another phone call reported that Isha's daughter Rabaca, mother of seven, at the age of forty suddenly and inexplicably died one morning as she stepped out of her hut in the refugee camp. The next year Sheikh Axmed Nur's second wife died, leaving him a widower with numerous young children. In November 2013, Sheik Axmed Nur died, after twenty-two years in Kakuma refugee camp. Ciise and his family still remain in Kakuma, beginning their third decade of life in a refugee camp. Funerals are held monthly in Lewiston for those long-separated family members who die in the refugee camps, separated from their loved ones in the United States by an ocean, a continent, and the borders against refugee mobility that condemn refugees to die in refugee camps.

Arrival Surprises

After passing the final interview and promising to pay back the $3,200 loan for their airfare, Isha's family finally began their journey to the United States in 2005 when they were sent to Atlanta. Their recollections of their airport arrivals buzz with uncertainty about how to navigate the new setting. Deplaning along with everyone else, the family walked through the airport to board a small train. But because they could not read or understand English and no one helped them, they remained on the train circling the airport over and over before finally figuring out where to exit, even though the escalator stymied them until they felt bold enough to step on after carefully watching how others navigated the moving stairs.[1]

Isha's sons Iman and Cabdulkadir, who left Kenya together a few months after Isha's voyage, did not realize their destination was Atlanta until they arrived. After deplaning they were immediately whisked away by armed immigration and police officers, who marched them to a locked room where they were guarded by white men with guns, so frightening fifteen-year-old Iman that he forgot all of his hard-earned English language skills. He thought that they were taking them away to kill them, a not unrealistic possibility in the experience of a young war survivor. Eventually the brothers were released, but since they had been kept so long in custody the caseworker sent from the resettlement agency to pick them up at the airport had given up and gone home. Iman was allowed to phone Isha, who was thrilled because no one had informed her that they were arriving in Atlanta. Another relative, Ahmed, remembers stepping outside the airport into the February evening in his T-shirt to wait for his ride and realizing that his body was beginning to shake uncontrollably. "I didn't know what was happening!" he recalls. "I thought I was becoming really sick." Only later did he learn that he was freezing. He had never experienced cold before.

Refugee resettlement in the United States is managed by eleven federally approved voluntary agencies, called VOLAGs, that are contracted by the federal government to provide arriving refugees with modest assistance during their first weeks in the United States. The agencies, which are mostly faith-based nationwide organizations such as Catholic Charities, Lutheran Immigration and Refugee Services, and Hebrew Immigrant Aid Society, bid on contracts with the U.S. State Department to resettle refugees in the cities where they have offices. The VOLAGs are responsible for meeting arriving refugees at the airport, providing some cultural orientation training, settling them in housing, and enrolling children in school and non-English-speaking adults in English language classes, a welcome that ends when the ninety-day resettlement contract between VOLAGs and the U.S. government concludes. As a VOLAG manager in Maine told me, "The ultimate goal of the reception and placement program is that clients will be self-sufficient within ninety days." When I expressed astonishment about this expectation for illiterate, non-English-speaking refugees to the director of the VOLAG in Syracuse, he shrugged and said, "Well, that's what they pay us for. After ninety days we move on to the next group of arrivals."

The VOLAGs are not responsible for placing resettled refugees in jobs, although they often attempt to connect their clients with job training and career services programs. The Office of Refugee Resettlement (ORR) offers a modest reprieve for some refugees struggling to attain self-sufficiency: during their first eight months in the United States, those who fail to find employment and who do not qualify for Temporary Assistance for Needy Families may apply for additional assistance ($230 per adult per month in 2010) through the federal Refugee Cash Assistance Program. But ORR is quite clear that by their eighth month, when this assistance ends, "Self-sufficiency must be achieved without accessing [further] public cash assistance."[2] Whereas Hmong refugees, who arrived in the 1970s and 1980s with a similar background as non-English-speaking illiterate farmers, received up to three years of direct federal support as well as greater support for English language classes, how Somali Bantus were to become immediately economically self-sufficient was unclear to everyone. Although the news accounts mentioned in chapter 3 had warned that Somali Bantu refugees were poorly prepared for life in the United States, such warnings did not translate into greater assistance for their transition; to the contrary, they arrived on the heels of deep budget cuts for economic support during their adjustment, including intensive English classes, job training programs, and child care and transport for adults in programs. Their experience reveals an ironic contradiction of the refugee resettlement program: the very people who must present themselves as dependent recipients of charity in order to gain resettlement must, within the space of a few weeks, become economically independent and productive residents who make no demands on their American host communities.

The refugees from the Banta-Bu'aale area were resettled by VOLAGs all over the United States, finding themselves in Atlanta, Columbus, Syracuse, Tucson, Portland (Oregon), Houston, Dallas, Denver, Hartford, Springfield (Connecticut), and other places. Their stories about their first weeks, while retold with humor, reveal just how unprepared they were to become self-sufficient within ninety days. Before arriving in the United States, refugees attend a few cultural orientation classes in the refugee camp to prepare them for the expected rapid transition to American life. Friends from Banta recall learning about new technologies (light switches, elevators, toilets, electric and gas stoves, refrigerators, thermostats) and new rules for family life, but nothing about the racism and discrimination they would experience in their new host communities or in the workplace.

As it turned out, the lessons on technology offered inadequate preparation because they were either inaccurate or incomprehensible in the context of the refugee camp. Sadiq remembers the emphasis on cleanliness and abundance: "The stoves were white and clean and beautiful. We were all amazed by how clean everything was. And we learned there was plenty of food. They showed us an open fridge, and it was full of food!" Iman had heard that everyone uses computers in the United States, so with remittances from Isha of $20 per month he paid for a privately run computer course in the refugee camp so he would arrive prepared. The course, which ran for five weeks, taught him how to turn the computer on and off and use the keyboard, but neglected to teach him about the Internet, printing, or word processing because the teachers in the refugee camp had procured no Internet connection, paper, or software. People tell funny stories of living in the dark for days after their arrival before relearning how to use light switches, or sweltering in apartments where the thermostat was accidentally set at 90 degrees because they couldn't remember how to control the heat, or racking up hundreds of dollars in long-distance phone charges from calling their relatives all over the country before learning that long distance calls cost extra.

After their early mistakes, resettled Somali Bantus shared their stories to help each other adjust, and within a few months many adults were adept at household technology, learned to shop at Walmart ("We know which aisle is the one with the foods we recognize," explained one woman), and use public transport. Sadiq arrived in Syracuse determined to find the local community college, so after dropping his children off at school during his first week he boarded the first bus he saw because someone had told him the college was at the end of the bus line. "I rode the bus to the end of the line, but there was no college!" he recounted, laughing. The kind driver realized he was lost and explained to him that Syracuse had many bus lines that went many different places in the city. For the next few weeks Sadiq rode the buses every day after taking his kids to school so he could learn all the routes.

Far more challenging and surprising than learning about technology and transport was the structure of education and the growing realization that they would be living in poverty in the land of opportunity. Cultural orientation classes in the camps had stressed that living in the United States meant having a job and the opportunity to attend school, but had failed to clarify that barriers to both would be very high, that the kinds of jobs available to Somali Bantus would not cover their living expenses, that education would not be accessible to everyone, and that the expectation of a job took priority over the opportunity for education.

Although the promise of education was a huge draw for those who signed up for resettlement, the reality after arrival was a crushing disappointment for many. As the second Somali Bantu to graduate from high school in the refugee camp, Sadiq could hardly wait to enroll in college after resettling in Syracuse, but he also went to work right away as was expected of him, at Stickley Furniture, where he milled trees into lumber while wearing earplugs, breathing filters, and big goggles. He worked from 5 AM to 3:30 PM, heading straight to Onondaga Community College after work, where he took classes until 9 PM. Returning home at 10 PM, he slept from 11 PM until 3:30 AM before rising to get to work on time. He rarely saw his wife and children when they were all awake. His job, which required him to work fifty-five hours a week, Monday to Saturday, paid him $420 per week, which was not enough to support his family. He soon realized that coming to America did not really mean getting an education. It meant manual labor and poverty.[3]

Many Somali Bantu refugees did not initially realize that students in the United States are assigned to educational levels on the basis of age rather than ability, which meant that refugee students were placed in grade levels far above their abilities, producing terrible frustration and humiliation as they flailed and failed year after year. The expectation that a fifteen-year-old who had never been to school must be placed in tenth grade, even if that would only ensure his failure, simply made no sense to the resettled refugees, who understood that such a system would doom their older children and offer nothing to young adults. They had thought that all who wished would be able to attend school, entering whatever grade level was appropriate for their reading, writing, and speaking ability, as was the case in the refugee camp schools. The principal of Lewiston's high school sympathized with their dilemma, telling me that it is ridiculous and harmful to expect a teenager with no educational background to be able to achieve enough quickly enough to graduate within the mandated time frame. He said, "It just won't happen. They won't graduate, but the expectation that they should is terrible for everyone," by which he meant that not only are the students and their parents horribly disappointed, but their failure also counts against the school's graduation statistics. "It's a rotten system," he concluded. Even young adults arriving in the United States from the refugee camps expected to be able to progress through elementary school to high school to college. As a forty-year-old non-English-speaking man from Banta lamented when he realized that education would never be an option for him in the United States and that his lack of education would doom his prospects for a decent job, "It is over for us [adults] here. This place is for our children."

Because all resettled refugees over the age of sixteen are expected to seek work, even if attending school, many high school students faced additional barriers to educational success. Caliyow Isaaq's sixteen-year-old son, Musle, had been greatly excited to attend high school when he arrived in the United States with Mohamed and Xawo, but his resettlement caseworker refused to enroll him in high school because of his age. After months of arguing with the resettlement agency, he finally appealed to school authorities, begging to be allowed to enroll in high school. Although he ultimately won the right to attend school, he could barely pass his courses because he was placed in ninth grade after only completing third grade in the refugee camp. One day he showed me his coursework, which included, for his social studies class, pages and pages in his careful neat lettering of the assigned phrases, "I want to be an American Citizen," and "I am patriotic." Almost all of the young Somali Bantu refugees who came to the United States as teenagers failed to graduate from high school.

In short, Somali Bantus faced nearly insurmountable barriers in achieving economic self-sufficiency through employment and education, the two things they had been promised as opportunities available to them in the United States, learning, instead, that their illiteracy, lack of English, lack of education, and subsistence farming skills were a poor fit for life in America, that fears of their foreignness constrained their access to employment and school, and that no one had a plan for closing that yawning gap. They were, in the words of a 2010 report about the refugee resettlement program prepared for the U.S. Senate Committee on Foreign Relations, "Abandoned upon Arrival."[4] Four years after the Somali Bantus began arriving in the United States, ORR sponsored a national conference of Somali Bantu refugee immigrants to assess their resettlement successes and experiences. Somali Bantu representatives from all over the country attended, where they listened to speakers, participated in workshops on subjects ranging from jobs to education, networked to form a national Somali Bantu organization, and had the opportunity to ask questions of ORR staff.

After a panel called "Somali Experiences in Somalia and the Diaspora," audience members talked about their initial challenges with sky-high utility and telephone bills and other financial and educational issues. One man stood up to ask, "I am wondering about the fact that we came from the poorest country to the poorest refugee camp to the poorest towns where our children were placed in the poorest schools where other children were already failing. I am wondering why this is." Many resettled refugees wondered the same thing; why were they brought to America only to be poor? Why were they brought to America to be placed in impoverished, dangerous housing projects and failing schools? Why were they brought to this country and abandoned? As David Haines observes in his review of refugee experience in America, spare support for resettled refugees struggling to make ends meet means poor housing, dangerous neighborhoods, poor transport, and poor schools: "It is 'welcome to the other America.'"[5]

Choosing Lewiston

Isha's family had a rough start in Atlanta. Iman was attacked several times on his way home from junior high school by young men in their public housing project; Isha was abused by their neighbors; and the family struggled financially on the meager assistance they received. Frightened and intimidated by their African American neighbors, they decided within a few months of their arrival to relocate to Lewiston, which had been identified by other resettled Somali and Somali Bantu refugees as an affordable and livable small city with good public housing, safe schools, a very affordable cost of living, more financial support than in other cities, and the familiarity of a growing Somali community. That Somalis and Somali Bantus would choose to move to one of the whitest states in the country made perfect sense to those refugees who wished to distinguish themselves from the African Americans they met in public housing projects in large cities, reflecting a broader pattern among black immigrants from Africa and the Caribbean.[6]

When Isha's family decided to move to Lewiston, their VOLAG caseworker in Atlanta arranged for someone to drive them in a minibus all the way to Lewiston, where they were dropped off at the apartment of friends. Within a few weeks, Isha moved her family into a tiny downtown apartment within walking distance of the downtown shops, park, high school, police station, Adult Education, International Health Clinic, and Trinity Jubilee Center, where Isha joined hundreds of other people every Thursday for the food pantry. Iman enrolled in high school and her grandson Abshir enrolled in grade school, but Isha gave up on the effort to learn English at adult education classes, having spent several unsuccessful months in adult English language learner classes in

Atlanta. "I'm an old woman," she explained, "and my mind is back in Africa, with my other children I had to leave there." Iman found an after-school job at L.L.Bean working 4 PM to midnight; no time for homework. Idris, adept at English from studying hard in the refugee camp, joined an interpreting agency as a translator, while Isha continued her community work as a spiritual healer, cared for her grandchildren, cooked and kept house, and mediated family disputes in her community.

Isha's apartment in an old downtown tenement building sits between the upstairs apartment of her nephew (Cali Osman's sister's son) and his wife and five children, the downstairs apartment of her other nephew (my former field assistant Garad) and his wife and nine children, and a neighboring apartment housing her son, Cabdulkadir, and his family. In all, thirty members of her extended family moved into the building to live together again. Despite its location in a dilapidated building with peeling paint and listing porches, Isha's home is filled with reminders of the family life I remember from Banta: a large extended family compound, segregated gender roles, a matriarchal presence watching over grandchildren, a constant stream of visitors, an olfactory aura of frankincense, cardamom, and tea mixed with roasted meats and boiled corn, an incense dish used for healing rituals always present and ready. Isha's parlor is always busy as she serves tea and snacks to family and friends in a room draped with brightly printed nylon wall coverings and lined with colorful plastic woven floor mats. Isha's two dozen grandchildren from all four apartments constantly dart in and out to play and greet visitors. When the kids get too rambunctious, Isha silences them with a quick word or movement. The rooms initially held little more than floor mats and a TV, but gradually the family acquired mattresses, bed frames, and, finally, a huge wraparound velour sofa in a style popular with Somali families.

The apartment connects memories of Somalia to other places—the spiritual world, the diaspora world, Kenya, and, of course, America. The TV is usually blaring a video of a wedding in Somalia, the refugee camp, or elsewhere in the diaspora—the ubiquitous entertainment in Somali homes. Loud, modernized new versions of classical Somali music from the video compete for sensory awareness with the goat meat and corn porridge often bubbling on the electric stove. Isha doesn't keep much in her cupboards because she is too short to reach above the first shelf, so although her kitchen is typically American, life in this room is still lived on the floor, where everyone sits, plays, prepares food, and rests.

Isha and her extended family had joined a flow of Somali Bantu refugees from Syracuse, Dallas, Houston, Denver, Columbus, Springfield, Atlanta, Hartford, and elsewhere who began moving to Lewiston in 2005 after learning about Lewiston's amenities from Somalis they had known in the refugee camps, who had themselves resettled in Lewiston from 2001 to 2004, making the city a gathering place for former neighbors seeking once again to live near each other and for families and polygynous marriages separated by the resettlement process to reconstitute themselves. Many Somalis and Somali Bantus joined the migration to Lewiston because they found they could not possibly support themselves in their new cities on minimum wage jobs or welfare support and they hoped the lower cost of living in Maine and the ability to re-create community support structures based on sharing resources would make life more manageable. Given that their bid for resettlement was predicated on their ethnic distinctiveness from and abuse by other Somalis, the choice by resettled Somali Bantus to join a Somali community in the diaspora points to the tensions inherent to Somali Bantu identity as racially marked but still culturally, linguistically, and religiously Somali. These tensions would find expression in Lewiston as well.

Outlining Lewiston's Stories

The arrival in Lewiston of so many poor, uneducated, illiterate, and unexpected residents sent a shock wave through a city already struggling with years of economic decline following the closure of the mills that had employed 70 percent of the city's workforce a century earlier.[7] The national conversation about immigrants, focused so intently on their economic and cultural impact, is reproduced in the different versions of Lewiston's story about the first decade of Somali refugee immigration told by residents. Since the federal government tries to achieve refugee economic self-sufficiency by cutting off financial support to resettled refugees within a few weeks of their arrival, the details of their longer-term economic sustainability are left to local communities to sort out. "Integration" is a muddy term, stretched between visions of assimilation that many Euro-Americans believe characterized the experiences of their immigrant ancestors and hopes for a multiculturalism that includes economic assimilation to property ownership, wage-paying employment, and capitalist values alongside the celebration of cultural traditions like dances, songs, and special foods. Concerns about economic sustainability and integration play out in different versions of Lewiston's story. The next three chapters each tell a different version of Lewiston's story of the first decade (2001–12) of Somali and Somali Bantu immigration from the vantage point of different groups of residents.

In the first version, city officials highlight the financial burden on the city of accommodating unexpected impoverished refugees in the context of a retreating welfare state, emphasizing the pressure they faced to develop programs for refugees that conformed to federal legal requirements for accommodating diversity in the absence of outside financial support, local refugee resettlement agencies willing to apply for grants, and any previous experience with managing refugees and cultural difference, all while responding to the concerns of Lewiston's citizens about the cost to the city of meeting the needs of refugees. Since the refugees chose Lewiston and not the other way around, Lewiston's city officials emphasize how the city has tolerated their presence while adopting a business-as-usual approach to minimize their potential disruption to the city's coffers and its way of life. Praise for Lewiston's generosity in accommodating difference and addressing the challenges posed by the unexpected arrival of so many refugees anchors this version, which honors the hard work of city and social services administrators who found themselves scrambling in 2001–6 to build programs for refugees from scratch in an environment of severe economic constraints and social hostility in a way that would not negatively impact the city's native residents. Chapter 4 introduces this "tolerant, business-as-usual" version, a story of legitimate self-congratulations that begins to crack when one reads the local newspaper or listens in on conversations between Lewiston's residents who are unhappy about their city's transformation.[8]

A second version characterizes Somali refugees as an uninvited, unwelcome, and dangerous intrusion into city life. In this xenophobic version, presented in chapter 5, refugees are bearers of economic, physical, and cultural insecurity who bring with them the uncivilized customs of their warring homeland, the threat of different moralities, and the danger of economic penury. Chapter 5 reviews anti-immigrant/refugee sentiment during Lewiston's first decade of Somali immigration in the form of ten insidious myths reiterated in editorial commentary and blogs in the local newspapers, by two of Lewiston's mayors during the first decade of Somali immigration, and circulated in public and private commentary by citizens who cite the blogs and mayoral pronouncements as the basis of their anti-immigrant views. I include a small selection of quotes from blogs and editorials to provide the flavor of the online commentary that paralleled and was often quoted in daily conversations about refugees. Although editorials were signed, blog comments were usually anonymous, but nevertheless infected and inflected private conversation, at least until one newspaper decided to shut down the possibility of anonymity late in the decade because of concerns about the public impact of persistently vitriolic anonymous commentary. The myths' tenacity reflects predominant American concerns about resettling refugees (and accepting immigrants) in "our" midst, concerns that trouble the idea of charity toward refugees with hostility to cultural difference and economic costs and raise questions about how to define community and collective moral responsibility in a globalized world characterized by mobility.

The third version, the communitarian story presented in chapter 6, pushes back against such hostile views by insisting on an expansive definition of community and a delight about the possibilities for social transformation that arriving refugees brought to Lewiston, while also betraying disappointment, disgust, and even rage about poor institutional support for indigent and marginalized immigrants, gatekeeping efforts to contain refugee agency and engagement in city life, and the hostility of colleagues and friends toward refugees. The people in this category, sometimes derided as out-of-touch liberals, social worker types, or even, in the colorful words of the current mayor, "boo-hoo white do-gooders and their carpetbagger friends,"[9] express frustration at the narrow, tolerance-based approach to building programs for refugees taken by institutional leaders, marked by an unwillingness to look to models from other cities that had more experience with diversity, refugees, or both. Chapter 6 profiles social workers, teachers, and community activists and advocates who see the future of the refugees as the future of Lewiston, who have found personal renewal and transformation through their work, and who advocate communitarianism rather than tolerance.

The Somali Bantu refugees' views of their first decade in Lewiston opens part III, which, in contrast to these three versions, highlights their hard work to make Lewiston their home by fighting for and negotiating their place and their rights. This "refugee agency" version speaks of their efforts to create life anew in Lewiston, access available resources, adjust to American cultural practices, and construct a new life designed by them. In this version, the refugees are the protagonists in creating their own refuge and the architects of their lives in Lewiston. As we shall see, their perspectives on self-sufficiency and integration vary considerably from the story of conformist assimilation that anchors the mainstream American view of Euro-American immigrants.

The versions contain different perspectives about the economic costs of refugees and the insecurity provoked by difference. The first (tolerance) version (chapter 4) emphasizes how Lewiston successfully accommodated different cultural practices within an overall framework of assimilation, becoming a model for other cities faced with large numbers of new immigrants while keeping a careful lid on costs. The second (xenophobia) version (chapter 5) blames refugees for Lewiston's ongoing economic ills, claiming that economic resources spent on assisting foreign refugees are starving deserving local community members of the help they have earned as hard-working citizens. The third (communitarian) version (chapter 6) promotes an expansive, inclusive definition of community and sees the refugees as a redemptive force for an ailing city, even while expressing anxiety about what the future holds for Lewiston's refugee population because of the impact of racism on Somali youth identity. This version reflects a belief that diversity and expanded support for the poor are desirable and that the city, state, and federal governments should expend more resources to support the refugee community. The version that opens part III shows how refuge is created by the refugees themselves rather than provided by the host country, through their hard work to build community support structures, negotiate among themselves about changing practices of self-governance and intracommunity support, and demand equality and respect from their new neighbors.

All of these versions simultaneously are true and they have uneasily jostled against each other during Lewiston's first decade of Somali immigration. Lewiston's three mayors during the first decade of Somali settlement personified the different viewpoints: Mayor Raymond gained notoriety in 2002 for writing a letter against Somali immigration that sparked a neo-Nazi rally. Mayor Gilbert (2007–11) used his newspaper column as a bully pulpit to denounce anti-immigrant myths and celebrate the renewing potential of new immigrants to Lewiston. Mayor Macdonald was elected in 2011 (and reelected in 2013) on an explicitly anti-immigrant platform that promoted condescending caricatures of Somali immigrants. The radically different viewpoints about Somali immigration held by the mayors reflect the profound contradictions that Lewistonians, old and new, experience every day as the city continues its dramatic transformation and these narratives compete for ascendancy.

CHAPTER 4

We Have Responded Valiantly

"February 2001!" exclaimed Sue Charron, the director of Lewiston's General Assistance (GA) office, when I asked in 2010 if she could clearly remember back to the early days of Somali immigration to Lewiston. "It's *really* clear. We didn't have time to even think about what was happening. We just handled it. At the same time we were doing this we were also educating everyone else. We were educating DHHS [Department of Health and Human Services], who were denying people [benefits] because they didn't know they were eligible for assistance!" Like other city officials reminiscing about the shock of Somali immigration, Sue emphasized how unprepared they were to support refugees arriving with no place to stay, no jobs, and no English skills: "Never in my wildest dreams did I ever imagine we'd be doing this kind of work."

Refugees from Banta arrived in Lewiston right in the middle of roiling debates about the city's responsibilities and obligations toward uninvited refugee immigrants precipitated by the unexpected arrival in 2001 of the first thousand Somalis.[1] This chapter begins with recollections about the impact of that first wave by city administrators whose job descriptions placed them in key positions of engagement (staff in the GA and mayor's office, schools, and hospitals). The city's experience demonstrates how a neoliberal definition of refuge—such as the offer of refuge, but with scant economic, educational, or employment support—leaves local host communities responsible for supporting refugees whether or not they invited them. Lewiston's city officials promote Lewiston's first decade of Somali immigration as a success story, not because refugees attained "economic self-sufficiency" and "integration," but because violence was averted and federal mandates for accommodating diversity met. Accommodation to the law, however, can come with its own limitations.

"What Is Supposed to Happen if the City Is Unprepared to Work with Refugees?"

One of the shocks for the city of Lewiston was that the sole VOLAG in Maine initially refused to provide any assistance to the new arrivals because they did not have a government contract to help secondary migrants (refugees, like Lewiston's Somali immigrants, who voluntarily leave their first resettlement site to relocate to another town within three years of their arrival), and the agency feared a hostile backlash from Lewiston's citizens. After resettling in the United States, refugees are free to move wherever they wish, just like anyone else, although VOLAGs retain no enduring commitment to those they resettle, and the funds they receive to assist newly arriving refugees remain with the VOLAG in the place of initial resettlement and do not follow the refugees if they move. Funds allocated to local VOLAGs to help resettle Somali refugees thus did not follow the refugees when they moved to Lewiston, where the local VOLAG did not offer assistance because they lacked a federal contract to work with the new arrivals.

Unexpectedly, city staff had to become de facto resettlement workers even though the city had little institutional infrastructure in place for providing assistance to newly arriving refugees. Although Lewiston was not an officially designated refugee resettlement site for Somali refugees, the city of Portland, a few dozen miles to the south, was. In the 1990s some Somali families unhappy with their first resettlement site came to Portland to visit their relatives and decided to stay. Word circulated about Maine's quiet lifestyle, low cost of living, low crime rate, and the availability of immediate short-term assistance through GA funds, and Somali refugee families began moving to Maine as secondary migrants whose original VOLAGs were no longer responsible for assisting them.[2] By early 2001, public housing in Portland was full and city staff drove a few Somali families further north to Lewiston to be housed with assistance by Lewiston's GA office. Deciding Lewiston was a fine place to live, those families invited their relatives from across the country to join them, and within a few months several hundred more arrived, shocking the local schools when their doors opened in September and scores of new students unable to speak English showed up. Within a year the Somali population had grown to about a thousand.

Because many of the immigrants arrived with few resources, Lewiston's GA office became their primary point of entry. In the absence of an involved VOLAG, the GA staff helped new Somali arrivals locate housing and provided vouchers for food, diapers, utilities, and other goods for their first weeks in Maine. The year 2001 was particularly challenging because the arrival of a thousand Somalis coincided with a 50 percent reduction in the GA budget, a cut made before the city realized it would be extending support to so many new residents.

Sue Charron recalled the sense of bewilderment about how to help the newly arriving refugees in a context of no preparation or assistance from the state's sole VOLAG or any state agencies: "It was a brand new experience for us. It was incredible. You learn everything you can on the fly. There was no one willing to help us." Shaking her head, Sue said, "We had no idea what an I-94 [the official arrival-departure record used by U.S. Citizenship and Immigration Services] was. We had no idea what an EAD [Employment Authorization Document] was. We knew nothing! And it wasn't fun. We felt like we were an island. We didn't know what we were doing and yet we had to tell everyone else what to do." Another staff member who worked with new arrivals during this period recalled, "It took two years before Catholic Charities [the local VOLAG] was willing to provide some assistance, but even then only in carefully constrained ways, and even then their assistance was offered without Catholic support. Churches, the Catholic community, was not at all supportive of working with black Muslims in Maine. Not at all. [A close family relative] who works with priests refused when I asked him to get Catholic networks to help. And when they are the only VOLAG, and faith-based, accountable to their own leadership [as opposed to the host community], there are no other options." In addition to the lack of VOLAG support, the office of the state refugee coordinator was vacant during the early years of Somali immigration, which meant that the key position in the state that should have been able to offer assistance was also absent. The person quoted above echoes the sentiments I heard from many city administrators that Sue Charron, as the first stop for secondary migrants arriving in Lewiston, "was absolutely amazing."

Sue and her small staff had to learn on the job about how to help the refugees who were arriving daily get settled into housing and referred to school, job training, English courses, and DHHS to see if they qualified for Temporary Assistance to Needy Families and food stamps. One staff member remembered, "We'd show up to work on Monday morning wondering how many people would be sitting in the waiting room needing help." Sometimes several families would arrive each day. Processing each family for GA took hours, as did the constant stream of phone calls to potential landlords, hospitals, schools, DHHS, Adult Education, the local office of the state CareerCenter, and the Portland-based nonprofit Immigrant Legal Advocacy Project for questions about legal status and eligibility for assistance. In 2001, half the GA budget went to helping new refugee arrivals.

Echoing Sue's description of the impact on her office of the massive and unexpected arrival of so many Somalis seeking assistance, the coordinator of the city's adult English Language Learner (ELL) program told me, "Those were the worst years of my life," because of the scramble to provide English language and literacy classes on a constrained budget with no funding for child care or transport and a very small staff. Her funding had been cut just as the first Somali immigrants began to arrive, and her program had no models in place for teaching English to people illiterate in their own language. Managing on a razor-thin budget, the courses were soon swamped by new students.

In the absence of VOLAG support, at the end of 2001 Lewiston and Portland collaborated on a $1.2 million "Unanticipated Arrivals" grant from the U.S. Office of Refugee Resettlement to support additional staff for case management, cultural orientation programs, and community outreach for the two cities from 2001 to 2005. Their grant was the first to cities rather than a nonprofit or VOLAG, a fact many administrators note with pride. Lewiston-Auburn native Cheryl Hamilton, a recent college graduate, returned to her hometown to join the staff funded by the grant, excited to be part of the process of changing and diversifying her native city. Working with Sue and other staff hired through the grant, Cheryl coordinated cultural orientation classes for new arrivals and community outreach efforts to engage Lewiston's other residents in positive educational programs about their new neighbors. It was not an easy undertaking. Cheryl recalled how few models she could find for community outreach programs because such initiatives were not typically part of a VOLAG's contractual responsibilities, which focused on providing specific services to refugees and not general services, like community outreach, to host communities.

Some of Cheryl's efforts in the early years, such as panel presentations and community conversations, were aimed at confronting the mistrust and hostility from Lewiston's residents who were worried about the impact on their home city of so many Somalis. Sue recalled fielding constant phone calls and comments from citizens upset and concerned that in a context of shrinking financial resources and widespread poverty the refugees would take away resources from needy Maine citizens: "We had phone calls every day—ya ya ya. People complaining. Everybody thinks it's just a free ride. I explain, 'They have to do exactly the same things everyone else had to do [to get city support].' The ignorance has been the hardest thing for me, other than almost dying from the workload." While Cheryl, like Sue, remains proud of the community-building efforts she initiated, her memories also are clouded by the strain of constantly fighting against antagonistic community members. One public forum at the local Armory in 2002 brought hundreds of citizens who lined up at the microphone, one after another, to denounce the Somali presence. Cheryl recalls, "The worst thing we did was the public forum at the Armory with our 'who's who' panel. It was terrible. Lots of angry people came. . . . People stood at the microphone and said terrible things. My music teacher said terrible things. I sat there watching my town break my heart."

She acknowledges they made mistakes in managing some of the open forums that went awry with overwhelming hostility and complaints, but echoes Sue's recollection that everyone who was working to help resettle the new arrivals and facilitate public education programs had no blueprint for action and worked under the stress of constant community antagonism. "To be a local during that time was awful," Cheryl remembers. "You were never not defending Somalis wherever you went. You were never able to turn off your job." Family gatherings, local bars, friends' houses for dinner became contexts for demands that she explain and defend the presence of Somalis. Sue admits to becoming fed up with constantly having to educate her friends, sometimes just shutting down rather than engaging: "It's the weekend. Someone makes a stupid ignorant remark, pushes me about the burden of the refugees, and sometimes I just say"—she heaves a heavy sigh—"It's the weekend. Leave me alone on that."

Cheryl explained her growing frustration with the entire refugee resettlement system, which in her view relies on VOLAGs that are not accountable to the host communities and provide no support or assistance to host communities who may be unprepared to welcome new refugee arrivals. While refugee success is defined as self-sufficiency and integration, there is no way to hold refugee resettlement agencies accountable. The only way that VOLAGs account for their work is statistical, by recording how many refugees attended their programs or received caseworker assistance. Broad community-oriented programs like community outreach and integration initiatives are not part of a VOLAG's responsibilities, which is why she attempted to pioneer such programs through her job with the city. "But what does accountability mean?" she asks. "If we were held accountable for refugee integration 'success,' we'd have failed most days. If we were to be held accountable for no homelessness, then we won most days." And if no VOLAG is active in the city (as was the case in the initial years of Somali immigration to Lewiston), she continues, "What is supposed to happen if the city is unprepared to work with refugees? What about preparing cities and employers so they are willing to hire refugees? There is no allowance for things like fear, racism, discrimination, and insecurity.

Local education is left up to local VOLAGS, but what if they're not active or not capable due to limited resources?"[3]

In interviews and publications, Phil Nadeau, Lewiston's acting city administrator in 2000–2002, shared the frustrated view of other city officials that community, religious, and civic organizations avoided any initial engagement with the growing Somali community and any confrontation with the swirling rumors about how the Somali influx would harm Lewiston, leaving beleaguered city staff on their own to manage the influx and negative rumors.[4] Even the director of the downtown community organization that had received a $1 million grant from the federal Empowerment Zone program for highly distressed urban and rural communities called him to complain about potential problems from all the new Somali arrivals. The grant targeted the very neighborhood that was filling up with Somali immigrants, and the director wanted to know what the city was going to do about it. Phil recalled telling him, "What are *you* doing to help? You've got this big federal grant to do community work [in the neighborhood where the Somalis were living] and you're not doing anything!" Phil also maligned the state for its lack of support, which he attributed to Maine's lack of historical engagement with diversity, a sentiment he expressed more diplomatically in one of his published articles: "The state took a minimalist approach to services beyond Portland's borders. The state was certainly aware of immigrant populations in other parts of Maine, but its lack of any tangible assistance for Lewiston's Somalis in 2001 came as one of many surprises to Lewiston officials."[5]

The local hospitals and schools initially responded to the new arrivals with a determined attitude of business as usual: the refugees would just have to fit in and should not take away resources from Lewiston's other citizens. Treating the extension of services to Somali immigrants as additions to core programs already in place meant balancing the legal responsibility of providing welfare, health care, and education to Somali immigrants against the desire to ensure that such programs for Lewiston's other residents would not be compromised. Confusion about available federal assistance for supporting diversity meant hostility to offering things like translation services at the hospitals or additional ELL classes at the schools. Laughing in hindsight about the disastrous public meeting at the Armory, Sue Charron recalled, "Medical providers. Oh my God! 'We can't offer this! We can't offer that! We can't pay for interpreters!' 'Wait! MaineCare pays for interpreters!' 'What!?' That [was the] huge meeting at the Armory where doctors were yelling about costs [without realizing that the costs of translation would be borne by the state and federal government]." Just as the hospitals lacked a plan for providing adequate translation services, the school system had no plan for how to develop a comprehensive

English language program for such a large number of new students, allowing non-English-speaking students to languish in poorly structured, marginalized classes for years.

Neo-Nazis Come to Town

Facing an onslaught of complaints by city residents about city assistance to the new arrivals, by 2002 city staff felt administratively, economically, and socially overwhelmed by the continuing influx of Somalis despite the city's lack of preparation, financial support from the state, and support programs from the local VOLAG and other nonprofits. In a politically clumsy move, Mayor Raymond attempted to address the matter by writing an open letter in October 2002 to the Somali community asking them to stop moving to Lewiston, suggesting they had emptied the city's coffers and taxed the city to a breaking point:

> For some number of months, I have observed the continued movement of a substantial number of Somalis into the downtown area of our Community. I have applauded the efforts of our City staff in making available the existing services and the local citizenry for accepting and dealing with the influx.
>
> I assumed that it would become obvious to the new arrivals the effect the large numbers of new residents has had upon the existing Staff and City finances and that this would bring about a voluntary reduction of the number of new arrivals—it being evident that the burden has been, for the most part, cheerfully accepted, and every effort has been made to accommodate it.
>
> Our Department of Human Services has recently reported that the number of Somali families arriving into the City during the month of September is below the approximate monthly average that we have seen over the last year or so. It may be premature to assume that this may serve as a signal for future relocation activity, but the decline is welcome relief given increasing demands on city and school services.
>
> I feel that recent relocation activity over the summer has necessitated that I communicate directly with the Somali elders and leaders regarding our newest residents. If recent declining arrival numbers are the result of your outreach efforts to discourage relocation into the City, I applaud those efforts. If they are the product of other unrelated random events, I would ask that the Somali leadership make every effort to communicate my concerns on city and school service impacts with other friends and extended family who are considering a move to this community.
>
> To date, we have found the funds to accommodate the situation. A continued increased demand will tax the City's finances.

This large number of new arrivals cannot continue without negative results for all. The Somali community must exercise some discipline and reduce the stress on our limited finances and our generosity. I am well aware of the legal right of a U.S. resident to move anywhere he/she pleases, but it is time for the Somali community to exercise this discipline in view of the effort that has been made on its behalf.

We will continue to accommodate the present residents as best as we can, but we need self-discipline and cooperation from everyone.

Only with your help will we be successful in the future—please pass the word: We have been overwhelmed and have responded valiantly. Now we need breathing room. Our city is maxed-out financially, physically and emotionally.

I look forward to your cooperation.

Laurier T. Raymond, Jr.

Mayor, City of Lewiston, Maine[6]

The major news media, already fascinated by the apparent incongruity of so many Africans in Lewiston, contributed to the controversy through stories about the Letter by ABC News, *Time* magazine, the *New York Times*, the *Chicago Tribune*, the *Washington Post*, the *Los Angeles Times*, and elsewhere.[7] While many of Lewiston's residents applauded the mayor for finally speaking "the truth," Somali community members asked why the mayor had never asked to meet with them directly before making such a public statement against their community, and some appalled members of Lewiston's city staff rejected the implication that the city had run out of funds because of overuse by Somalis.[8]

National media coverage of the Letter caught the attention of the World Church of the Creator, a Midwestern neo-Nazi white supremacist group, whose members descended on Lewiston to rally in defense of the city's right to bar the door against black Muslim refugees. Their arrival shocked and upset many Lewistonians, who perceived the mayor's letter not as racist but rather as driven by budgetary concerns. Embarrassed activist and church groups in Lewiston responded by organizing a prodiversity Many and One Rally at Bates College, which drew about 4,000 people from throughout the state to show their support for diversity, including both of Maine's senators and the governor, but not the mayor, who had fled town on vacation. Several Somali friends told me that when news of the Letter and the white supremacist rally reached the international arena, their concerned relatives began phoning from Dadaab refugee camp to ask if they were safe and to suggest they should move elsewhere or return to Kenya. Other than some leading activists in the

Somali community, many Somalis chose to stay home during the rally, fearful of what the day might bring.

Then–acting city administrator Phil Nadeau believed the media coverage and neo-Nazi show of solidarity for the Letter "changed everything" because it provoked a greater engagement with refugee support from civic and community organizations that had been previously reluctant to become involved. He told me, "As difficult a situation as it was for the community to get through that [the fallout from the Letter], we're fortunate that if we had to pick the thing to galvanize the community it was a letter [and not a violent act]. The Letter got people talking to each other, talking about the issues."[9] He noted as evidence that despite its initial reluctance, Catholic Charities finally joined the city in providing case management services (after the city had been awarded the Unanticipated Arrivals grant), local agencies began to educate themselves about language access policies, and the local school system and hospitals finally expanded and professionalized their programs for non-English speakers. "We all had to play catch-up," he acknowledged. "Hell, we're the poster child for Sudden Ethnic Diversification!"[10]

Somali Bantus Come to Town

When Somali Bantu families began arriving in Lewiston in 2005, the city had weathered the neo-Nazi rally and the counter-rally show of support for diversity. The Unanticipated Arrivals grant brought Catholic Charities on board to offer case management services to secondary migrants by newly hired Somali-speaking caseworkers; the city's GA office had a functioning model for settling new arrivals into housing and signing them up for job training and/or English classes; and DHHS had begun to figure out the complicated benefits eligibility for resettled refugees. But whereas some Somali immigrants in 2001–4 were literate English speakers with professional skills, the Somali Bantus presented a brand new challenge because of their nearly universal background as illiterate non-English-speaking farmers completely dependent on the intervention of interpreters and cultural brokers to navigate life in the United States.

When I first met formally with Somali Bantu elders following the slide show in February 2006, their community in Lewiston had grown to around 500 people, and the elders had a list of priorities for which they were seeking my assistance. Jammed into a small apartment for a meeting that lasted for hours, the elders articulated their top goals: to learn English and become literate; to obtain jobs, because only four Somali Bantus had thus far obtained employment; to develop extended day or after-school programs for their children because they were so far behind their American peers; to advocate for better public transport, because everyone was trying to share cars to get to shopping centers, adult ed classes, DHHS, and the distant CareerCenter; to rent an office for community meetings; and to ensure that Somali Bantus could use their own translators in meetings with city institutions, hospitals, and schools rather than relying on Somali translators. They explained that their community of 500 people included nine adult English speakers whom they wished to use as translators, which I later learned was a dramatic exaggeration because many of the nine had only modest English skills. No one had a college degree, and only a few had a high school degree from the refugee camps. Driving home from our meeting, I pulled off the highway in tears, feeling almost undone as I considered the reality of 500 people depending on five English speakers and four people with paid jobs.

Many of Lewiston's authorities felt the same way. As the size of the Somali Bantu community doubled and then doubled again over the next two years, officials and social services providers uniformly remarked on how much help the Somali Bantus required because of the nearly universal lack of English language, literacy, and education among the adults and the high number of large families headed by illiterate single mothers, which constituted about a third of the population.[11] Everyone with whom I spoke, from staff at the hospitals to schools, remarked on the additional set of major challenges their arrival brought to public institutions struggling to accommodate the newcomers.

Learning to Swim with Sharks

Phil Nadeau is right that many city institutions had to play catch-up. Local hospitals, schools, and other organizations have long experience with Lewiston's history of English-French bilingualism and a clear understanding of the cultural and economic challenges faced by preceding generations of minority Franco-Americans, and many of those organizations are now staffed with people whose parents and grandparents were French-speaking immigrants. But the new arrivals—black Muslim war refugees who spoke Somali and Maay Maay—offered a novel and utterly foreign presence that challenged the ability of local institutions to accommodate new forms of difference. Initially only a few organizations in addition to the GA office and Adult Education wholly opened their doors to the new arrivals. The public library began offering after-school homework help sessions, as did Trinity Jubilee, a downtown day shelter that provides a daily free lunch, a weekly food pantry, and caseworker support for anyone who needs help. When the Somali Bantus began moving into the downtown neighborhood served by Trinity, the director hired Somali- and Maay Maay–speaking staff to help them with everything from reading mail to intervening with landlords, paying bills, supporting parents in school interactions, connecting refugees with services, and more, making Trinity the primary location for refugee assistance in the city after the GA office. Their after-school homework help program for elementary school children grew to accommodate up to a hundred, mostly Somali Bantu, students each day. Trinity received a trickle of grant funding from the city and from other nonprofits, but primarily relied on donations, volunteers, and its tiny but energetic staff to run its programs.[12]

But other city institutions took a slower approach to including Somalis and Somali Bantus in their programs or developing ways to engage with the refugee population. Despite the confusion about refugees' entitlements to benefits and the repeated intervention of the nonprofit Immigrant Legal Advocacy Project to educate about refugees' rights, the local DHHS office only assigned a supervisor to pay particular attention to refugees' entitlement to benefits in 2008 (although the agency had hired three Somali speakers earlier in the decade, who comprised about 2 percent of the staff). The downtown development project supported by a million-dollar federal grant (whose first director had complained to Phil Nadeau about the new downtown residents) initially denied all the grant applications by Somali Bantu community groups until complaints by activists forced them to reconsider. (Under the leadership of a new director, they did, first meeting in 2009 with the rejected applicants to review their grant applications before funding several and offering workshops to Somali Bantu community groups on grant writing and project design.) Under pressure from a couple of activist physicians, the local hospitals agreed to open an International Clinic one day a week in the downtown community clinic specifically for the new arrivals, but unfortunately the doctors' hopes were undermined by a staff unhappy about having to work with refugees and resentful of the "special treatment" provided to refugees in the weekly clinic. The physicians felt that the staff bullied the Somali cultural brokers and translators, denied them access to the computers, failed to include them in office birthday celebrations, and revolted when the physicians tried to reorient the annual Christmas party into a holiday party. Attitudes toward Somali staff and clients became so hostile that the doctors feared a breach in medical protocol. After battling with the hospital administration for a contract that affirmed the existence of the International Clinic and for better staffing and training, both doctors resigned in frustration, and the hospital closed the clinic in 2009 after only a few years in existence. A friend who attended the decisive meeting reported that one hospital administrator told another, "Now we can get back to serving the people we're supposed to be serving." Reflecting on this experience, one of the physicians told me, "Now I know what institutional racism means, but I don't know what to do about it. How do you make someone less racist?"

The public schools faced a special challenge, because their ELL offerings in 2001 were minimal and the school system did not expand the ELL program quickly or comprehensively enough to accommodate the large number of new non-English speakers in a manner that met federal and state requirements. From 2001 to 2007, the number of children enrolled in ELL classes grew from around 20 to 702.[13] As had happened in other cities, a complaint filed in 2006 against the school department for its failure to develop an appropriate ELL program brought in the U.S. Department of Justice to mandate its creation, which began with the hiring of a local former school principal to build a program that would comply with state and federal requirements.[14] While the school system was expanding its ELL programs, school leaders faced an onslaught of complaints from parents and community members about adding anything that looked like special programming or privileges for refugees, making the administration extremely sensitive to public scrutiny.

In an interview, the school superintendent recalled the first years of Somali settlement as "chaotic" since, as he explained, the schools "had no one to prewarn them, help them, or provide them with background information about the new arrivals." "When you have a teaching staff and suddenly demographics change overnight, it's a trauma for them!" he explained to me.[15] Shaking his head dismissively when I asked if he sought help from the federal Office of Refugee Resettlement, the state refugee coordinator, or other refugee support organizations or information clearinghouses, he emphasized that the priority was networking within local institutions, like the hospitals to assess public health risks, the local Department of Labor to help with adult education, the Portland-based Center for the Prevention of Hate Violence to help with in-school fighting, and leaders in the Lewiston community. Like many of the city administrators with whom I spoke, he stressed how the challenge to accommodate Somali immigrants forced local institutions to transcend territoriality and their historic silo pattern of management. Public schools are a particular site of community struggles over identity and values, and it was clear in our conversation that the superintendent felt that every action he took was under a microscope, including scrutiny by people and anti-immigrant activist groups beyond Lewiston who read blogs and news reports "ready to dive in whenever they read or hear something they don't like."

A refusal to bend the rules or loosen the standards to accommodate Somali newcomers emerged as a regular theme in my conversations with the superintendent and school leaders, who uniformly explained that "unlike other schools," Lewiston holds non- and limited English speakers to high standards of achievement, does not grant credit toward graduation for ELL classes except as electives after students have reached a certain level, and strictly monitors student progress with frequent testing to ensure students only pass to the next grade once they have demonstrated competency.[16] They want to make sure to confront possible perceptions that Somali newcomers are passed through the system for the sake of school statistics or because of a soft spot for diversity. One school principal, while expressing pride about their high standards, nevertheless acknowledged that the system is stacked against Somali Bantu children, telling me, "They come to us having never been in schools before, with no socialization and no understanding of school, and they don't have the skills to be in school. Now we live in a society with a razor blade at the throat of education and these kids—the new arrivals—are walking into a combat zone." It was a war that most Somali Bantu students lost during their first decade because so few managed to graduate from high school.

While maintaining standards, the superintendent also felt pressure to ensure that schools were not perceived as offering extras or special treatment to Somalis, refusing requests from Somali parents for a prayer room, the removal of pork from the school cafeteria, or an early departure on Friday for prayers. Remarking on a public flap about a student who claimed she was not allowed to pray in school, he noted that he "could easily get about twenty-five, thirty e-mails, phone calls a day, from all over the country from watchdog bloggers contacting me to say, we're with you! Stand firm!" Reporters with TV cameras arrived to cover the story about the prayer room request for Muslim students, followed by letters of outraged support from Christian groups in the South. He even received a call from someone who told him, "If you're going to [allow Muslims to have a prayer room,] then I want a prayer room for Satan!" Shaking his head about the vigilance of national anti-immigrant activists, he said, "It's out there. I'm sitting on a keg. I've got to learn to swim with the sharks."[17] (Remarking on the fear of Muslim prayer in schools, an ELL teacher dryly observed, "but we've long had a Christian Bible study group.") The schools overcame initial protests against head scarves while adhering to a school-wide rule against headwear that might be construed as gang related by defining head scarves as religious, like the yarmulkes that Jewish students would be allowed to wear. Although the schools refused to provide dedicated rooms for prayer, they allowed students to pray during the day, and the cafeterias began clearly labeling pork products. (Because U.S. government subsidies make pork products cheap, pork is a ubiquitous menu item in school cafeterias in poor communities.)

But such indications of tolerance and accommodation did not extend to anything that might be regarded as special or extra programming for Somali students. School administrators would not support new programs that targeted only refugee children. Noting the poverty indicators for children in the school district (e.g., the very high enrollments in the free lunch program), school authorities emphasized their commitment to providing programs that would benefit all students, not just the refugees, such as free summer school, free sports participation for everyone (rather than a pay-to-play model), and a free after-school homework help program. But using designated funding for underachieving students to pay for free summer school for everyone came at the expense of one-on-one tutoring with ELL students (an alternative option fundable through the earmarked grant); the free sports program did not include the majority of ELL students, who are prohibited by school policy from joining sports teams because most of their ELL courses do not count toward graduation; and the free after-school homework help program was a generalized program that did not offer targeted ELL help. The insistence on prioritizing programs for everyone meant a reluctance or refusal to pursue funding for programs that would specifically target non-English speakers or refugees, to the disappointment of some (including many of the refugee parents), who believed that since the refugee children arrived in the United States so poorly prepared, they needed and deserved extra assistance.

Writing about the significance of racial difference in a different context, education scholar Mica Pollock argues that using the language of "everyone" (she uses the term "all") allows a diversion away from identifying those students who struggle the most, but whose particular needs are not distinguished or identified in ways that would enable more specific targeting and intervention. The discourse of "everyone" becomes a way to avoid having to engage the thorny issue of how and why race matters in student achievement, because the talk of "everyone" papers over racial differences in performance. Ignoring the salience of race and refusing to orient interventions specifically toward those students who are most often struggling and most often racially marked thus has an implicitly racist outcome.[18] As we shall see in detail in chapter 6, in Lewiston the insistence that any new programming had to be developed for all students meant that school authorities consistently rejected appeals or proposals from Somali and Somali Bantu parents and ELL teachers to develop programs specifically for the (racially and linguistically marked) ELL students (such as special tutoring sessions, extended-day ELL programs, special parent-teacher committees for ELL students, culturally competent mental health and counseling services, and networking with other nonprofit agencies to apply for grants to target Somali-speaking children). Part III details the consequences.

Managing Diversity

Recognizing that Somali-speaking children faced particular and acute challenges that the school system would not fully address as it worked to expand and systemize its ELL program, a group of social services providers formed a collaborative to brainstorm and network about how to support the "New Mainers," particularly in the area of cultural competency for mental health and social services. The fluid group met monthly to report news and share suggestions for action. From 2008 to 2010, many monthly discussions focused on the experiences of Somali-speaking students in local schools.

Several ELL teachers, social workers, and immigrant caseworkers in the collaborative suggested the creation of a subcommittee specifically to deal with parent-school interactions, hoping, for example, to encourage the school system to create an ELL parent-teacher or parent advisory group. Defining its role as that of cultural broker and mediator, the subcommittee began by holding open meetings during 2009 with refugee parents to learn about their concerns. The meetings with parents were well attended, vibrant but calm, and generated widespread agreement about a few issues of significant concern (e.g., concerns about how long their children stayed in ELL before being moved into mainstream classes, their children's boredom in ELL classes with material that was too simple, the forced departure of a favorite teacher whom the parents and children trusted, the high rate of suspension for Somali and Somali Bantu children that left them further behind their peers, and the fact that not a single Somali Bantu student had graduated from high school in their five years in the city). Recognizing that many parents were frustrated that they had been expressing the same concerns for years but were seeing no progress, the group understood that the meetings would have to produce concrete results. The plan was to follow the initial small meetings with a larger open meeting where immigrant parents of ELL students could meet with school administrators to discuss their concerns and ask questions.

The open meeting between Somali and Somali Bantu parents and school administrators went badly off script, however. A few parents became increasingly upset as they felt their concerns were deflected by school officials, who refused to discuss personnel policies and talked about the ELL structure in highly technical language that parents found difficult to understand. When a couple of immigrant parents started shouting, the school officials became defensive and shut down discussion about the parents' allegations and questions. Chaos erupted as some school administrators began packing up to walk out while some parents continued yelling, other parents tried to calm the agitators, interpreters tried to intervene, and the meeting organizers conferred about what to do. One brave teacher tried to quell the growing commotion with a forceful intervention, telling the parents that the ELL teachers cared deeply about their children and parental concerns, but her words of solidarity got lost in the parents' frustrations with the lack of a satisfactory response from her supervisors. As some of the school administrators announced that the meeting was over, one of the interpreters protested in vain, "It's not our culture to limit discussion! You can say 5 to 7, but we stay until we're done. You can't just stop the discussion at 7 PM!"

Immediately following the meeting (which resulted in negative coverage of the parents' behavior in the local newspaper), the school authorities asked that all the participating teachers resign from the collaborative subcommittee. The social services staff member who chaired the subcommittee was also asked to resign, out of concern that her involvement in a committee that generated criticism of the school district would reflect negatively on her service organization. Other subcommittee members were told by school authorities never to participate in such an event again, not an idle threat for those service providers who depended on city funding for their programs. This experience clarified to everyone in the collaborative the scant opportunity for public and social services employees to engage in advocacy or critique and how threatened the school felt by angry Somali-speaking parents. One social services provider wryly observed that everyone would have supported the parents' right to yell and scream if the issue was a fired popular ice hockey coach. But because the meeting was about the concerns of ELL kids, refugee parents were supposed to be grateful, take what was offered, and not complain. Refugee parents yelling about school policy were unacceptable.

In the wake of their public loss of control over parents, school officials determined to avoid such forums in the future, steadfastly blocking the efforts of ELL teachers to build solidarity with parents through teacher-parent support groups or parent advisory committees. Administrative staff cited fears about unpredictable outcomes and demanding parents, and that such bodies could become sites of Somali tribal conflict. Uncertainty about how to contain unruly refugee parents gave pause as well to local social services agencies considering how to extend their programs to include the new immigrants. By 2010, only a few local organizations other than Trinity, the public library, a farming project that enabled refugees to access farming land, and Adult Education had begun to cautiously extend themselves to the refugee community by developing small, targeted programs for Somali speakers mediated by a Somali cultural broker or translator. An agency dedicated to supporting children assigned a staff member to work one-on-one with twelve toddlers in large Somali families to prepare them for attending school, while another organization created a nurturing program for five Somali mothers with infants. Another nonprofit hired a part-time family advocate to work as a home-school intermediary for three Somali families with children in the local school system. At the end of the decade, the school district allowed a staff member from a social services agency to invite ten boys who had lost a loved one in the refugee camp to participate in an after-school program oriented toward emotional development that met for one hour a week for ten weeks. Many local organizations offered no specific outreach to the refugee community at all, although refugee friends believe that most grant-seeking organizations in the city habitually mentioned the large refugee population in their grant proposals to ensure that their description of the context in which they worked sounded dire and challenging. Refugees are good for raising money, says one activist friend, even if the grants are not used to extend programming to them.

Accommodation Is about Containment

While the predominant narrative from Lewiston city officials rightfully emphasizes their hard work and dedication to accommodate the Somali immigrants and their success at averting the potential for violence, voices of dissent argue that accommodation can also include resistance to change, take the form of "othering," and feel profoundly undemocratic to those being accommodated. Those of this opinion ask, for example, why Lewiston's institutions, like schools and hospitals, initially seemed so unwilling to develop programs specifically for Somali speakers and to hire Somalis for jobs other than as cultural brokers and translators. They note the resistance of school officials to support ELL parent outreach or advisory groups or to develop additional programs directed at ELL children, that the hospital failed to support the fledgling International Clinic, and that city and nonprofit agencies who received funding for programs targeting refugees failed to train and promote Somali cultural brokers and translators. They point out that although Somalis are nearly 20 percent of the school body, there are no Somali teachers or administrators. One frustrated Somali activist asks, "Why are Somalis not receiving higher-level jobs, supervisors, managers, administrators? No refugees, after ten years, are in a position of authority! Why not?" Indeed, I was astonished to discover in 2010 that the web page for the Lewiston public school system did not even include the names of any of the district's Somali employees who worked as translators, tutors, and parent outreach coordinators, supporting the ELL program and the 1,000 Somali-speaking students in the district (an oversight that has since been corrected). The activist is angry that the official story of Lewiston's success ignores the role of Somalis themselves in making their lives in Lewiston, and that many of the local institutions that emphasize their success at accommodating Somalis have failed to hire Somalis into positions of authority or to engage in internal transformations beyond hiring translators and cultural brokers. Translators and brokers are mediators who are employed to manage outreach to the Somali population, but they are not treated as integral to the internal functioning, decision making, or priorities of the organizations that employ them. These critics lament the silencing of critical discussion, as we saw in the outcome of the large parent meeting with school administrators, and the ways in which accommodation feels like containment.

I return to these particular points again in later chapters, but here want to highlight one criticism in particular: that a reactive approach of accommodation without transformation—of treating diversity, multiculturalism, and outreach to foreign immigrants as add-ons rather than integral to institutional culture—silenced other approaches that might have introduced reforms or transformations of local institutions. People frustrated with the slow pace of change berated Lewiston's approach as guarded, self-protective, insular, and parochial, especially in comparison with cities like Portland, where numerous strong advocacy groups for refugees and immigrants had formed, whose public school system quickly developed a robust multicultural program, and whose citizens were discussing the extension of voting rights to resident noncitizens (a ballot proposal ultimately rejected in 2010 by a vote of 52 to 48 percent). By comparison, critics note that institutions like hospitals and schools in Lewiston added translation services and ELL programs as their effort toward diversity, but did not transform their normal operating culture, allowing staff who subscribed to the anti-Somali myths detailed in chapter 5 to remain hostile and resistant to Somali patients, students, and staff. Bringing the provision of social services, medical care, and schools in line with bureaucratic mandates for language access did not mean changing institutional culture, and critics suggest the result has been an outward appearance of accommodation while, as we will see in chapter 5, racism and hostility rage within.

Discussing the resistance in Lewiston to adapting or learning from models developed in other cities for embracing multiculturalism and refugee outreach, a woman from Lewiston who is heavily involved in refugee resettlement initiatives explained the attitude of her colleagues: "They don't want people from Portland to come tell them what to do. They don't want intellectual outsiders to come in." People in Lewiston, she suggested, "don't want to ask for help because that might reveal ignorance or lack of capacity. Lewiston fears it's unqualified and lacks the intellectual resources to make things work. Doing the right thing might mean the person supposed to be doing it is unqualified and someone else should actually be doing it." Like the activist quoted above and others, it is frustrating to her that throughout the city's first decade of

Somali settlement, many of the major public institutions remained staffed by people hostile to refugees, unwilling to learn from well-functioning models elsewhere of refugee outreach (whether through language access and interpretation services, new school models for ELL and multiculturalism, or new multicultural approaches to physical and mental health care), and closed to the upward mobility of Somali cultural brokers and professionals. Another woman who has a long history in education and health care administration in the city described to me her frustrations with her colleagues' conservative, constrained orientation toward change: "Portland has so many innovative programs [for immigrants], but the attitude of Lewiston's service providers is, 'We aren't Portland! We don't want to be Portland! Don't talk to us about Portland!'" She continued in a tone of exasperation, "If Portland has developed a program, then Lewiston wants nothing to do with it. They won't even learn about it!" She's anxious about Lewiston's refusal to innovate because she thinks the city is "sitting on a time bomb" because the approach to containing and managing the new immigrants rather than integrating them through innovative programs that will transform public institutions like schools will end badly, as immigrant kids become increasingly alienated. These concerns escalated in 2009–10 when police began arresting Somali Bantu kids for criminal activities and city officials became concerned that Somali immigrant youths were forming criminal gangs. A frustrated social studies teacher who quit her job to move to a more innovative and dynamic school district in Portland summed up her experience with initiatives to expand multicultural programming and social justice initiatives that would support alienated immigrant youths in the schools: "No one in Lewiston is on board with anything."

The critics are frustrated that tolerance and accommodation in Lewiston during the city's first decade of Somali immigration took the form of meeting legal requirements for managing diversity rather than intercultural collaboration and institutional transformation. Writing about the dangers of "tolerance" as a foundation of multiculturalism, political scientist Wendy Brown argues that tolerance is also often about superiority, "the marking of subjects of tolerance as inferior, deviant, or marginal vis-à-vis those practicing tolerance."[19] She continues, "Moreover, since tolerance requires that the tolerated refrain from demands or incursions on public or political life that issue from their 'difference,' the subject of tolerance is tolerated only so long as it does not make a political claim, that is, so long as it lives and practices its 'difference' in a depoliticized or private fashion."[20] In the first decade of Somali immigration, tolerance as accommodation meant policing the boundaries of Somali involvement in decision making about their lives in Lewiston to ensure their inclusion in city institutions met the letter of the law but did not change institutional practice or culture.

Lewiston as a Model for America

And yet, as one ELL teacher, who herself has many complaints about the management of non-English speakers in the school system, observed to me, "I don't think Lewiston gets enough credit for how well it has done." Assessing Lewiston's successes and failures in adopting a proactive approach to embracing refugees depends on one's expectations about the general American attitude toward diversity and bilingualism. While one white woman rages about blocked parental involvement in ELL programs and the absence of Somalis in positions of authority in city institutions—"This is the twenty-first century! It's just totally unacceptable for any town in America to be unprepared for multiculturalism!"—others note that many towns in America are insular and unversed in accommodating difference and that, in fact, Lewiston has done quite well in terms of a low incidence of violence and a strong voice of support for refugees by activists and some city leaders. As one Somali culture broker acknowledged, "Things *have* really improved here since the Many and One Rally." Condemning Lewiston for its failures to be even more proactive seems to some like just a continuation of the long-standing jokes across the state about Franco-American Lewiston being poor, parochial, and backward.

As befits a city administrator, Phil Nadeau clearly wants to emphasize Lewiston's success at valiantly and generously managing the unexpected arrival of thousands of Somalis in the absence of directed state and federal support. Praising the efforts of the local schools, hospitals, and social services agencies for expanding their programming to refugees, Nadeau acknowledges, "They weren't quite where they needed to be in the early days. Now they're on top of things. It's a complete waste of time to criticize these people." He is proud that he has been contacted by other city administrators in the United States and abroad who have heard Lewiston's story for advice about how to manage the arrival of immigrants. He also wishes to undermine the claims in several national news stories, such as a 2009 *Newsweek* article called "The Refugees Who Saved Lewiston," that celebrate the revitalizing energy of immigrants in rejuvenating a dying town rather than the generosity of Lewiston's resident-hosts in accommodating uninvited refugees.[21]

Mayor Larry Gilbert, a strong voice of support for immigrants during his tenure (2007–11), echoes the story of Lewiston's success at welcoming refugees in his public presentations, and publicity about Lewiston as a success story has entered the national arena at conferences and workshops about immigrant integration. When I give public talks about Lewiston's experience, I inevitably meet people in the world of refugee resettlement who tell me how fascinated they are by Lewiston's successful story of immigration integration.[22]

Other organizations also sought to market the story of Lewiston's success in accommodating difference. Maine's (now defunct) nonprofit Center for the Prevention of Hate Violence (CPHV) won a large ORR grant to take Lewiston's story to a national audience, beginning with a well-publicized 2010 conference in Lewiston called "Advice for America: What Lewiston–Auburn Has Learned since 2000 about Fostering Relationships between Residents and Newcomers." The CPHV had held "conversation groups" early in the decade to bring together Somali immigrants and non-Somali locals, offered workplace workshops on diversity, and worked in Lewiston's schools to confront youth racism and violence, culminating their efforts in a national tour to promote Lewiston as a model of immigrant integration. Cheryl Hamilton, who led the CPHV projects after leaving her job with the city, hoped the conference would remove "the blot" on the city's name left by the Letter incident, which she believes continued to hinder the ability of city organizations to attract national funding for refugee assistance because of the media portrayal of Lewiston as "refugee resettlement gone wrong." The Advice for America conference aimed to summarize everything that went right in Lewiston, helping to promote the emerging new narrative about Lewiston's success at accommodating thousands of uninvited refugee immigrants.

Conclusion

The feelings held by many of Lewiston's leaders and citizens that they valiantly adapted to the arrival of a large number of illiterate, black, Muslim people who needed or were entitled to benefits and services that did not previously exist (such as a full-fledged ELL program and translation services) reflect the fact that host communities shoulder the economic and cultural responsibility of welcoming and accommodating resettled refugees whom they did not invite. Yet this is the very heart of the humanitarian basis of the U.S. refugee resettlement program, which states that the objectives of refugee resettlement are rapid achievement of economic self-sufficiency and integration while leaving the details up to host communities and refugee self-help groups.

So what, exactly, does refugee resettlement as a form of humanitarianism mean in this context? If it means allocating public resources to support and welcome strangers, people in Lewiston feel like they got caught holding the humanitarian bag, so to speak, in which humanitarianism toward strangers competes with commitments to citizens in a context of economic decline for all. The paramount concerns of Lewiston city officials were to minimize the financial burden to the city of uninvited indigent refugees in the absence of sufficient federal funding, to meet legal mandates for how public institutions and hospitals are to serve non-English speakers, and to manage Lewiston's public image and citizens' criticisms of city assistance to refugees. While they were gravely concerned about the ability of refugees to become economically self-sufficient, they felt their only recourse was to ensure refugees could access benefits to which they were entitled and to plead for state and federal support for job-training programs. For many of the city's organizations and citizens, integration also meant ensuring that refugee claims to benefits did not compromise or displace the rights and entitlements of citizens, which meant the slow, cautious, uncertain, and sometimes grudging extension of social services to refugees.

The practical effects of refugee resettlement appear to suggest that humanitarianism is actually defined only by geography, to the concept of refuge in a physical sense: that the United States will provide a relatively safe physical environment within which refugees can attempt, with little assistance, to create a new future. Providing refuge is a form of humanitarianism fundamentally based on exclusion and exclusivity; the decision to take in refugees is the exception to the normal practice of exclusion and containment. In this way humanitarianism toward refugees is simply exceptionalism, a choice to violate national integrity by allowing in people who do not belong. When such exceptions move to a town whose citizens already feel forgotten and marginalized by their own history of struggle and economic disintegration, expecting a clear route to economic self-sufficiency and integration for newly arrived refugees seems like little more than a bad-faith demand.

The United States has a complicated orientation toward refugees, as noted in chapter 2, because of the competing meanings of refuge, especially in the context of heightened security fears post-9/11. While the concept of refuge has an ancient history as protection offered by religious communities to escaping slaves or those cast out of their own communities, today's offer of refuge by governments ensures that refugee resettlement accords with reigning ideologies about the obligations of citizens, which in the United States means a dominant orientation toward neoliberal values such as self-help, individual responsibility, and spare government support for the unemployed.[23] Refuge, for Somali Bantus, meant paying for their airfare to the United States, redefining their identities and family relationships to meet American criteria for resettlement, leaving behind family members who failed to meet the criteria, and, for everyone over the age of sixteen, subverting the dream of education to the demands of low-wage, undesirable, dead-end jobs. (In the Orwellian words of one resettled Somali Bantu woman, "There is freedom here. But you need a job to be free.")[24] That refuge might include support for the enormous life transformation resettled refugees experience and to ensure that refugees have adequate time to develop language and job skills is absent because the

United States lacks a developed public discourse that refuge should include anything other than the opportunity for legal border crossing. An educated Somali caseworker who helped settle Somali Bantus in the United States told me in exasperation, "Now I see how marginalization works. I see the impact it has on people. Somali Bantus were brought here and there's no support! There's no support for them here!" Eloquently summarizing the confounding experience of people who wonder why they were brought to the United States to be abandoned, he asked, on their behalf, "What is the basic reason that you bring me to an ocean and then tell me to go swim by myself?" The sink-or-swim attitude is a neoliberal definition of refuge, steeped in economic rationalities and valuations.

Lewiston's experience reads like an object lesson in abandonment, where "economies of abandonment," to borrow Elizabeth Povinelli's useful phrase,[25] are everywhere in abundance: a town abandoned by industry, inhabited by citizens who feel abandoned by the economy they helped to build, taking in refugees who have been abandoned by the government that admitted them, and then feeling abandoned by that government in their effort to provide support for those refugees. The city leaders have to adhere to federal mandates for the accommodation of diversity (through medical translation and ELL programs in public schools)—an accommodation resisted by many residents—but, cruelly, support for bewildered refugees who fail in school and are rejected over and over by employers is absent. Instead, federal and state programs that fund support for refugees are facing cuts because of the neoliberal logic that claims economic support inhibits refugee self-help and integration.[26] To city authorities who are wedged between federal mandates to accommodate diversity, the lack of economic assistance to support indigent refugees while they become settled, the reality of the extreme poverty of refugees, and citizen hostility to the provision of support to refugees, the entire system of refugee resettlement feels like a bad-faith effort of humanitarian rescue. That they define success as the absence of violence reflects an austere American definition of refuge as legal border crossing rather than intentional life enhancement, care, or opportunity.

A city abandoned by economic growth unexpectedly and valiantly absorbing foreigners abandoned by the government that brought them to American shores is indeed an American success story of perseverance, hard work, and responsibility. But the costs of a sink-or-swim attitude means some people are left to sink, many people live in fear of sinking, and everyone wonders how far their responsibility to save those who are sinking extends. Such insecurities strike at the heart of community life, nurturing the rumors and myths about the dangerous insecurities brought by indigent foreign refugees that I explore in chapter 5.

CHAPTER 5

Strangers in Our Midst

Herein lies their radical difference, the demonstration that they have never been, and never will be, a
part of us.
—Achille Mbembe, "Provincializing France?"

While the city representatives quoted in chapter 4 are eager to champion a
positive image of Lewiston's management of difference that can be exported to
other cities, a very loud background conversation circulated in local newspapers and private conversations asserting that Somali refugees were deepening
Lewiston's economic insecurity and weakening the city's cultural integrity.[1] In
a blistering editorial, the managing editor of the city newspaper challenged
the 2010 Advice for America conference representation of multicultural success, suggesting that "the social workers and educators" in attendance were
deaf to the broader and much more pervasive antagonistic feelings about
refugees in Lewiston:

> I have a little news for advice-givers who attended last week's Advice for
> America conference hosted by the Center for Preventing Hate. They may
> believe the Somali integration post-2006 here has been a success worthy
> of national model, but that view is not wholly shared in the Twin Cities

[Lewiston and Auburn]. . . . I hear negative comments every day. Every. Day. . . . I saw with great clarity a gap in how this group perceives the climate of acceptance in Lewiston and what that climate actually is in multiple corners of this city. . . . Any advice coming out of Lewiston should be viewed as through a kaleidoscope of distorted views.[2]

A set of powerful myths (by which I mean shared beliefs) about the refugees that capture "what the climate actually is" reveals the ways in which unhappy Lewistonians felt that their city was under economic and cultural siege. The myths rest on the assertion that, in contrast to the Somali refugees, the earlier French Canadian immigrants were a model of determined economic self-sufficiency and integration, the two pillars of the refugee resettlement model. Commentary on this point became especially heated in response to articles in *Mother Jones* (2004) and *Newsweek* (2009) suggesting that the refugees were rescuing Lewiston, a view that contradicted the perception held by many that the city of hardworking residents was draining its coffers to provide for economically dependent refugees, as the mayor's 2002 letter had suggested.[3] The *Newsweek* article alone generated over 150 pages of mostly vituperative blog comments railing against the article's suggestion that refugees saved Lewiston by bringing economic and cultural revitalization to a dying mill town. A few typical examples, with original spelling, set the tone:

Revived my ass! They have done nothing good for our city! We have lost jobs. People who actually need state assistance can't get it because them and their ten kids have used up what little there was to begin with. Areas that used to be decent to live in are now infested with them. Seriously, find twenty people in Lewiston who are glad they are here. I know I can't.—domnemmasmama, January 30, 2009

Am I disgruntled that federal and state dollars are being used to supply immigrants with housing food clothes and vehicles? YOUR DAMN STRAIGHT.—Dee In Maine, January 30, 2009

They [Somali refugees] are human leaches brought her to suck off the liberal maine system. . . . When did maine become the welfare state to house and feed the worlds misfits.—Megalito, January 30, 2009

The Somalis over-populated Lewiston, drained it's money and resources, and cried discrimination constantly. . . . They are at DHHS [Department of Health and Human Services] requesting welfare daily. The majority of Somalis are unemployed. Our schools are overcrowded with children who don't speak English. Lewiston . . . is down the tubes.—cojr, January 26, 2009[4]

During my research in Lewiston I constantly encountered these myths, which circulated despite news articles and op-eds challenging their veracity, as well as the dialogues sponsored by CPHV early in the decade and ongoing community meetings and panel presentations throughout the decade offered by refugees at myriad events and institutions to teach people about their background.[5] Although these events offered opportunities for Lewiston's residents to confront stereotypes about their new Somali neighbors, the myths' stubborn persistence from 2006 to 2011 indicates they speak to deeply held suspicions about charity for illegitimate recipients, fears of cultural difference, and the danger of the resident foreigner for American civic life.

This chapter draws on conversations, interviews, editorials, and letters to the editor in the daily *Lewiston Sun Journal* and the conservative-leaning local weekly *Twin City Times*, and, most obnoxiously and extremely, the online comments that accompanied every news story about the refugees (until the *Sun Journal* closed off the ability to make anonymous comments), to explore the most widespread myths and analyze their peculiar potency.[6] The discussion of each myth also offers contrary empirical evidence from research I conducted with Ismail Ahmed and Rilwan Osman, as well as ethnographic observations about the quotidian experience of these myths for Somalis and Somali Bantus in Lewiston. Because most of the myths are not particular to Lewiston but echo nationwide allegations about how immigrants introduce financial and cultural insecurity into American communities, I conclude with a reflective analysis of the insecurities contained in American mythologies of immigrant foreigners, situating the material presented here within broader American nativist and racist discourses against immigrants.[7]

Free Cars and Apartments! Chickens in the Cupboards!

On June 24, 2010, Rilwan Osman e-mailed me a copy of a letter to the editor from a local resident that appeared in the *Twin City Times*. The letter read:

> The Somalis received more money than they deserved upon setting foot here, and most never pay a cent into the system. It makes me sick that we are supporting them and seeing them living a better life than most of us. Some lie to receive money when they go for help. . . . Most of them claim that they don't speak English, but they can all say "City pays." . . . Besides food stamps, why do they receive vouchers for car repairs and other things? . . . Why is it so easy for them to start up in a business while on welfare? . . . Do they pay taxes on the money they make, or is that another thing being kept secret? And most of their stores refuse to serve white people (not that I'd ever go there). . . . I think it's time someone puts them

in their place. I would put them on a ship back to their uncivilized country because I don't trust them as far as I can throw them.

Fed up with the constant repetition of such allegations, Rilwan wanted us to draft a response. Together with Somali activist Ismail Ahmed, we generated a list of the claims we heard most often, and then gathered evidence to attempt to debunk them. Our response, "The Top Ten Myths about Somalis and Why They Are Wrong," appeared in the local newspaper and was circulated in government and social services offices and posted online by Catholic Charities. Ismail and I also collaborated on a publicly circulated financial study about the economic impact on Lewiston of the Somali presence, demonstrating that the influx of Somalis brought economic advantages rather than distress.[8] Here are the top ten myths.

I. SOMALIS GOT A FREE RIDE TO COME TO AMERICA.

The basis of this complaint is that Somali refugees have not earned the right to live in America, an assertion that is sometimes accompanied by a reminder about the young soldier from the Lewiston area who was killed in Mogadishu during the Black Hawk Down debacle.[9] Obviously this myth refers most generally to concerns about giving foreigners the right to cross America's borders—suspicion about the wisdom of the exception noted in chapter 4— but it also reveals a belief that Somalis (the very people who killed Maine soldiers ostensibly sent to help them) received easy access to America, unlike the ancestors of Lewiston's residents whose immigrant struggles are memorialized in family stories and the exhibitions of the local Museum LA. The difference between the two waves of immigrants to Lewiston rests on the claim that whereas French Canadians came to work, Somalis came for security, which makes the latter's presence in the community less legitimate because it is not based on a commitment to economic productivity.

In 2009, the Museum LA, whose mission is to tell "the story of work and community in Lewiston-Auburn," agreed to mount a collaborative exhibit on the history of immigration to Lewiston, using as its core the exhibition *The Somali Bantu Experience: From East Africa to Maine*, created by Somali Bantu community members, my students, and myself for the Colby College Museum of Art. The exhibition for the Museum LA, called *Rivers of Immigration: From the Jubba to the Androscoggin*, included immigrant stories from other newcomers as well as Somalis and an immigration timeline that charted the history of foreign arrivals in Lewiston over the past two centuries. For museum staff, the goal was visibly to place the Somali arrivals within a single timeline of immigration to Lewiston that included the earlier wave of French

Canadians, a risky move for the museum because some Lewiston residents found it offensive to place the Somali immigrant experience alongside the experiences of their hardworking parents and grandparents. As Mayor Macdonald explained in one of his editorials, "equating safety-seeking Somalis with job-seeking French Canadians . . . so outraged Lewiston's established community that even today this statement is held against the Somali population."[10]

When the exhibition was announced, staff members received complaints from the museum's regular visitors that their museum was showcasing the Somali arrivals. (One of the staff members mimicked a common response: "Too much Somalis! Everything's about the Somalis!") At the close of the year-long show, the museum director reflected that the exhibit successfully challenged the myth that Somalis, as refugees, had an easy and direct trip to the United States, where everything was arranged for their care. After acknowledging that although she continues to hear "the same shpiel, that they're taking all the welfare meant for our people" from her Franco-American neighbors and family, she said,

> Those who have gone through the exhibit have learned from it. I gave a tour to a group who said, "Wow, we didn't realize they'd been through so much." They don't know. No one's ever explained it to them. . . . [Our museum visitors] didn't have any idea they spent time in refugee camps and how horrible it was. They didn't know about the war, about the loss, the horror. . . . Viewers never realized how hard they had it in their country and why they had to leave. Genocide was never on their radar. Rape was never on their radar.

Her staff assistant interjected, "All the stories about walking for hundreds of miles. They thought they just got on a plane and came straight here! Having to stay in refugee camps for years, people didn't know that. That was a big learning curve. People don't know. They don't know that story. The news doesn't tell them. The news just says, 2,000 Somalis arrived. They didn't know they went somewhere else first and didn't just come here directly."[11] And almost no one realized that Somali refugees must repay the full cost of their airfare (with mandatory travel on American carriers). Many thus arrive in the United States already thousands of dollars in debt, paying off their travel loan for years and years after resettlement.

Criticizing the border crossing into America of Somalis in search of security raises a fundamental question about the basis of humanitarianism. Under debate here is the question of who has the right to mobility and who has the right to residence in the United States. It is difficult not to interpret these debates within a broader racialized, imperialist frame that positions Somalia as a chaotic African country of uncivilized, irresponsible people, as implied in the quote that opened this section, who destroyed their own country and killed the Americans sent to rescue them. The racialized imperialist lens thus sees Somalis as illegitimate invaders whose mobility is not motivated by the values of hard work and personal sacrifice that Lewiston's citizens believe defined the earlier generation of French Canadian immigrants. The obvious result is myths 2–5, which insist that Somalis are accessing resources to which they should not be entitled.

2. SOMALIS ARE DRAINING THE WELFARE COFFERS.

In the words of "liam," in his online post in response to a January 30, 2010, *Sun Journal* article about Lewiston's experience with refugees, "My family came here without a dime in their pocket. There was no welfare system to leech off. They had to make it work and they did. They made Lewiston/Auburn what it is today. They didn't do it so refugees could rape our system till it's dry." Liam's comment is so commonly expressed by Lewiston's residents that local newspapers have published several articles investigating the use of welfare by Somalis, the most recent of which included a link to the economic impact study I did with Ismail Ahmed in which we used Freedom of Information Act requests to estimate how much money Somalis in Lewiston were actually receiving in welfare payments (including GA, Temporary Assistance to Needy Families or TANF, and food stamps) in comparison with the rest of the population.[12]

Allegations about Somali use of welfare condenses two common arguments: that Somalis are moving to Maine because it has more generous welfare benefits (a sentiment endorsed by Governor LePage and Mayor Macdonald) and that Somalis are taking welfare resources away "from our people, the ones who really need it." Since everyone but Somalis seems to find it incredible that Africans would choose to move to Maine, a cunning effort to access welfare benefits offers a more likely sounding reason and places Lewiston's newest immigrants in contrast to the previous wave of Franco-Americans, who moved to the city to work rather than to receive welfare. Sadiq has become increasingly annoyed by the question he most consistently receives: "Why did you come to Maine?" "No matter what you say," he tells me, "there is only one right answer." In one conversation I overheard with a hostile administrator of a doctor's office with whom he was negotiating for Somali Bantu translators, Sadiq showed his frustration to the standard question by asking the administrator, testily, "Why are you asking me this question when you have already decided the answer?" Next to myth no. 1, this claim was the most frequent criticism I heard about Somalis during my years of research, many of whom cited the bloggers who post online comments to newspaper articles when I asked for verification of their claims.

The data (obtained through Freedom of Information Act requests and records maintained by the city of Lewiston) reveal that after heavy use of GA funds in the early years of their migration to Lewiston, by 2010 Somalis drew welfare at lower rates than the rest of the population. During 2001, the first year of refugee arrivals in Lewiston, refugees accounted for half the GA budget (which, as noted earlier, had been cut in half that year from the previous year), then 40 percent of the next year's budget, and 35 percent of the following year's budget before dropping over the rest of the decade to 16 percent in 2009. City officials state that no one who qualified for assistance from the city was ever turned away, or, in other words, that Somalis are not taking all the available resources for emergency support. In 2009, noncitizens (who are mostly adult refugees) received 6.8 percent of TANF expenditures in Lewiston-Auburn, and 5.4 percent of TANF expenditures in Androscoggin County, as well as 3 percent of the food stamp budget in Lewiston-Auburn and 2.1 percent of the food stamp budget for Androscoggin County. Recognizing that children of Somali refugees are citizens and thus not counted as noncitizens, these statistics suggest that Somali families draw assistance more or less in proportion to their demographic representation.[13] While Somalis do acknowledge that immediate access to assistance through the GA office enabled their resettlement in Lewiston, the facts indicate that claims about their long-term dependence on welfare are wildly exaggerated.

To confront the persistent distortion of the facts by private citizens as well as public figures, Maine's DHHS prepared a document, "The Real Facts," that reported the following in 2010:

- Maine's maximum TANF benefit is $485 a month, which is the lowest in New England. When combined with food stamps, recipients reach only 65 percent of the federal poverty level.
- Over 70 percent of Mainers who receive TANF do so for less than a year, and 85 percent receive TANF for less than two years. Only 4 percent of recipients have received TANF for over five years, most of whom are permanently disabled.
- Over a five-year period, five times more recipients left Maine each month than the number who arrived and received benefits.[14]

The DHHS point person for refugee benefits in Lewiston is clear that everyone receives benefits according to their eligibility: "I know what the guidelines are and I know the verification process and I know people are not coming in here getting benefits they are not entitled to. Only those who are eligible are getting assistance." When non-Somali clients whose TANF benefits are reduced or denied because of household changes blame Somalis for their loss of benefits, he patiently explains that "everyone is getting exactly what they're eligible for and Somalis don't get any more than anyone else." He is frustrated by the accusations that somehow Somali eligibility impacts the eligibility of other Mainers, and when I suggest it may reflect a perception of a zero-sum game—the more they get, the less there is for me—he replies, "It's not about the division of resources. It's about prejudice." The anger derives not only from a belief that Somalis are using up welfare benefits not meant for them, but also about the fact that Somali immigrants have the right to be eligible for benefits in the first place.

Whether or not they draw welfare, many of my Somali friends are embarrassed by the perception that they are dependent on welfare and that their use of welfare is somehow illegitimate. In a 2010 conversation with Somali Bantu teenagers about what they most enjoyed and most disliked in Lewiston, many participants mentioned their shame about the perception of Somalis as welfare cheats. Some students had even demanded that their parents stop using food stamps because they were being attacked at school as welfare users with taunts like, "My dad bought you those shoes!" In 2012, a Somali Bantu college student recounted his humiliation in a high school government class when the teacher staged a debate about welfare. Students lined up to denounce welfare as an unfair entitlement program for lazy people. My friend, the eldest of five boys raised by a single, illiterate, non-English-speaking refugee mother who fed her family with food stamps and lived in subsidized housing, was shocked and mortified at their hostility. When the teacher asked if anyone in class was willing to mount a defense of welfare, my normally gregarious and confident young friend stared at the floor in mute shame. "How can they not understand what it's like for people with no income? What are they supposed to do if there are no jobs?" he asked me. We discussed the sentiment that people who work and pay taxes are angry that their tax money supports others who don't work. "So, if they cut welfare will people pay less taxes?" he asks, and I admit that a reduction in welfare would probably only translate into a minuscule tax decrease, if any. He was incredulous that anyone would want to "just cut off a struggling family with no job and say, 'Too bad!'"

The myth about Somali welfare dependence is coupled with persistent claims that people see Somalis leaving stores with carts full of food they have been given for free. Even the superintendent of schools mentioned to me that Somalis "overbuying" in the supermarket was one of the common complaints he heard from local parents. Somali families often pool money to buy groceries in bulk, leaving local residents to speculate that people (presumably) on welfare who can afford carts full of food must be receiving enormous welfare payments. Police officer Bill Rousseau, a member of Lewiston's downtown Community Resource Unit, laughed as he recounted police efforts to track down this rumor:

It's just like those stereotypes about the police. You know the story of the guy pulled up at the red light, and a police car drives up alongside him and puts on his lights, drives through the intersection, and turns into Dunkin' Donuts? When different groups come in there's a newness, an unknown, and the rumors start. You heard about that lady with the cart filled with food in the store? She said the government was giving her the food for free and they let her leave the store with all the food. Everyone saw it! Everyone was in the store that day! Everyone you talk to saw that happen! There must have been a huge line at the store that day! We looked into this story. It never happened! It's a bunch of crap! It's an urban legend. I arm myself with the facts. Less than 15 percent of the Somali population is on welfare. If you look at old Mainers, more of *them* are on welfare! We're seeing second- and even third-generation Mainers who are on welfare!

Like myths 4 and 5 below, the claims that Somalis live on welfare and somehow get more of it than local people encapsulate several sentiments about growing economic insecurity: that local people who worked hard their entire lives are being abandoned by their government as the local economy contracts and that instead of honoring its commitments to hardworking citizens the government is funding foreign nonproductive interlopers who should not have the right to receive assistance because they are not members of the community.

3. SOMALIS REFUSE TO WORK AND ARE NOT SEEKING JOBS.

A 2008 Maine Department of Labor (DOL) report estimated that the unemployment rate for Somalis in Maine was around 50 percent, setting off a firestorm of accusations that Lewiston's high poverty level resulted from Somalis unwilling to look for jobs because of their happy dependence on welfare.[15] Since employment is seen as the path to economic self-sufficiency, city officials have been particularly concerned about how to employ Somalis with limited English and literacy skills, a concern that became acute in middecade when state officials inexplicably missed a deadline for providing information to the federal government that would have allowed the city to apply for special federal funds for refugee-targeted job skills training programs.[16]

Lewiston's challenging economic environment means that concerns about jobs resonate powerfully. As Mary LaFontaine, the director of Lewiston's

CareerCenter, suggested to me, an unemployment rate of 50 percent is probably accurate for the downtown population more generally, not just the Somalis, due to a regional lack of low-skilled jobs: "We do not have [enough] low-skilled or unskilled labor jobs here. All our jobs are computer-based and high-tech jobs. Even Walmart uses computers in the warehouse to manage the goods. . . . We don't have a meat manufacturer. There is no garment sewing industry. We don't have jobs that can be easily shown with visual cues. This is putting our population at risk."[17] The DOL report also acknowledged that employed Somalis receive lower wages than other workers, contributing to the perception that the Somali presence accentuates unemployment levels by ensuring more competition for the lowest-skilled jobs.

Complaints about Somalis in the job market even extend into school classrooms. During a visit to *The Somali Bantu Experience* museum exhibit at Colby College Museum of Art by Lewiston's junior high school, I overheard a teacher say, sotto voce in a roomful of Somali students looking at a photograph of a smiling Somali Bantu parent at his post in L.L.Bean's order fulfillment center, "He took a job away from our people." The child of a Somali friend reported to her mom that her fifth grade teacher says she should not have been allowed to come to America because her parents are taking jobs and resources away from "real Americans." While the child is confused about what it means to be a real American, the adults in the room have all heard this complaint many times. In a no-win assessment that echoes American complaints about immigrants more generally, residents decry Somali use of welfare because of a supposed aversion to work while simultaneously accusing Somalis of taking away jobs from local citizens.

Evidence from Somali enrollment in job training programs, use of the city's CareerCenter, the rush to seasonal work, the large number of new Somali-owned businesses, and the constant requests at Aliyow's, the store I frequent, for help with job applications indicate that refugee community members are eager to find jobs. One of the most common complaints from the ELL adult education teachers is the inconsistency in attendance of their students because their classes empty as students flock to short-term seasonal jobs at L.L.Bean, a wreath-making company, coastal hotels, and to the Cultivating Community nonprofit farming project.[18] While seasonal jobs cut into the ability of Somalis to attend ELL classes consistently, refugees with limited English also tend to get the most demanding, physically grueling jobs, which often leave them too exhausted to attend English classes. A vicious cycle ensues, as limited English translates into limited job opportunities, ensuring that refugees with limited English will only be able to get short-term, arduous work.[19]

FIGURE 5.1 Nur Libah at his post in L.L.Bean, 2008. Photograph by Catherine Besteman.

Abdiya is typical of many women: she attends adult ed ELL classes to improve her English, applies for every seasonal job available even when a successful application means suspending her English classes, joined an intensive
job skills training program in computer literacy and workplace expectations,
visits the CareerCenter to learn about new job possibilities, and yet, despite
her obvious intelligence and work ethic, cannot even find a permanent job
as a housekeeper. After being told by a potential employer that her lack of a
GED and advanced computer skills makes her unqualified for a housekeeper
job, she asked me, "Why do I need a high school degree and advanced computer skills to clean hotel rooms?" At Somali Bantu community meetings, the
desperate need to find jobs dominated most of the discussions I attended in
2006–8, when people regularly asked me to tell people in Lewiston that since
they used to be farmers they are hard workers who can do any kind of physical labor. At a 2007 meeting with a school administrator, a parent begged the
school to offer Somali parents simple jobs like grass cutting, but the administrator responded that the school requires literacy even for gardening. The
parent explained that, like many others, he had applied for many jobs, but no
one would hire him because of his lack of English and prior work experience
in America. "How will I ever get a job without prior work experience and

with only one hour of ELL class a day?" he asked, which the Somali translator augmented, for clarity, "He's in a catch-22!" Gesturing at the huge vacant mill across the river from his store, the Somali Bantu owner of Aliyow's store told me, "I thought President Obama promised to reopen the workplace if he got elected. Well, I've been waiting for that factory to reopen. It's been a year since Obama said that and it hasn't happened. Everyone here would work there" (a sentiment my friend undoubtedly shares with many non-Somali residents).

Addressing the high unemployment rate in the face of evidence that Somalis are avidly seeking jobs, the DOL report and subsequent research by an anthropology class at Bates College attempted to define the barriers to employment specifically faced by Somalis in Lewiston, offering explanations that resonate with accounts from career training and job development professionals as well as Somali job seekers like Abdiya.[20] As one would expect, employers say they fear language, cultural, and religious differences, expressing concern about the potential for miscommunication and that daily prayers and a different conception of time and work expectations will interrupt work schedules. CareerCenter director Mary LaFontaine argues that she can train any employer to work with limited English speakers and accommodate things like praying, but few employers seem willing to try. Although L.L.Bean regularly hires Somalis as seasonal workers, outfitting them with audio devices that provide work instructions in Somali, Walmart and other large employers have resisted such technologies.[21] When in 2009 the city of Lewiston funded a special job skills training program for refugees, 180 Somalis (including Abdiya) completed 144 hours of training before transitioning to the Work Ready program for another seven weeks, after which they were supposed to be able to get jobs.[22] But the trainer, Ismail, says, "Even after all this training they still weren't able to get jobs! Not even entry-level jobs that they are perfectly capable of doing, like laundry, housekeeping, warehousing." He tried to negotiate with Walmart for warehouse jobs, but the store insisted that Somalis had to start as cart pushers, cleaning up and organizing the shopping carts, and that they would only hire a few but not a group. After years of working in Lewiston to help Somalis find employment, he eventually abandoned the city in frustration. Noting other cities where Somalis have been able to move quickly into entry-level jobs, Ismail says, "My biggest frustration [in Lewiston] is with employers. They set a bar, and I train the workers to meet that bar. At first, they said Somalis had to have working English to qualify to apply for jobs. Okay. I train them to have working English. Then employers say they need a GED, or an algebra test. They create competencies for us to follow, and we follow it, and then they change their expectations. Then they blame Somalis for not wanting to work!" Reflecting Ismail's experience, numerous Somali friends, like Abdiya, believe that GED requirements for housekeeping and custodial jobs are a disguised way of rejecting Somali applicants.

After years of training Somalis and Somali Bantus in work-ready programs, Ismail summarized his frustration with local businesses: "They don't want us here. They don't want to hire us. The idea is to frustrate us. It is the open secret of hiring here in Lewiston. They advertise a job, you go and apply, and the job disappears, or has new requirements, or they are too busy to deal with you, or they aren't taking applications at that time. The employers are resentful that Somalis are trying to get jobs, and they just want them to go away." After working with refugee resettlement in Lewiston, Cheryl Hamilton took a job with RefugeeWorks, a nonprofit dedicated to employment training and initiatives for resettled refugees.[23] She too expresses frustration that the ORR-mandated path to rapid economic self-sufficiency overlooks racism and discrimination and offers local communities and resettled refugees no assistance to confront these barriers. She insists that the relevant question should be "How does discrimination affect employment?" rather than "How should refugees get more jobs?"

The Bates College study offered suggestions for how local employers could be more proactive about hiring Somalis, including hiring translators, offering better training programs, scheduling work breaks in conjunction with prayer times, offering greater flexibility for family needs, and more. Predictably, their report was lambasted in a hostile editorial in the *Twin City Times* titled "Employers Should Relax Standards to Hire Somalis," which mocked the Bates study for suggesting "that employers should ignore requirements for speaking English, pay for mediators and translators; relax their application process; and abandon standard workweek hours to make it easier to hire Somalis."[24] A flurry of op-eds, editorials, and conversations that pilloried the Bates study as pandering to ungrateful refugees dominated the newspapers and private talk for months.

In her coverage of the Advice for America conference, the Lewiston *Sun Journal*'s managing editor expressed similar disgust at the suggestion by conference participants that the problem with Somali employment resulted from employer discrimination rather than refugee resistance to work:

There was a real focus that businesses must share a greater responsibility for integrating the new Mainers into the workforce by providing childcare, transportation and other amenities to ease the step from welfare to work. . . . There was, at the end of the day, a platform of recommendations developed that put the responsibility of peaceful integration at the feet of existing communities, not that of newcomers. That, instead of immigrants stepping into this land of opportunity and making their own way as pioneers, that there is a great need to develop more networks to cocoon and protect immigrants when they arrive and for years afterward.[25]

While the view that employers should find ways to accommodate Somali employees largely failed to gain traction in Lewiston, Somalis found multiple ways to earn a living in addition to unskilled wage labor jobs, especially by creating new businesses and finding cultural broker, translator, and caseworker jobs. Dozens of Somalis started businesses as store and café owners, butchers, truck drivers, and importers, or, informally, as accountants, child care providers, caterers, and healers. Those who work as cultural brokers, caseworkers, and translators for the local schools, hospitals, and mental health care and social services agencies often find their opportunities for upward mobility constrained, leaving job trainers like Ismail frustrated that with the grant funding that came into Lewiston over the 2001–10 decade in part to support outreach to Somali refugees, so little of it was used for capacity building for the refugees themselves, who remained caseworkers and translators on an hourly wage: "There is no progress in the workplace for Somalis [here]. No upward mobility," he complained.[26]

I watched as the careers of several Somali Bantu friends employed as caseworkers suffered from a combination of no training and what Ismail calls "microsupervision." One bright, ambitious friend was hired as an outreach coordinator to do "social marketing" to the refugee community for a community assistance agency's programs, but received no training or mentoring in agency expectations. With no clear instructions, he interpreted his job to mean community caseworking, so he spent his days in an exhausting whirlwind, helping refugee families with everything from rent negotiations with landlords to parent-teacher meetings about discipline problems at school. An older white woman at the agency shook her head as she told me that because the agency provided no guidance or training, my friend looked incompetent because he was always running around trying to solve daily problems rather than building programs of social outreach.

Another quiet, hardworking friend landed his dream job as a caseworker at a medical office while he studied nursing at the local college, but became increasingly unsettled as his colleagues constantly questioned and challenged his interpersonal style. The only male, Muslim, and person of color in his unit, he found it difficult to adjust to a work environment where his female colleagues went out drinking together after work, talked about their boyfriends and what they did with them on the weekends, and "kicked each other in the ass" (a phrase he learned from his coworkers). Because he doesn't participate in these activities (explaining to them that he is a quiet, religious person who doesn't drink, is uncomfortable sharing private stories about his wife, and will never be able to kick his supervisor in her ass) his colleagues repeatedly filed complaints against him for "refusing to be a team player" and for "poor workplace social skills." The office eventually fired him for his "inability to integrate into office culture." Other friends tell me about how their supervisors stand over them while they type e-mails to ensure they are not attending to personal business or gaming. Ismail jokes in frustration, "We're trying to learn to type, not to play FreeCell! We are not the ones they should be watching!"

Idris's family provides a snapshot of typical employment. In 2010, Isha worked as a farmer during the growing months in addition to her informal activities as a child care provider and healer. Idris worked as a translator in the hospital, a parent liaison-translator in local schools, and a translator-caseworker for a mental health agency while taking classes toward a social work degree at the local college. Only the caseworker position was salaried; the others were based on an hourly wage and offered no opportunity for further training or career development. Idris's wife Fatuma volunteered at the Somali Bantu Youth Association as a mentor. Idris's younger brother Iman worked evenings at Tambrands and seasonally at L.L.Bean in hourly wage jobs while attending school and volunteering in the Somali Bantu community office; another brother, Bashir, worked as a community volunteer for the Somali Bantu community office, and cousins Garad and Mohamed held hourly wage jobs, respectively, as a cart pusher at Walmart and a food services worker at Bowdoin College. The wives of Bashir, Garad, and Mohamed cared for their preschool-aged children at home.

The DOL report failed adequately to capture the work of women who care for small children, some forms of seasonal employment, out-of-town employment, newly arrived Somalis still completing their ELL courses, and Somalis in job training programs, high school, and college. It also made no attempt to acknowledge the thousands of hours of free and volunteer work like translating, casework, chauffeuring, child care, or wedding and festival catering that Somalis do all the time for each other. It did not include the grant-funded projects run by community members through community-based organizations, nor does it recognize the volunteer time Somali community members spend running youth sports programs; holding citizenship, tutoring, and adult literacy classes; and staffing the Somali and Somali Bantu community offices for troubleshooting and assistance (discussed in chapter 7). The DOL report also did not include the time Somalis donate to the city, through participating in the numerous focus groups of researchers and other organizations, giving (uncompensated) presentations to local organizations and schools, and volunteering in support of other city projects.

Aware of the negative stereotype that the refugee community are welfare dependents, Somali Bantu leaders have begun placing ads and articles in the local newspapers to showcase their grant-funded and volunteer programs, attempting to counter the insistence that wage labor is the only labor worth counting as work and to demonstrate the wide variety of ways in which they are working, "giving back," and participating in civic initiatives. Nevertheless, when Robert Macdonald announced in 2011 that he was running for mayor, he told the local newspaper that he intended to be aggressive about jobs and welfare in his campaign: "Lewiston taxpayers can no longer afford to support people who are unable or refuse to support themselves. If you come to Lewiston, come with a job or a sponsor—not with your hand out."[27] Everyone knew whom he was talking about.

4. SOMALIS GET FREE APARTMENTS FROM THE GOVERNMENT.

Fears about housing, along the lines of the often-heard claim that "Somalis are taking all the apartments and there won't be anything left for our people," reflect concerns similar to fears about welfare: that Somalis are illegitimate claimants who will use up a scarce resource (either low-rent public housing, low-income housing vouchers, or Section 8 assistance) that should be reserved for local people. And, like welfare, some people claim that generous Section 8 housing subsidies lure more Somalis to Lewiston, as mayoral candidate Robert Macdonald asserted during a 2011 debate: "Many are unemployable, as they are unskilled, illiterate and speak little or no English. And what is the response from our city leaders? Avoid confrontational issues and encourage more of these layabouts to settle here by providing new and more spacious Section 8 housing."[28] Four weeks later Macdonald was elected mayor.[29]

Many Somali refugees do receive housing subsidies, paying rent at the same scale as everyone else. Housing assistance is available in the form of housing units that come with a subsidy as well as vouchers that provide rent support but allow families to choose where to live. The latter are in great demand and the program has maintained a waiting list since before the Somalis arrived. The director of Lewiston Housing Authority, Jim Dowling, estimated that in 2010 Somalis held perhaps a fifth of the available vouchers, noting that the pressure in this program is real but primarily due to unpredictable fluctuations in federal funding from year to year. The biggest change in the low-income housing scene in Lewiston is in subsidized housing, which never had full occupancy until Somalis began moving to town. About the positive benefits of full occupancy, Dowling observed, "A vacant unit collects no subsidy. When a family moves in, the subsidy starts to flow, and those funds enter the community and circulate."[30]

The director of Trinity Jubilee, Kim Wettlaufer, whose work ensures a detailed knowledge of downtown demographics, offered an additional suggestion in a conversation about why the shift to nearly full occupancy might anger local people. Low vacancy rates have hindered the formerly popular practice of apartment hopping, whereby some tenants in downtown apartments avoid paying rent by falling behind on rent payments while staying in an apartment until they receive an eviction notice, then hopping to another apartment to do the same thing. Because there was so much available housing, it was an easy rent-aversion strategy. So, in a way, the Somali influx has made it more difficult for other Lewiston residents to shirk on paying rent.

5. SOMALIS GET FREE CARS FROM THE GOVERNMENT.

When I asked Mary LaFontaine, the director of Lewiston's CareerCenter, about rumors she hears most often about Somalis, she immediately responded, "The car thing! All the time!" She recounts that she was at a car dealer recently and even the dealer was complaining about the Somalis getting free cars. She says she told him, "Knock it off! They don't get free cars! How can you think that?" LaFontaine's observation is echoed by GA director Sue Charron, who similarly expressed her exasperation with the persistence of this rumor. In response to the questions she regularly receives about new cars given to the refugees, Sue Charron sometimes says, "Oh, we give the new models to the Americans and the used models from last year to the refugees." People stop and look at her for a minute before realizing the joke. "Ask me a stupid question and I'll give you a stupid response," she says, with an innocent smile.

Even though the myth of free cars seems ridiculous, rumors are rampant that the government gives Somalis free cars as well as vouchers for cars, car repairs, and gas, and the blogs are filled with comments asking why Somalis have cars if they are refugees and receive welfare. Reports in the paper of car accidents involving Somalis always provoke a slew of comments that they should not be allowed to drive at all.

Along with their use of cell phones, the visible fact of Somalis driving cars inspires enormous ire in people whose comments suggest they believe that refugees either do not have the right to drive cars or should not have the money to buy a car. Driving is envisioned as a right of citizenship that should not be available to refugees. Cars imply ownership and property, and if Somalis are recipients of charity, as the myths insist they are, perhaps they are visibly to appear disenfranchised (by walking rather than driving). Since Lewiston has a poor public transportation system, car ownership dramatically enhances freedom of movement and independence. Cars imply mobility, which is a form of freedom, but also invisibility, which is frightening in an age of terrorism panics.

Since American culture is car culture, I wonder if Somali car ownership implies that Somalis smuggled themselves into American culture without passing through the appropriate stages: citizenship, English capability, pulling themselves up through poverty to property ownership. Does their car ownership make visible their illicit entry through the back door as refugees by an inappropriate appropriation of American culture? Is car ownership a material signification, a visible indication, of the appropriation of American culture by the illegitimate, who are first expected to exhibit gratitude and patriotism?

In 2010, the *Sun Journal* ran a front-page article, with color photos, about the hearing of a Somali Bantu woman who had accidentally hit and badly injured a student in the high school parking lot. Buried inside the paper was an article about an arraignment of a local man caught running a meth lab in his house. "Since when does a car accident outrank a meth lab in the middle of town?" asked Kim Wettlaufer, answering his own question, "When it's a Somali driver!"

6. SOMALIS ARE RESPONSIBLE FOR A RISE IN CRIME.

Early in the decade, concerns about Somali criminality rested on claims that since Somalis had destroyed their own country, they would do the same to America. By the end of the decade, the significance of their foreignness as a route to criminality seemed to give way to popular associations of blackness and crime. A front-page headline in the December 17, 2009, issue of the *Sun Journal* screamed, in huge letters, "Police Investigate Somali Attacks." The article reported a number of assaults on people downtown by Somali boys, introducing the word "gang" to describe "the Somali attacks." Within hours, Somali Bantu friends in Lewiston e-mailed and phoned me, upset about the allegations in the article, which was followed the next day with an editorial that said, "We are angered and disappointed by revelations Wednesday that roving bands of Somali youngsters are mugging vulnerable white people in the area around Kennedy Park." The online comments were, predictably, vicious, calling for deportation and insisting that Somalis were terrorists and a threat to national security. When I wrote to the paper's managing editor to complain that no Somalis were interviewed for the article, that the article made no mention of the violence against Somalis (there had been numerous cases of assaults and dog attacks on Somalis),[31] and that the article was sensationalistic, she responded that people in the city had a right to know "that the trend of these Somali youth gangs was real. . . . If there were gangs in your neighborhood, wouldn't you want to know?"[32]

The language about Somali gangs continued to simmer over the next year, resurging in a memo written by an investigator at one of the public housing projects with a high percentage of Somali residents warning that Somali "GANG" activity was on the rise and listing the individual GANG names (GANG always appeared in caps in the memo). The memo, which was circulated in the school system, suggested that the police should be prepared for "some type of GANG war" in the upcoming months and that schoolteachers should be vigilant to report anything suspicious, setting off a wave of panic among some of the schoolteachers who did not regularly interact with Somali students and who, according to their ELL teacher colleagues, were afraid of Somali children.

When Janet Saliba, the woman who ran the after-school tutoring program for Trinity Jubilee, saw the memo, she realized that the "GANGs" listed in the memo were the names her charges used among themselves, one of which had even been adopted for the Somali girls' soccer team. In a meeting of the community collaborative mentioned in chapter 4 that included social services staff and police officers, Janet challenged the use of the word "GANG" to describe Somali kids who were, she admitted, engaging in bad behavior. "I know these kids, their struggles, what they've been through, what their parents have been through, how hard they are trying. Most of them don't have dads. They are vulnerable kids trying to be tough, and making some bad choices." She described the derivation of the local "GANG" names, explaining that it was kids' play that became something else entirely when the police and the public adopted the culturally symbolic term, stigmatizing the kids by connecting them to violent images of gangs in popular culture. Acknowledging that some of the kids behaved as bullies and commanded younger kids to do their bidding, she cautioned against using the term "GANG" but did not reveal that the kids who belonged to the so-called gangs were the very kids tutored by several of the police officers who volunteered in her after-school tutoring program.

One day in 2010 as Janet and I sat chatting in my car outside Trinity while kids were arriving for the after-school program, a Somali Bantu boy wearing a hoodie over an oversized T-shirt came up and pounded on the window, yelling, "Hey! Whatcha doin'? Open up!" Janet opened the door and told him she'd be in soon, to which he responded, "You better! I gonna beat you up!" Janet laughed and told him to tell Kim she'd be inside in a minute. The boy returned a few minutes later, pounding on the window again while yelling, "Kim gonna kill you if you don't get in here!" Chuckling at the idea of Kim killing anyone, Janet recognized that the boy was eager to connect with her after his long day in school. Making sure she was watching him, the boy picked up a rock and threw it at a passing school bus, hitting the back bumper. As Janet opened the door to tell him to knock it off, he ran into the street to retrieve the rock. Janet turned to me and said, "Being the tough kid, throwing a little rock, and then picking it up." We had just witnessed exactly what she was expressing in her cautionary lecture against the use of the word "GANG" to describe the kids' antics. She suspects the average white Lewistonian watching that kid would not see how hard he was working to look tough on the outside, would not see the sweet kid he actually was, would not take note that he threw the rock gently and picked it up after it bounced off the bus, but rather would likely only see a black youth in a hoodie throwing a rock at the school bus. In the community collaborative meeting, Janet was demanding that the police officers see through the performative swagger and faux violence to connect with kids rather than stereotype them.

The community resource police officers, in fact, were extremely receptive to Janet's argument about the symbolic weight of the term "GANG" and attempted to dampen the semihysterical tone of the warning memo as well as injecting common sense into the tendency by some community leaders to see Somali youths as inherently dangerous. One officer told me that a top school official even asked for a daily police patrol to supervise the sidewalks and parking lot of the downtown elementary school when school let out for the day: "He talks about the school like it's a war zone . . . but it's just a couple of car keying incidents and the fights that break out on the way home. It's only because they walk home in groups and sometimes a few start shoving at each other. The school is mostly Somali, so when fighting breaks out it's mostly Somali kids who are fighting, but the reaction is: Oh! The Somali kids are fighting! Like it's something different from other kids who fight." Another officer agreed. "Kids have always fought, but now when Somali kids do it, it's a catastrophe!"

Although the police attempted to dispel rumors about Somali crime and violence, rumors about Somali gangs, terrorism, and crime remained powerful even though actual crime statistics tell a totally different story. Overall crime rates were falling during the first decade of Somali immigration to Lewiston, and my scrutiny of county grand jury indictments gave no indication that Somalis were buoying the crime that did occur. While things began to change in 2011–12 with the entry of some juveniles into the system, during the first decade fears of Somali criminality were, like claims about their welfare dependence, wildly exaggerated.

7. SOMALIS KEEP LIVE CHICKENS IN THEIR KITCHEN CUPBOARDS.

People who claim to know people who have seen kitchen cupboards turned into chicken coops keep this myth alive. Even though I initially thought this myth was too silly to include in our study, Rilwan insisted it was important because he heard it so often. This myth resonates with other accusations that Somalis are uncivilized, unprepared for life in America, that they sacrifice and butcher animals in their backyards, and that their eating habits are filthy. For example, many families were mystified when a public health nurse who visited their homes berated them for eating with their hands from a communal bowl while sitting on the floor, which is the normal way for Somali families to eat together. One concerned father e-mailed me to ask if it is true that, in America, sharing food while sitting on the floor will hurt their children.

8. SOMALIS REFUSE TO LEARN ENGLISH.

This rumor persists despite the fact that over 1,000 Somali-speaking children attend Lewiston schools and that hundreds of them flock to after-school homework help programs at Trinity Jubilee, the public library, a public housing community center, and in the schools. In their early years in Lewiston, Somali parents ran academic summer camps so their kids could continue to study English during the summer break. Because of the high demand for ELL classes at Lewiston Adult Education, the program is full and has a waiting list, and Somali adults are enrolling in ELL programs in neighboring cities. In a 2010 survey conducted by the community collaborative mentioned in chapter 4, 100 percent of Somali respondents said learning English was their top priority.

I found this myth particularly intriguing as it was often accompanied, in my conversations with Lewiston residents, by stories about Franco-American parents and grandparents who struggled with or never learned English, even as their children were learning English in school. The director of the Museum LA reminisced about how Lisbon Street used to be French-speaking because all the major stores ensured they had a French-speaking staff for their non-English-speaking customers. Many older residents, including Maine's first Franco-American governor, recall attending elementary Catholic schools where the only language spoken was French. Governor LePage even successfully fought to be allowed to take his entrance exam to a Maine college in French rather than English.

9. SOMALIS REFUSE TO BECOME CITIZENS.

Refugees can apply for citizenship only after residing in the United States for five years, and when they hit the five-year mark many Somalis began pursuing the process although no local organizations offered assistance with citizenship applications until late in the decade.[33] The Somali Bantu Youth Association began offering classes in 2008, which were soon flooded with aspiring applicants. By 2010, hundreds of Somalis were enrolled in citizenship classes offered by three organizations at four different locations in the city. Citizenship tests must be taken in English, which means a massive amount of preparation for people whose English-language skills are poor. By the end of the decade I was always running into Somali Bantu friends shopping downtown while listening through headphones to citizenship questions and answers, muttering to themselves things like, "WhoischiefjusticeoftheSupremeCourtJohnRoberts" or "Presidentdievicepresidentdiewhorulesspeakerofthehouse."[34]

Allegations about citizenship are, again, about questioning the legitimacy of border crossing as a form of humanitarianism, as well as the fear that Somalis are not invested in adopting American cultural practices and norms, discussed further in myth no. 10.

10. SOMALIS REJECT AMERICAN CULTURE AND DO NOT WANT TO PARTICIPATE IN COMMUNITY LIFE.

Lewiston's newly elected mayor, Robert Macdonald, got himself into hot water in one of his first major postelection interviews in 2012, when, referring to Somali immigrants, he told a BBC reporter, "You come and accept our culture, and you leave your culture at the door." He went on to clarify: "Don't try to insert your culture, which obviously isn't working, into ours, which does."[35] As with their response to the Letter a decade earlier, proimmigrant activist groups were quick to criticize the mayor's remarks, although the mayor's views captured a sentiment shared by many others in Lewiston. Complaints about the lack of Somali participation in American cultural and community life range across a wide landscape but seem to focus most acutely on aesthetics, assumptions about gender norms, and visible participation in civic life. This final myth encapsulates a variety of claims about Somali failures to assimilate, evincing what Ismail Ahmed calls "cultural insecurity" produced by fears about difference.

Public harassment of Somali women for their dress has declined over the decade, although distress about their continued practice of wearing hijab dominated the early years of Somali settlement in Lewiston when passersby regularly criticized women out in public. Women initially did not understand what people were yelling at them when they walked their kids to school and shopped downtown, but soon learned the meaning of phrases like "Go home!" and "Dress like an American!" Remembering her feelings of shock and humiliation after being targeted in public during her first few months after moving to the United States, Abdiya asked me, "Why did they bring us here if they don't want us?" The teacher of one young Somali Bantu friend told her that she was being "a hater" by wearing a head scarf to school. Almost all the Somali Bantu women I know have been yelled at in public because of their dress.

Concerns about women's dress signal broader unease about Somali gender norms, which many non-Somalis assume are patriarchal and sexist. Blog comments state that non-Somali women are afraid of dealing with male Somali customers in their workplace or engaging with Somali men if they enter Somali stores. Several female teachers told me that they were warned by their white superiors to expect sexist behavior from male Somali youths, although none ever did. Mayor Macdonald stated in one of his news columns what many others discussed more privately: "Living in America, the Somalis must conform to our culture. Here men and women are equal. In many places of employment, women are the boss. Somali men will have to get over it and conform. There can only be one dominant central culture: American."[36] Assumptions about Somali patriarchy and female submission make the visible difference of Somali women's dress an affront to American sensibilities regarding gender.[37]

The anger about women's dress styles, seen as an explicit rejection of American culture and liberal values, gradually shifted to the aesthetics of Somali stores, most of which cover their windows with colorful fabrics (including women's clothing) and sell products labeled in languages other than English. Lisbon Street hosts as many Somali-owned stores as other businesses and offices, causing non-Somali residents to grumble that it has become "Little Somalia" in a not-quite-hostile takeover. The chamber of commerce is concerned about complaints from Lewiston's non-Somali residents that they are uncomfortable entering or passing the Somali stores because their windows are obscured by fabric and their entryways filled with idle men. People say things like, "I don't know what goes on inside those stores," and "I'm afraid if I go into one they'll harass me." A 2010 editorial in the *Twin City Times* decrying Lewiston's downtown as "an inner-city ghetto of low income, non-working residents" asked readers, "Do you stop to peek in one of the 'New Mainer' shops with their windows completely covered by fabric? No, you hop in your car and get the heck out of there!"[38] To address the situation, the chamber of commerce approached a number of Somali store owners to ask if they would be willing to make changes, such as removing the window coverings and posting photographs of items for sale in order to make their stores more legible to non-Somalis and to make Lisbon Street look more like an American shopping center. Thus, although store ownership is a robust form of participation in civic life, instead many of Lewiston's residents experienced Somali aesthetics as an unacceptable intrusion of Somali culture into Lewiston's downtown civic and commercial culture.

The small businessman in American political and economic iconography stands as the quintessential American, the hero of the American economic story. But if so many Somalis are small business owners, then are they the heroes of the American story? How are they succeeding when so many others have failed? The only explanation is that they must be doing something illicit in their stores. Concerns about Somali stores spill over into accusations that Somalis do not shop at American-owned stores (except for the claims about their full grocery carts at Walmart). As one woman complained during a conversation about Somali involvement in civic life, "I don't see them at our restaurants! Where are they eating?"

As with store ownership, there are many indications that Somalis are embracing an active civic role, although perhaps not in ways non-Somalis grasp or accept. While Lewiston's residents complain that Somalis remain isolated in their ethnic enclaves and do not attend the signature annual balloon festival, the Dempsey Challenge bicycle race, or high school sporting events, Somali efforts to engage in other civic ventures have faced resistance. Even though Somalis are perhaps 15–20 percent of the city's population, at the end of their first decade in Lewiston the city school board still refused to provide interpreters for their meetings; the local school district still refused to allow the creation of ELL teacher-parent support groups despite urgent requests from teachers and Somali parents for such groups; and the city council refused to allow the appointment of noncitizen Somalis to city task forces despite their desire to serve (and recall that the federally designated downtown urban poverty zone initially refused to fund any grant proposals by Somali community action groups even though Somalis made up the majority of residents in the targeted zone).[39] Somalis had valiantly weathered being yelled at on public streets, publicly chastised as overconsumers in grocery checkout lines, and chased by loose dogs in public parks. They had responded calmly when their two mosques faced assaults: one by a disturbed white man who flung a frozen pig head into one mosque, and another by a businessman who threatened Somali Bantus at their mosque because he was angry about their use of his parking lot. They had endured the incredibly nasty comments that always accompanied local newspaper articles about Somali residents in Lewiston (until the newspaper altered the rules for posting responses). Somalis accepted invitations to participate in panel discussions and focus groups for city or social services agencies, and, as noted above, many donated countless hours to volunteer initiatives run by Somali community organizations. While Somalis may not always participate in community life in ways desired by other Lewiston residents, by the beginning of their second decade in Lewiston they had finally begun to claim the right to a public political voice. In a striking display of civic engagement, and after staying out of the spotlight during the protests over the Letter a decade earlier, Somalis led the response against Mayor Macdonald's condescending remarks in 2012 about failed Somali culture and the need to assimilate by writing letters of complaint in the local newspaper, giving interviews to denounce the mayor's comments, and organizing a protest march down Lisbon Street. Activism is, of course, a mark of democratic civic engagement.

On the Role of the Foreigner

In her book *Democracy and the Foreigner*, Bonnie Honig argues that the point of philosophical and popular democracy origin stories involving foreigners is to resolve or make sense of the tensions and contradictions of the role of the foreigner, where the foreigner both redeems the democracy and threatens it, replenishes the democracy while taking from it. Foreigners appear in American democratic theory literature as the founders and renewers of America, the backbone of American exceptionalism as a nation based on consent, individualism, and liberty. In this literature, Honig writes, America needs foreigner-immigrants, who fulfill important roles in the popular versions of America's origin myths, including the myth of capitalist success, in which the foreigner-immigrant outworks everyone else as a devoted entrepreneur, affirming the possibility of upward mobility for others; the communitarian myth, in which the foreigner models community solidarity for those alienated by the predations of capitalism; the patriarchal family myth, in which immigrants renew traditional family values and gender roles; and the myth of liberalism, confirmed by the desire of the foreigner-immigrant to live in America. The four myths each contain within them threats as well: that the capitalist immigrant is an instrumentalist taker, only out for himself; that the communitarian immigrant self-isolates in an ethnic enclave; that the patriarchal immigrant imports illiberal traditional backward values; and that "their" naturalization threatens to overwhelm "us."[40]

If Honig's insights are right, then perhaps the myths about Somalis make sense if they emerge, in part, from a fear that Somalis are the renewing force that will displace those rendered impotent, disempowered, and atomized by Lewiston's long years of economic decline and marginalization. The very things for which Somalis are chastised—opening stores, buying cars, creating community organizations, trying to serve on task forces and participate in community meetings, demanding and demonstrating for their civil rights—suggest their potential power as the force of renewal and backbone of a new community. The myths then become a way to denounce Somalis as potential renewers by insisting on their status as guests, and specifically as recipients of charity, burdened by the gift of humanitarianism.

The myths promote hostility about allegations that Somali refugees are ungrateful beneficiaries of charity who refuse to fulfill the proper role of charity recipients. The contradictions created by the hostile resentment against Somalis for receiving charity because they are refugees, the hostile suspicion that Somali refugees do not want to participate in community life in the ways in which they are expected, and the hostile response to Somali efforts to participate in community life on their own terms only makes sense if Somalis are, in fact, behaving as ingrates while receiving substantial charity.[41] For the myths to resonate, Somalis must be seen as receiving charity rather than benefits to which they are legally and legitimately entitled as full community members. Situating Somalis as charity recipients enables a community-wide response of what Derrida has called "hostipitality,"[42] the hostility that is always contained within hospitality, where, as Michael Herzfeld has shown, hospitality is an act of othering that implies a moral indebtedness on the part of the recipient and the expectation of eventual reciprocity.[43] Positioning Somalis as foreign, disempowered refugees burdens them as unworthy recipients of hospitality because dispossessed refugees are presumed to be unable to reciprocate.[44] Additionally, in return for charity, humanitarianism demands silence, dependence, and the renunciation of civic and political rights, an expectation that extends from the refugee camps to the new homes of resettled refugees, where their welcome demands an apolitical life of silence, docility, conformity, and unending gratitude.[45]

This is more than just conjecture. Somali failures to conform to American standards of etiquette, civility, and gratitude are a steady topic of complaint. A common question from the audience at public presentations offered by Somalis to explain their history is, "Are you grateful to be here?" People have suggested to me that Somalis should publish thank-you letters in the local newspapers to let other Lewiston residents know how grateful they are. The repeated failure of Somalis to participate in the annual Dempsey Challenge bicycle race and the balloon festival is interpreted as ingratitude to the host community (although bloggers express outrage that Somalis hold their own independence day celebration, but on Somali and not American independence day). Constant expressions of appreciation, including the ubiquitous use of words like "please" and "thank you" are abnormal in Somali speech, which heightens the perception that Somalis do not express their appreciation properly or enthusiastically enough. In Somali, Somalis say, "Give me that," a matter-of-fact command that relies on clarity rather than some formulation like "Could you please pass me that?," which to many Somalis sounds oddly and unnecessarily obsequious. That Somalis in stores or service centers sound demanding rather than gracious feeds talk about Somali pushiness and aggression in making demands, most especially the women.[46] In one of his editorials, Mayor Macdonald asked, "How do submissive Somali women turn into obnoxious customers at the grocery store cash register?" (In an effort not to appear racist, however, he suggests that "extremist" white liberals are to blame, for telling "submissive" Somali women, "Stand up for your rights!")[47]

Concerns about standards of etiquette extend to other public spaces as well, such as school events, where Somali participants are maligned for talking during ceremonies and failing to observe cues to be silent. During the opening of Museum LA's *Rivers of Immigration* exhibit, people in the audience yelled "Shut up!" at the Somali Bantu dance troupe when some troupe members were talking among themselves while another member attempted to explain to the audience the meaning of the dance.

As Honig notes, the figure of the foreigner as a central figure for the story of American democracy is simultaneously ambivalent and frightening. In Lewiston, positioning Somalis as foreigners, in addition to as charity recipients, partitions them off from the community in another important way. The hostile discourses in Lewiston about charity for refugees mirror broader accusations about welfare in general, but with a slight twist. In Lewiston, the complaint about refugee use of welfare is that there will not be enough left over for "our people." The debate in Lewiston is not about whether welfare is good or bad; it is about whether or not refugee immigrants should count as community members who legitimately qualify for help.[48] It is about determining who belongs to the community, and thus complaining about refugee use of state assistance is easier if refugees are denied other forms of community membership, such as on task forces or parent school committees. Defining refugees as charity recipients thus ensures that they remain outside the community defined by moral responsibility.

The exclusion of Somalis from the moral community, and thus the community of legitimate welfare recipients, is deepened by the ways in which Somali support structures are visible to non-Somalis in Lewiston who express resentment and longing for such networks of care and mutual support. A wistful discourse has emerged among some of Lewiston's poorer residents at the sight of Somali sociality, which is obvious in public arenas where men gather every day on the sidewalks outside Somali shops to talk, and where women always shop in groups, care for each other's children, and constantly gather in each other's apartments. Listening to Somalis talking in an Adult Education class about solving a community issue by asking the elders to step in, a local non-Somali woman turns to a classmate and says, "I wish we had elders." A teacher in the Adult Education ELL program remarks that each new Somali arrival in Lewiston is embraced by resident Somalis, who offer help with shopping, transport, child care, and the challenges of settling into a new city. Everyone else in the Adult Education classes can see that every new Somali arrival in Lewiston instantly "has people," a display of conviviality that does not include them. The teacher wonders if her Somali students might be able to extend their welcoming efforts to other, non-Somali newcomers as well.

Kim Wettlaufer, the director of Trinity day shelter and food pantry, similarly notes the gulf between his Somali and non-Somali clients in their access to social support networks. One day when I was visiting Trinity, a very young white woman appeared at Kim's door to ask for help. She explained she was struggling to take care of her two special needs children. Apologetic and embarrassed about asking for help, she explained that her husband was unemployed, repeating several times, "I have no one to help me. I have no one." Kim sees that the strong Somali community support structures offer a palpable sense of community that many of his non-Somali clients utterly lack. This may be why it is so challenging for people to grasp that the overflowing shopping carts of Somalis represent the careful pooling of resources by many families who buy together in bulk and divide the food when they get home or that Somali car ownership is often the result of several families combining resources to purchase a car they share.[49] Perhaps the apparent vitality of the Somali community suggests something uncomfortable about the non-Somali community, provoking a backlash about "their" ability to benefit from "our welfare." Fears of gangs of Somali children relate to fears of being outnumbered. Each of the myths I list above speaks to Honig's four myths of the foreigner-renewer of American democracy, by insisting that Somali entrepreneurialism must be dangerous and related to illegitimate access to public resources, that Somali community structures are exclusionary, that Somali cultural and aesthetic practices are unacceptably traditional or disgusting, and that they did not struggle to get here and do not want to naturalize.

The fact of Somali physical difference as black people in a white city offers another unmistakable marker of their foreignness, and racist views obviously pervade the myths, especially in a country where welfare dependence and criminality have long been associated with blackness. Racial difference is where the unifying story of America as a nation of immigrants falters and breaks. African immigration has remained comparatively tiny since the era of the slave trade until recent years, which in the racial calculus of the contemporary United States positions Somali refugee immigrants as African Americans and not Euro-Americans who will assimilate into mainstream whiteness. Their blackness in U.S. racial ideology combined with their identity as "refugees" labels them as charity recipients rather than workers, positioning them within broader American popular discourses about lazy and criminal black people dependent on welfare, refusing to join mainstream (white) American culture.

Honig argues that democracy, like the history of immigration, is all about claiming rights, claiming participation, and insisting on voice, and is crafted and learned by fighting for voice and rights rather than through things like citizenship classes for immigrants.[50] She wonders whether myths of the immigrant's value to the nation can be, in effect, repurposed for the benefit of a more expansive democracy rather than to shore up the nation, sharing a hopeful vision of democratic cosmopolitanism in which immigrants stretch political practice into a form of border-crossing democratic practice. Somali refugees in Lewiston reject the imposition of a localized subjectivity as charity recipients who ought to express gratitude and docility for the right to live in Lewiston, insisting, instead, that they have the right as human beings to live a decent life and to keep their (transnational) families safe. They argue that they are not responsible for the war that destroyed Somalia and do not need to be especially grateful to be living in the United States, where they are suffering and working hard to support families in Lewiston, Kenya, and Somalia. Somalis view the right to be mobile as a human right, not a humanitarian gift, and contest the idea that resettlement, which they feel they have worked very hard for, is a form of charity.

In addition to rejecting the presumption of gratitude, they also fight back against the imposition of a narrowly defined understanding of blackness in America, as well as the neoliberal calculus that defines economic productivity as the sole measure of human worth and individual autonomy and consumption as laudable goals. Through demonstrating alternative modes of blackness, alternative models of reciprocity, sharing, and collectivity, and a persistent insistence on mobility as normal to human life, as part of the largest group of African refugees in America, Somali and Somali Bantu refugee immigrants may very well begin to stretch democratic practice in ways foreseen by Honig. We shall return to these points in part III.

CHAPTER 6

Helpers in the Neoliberal Borderlands

The recipient of hospitality, no less than the recipient of the bureaucrat's rude rejection, remains
"other" until the groaning tables can be turned, or
until both chairs are moved to the same side of
the desk.
—Michael Herzfeld, *The Social Production
of Indifference*

It is a typical Thursday at Trinity Jubilee Center on a winter morning: freezing outside, the kind of bone-rattling Maine cold that makes your eyeballs
feel frozen and your throat raw. Inside, the large basement room is packed,
as usual on food pantry Thursdays, with a vast array of people. The long
food pantry line of refugee moms and kids, old homeless alcoholics, young
scarred men, middle-aged men and women down on their luck, and very
young white families with babies in tow snakes from the kitchen to the outer
room, where people in line compete for space with those sorting through the
mounds of donated winter clothing piled on the tables on either side of the
line. Somali women move up and down the line greeting each other, their
kids trailing behind with mittens dangling, snow boots leaking water, parkas
partially unzipped, noses running. Everything is muddy today. Many of the

Somali women wear sweatpants under their thin dresses and long underwear under their sweatpants, although, astonishingly, some continue to wear sandals throughout the winter. The center is also a gathering place for people who live on the street or in homeless shelters with lockout hours during the day, some of whom struggle with substance dependence or mental illness. While the food pantry line slowly moves, some of Trinity's other clients mill about the room as they wait for lunch, talking to themselves, humming, chatting with each other, watching TV, looking at the wall, gently rocking. A few munch on the free doughnuts available at a side table. The director, Kim Wettlaufer, perches on his stool at his usual place, struggling to keep order in the food pantry line as women continually abandon their spots to talk to friends and as people in line push against people sorting through clothing. When an unstable man begins yelling his suspicions that Somali women are cutting in line in the course of greeting each other, a couple of the Somali women try to engage with him, saying in a way they intend to be friendly, "Sorry my friend" and "What's your problem?" while other Somali women giggle at their attempts to speak English. Other men kindly invite young Somali moms with toddlers to move ahead of them in line. Patsy, a Trinity regular who once accused Kim of favoring the refugees over his other clients, is busy pointing out nice things in the donated clothing pile to a Somali woman.

Kim asks me to take over monitoring the line while he attends to some office chores. I shiver as I climb onto the stool, placed in front of the room's only entrance, which is constantly opening as people stream in and out. Kim notices my shivering and confides that he is never not cold during the winter at Trinity because the door is rarely closed for long. The kitchen is busy preparing the day's free lunch, and the smell of good food mingles with the rancid smell of the buckets used to mop the old linoleum floors. At noon, as the food pantry line winds down, the man in charge of the hot lunch program tells everyone to stand and gives a short rousing prayer before the lunch line opens. A skinny older white woman wearing a fringed faux leather jacket says to the man in front of her, "I'm too drunk to pay attention."

Despite, or maybe because of, the mingling of bodies, voices, smells, and stuff, Trinity always has a relaxed feel, even when women in the line are fighting over a spot, even when a young man high on drugs begins causing trouble and is quietly ejected by Kim, even when the woman who responds to voices only she can hear starts talking out loud, even with the TV blaring, the phone ringing, the kitchen staff hollering to each other, the little kids squealing, the door constantly flapping open, and the anthropologist trying out her rusty Somali on her old friends. Trinity's uniqueness is its universal welcome, where visitors are subject to no expectations or demands other than mutual consideration.

This chapter looks at people like Kim who work in the wholly or partially state-funded neoliberal borderlands to patch together a fraying safety net for those living in economic precarity and social marginality, including impoverished refugees. Neoliberal borderlands are fraught, contested spaces, where the provision of assistance by the welfare state to those living in precarity confronts neoliberal reforms and rhetoric that pillories those who receive assistance for their dependence on "government handouts." As the welfare state contracts with curtailments in food stamps, TANF, General Assistance, unemployment assistance, Head Start, and public funding for education, and the extension of some social services shifts to nonprofits and other agencies that compete for shrinking government support, people like Kim network with each other and with public employees in the schools, hospitals, courts, and welfare offices to pick up the pieces by trying to provide assistance to those who need it. My years of fieldwork in Lewiston ensured I spent a lot of time in the neoliberal borderlands as well, volunteering in Trinity's food pantry and in ELL classes at local public schools, serving on statewide boards concerned with multiculturalism in state agencies and the provision of legal services and advocacy for immigrants and refugees, and joining committees with local caseworkers, social workers, mental health counselors, health care workers, and teachers to discuss how better to extend educational, social services, and health care support for "New Mainers."[1] This chapter explores what is happening in the neoliberal borderlands where people who are being crushed by some combination of poverty, homelessness, mental illness, illness, racism, and xenophobia go to seek help and support, and where frontline social service providers in schools, hospitals, police, and social welfare agencies engage them. This interface is the location of a third narrative about Lewiston's experience with Somali refugees, a narrative that sees the offer of assistance to refugees as a component of community responsibility for assisting the poor and the marginalized.

Many studies of social support agencies that operate in the neoliberal borderlands reveal the ways in which case workers, social workers, and street-level bureaucrats are often forced to operate as agents of neoliberal reform, mandating expectations such as work requirements and obedient subjection to state surveillance (for substance use, household membership, unreported income), and more. These studies make sense of how the "helping professions" simultaneously help and police, offer care and cruelty.[2] Somali refugees fully recognize the ways in which they are regulated and monitored by the agencies that offer them help. My field notes are filled with examples: rumors about families in danger of losing their children to the state because of one infraction or another; fears that shoplifting by little kids could result in deportation; a Somali man at a cultural orientation meeting offered by Catholic Charities in Lewiston elegantly voicing his experience: "In Africa children listened to and respected adults. In Africa I was the head of the household, with my wife beside me, and the children listened to me. Not here. Back home the government wasn't involved in the families but here the government is the head of the family." He and others describe the ways in which caseworkers scrutinize family life, observing interactions between parents and children, policing parental discipline, imposing standards for hygiene and domestic cleanliness, recording births, deaths, marriages, divorces, and any other changes in household membership, monitoring wages gained and lost, and conducting regular inspections of family homes in public housing projects. Talking about the treatment of newly resettled Somali Bantu families in Lewiston, a Somali social worker ranted to me one day about the government surveillance that accompanies public assistance:

> Public assistance allows people to come in and inspect and question everything about your private life. My private life is nobody's business! All the people who are on welfare are brutalized by it. They are just beaten down by it. It is punishing, and demeaning, and makes them dependent and unable to make a decision on their own. If anything happens in my life I'm not going to have a caseworker coming down the hallway to inspect my house, interview my children. Housing agents have their own keys and can come in whenever they want! They claim that they are inspecting things, that there are bed bugs. They tell a poor Somali Bantu guy that he has to throw away all his mattresses and bedding and rugs and everything! What is he supposed to do! Oh! it makes me cry!

Resettled refugees who depend on social services and publicly funded programs during their adjustment to life in the United States are utterly exposed to the surveillance of government authorities in their lives.

But in addition to discipline, judgment, surveillance, and control, the encounter between those seeking assistance and those employed to offer assistance might also be characterized by care, mutuality, affection, and respect. This chapter draws attention to those who work in publicly funded neoliberal border zones, like public school ELL programs, social services agencies, welfare offices, and day shelters, who see themselves as struggling, alongside their clients, against the marginalizing forces of xenophobia, racism, and neoliberal reforms to welfare. The pressures in the state-funded neoliberal borderlands are acute in Maine, where the current governor (Paul LePage) ran for office on a promise to reduce the number of people receiving welfare, disability, unemployment, and MaineCare (the state's public assistance program for health care), to put state employees in the unemployment line themselves, to deny many noncitizen immigrants access to welfare assistance, to reduce state funding for public schools (expressing his desire to close down the state's Department of Education), to break the remaining vestiges of union power, and to deregulate everything that hinders business. Even though he won his first term with only 38 percent of the vote, his policies and rhetoric demand compliance from state employees, many of whom are horrified about the proposed and intended cuts to public support programs.[3] As funding for welfare programs, public housing, and public schools repeatedly comes under attack, and as the rhetoric from some of the city's and state's leading politicians persistently identifies immigrants as a problem to be eradicated, those who work in the social services sector with immigrants and the poor feel acutely the unstable, insecure provision of assistance to people living in economic precarity and social marginality. People whose career choices were motivated by a belief that those who need help should get it, yet who work in an environment where people who seek public assistance are negatively judged for their failure to achieve self-sufficiency, responsibility, and autonomy, are also being crushed.

Focusing on those derided by Lewiston's Mayor Macdonald as "boo-hoo white do-gooders" and by the city newspaper's managing editor as out-of-touch "insulated" social workers and educators, this chapter offers short profiles of people who, through their jobs and personal philosophies, contest the xenophobic discourses described in chapter 5.[4] The people described here extend care and support to immigrants and poor people through poorly compensated work that is often challenging, depressing, subject to bureaucratic assessment pressures, and met with hostility by those opposed to the provision of social services to the poor and those perceived as foreign. Many live materially modest lives and some live in the same neighborhoods as the Somali immigrants with whom they work. My focus here is not on their economic circumstances as employees, but rather on the affect they bring to the neoliberal borderland where they extend help and care to resettled refugees. Watching them try to locate sources of economic assistance for people unable to pay their utility bills, to provide extra child care for toddlers to mothers with many other children to care for, to connect hungry families to food pantry provisions, to offer extra educational support to children whose language and family background stymie their progress in school, to guarantee safety and security and trust in the law, I was repeatedly struck by their insistent devotion to an expansive understanding of community and to the provision of professional services to people stigmatized as economically unproductive, in a social and work context where neoliberal rhetoric blames their clients for their poverty and marginalization and pillories them for complicity in welfare dependence. The profiles below try to explain why they do this work and what they struggle against to extend help and care.

A conversation in 2010 with a local welfare supervisor opened my eyes to the professional pride that I highlight here. After several years of bureaucratic confusion in Lewiston's welfare office about the rights of immigrants and refugees to welfare assistance, this man volunteered to take on the extra responsibility for overseeing and coordinating benefits for refugees in the Lewiston-Auburn area. He explained to me his special interest in working with refugees: "You don't want to have the reputation of not being able to give people the assistance they are eligible for. These people have experienced a lot of stress and we don't want to give them any more. This is very rewarding work, seeing the hardships these people have gone through lessen because of this agency [DHHS]. I get a lot of joy out of it."[5] While attending every diversity training offered by his department and educating himself about the benefit structure available to refugees, he was upset to see, early in the first decade of Somali immigration, "clients coming in and not getting assistance for benefits they are eligible for and just breaking down. *That can't happen.* I take pride in this. I take pride in making sure they're not left out or excluded, because they are part of the community." Reflecting on his thirty years of work in welfare assistance, he explained that as "a die-hard Democrat" he really believes in the safety net and the responsibility of the government to help people in need, expressing frustration at people who say, "If they don't have a job, cut them off!" "Look around!" he tells me in response. "Look at the unemployment here! Look at the businesses closing! If the government doesn't help out-of-work people, what will happen to them? If your neighbor loses his job, are you going to take in his family, give them shelter and food? You better be glad we have a government who offers support, who ensures a safety net for people who run into hardships. If the state doesn't help who will?" He is infuriated at the unfounded complaints about Somali welfare fraud and unworthiness, remarking that in his long history of home visits, he never once visited a family whom he believed to be fraudulently requesting assistance. And yet he faces, daily, accusations from other citizens and from the state's politicians that his clients are undeserving, that their benefits are negatively impacting the benefits of "real" Mainers, and that he is complicit in supporting people making illegitimate claims to assistance.

I found echoes of the welfare officer's insistence that people who need assistance deserve assistance in the frustration I heard from some of the publicly funded job skills and CareerCenter counselors I knew, who expressed far more irritation with close-minded or racist employers than with job seekers, as discussed in chapter 5. In standing up for the people they assist, several city, state, and federal employees who work in welfare, employment, and public housing offices clearly articulated to me, over numerous interviews, their views about deleterious effects on poor people of budget cuts to critical social programs, especially in the face of tax cuts for the rich and special state-supported financial benefits for corporations. As professionals who work to alleviate poverty through the provision of welfare support and job training, these service providers insist on an understanding of community that situates the refugee newcomers as equally legitimate and deserving recipients of support, a sometimes exhausting position to hold in the face of constant assertions to the contrary.

In short, while the ethnographic accounts of how the helping professions police and discipline refugee subjects are undoubtedly true, of equal importance are those in the helping professions who, feeling the weight of injustice and exclusion deep in their hearts and souls, work to subvert and maneuver within a system that constrains them just as it constrains the refugees. Those caseworkers and public employees who hold those jobs because they believe strongly in the value of a welfare state rather than because they see themselves as the shock troops of neoliberal reform are fighting such reforms, alongside their clients, every step of the way. Often they struggle against colleagues who do not share their view, and sometimes they work in environments where they are lone voices of resistance, but that does not make their actions or philosophical orientations marginal or unimportant. Recognizing the emotional lives and personal philosophies of teachers, welfare officers, police, and other social services providers is important because, as part of the bureaucratic machinery that reproduces social hierarchies, patterns of exclusion, and the governmental production of subjectivity, their subjectivity is often erased in accounts of bureaucratic racism and the imposition of neoliberal reforms.

The snapshots below highlight three dimensions of the attitudes and motivations of those profiled here: professionalism, an expansive and future-oriented understanding of community, and reflexive mutuality. Some people mentioned here, like the welfare officer, explain their orientation as a commitment to professionalism defined by the belief that the state exists to provide for and protect those who need help, that those who need welfare or extra schooling or health care should get it, and that their job is to ensure everyone gets access to the support they need. They are proud of their ability to solve problems and ensure access to food, housing, diapers, health care, security, or quality education. Some people, like Kim Wettlaufer and former Mayor Gilbert, are clearly motivated by a profound sense of responsibility for those marginalized by mainstream society, a compassionate orientation that they feel particularly acutely for refugee immigrants struggling to adjust. Defining "community" as inclusive of difference and alterity offers a very different vision of Lewiston's future than the one presented in chapter 5.

Finally, some of those profiled here emphasize how they have grown personally through their relationships with refugees and meaningful engagements with difference. Their motivation emerges from a sense of mutual human connection through which they are creating a new self. When Cheryl Hamilton says, "Refugees saved my spirit," or Janet Saliba describes her commitment to her community work by saying, "This isn't a job. It's a lifestyle," they are expressing an alternative understanding of personhood, engagement, and community to the one pressing in from broader discourses of self-help, independence, autonomy, and xenophobia. They are trying to work toward a community in which diversity is not something to accommodate but is, rather, at the heart of community life, where Somali immigrants are fellow community members rather than needy clients or guests and where engaging alterity is about mutuality rather than difference.

Glimpses of their moments of despair also appear in the profiles below, when their compassion, desire for professionalism, and experiences of mutuality are squashed by the hostility, denigration, or resistance of their colleagues or by the mechanisms of accommodation that enforce hierarchies of human value. Fragile and earnest people get bruised, including not only the refugees but others who define their lives in tandem with them.

The Day Shelter Director, 2009–2010

The tone at Trinity is set by its director, Kim Wettlaufer, a kind, gentle man who admires and respects the people he serves. For years, Trinity, located in the basement of an Episcopal church but maintaining a nonreligious identity, has provided assistance with life's necessities and challenges to Lewiston's downtown population, offering a welcoming place to hang out during the day, a free hot lunch, (pre-owned) clothing and toys, and free caseworker assistance with landlords, the courts, lawyers, the police, schools, utility companies, bills, doctors, counselors, and more. When the refugees began moving in downtown, Kim went door to door to meet the new arrivals, hired Somali-speaking caseworkers to ensure the center's services were accessible and available to them, and started the city's first after-school homework help program for Somali-speaking kids. The tiny Trinity staff, which for years included Janet Saliba, a feisty Bates college student, and Jama Mahmood, a Somali Bantu refugee and founding member of SBYAM, along with a few other Somali and non-Somali staff and volunteers, act as counselors, job skills trainers, translators, listeners, drivers, advocates, scribes, tutors, mentors, and friends. During the day a constant stream of people passes through Trinity seeking help with everything from reading mail to paying bills to responding to a legal summons to asking for money to cover a shortfall. Kim regularly opens his wallet to offer small loans, proudly noting the full repayment rate of his clients. Trinity is usually the first stop for other NGOs and city institutions seeking to make contacts with the refugee population. Coaches at the city's schools depend on Trinity to make sure the Somali kids have completed their physicals before the start of each athletic season; school principals call Trinity when Somali kids are in trouble and for help meeting with Somali parents; social services staff from local agencies shadow Kim to meet the city's downtown Somali residents and use Trinity's interpreters; the public health authorities use Trinity to give vaccines and public health information; local businesses with goods to donate (mattresses, shoes, food, electronics) go through Trinity to manage the distribution; and the juvenile justice staff depend on Trinity to shepherd families through the system when their kids get arrested. While many other organizations in the city dithered about how to extend their services to Somalis, Kim spent little time making plans but rather just said yes to things if he thought they would help his constituency. His attitude seems to be one of generous faith that good intentions will work. For example, one day a local physician dropped by while I was at Trinity to ask if she could open a public clinic in Trinity's basement room for the downtown population. After resigning her position at the short-lived downtown International Clinic in frustration over management issues, she hoped to start a new free medical clinic. Surveying the modestly sized space, Kim answered "Sure" without hesitation, as I looked around with uncertainty about where the clinic would be located. Although their meeting lasted less than half an hour, it was a stunning departure from the many meetings I had witnessed elsewhere in Lewiston in which participants' worries about logistical, legal, social, linguistic, and economic challenges repeatedly derailed new refugee-oriented program suggestions. The medical clinic was up and running within months.

A typical Thursday begins with the lineup for the food pantry as up to three hundred people file through to collect whatever is on offer that week. Donations determine much of what is available, which may vary from hundreds of pounds of rapidly thawing potatoes one week to hundreds of jars of peaches in syrup the next, along with diapers, canned foods, occasional vegetables, and, sometimes, hotel-sized body products. There is often an abundance of things like canned sauerkraut and bottled salad dressings in uncommon flavors (blueberry ginger, pomegranate, chipotle ranch). When I volunteered at Trinity in

2009–10, staff members Janet and Erica usually worked the pantry, along with the occasional Somali student volunteering during school vacations, greeting each client by name with hugs, handshakes, and smiles, and using the moment to check in about recent or upcoming doctor's appointments, kids who might be old enough to qualify for Head Start, school paperwork to be signed, or other pending matters. Working the pantry was exhausting—individualized socializing across language barriers combined with the physical monotony of four hours of turning, bending, lifting, handing, turning, bending, lifting, handing. Janet and Erica seemed to love it.

While the food pantry line weaves through the basement and the kitchen, another line forms for the hot lunch served at midday. After school the room fills with up to a hundred kids, along with the volunteers who help them with homework, while women sort through the donated clothing and Kim runs errands for his clients—taking food to a sick mother, taking a young man for his driver's test, seeing a lawyer about a recalcitrant landlord, visiting people in the hospital and in jail, tracking down a kid whose worried mother can't find him, attending sporting events and citizenship ceremonies of his clients. Over the course of an hour-long conversation with Kim in the office, his phone might ring a half dozen times and over a dozen people will peek through the door to ask for his help, while students working on homework line up to use the computer or borrow office supplies. Attendees at the Advice for America conference were asked to name the most important organizations in Lewiston for supporting the refugee population, and Trinity topped the list, a sentiment repeated in a 2010 meeting with Somali Bantu teenagers who immediately said "Trinity" and "Kim" when they were asked to name the best things in Lewiston.

The staff at Trinity actively rejects the myths reviewed in chapter 5 that castigate foreigners as the enemy within. In addition to standing against xenophobia, Trinity stands with the poor more generally by rejecting neoliberal discourses that equate poverty with laziness and irresponsibility. In Kim's view, the new refugees and Lewiston's historically impoverished population have much in common because of the social and economic calculus of marginality that bundles together and stigmatizes the poor, minorities, and foreigners as marginal and threatening to national security. While some of Kim's non-Somali clients occasionally grumble that the refugees get undeserved special treatment, during my days at Trinity I noticed many small moments of mutuality. One day, for example, I chatted with Lucien, a crusty old Trinity regular, as he watched Xawo's little grandson, decked out in a tiny denim jacket dotted with sequins that spelled out "Pretty Girl" in looping script, playing hide and seek between the racks of donated clothing. Smiling—Lucien is always smiling—he said to me, "All kids are alike, aren't they?" After a pause to chuckle at the boy's antics, he continued, "Underneath this [skin and clothing] we're all the same, that's what I say. I came here from Canada; they came here from Somalia; but we're all alike." Lucien has lived in Lewiston nearly all his life, mostly in the downtown neighborhood. "I hear the others say bad things about the Somalis," he confided. "They call them the Salamies, and I tell them to stop it. I tell them, if you don't want the Somalis here, then you don't want me here either. We're all the same. If you treat them bad, then you're treating me bad. We're all the same." Lucien's jovial attitude is infectious. Shifting his attention from Xawo's grandson to an elderly Asian American woman, another Trinity regular, he grins and propositions her. She laughs. Then he flirts with me and I laugh.

Kim agrees with Lucien that all the families living downtown "have a lot in common," listing the issues that arrest the lives of all the people with whom he works—extreme poverty, fragmented families, illiteracy or little education, poor health, economic and emotional instability, children getting into trouble— and noting that Trinity is the only place in the city, apart from Walmart, where adult white Lewistonians and Somalis come together every single day. Because of their poverty, Kim says, "These folks, on a day-to-day basis, are the exact same way. Their biggest barrier with each other is communication."[6]

Kim's job at Trinity is really more like his life. Along with his small staff of caseworkers, he is always on call, running errands or meeting with clients until late in the evening and on weekends. After I'd known him several years, I asked Kim to explain why he does the work he does. He became the full-time director at Trinity after almost twenty years as a successful businessman, trading a routine working day for a 24/7 job with people struggling with some of life's greatest trials. Looking away, he knitted his eyebrows and responded, "Hmm. No one has ever asked me that before." The next week he recounted his path to Trinity, which began with volunteer work at a local hospice, then delivering food to elderly people, and then learning about Trinity and joining the board, volunteering a few hours a week, which grew to a few days a week, which became a full-time job when he agreed to step in as director and committed to running Trinity seven days a week as a day shelter. When he began to spend time in the homes of some of the first Somali arrivals in the downtown neighborhood, he was deeply moved by their resilience in the face of enormous pain, physical ailments, and huge cultural and linguistic barriers. He offered special support to one refugee mother, whose loving care and affection for her severely disabled wheelchair-bound child particularly touched him. "Some of the things we've seen are just amazing. And to be treated as part of the family . . ." he broke off, emotional. "To say it changed my life is an understatement." Kim's work, and routine involvement with car accidents, injuries, arrests, violence, psychological breakdowns, evictions, and other life catastrophes, has inoculated him against crisis: "Now I don't sweat the small stuff. The little things that used to upset me, like my basement flooding or something wrong with my car, are put into perspective. It makes you realize how lucky you are. When you hear the stories and know what people have been through, it puts things in perspective. Not just the refugee population, but everyone I work with at Trinity."

While Trinity offers a model of collaborative, inclusive community building, Kim is unable to extend this practice into a more activist form of politics because Trinity is dependent on public and private funding for its tiny budget. After Trinity helped to organize the public meeting where refugee parents yelled at school authorities, Kim experienced enough of a backlash from those authorities to convince him that Trinity must steer clear of activist politics and, instead, continue to maintain its public profile as modeling a preference for the poor. In this sense Kim's orientation is more reactive rather than proactive; he ensures Trinity is able to offer support and advocacy (with landlords, for example), but he does not define himself as an activist. As a space of refuge and nonjudgmental care based on a fundamental commitment to compassion, Trinity can offer a buffer but not a solution to poverty and precarity.

The Mayor, 2007–2011

During his two terms as Lewiston's mayor (2007–2011), former chief of police Larry Gilbert maintained an insistently positive attitude about Lewiston's transformation by the arrival of Somali immigrants, in stark contrast to the mayors who preceded and followed him (Mayor Raymond of the Letter fame and "leave your culture at the door" Mayor Macdonald). Mayor Gilbert used his regular column in the *Twin City Times* to express support and admiration for Lewiston's newest immigrants, to decry "corporate welfare," corporate greed, and tax cuts for the prosperous, to promote progressive immigration reform, and to offer expansive definitions of community.[7] Mayor Gilbert explained to me that his attitude emerged from two formative dimensions of his life: his immigrant ancestry and his Catholicism.

> I see so many similarities to Franco-Americans and people get upset with me for saying that. Francos came here to work. Somalis came here out of necessity and to feel safe. They are both good family people. The number one thing they'll say about choosing Lewiston is safety. They fled a civil war. Terrible things happened to them, and then they fled the gangs

and drugs of the cities where they were first settled in the U.S. By word of mouth they learned it's nice here—the people are good; the education is good; and it's safe. They came from an area where, when the police come to get you, you're never seen again. Here the police are working with them on community issues. When they came here, after getting their kids into schools, the first thing they wanted to do was build a mosque. What was the first thing the Catholics did?[8]

The answer, of course, is that they built a church. Noting that the Ku Klux Klan in Maine targeted Catholic Irish and Franco-American immigrants, Mayor Gilbert argues that each new immigrant group experiences xenophobic hatred despite all the values they hold in common with previous arrivals. In his newspaper columns, Mayor Gilbert was clear that the real problems are not immigrants and the differences they bring, but rather state-supported corporate greed and its withering effect on communities, a political perspective he actively promotes in his vigorous public and online presence and political activism. The role of government, according to Gilbert, is to lead, which he understands to mean fighting inequality, caring for those who need help, and promoting an inclusive definition of community.

During his tenure with the police department, Gilbert inaugurated a cultural training program that emphasized the commonalities shared by people who, despite their different cultural backgrounds, care about similar community-oriented issues like family, safety, religion, education, and decent jobs. "We're all one humanity. If people would just take time and communicate! Communication is critical," he explains, regularly chastising complaining constituents who acknowledged to him they had never actually talked with a Somali immigrant before making generalized character judgments about the newcomers. One day he recounted to me his dismay when, the previous Sunday, his priest asked in Mass for a show of hands by congregants who had spoken with a new immigrant during the previous week. Gilbert's was the sole raised hand. During his campaign and after assuming office, he made a point of getting to know as many Somali residents as possible, placing Somalis on his advisory boards, greeting Somalis in Somali in public, and finding in their life stories and hopes and dreams for the future resonances with his own background in a French-speaking working-class immigrant family. In one conversation about his background, he told me his memory of watching his mother, a shoe stitcher, walking to the bus station in the dark every morning to go to work, where despite her skill she always struggled to master new patterns, knowing she stuck with it to provide for her family. "I see that they [Somali immigrants] are doing the same thing and we are all

God's children. . . . I believe in God and I believe in life after death and that you will meet your maker one day and it's all going to depend on how you live your life. When God asks you, "I sent my children to live among you and how did you treat them?," you had better know how to answer that question."

Mayor Gilbert's stance contains a religious philosophy of mutual humanity and care as well as a belief that Lewiston's future, as was its past, is intimately bound with immigrant participation. Because of his belief in an expansive notion of community and collaboration, inflected with compassion, empathy, and an ethic of social justice toward all of Lewiston's poor, Gilbert shares with Kim Wettlaufer the conviction that communities must provide for their poorest members and that the role of government is to offer assistance and care rather than exclusion and judgment.

In a searing editorial denouncing the claims of a local newspaper editor that Lewiston's immigrants and poor are welfare cheats who are destroying the city, Maine's Roman Catholic bishop, Richard Malone, supported the alternative vision promoted in Mayor Gilbert's newspaper columns. Bishop Malone's editorial articulated an understanding of community based in an effort to create a "just and compassionate humanity" in the midst of an economic recession and growing inequality, noting that the answer is not gentrification to displace Lewiston's poor, as the newspaper argued, but rather "a recommitment to the principle of the common good that is at the heart of Catholic social teaching." Rejecting the newspaper's call for a residency requirement for welfare assistance, Bishop Malone promoted instead a "covenant of caring" that offers assistance to those in need regardless of their length of residence in the community.[9] While no one would suggest Catholic churches have been particularly proactive in connecting with Lewiston's newest immigrants, these men have used their positions of leadership to promote an image of collaborative community based in their religious understandings of shared humanity.[10] Theirs is a moral statement about community building as expansive and inclusive of the economically and socially marginalized, and about who should benefit from the welfare state (the poor and not the rich).

Mayor Gilbert's vigorous battle against the anti-immigrant rhetoric analyzed in chapter 5 remains tough: he was followed in public office by the right-wing Mayor Macdonald, whose campaign rhetoric denounced immigrants. When Mayor Gilbert decided to run in 2013 against Mayor Macdonald in the latter's bid for a second term, voters indicated whose views on immigration they support. Mayor Gilbert lost, 39 percent to 61 percent.

The Police, 2010

In light of concerns about possible criminality in the heavily Somali-populated neighborhoods, in 2010 Lewiston's police department created a special substation downtown staffed by community resource officers. Prior to its creation, popular attitudes among the Somali Bantu refugee population toward the police were negative at best: at community meetings people complained that the police typically protected white Lewistonians but not black Somali immigrants. The new community resource officers had a lot to prove.

Police lieutenant Marc Robitaille, the freshly appointed leader of the substation, shared Bishop Malone's "covenant of caring" in his approach to building the community resource police squad. His officers began their tenure by taking Somali language classes (to the consternation of online commentators to the local newspaper's story about the new substation), tutoring kids in Trinity's after-school program, going door to door to meet refugee families and learn names, and partnering with SBYAM and Trinity's Janet Saliba to provide informational programs for parents and youths. Allowing the kids to call them by their first names (although, appropriately, they called Lt. Robitaille "Baldy") and appearing at events both in and out of uniform, the officers tried to "police from the heart," in Lt. Robitaille's words.

For Lt. Robitaille, policing from the heart meant developing a relationship of mutuality and community building with the population they were serving. In a conversation at the substation, he shared a story about one of his first experiences in a Somali home in response to a midnight call about a vicious rat attack on a baby in one of the downtown tenement buildings. After tunneling through the wall to capture the huge rat and calming the horrified parents, Lt. Robitaille and his partner returned to the police station, where the baby's father showed up at 2 AM, on foot, to return the flashlight the officers had inadvertently left behind. For him, the gesture symbolized the kind of relationship he wants with his community, where policing from the heart is about loving his community and demonstrating a commitment to a shared future. "Lewiston is my town and the Somalis are part of my town," he told me. "The future of Lewiston is tied into how Somalis manage here."[11] He believes it is his responsibility as a community police officer to facilitate that process. (During this conversation, one of his officers interjected, laughing, "And now I've become a social worker!") To enhance community involvement, he placed his officers in the schools, at parent meetings, on bicycles peddling the streets, and in community action groups, where they worked long hours that regularly extended beyond the normal workday. One of his officers told me, "I could be working all day at the muffler factory where I'd be demanding overtime pay for any extra hours and going out of my mind. But here, I love this."

While a primary purpose of the community resource team was outreach to the Somali community and to overcome antipolice prejudice ("so they know we're not thugs or taking bribes," one officer explained), the officers also talk about how their work forges new interpersonal connections. One officer who spent a lot of time in an elderly housing complex near the downtown with many Franco-American residents became frustrated with the anti-Somali grumblings in the building. He recounted to me his response: "One time this old lady goes off on the Somalis. I said to her, 'Get in the car.' I take her downtown, take her to the Somali café for lunch. I take her for some Somali tea. I take her to two shops. About an hour later I drop her off at home and she has her bags of purchases, spices and some fabric, and she's telling everyone she got these things in Somali stores. Now Mohamed has nine elderly people [from that housing complex] coming in to buy things!" Drawing on a local stereotype (despite the disapproving look from Lt. Robitaille) to make his point about how to change people's minds about Somalis, he joked, "There are three forms of communication: telephone, e-mail, and an old French woman." Another officer interjected, "Not only is it people we bring on a daily basis to meet members of the Somali community, but it has also stemmed into the family dynamic too." He described bringing Somali food home to his wife and introducing her to his Somali professional acquaintances at the grocery store. "You're educating people in your own family as you're educating yourself! I can see that change." The officers' point is that such small acts—taking someone to buy spices at a Somali store, introducing a family member to a Somali colleague at the grocery store—are the incremental changes that will transform Lewiston.

The community resource officers worked hard to build trust and confront stereotypes. One of Lt. Robitaille's officers schooled me one day on this very point. Hearing that he was the newly assigned high school resource officer, I offered my congratulations and joked with him, "Ooh! You get the new class of ninth graders!," an allusion to the general school consensus that the rising ELL ninth graders came with particularly acute behavioral challenges. He smiled and gently reminded me, "They're not bad. I know them all. There are a few who make some problems, but they're all good kids." Viewing all residents, regardless of citizenship status or origin, as equally entitled to policing with compassion and protection from stereotypes, and understanding that community building rather than bracketing is a fundamental component of community security has produced, for these officers, a strong sense of police professionalism and rewarding personal journeys.

And yet, their efforts remain challenged, as Somali youths in focus groups name "the police" and "the schools" as their primary antagonists, and as some city leaders demand that the police take a hardline attitude against Somali juvenile misbehavior. When other officers arrest Somali youths, or when another officer promotes the idea that Somali kids have formed dangerous criminal GANGS, or when ICE (U.S. Immigration and Customs Enforcement) raids a Somali-owned store for undisclosed reasons, all police are blamed as the enemy.[12] Building trust in an environment of mistrust, legal insecurity, terrorism panics, and ICE raids conducted with no advance warning means the community resource officers are constantly fighting an uphill battle. The officers are also stuck between policing with compassion and their professional obligation to hold people accountable who commit crimes, including the refugee youths they are attempting to befriend. Despite their initial obvious excitement and the success of their collaborations with SBYAM to reach out to refugee parents (described in chapter 7), by 2013 all had left the substation for other jobs.

The Social Worker, 2009

Beth, a young woman from southern Maine with an advanced degree in child studies and training in Africa, found her dream job in Lewiston with an agency that assigned her to work on child development with Somali refugee families with many small children. Her position was brokered by Kim Wettlaufer, who wanted to connect early childhood development specialists with newly arrived Somali-speaking parents with large families. Kim matched Beth with twelve Somali-speaking families, where her role was to work with one preschool child in each family, introducing games that parents could play with their preschoolers to nurture cognitive development and prepare them for the classroom environment. Although her focus was to be with one child in each family, she was quickly overwhelmed with the pressing concerns of the families themselves, who, between them, included seventy-two children, although few families included fathers who lived with the mother and children. When she began visiting the families at home, she learned that some lived in apartments with no heat, no screens on upper-floor windows, leaking or collapsing ceilings, or stairwells in such disrepair that they were dangerous to navigate. Some of the children she worked with had skin rashes from bedbugs, cockroaches, and rats, had no winter clothing at all, or had blood tests for lead that were extremely high but whose siblings had never been tested.[13] One of the families with whom she worked lived in a tenement where doorways were boarded up with plywood sprayed with warnings: "High Lead Levels." One week, invading rats mauled a baby in one of the families with whom she worked. Although her job was to play for one hour per week with one preschool child in each family, she was quickly swamped with requests for all kinds of help: reading mail, paying bills, talking with landlords, interacting with schools, calling doctors, understanding unfamiliar cleaning supplies, and more. Because the social services agency that employed her would not offer additional support, she appealed to Kim for caseworker assistance to ensure the families received follow-up care from doctors, proper repairs from landlords, appropriate winter clothing, pest control, assistance with utility companies that were constantly threatening to turn off heat and electricity, and help with interacting with the schools about the children. Trinity funded the translator and caseworker.

During her first two years on the job, Beth's horror grew at a social system that offered so little care to struggling refugee immigrants. The mothers with whom she worked regularly broke down telling her about their exhaustion and frustration trying to parent many children in a new country with little support. On many of her weekly visits, she found moms critically depressed about the difficulties their older children were facing with school suspensions. "They had thought life would be better here," she says, with sympathetic anger. "I keep thinking, this week I'm going to meet a group who has a plan. They've been here long enough that there must be some system. But there's no system! They're being discriminated against, badly. I'm really angry about their treatment. The lack of understanding about why they're here. What they've been through. The lack of understanding at every level. People you would expect to have understanding and compassion don't. How is this allowed to go on?" Beth remembered that when she accepted the job, her friends predicted she would experience a huge culture shock, but, she told me, "My greatest culture shock wasn't my clients. It was my coworkers. I've never worked with people with such a limited worldview." At work, she endured the anti-immigrant remarks of her social services colleagues while fantasizing about creating a wraparound clinic that would provide coordinated care, ensuring each family access to a parent-school coordinator, health care workers, literacy volunteers, and caseworkers. Like Kim, she saw how the struggles of her clients related to the struggles of other poor people in Lewiston: "What the refugee population teaches us is what aspects of our system don't work. I would hope we could learn. It's glaringly obvious when we look at refugee populations, but these are problems for mainstream people also."

Although her job afforded her weekly debriefings, she still found that her on-the-job experiences radically altered her sense of a normal life, as, like Kim, she reconstructed her expectations: "I can't do baby showers anymore, or even weddings . . . realizing how little you need to live and be happy. Something horrible might happen to me, but I realize it's really nothing. Sometimes I feel childish when I'm with one of the families because of what they've been through. I'm aware of my privilege. I'm aware of how resourceful and resilient they are. Their humor! I really appreciate that they laugh and joke around: that after all they've been through they can still do that. Now I have very little patience for people who complain."

Hoping to contribute to building a community of wraparound services, Beth was instrumental in forming and leading the community collaborative mentioned in chapter 4, the goal of which was to ensure equal access to health care and education for New Mainers. But after the public meeting when parents yelled at school administrators, the collaborative's appetite dimmed for activist or advocacy work that might be impolitic, because so many in the group, like Kim and Beth, were employed by organizations that depended on city, state, or federal funding. Like Kim, Beth also realized the limits of advocacy work by organizations that depend on the support of local leaders.

The Teachers, 2008–2011

One of the ongoing concerns of the collaborative was the situation faced by refugee ELL students in school.[14] To comply with the 2006 agreement with the U.S. Department of Justice, the school system had to build an ELL program that reflected the growth of the district's ELL demographic from 1 percent of the student body in 2000 to 20 percent by 2010 and that complied with curricular and testing expectations set by No Child Left Behind. Rapid transformation was a tall order. For school administrators, as we saw in chapter 4, top priorities were control and management of the new population, compliance with federal and state requirements for testing and provision of ELL classes, containing parent complaints, and ensuring loyalty from staff during the challenging period of program building. But for some teachers and staff, an additional set of goals emerged as priorities because they felt their ability to do their jobs well was compromised by the lack of useful training about ELL and diversity for all faculty and staff, by the lack of focused, informed, directed, culturally appropriate support for ELL students, and by the lack of meaningful engagement with parents. These deficits produced, in the eyes of distressed teachers, community workers, and parents alike, an escalating spiral of punishment and misbehavior precipitated by cultural misunderstandings, frustration, and the unacknowledged effects of trauma in some children from refugee families. Over the course of the first decade of Somali settlement in Lewiston, suspension rates for Somali children relative to non-Somali children skyrocketed, despite valiant efforts by some of the ELL teachers to shield children, protest suspensions, reach out to parents, and seek support from nonprofit agencies that work with children. As one school employee told me, in distress, "It's easy to kick kids out of school. It's harder to deal with them."

After hearing parent and teacher worries about suspension practices in the schools, it dawned on me that every time I visited a Somali Bantu friend in Lewiston, there was a child at home who had been suspended. Somali friends were quick to note that all Somali-speaking children were subject to high suspension rates. Anecdotal observations gathered over the course of a few weeks included a wide range of infractions. A friend's child who had gone to tell a group of boys on the playground to hurry into the classroom at the end of recess was suspended along with the entire group for their tardy return. The child, a serious student at the top of her class, was so devastated and humiliated that her grades suffered and her parents sought psychological support. A middle school child was suspended for failing to wear his winter coat to recess. The five-year-old son of a friend was suspended for a week for saying, in a language he does not yet understand, "I will kill you." Another child received a three-day suspension for failing to serve an office detention and then immediately an additional ten-day suspension for failing to put away his iPod and for "giving attitude." A daughter of a friend was suspended for two days for writing a song in math class rather than attending to her math assignment. I heard of one parent who was so mortified by her child's suspension that she decided to stop sending her child to school in an effort to avoid any future suspensions. A teacher mentioned parent-teacher conferences where the parents just sat and cried in embarrassment, apologizing for their child's behavior and their shortcomings as parents. In my conversations with parents, many struggled to understand the significance of so many suspensions: Are their children terrible? Are they failures as parents? Or is the problem with the school?

Wondering about the actual facts, I filed a Freedom of Information Act request from the Maine Department of Education to obtain suspension statistics. They are grim. In the 2007–8 school year, Somalis were 9 percent of high school students and had 20 percent of suspensions, 14 percent of middle school students (grades six–eight) and 24 percent of suspensions, and 16 percent of elementary school students and 24 percent of suspensions. The next year, numbers in the middle and elementary schools shot up even higher: Somalis were 15 percent of the student body in the middle school but had 70 percent of the suspensions,[15] and 18 percent of the elementary student body but 65 percent of the suspensions. By 2010–11, schools began recording number of suspension incidents as well as number of total days suspended, and the numbers continued to be bleak. That year, Somalis were 13 percent of high school students but had 38 percent of total suspension incidents and 45 percent of total days, in the middle school Somalis were 19 percent of students but had 37 percent of incidents and 40 percent of days, and in the elementary school Somalis were 21 percent of students but had 53 percent of incidents and 45 percent of days.[16]

The ELL teachers, who have the most contact with Somali children in the school system, expressed constant distress about the number of suspensions meted out to ELL students by their colleagues and the impact of suspensions on their students. Suspensions were most frequently for infractions like disobeying, fighting, and displaying inappropriate attitudes like threats and intimidation. "Throughout the United States, schools tend disproportionately to punish the students who have the greatest academic, social, economic, and emotional needs," writes education scholar Pedro Noguera. Noting that minority students in particular are disproportionately disciplined for minor infractions and behaviors identified as disrespectful, and that students of color, boys, and low-achieving students are disproportionately suspended, expelled, or removed from the classroom, he continues, "In many schools, it is common for the neediest students to be disciplined and for the needs driving their misbehavior to be ignored." Yet, he argues, research suggests that such forms of discipline only further alienate students and rarely contribute to improved behaviors, including among students who are not often suspended, because high suspension rates suggest more pervasive problems in the school between adults and students.[17]

Only after I spent time in ELL classrooms did I really understand how the bodily discipline required at school posed severe challenges to some students unaccustomed to such an environment in ways that vigilant teachers uncertain about engaging with ELL students marked as black and foreign might find cause for suspension. For example, one day a new child joined the lowest-level ELL class. He had never attended school before and absolutely could not sit in his seat. The Somali tutor followed him as he moved throughout the classroom during the lessons, constantly shifting between standing, squatting, kneeling on his seat, lying across his desk, and pacing. Despite the tutor's quiet efforts to get him back to his desk, it was clearly beyond his physical abilities. (As one ELL teacher to whom I told this story reminded me, "Simply learning to be in a classroom is not intuitive." She likened the physical discipline of school to her experience with a Japanese host family, where she constantly fidgeted during long meals while family members sat on the floor with their legs neatly tucked under them.) While the ELL teacher in class that day, familiar with this issue, was willing to accommodate the child while he adjusted, a staff member in a non-ELL setting might not be, a suspicion corroborated by the stories of many ELL teachers who believe that some mainstream teachers and staff are far too quick to dole out suspensions for bodily indiscipline in Somali students. "The ELL teachers are great," one Somali tutor told me. "It's with the other teachers where the problems start."

The ELL teachers recognize how difficult it can be for a child who has never been to school to learn to conform to the bodily requirements for school: to walk and never run, to raise your hand and wait to speak until called on, to obey the precise time requirements for each activity, to sit still for an entire class period, to obey shouted instructions in the lunchroom, hallways, or playground in a language one barely understands. Everything about school is physically and intellectually hard for many children who have never experienced school, and children who fail to follow the rules get suspended. The ELL teachers concerned about high suspension rates tried to protect their students in the zones where mainstream teachers were inclined to distribute suspension slips, like hallways and playgrounds, while protesting what appeared to be an almost arbitrary pattern of suspension because of the lack of clear documentation about the relationship between actions and consequences.

But of course not all suspensions were for new students who broke rules of bodily control; even the most sympathetic ELL teachers knew that some students acted out to get attention, primarily because of things that the counselors, social workers, and ELL teachers identified as related to frustration, trauma, and racism but that other teachers and administrators treated as disciplinary problems to be punished rather than as evidence of the need for support and intervention. I witnessed boys arriving late to class with attitude and swagger, dropping books loudly on their desks, or offering a running background commentary sprinkled with curses or offensive language as the teacher tried to teach. Some of the girls teased, giggled, and provoked each other into arguments. Some students simply withdrew altogether, refusing to engage, talk, or attend to their work. While such behaviors meant a challenging teaching environment, many ELL teachers developed a range of strategies for managing disruptive students that rarely resulted in suspensions, treating them as frustrated, needy, or emotional adolescents rather than "bad" kids. One dedicated teacher who is beloved by her students resorted to yelling on occasion in one particularly difficult class, for which she felt terrible, but the students consistently remarked on how nice and kind she was. She felt she was anything but nice, and told them she felt bad about yelling: "When I hear other teachers yelling, it's definitely not nice!" She told me that her students responded, "But you don't call us names. You don't insult us. Other teachers say, 'You Somalis are all blank blank blank' or 'You people always blank blank blank.'"

Stereotyping is an insidious way to malign an entire category of students as a problem, and its destructive nature is recognized by ELL teachers and staff as well as parents and the counselors with whom some of them work. The ELL teachers felt that the ELL wings of local schools were treated as completely separate zones, avoided by mainstream teachers, mysterious (or even frightening) to others in the school who never engaged with the ELL program, and disarticulated from broader school activities, expressing frustration that non-ELL teachers and staff repeatedly came to the ELL teachers to demand, "Tell the Somalis X, Y, or Z," rather than learning how to work with the ELL students themselves. Some Somali staff members are frustrated by a school administrator responsible for discipline at one school who tells Somali kids, "In this country we don't behave this way," which implies that swearing, disrespect, or disruptive behavior would be acceptable in African schools. The Somali staff understand that telling kids, in effect, "You come from somewhere else where this is allowed—you don't belong here and you don't know the rules here," alienates them by placing them outside local culture and within some other, uncivilized culture, which reinforces problem behavior. When the school loudspeaker squawks, "Will the following *Somali* boys report to the principal's office," or when teachers make blanket remarks about Somalis taking away jobs from more deserving Americans, or when a high school social studies teacher screens the film *Black Hawk Down*, pausing the projection to point out the actor portraying the dead soldier from the Lewiston area while offering no guidance for how the class of white and Somali students are to discuss this incident, Somali students feel held up to public scrutiny and condemned. Not surprisingly, the education literature is clear that students who feel their cultural backgrounds are validated rather than ignored or denigrated in school are more successful.[18]

Even though a new discipline policy was supposedly launched in 2011–12, the suspension statistics remained high that year and ELL teachers struggled with classes where as many as half of their students were absent on any given day because of suspensions. At the end of 2012, a normally quiet and contained leader in the Somali community sent me an e-mail message screaming in frustration: "Many kids are suspended and expelled from school. I DON'T KNOW WHAT TO DO ABOUT THIS SUSPENSION/EXPULSION."

THWARTED EFFORTS

The ELL teachers, of course, knew exactly what would make a difference, and many with whom I talked about these issues easily drew up a list: extended day and more one-on-one tutoring for ELL students to help them catch up, greater involvement of parents, more staff training about ELL and the background of Somali kids (which, for most of the period of fieldwork, consisted of about 1.5 hours of training as part of the orientation for new teachers, described by several teachers with whom I spoke as based on the deficit model),[19] valida-tion of Somali culture in school, and allowing ELL students to participate in school sports. Some teachers felt the testing regime used by the school kept students in ELL classes too long, which frustrated them and ensured some would age out before attaining enough credits for graduation because only mainstream classes counted toward graduation.

In 2008 a few teachers tried to search for grant funding that would enable them to offer extended-day programming, devoting hours of personal time to researching models developed elsewhere for refugee kids who enter school with limited English, literacy, and previous experience with schooling. The teachers pulled together a series of meetings with enthusiastic local advocates, social services providers, and others to develop a grant proposal for the Office of Refugee Resettlement to fund an extended-day program. Their efforts de-railed when the group was informed that the school system would not pursue grants targeted solely or primarily at refugee children, but would only seek funding for programs accessible to all students.

The following year, the schools received a major grant of nearly $1.2 million to develop evidence-based programs focused on violence prevention, substance abuse prevention, behavioral support, mental health services, and early child-hood development. Although the grant was a great coup for the school, it left the particular needs of the ELL students—almost 20 percent of the student body—to the discretion of contractors who submitted bids for the different programs to decide how to include them, if at all. Frustrated Somali transla-tors and caseworkers found some of the programs and models implemented by contractors inaccessible to Somali-speaking students and their parents. Al-though ELL teachers are clear that some of the school counselors tried very hard to work with Somali-speaking students, in the absence of substantive and thorough antiracism and cultural competency training for school coun-selors, many floundered, leaving the ELL teachers poorly supported in their efforts to manage the emotional and psychological issues of their students.

But in a discussion about better cross-cultural training for school counsel-ors, one school official reminded me, "Schools are for education. That is our mission. We aren't here to provide mental health services." Despite the focus on behavioral and mental health programs financed by the major external grant, this is a valid point. While schools struggle under the twin burdens of reduced funding and heightened requirements for standardized testing, managing the emotional and psychological difficulties that students bring to school may be an unfair expectation. Nevertheless, ELL teachers devoted to supporting students from Somali families fought to be able to build construc-tive ways better to engage with Somali parents, even after being forbidden from doing so, because they believed so strongly that better relations with parents could only help struggling students. One teacher drew up a list of parents who could be invited to an inaugural parent-teacher support group, to be held just after the distribution of report cards, with the initial goal of reviewing the system of grades and the online system for tracking student progress as well as to discuss homework. Parents were eager, but the school canceled the meeting with the stiff reminder that after the experience of the large parent meeting the previous year, there would be no further such meetings hosted outside the school attended by teachers. The reprimand explained that teachers cannot handpick parents to participate, and because parents come to meetings with a variety of issues to discuss it is impossible to control what happens, and teachers with no sense of local politics cannot be put in such positions.[20] A school administrator canceled another evening event planned by ELL teachers for ELL students to share poetry and essays with their parents over fears that the inclusion of poems in Af-Maay Maay, one of the languages spoken by a minority of Somalis, might be overly political. Concerns about language politics relate to more general concerns that meetings with Somali parents might become riven with tribalism and internal community politics.

While protesting the profligate use of suspensions, exclusionary treatment, and barriers to better parent outreach, ELL teachers are also subject to the hegemony of standardized testing, which is required of all students no matter how long they have been in the United States or whether or not they speak English. Thus ELL teachers must ensure their classes are oriented toward standardized test materials and formats, an absurdity captured by one ELL teacher in a blog post worth quoting in full:

> Whether you sat for your O-Levels and A-Levels, took the SAT or ACT, the dreaded Bac, or perhaps some other equivalent rite-of-educational-passage, one of the concepts you absolutely had to know and fully understand was how to compare and contrast. You might have faced a question that asked you to compare and contrast the lives of Juliette and Madame Bovary. Alternatively you could have been asked to compare and contrast gneiss and shale perhaps. In any event the concept of compare and contrast was one you had become very familiar with. Amongst teachers of English Language in the school and college settings today this is known as "academic language." If you sit in the SAT examination hall for 4 hours and don't know this concept you are well and truly lost. In our classrooms we aren't teaching every day speech, such as, "How are you? It is so nice to meet you." Nor are we teaching the skills required to drive a car and read road signs, nor the vocabulary necessary to purchase groceries or get a job.

We are teaching students to compete in the academic world, to strive to better themselves through the educational arena, to engage in scholastic and intellectual discourse. For many refugees this is a monumental challenge, but it is a challenge worth making. Our students have had little or no background to prepare them for the daunting task that awaits them. On May 1st in Maine all high school juniors (Year 11 students) will spend a Saturday morning struggling with tests that were developed to measure their ability to do well in an academic college setting. No matter if you have only been in an English speaking country for 12 months, no matter if you had no lessons in literacy prior to your arrival, you will take the 4-hour test along with everyone else. Compare and contrast, describe, explain, elaborate. It makes as much sense as the Red Queen and the White Queen in "Alice Through the Looking Glass" when they were testing Alice's ability to do Subtraction:

"Take a bone from a dog: what remains?" Alice considered. "The bone wouldn't remain, of course, if I took it—and the dog wouldn't remain: it would come to bite me—and I'm sure I shouldn't remain!" . . . "Wrong, as usual," said the Red Queen: "the dog's temper would remain."

Our perceptions, our cultural background, our linguistic competence are all at variance with each other. We lack so many commonalities, and we're constantly striving to close the gaps. Poor Alice, she tried so hard.[21]

Lewiston schools must teach to the test because test results have implications for how schools are evaluated. When schools failed to demonstrate adequate progress, letters to inform parents of the schools' failure mentioned the poor test performance of ELL students, upsetting some ELL teachers, Somali staff, and Somali students and parents because of the implication that they were the problem. In classes I witnessed how hard ELL teachers worked to encourage and embolden their students facing the severity of standardized tests and the constant messages that they are the problem. One day when I arrived in a high school ELL English class, for example, the teacher was beaming with affection and encouragement to her hard-working students, telling them that they are smart, that by following the instructions carefully they can figure things out on their own as she took them through exercises to identify which terms in a list (protagonist, climax, rising action, theme, genre) pertain to each in a list of sentences and phrases. The lesson ended with a tutorial on irony and a reminder that this is the kind of material they must master to enter mainstream classes and perform well on standardized tests. Trying to build their self-confidence, she insisted, "You can do this! I believe in you!"

As suspensions continued unabated at the end of the decade and the efforts of some teachers to reach out to the parents of their Somali students remained blocked, several turned to local activists, community workers, and social workers for help. Several area therapists with Somali clients joined the conversation because their clients' mental health challenges were exacerbated by concerns about the experiences of their children in school. After the community collaborative chaired by Beth pulled back from advocacy on parent-school relations, a nonprofit organization dedicated to health care access for poor or marginalized community members stepped into the breach to try to figure out ways to bridge the yawning gap between parents and schools around the issue of behavior by brokering help from a nonprofit parent advocacy organization. A series of meetings and small efforts emerged over the next couple years, as these "helpers" (social and community workers) worked under the auspices of the collaborative to talk about how to better support Somali parents and their kids in their engagements with the schools.

THE COLLABORATIVE'S EFFORTS, 2010–2012

At one of the first meetings between the helpers and the parent advocacy representative, frustration boiled over during a discussion about school hostility to better parental outreach and reformed approaches to working with behavioral issues of kids from refugee families. "Do you mean, when these people are brought here as refugees, they aren't given any resources? Any help? They're brought here from a war, they're traumatized and grieving, and they're just dumped and abandoned? They've been here ten years and there's nothing being done to help them adjust?" the incredulous parent advocacy representative asked. She persisted with further questions: why hadn't the schools instilled any kind of substantive cultural orientation for teachers and guidance counselors, put sufficient programs in place to handle trauma among the kids, or engineered effective opportunities to involve parents? Social workers from other agencies chimed in to ask why, during the first decade of Somali immigration, didn't the schools, hospitals, Catholic Charities, or other large agencies come up with an overall plan for extra outreach and assistance for children entering school for the first time and their parents, enhancing ELL education with extracurricular programs, developing coherent approaches to assisting families making the transition to life in America, or developing culturally appropriate forms of support for immigrants struggling with mental health challenges? We were seeing, in the suspension practices for children and mental health challenges of parents, the staggering effects of a business-as-usual approach on children who foundered and floundered in school for a decade.

A grief counselor from a local nonprofit who was allowed to run one after-school program for ten boys from refugee families who had lost a loved one described the distress he read in the children with whom he worked: fear, insecurity, anger, uncertainty about their future, and instability. His ten-week program of weekly hour-long meetings, based on a model pioneered in Portland schools, helped the participating boys develop strategies for managing their emotions and especially their anger, and was coupled with home visits to meet the families and involve the parents in the program. Because the Lewiston school system does not allow ELL students to participate in school sports, the counselor was particularly attentive to the kids' lives after school: "At home they're so bored! There's nothing to do after school. They have no activities, no programs, nowhere to go." Shaking his head, says, "I can't believe that ten years after they started arriving, there are still so few programs for them! Only the homework help programs at the library, middle school, and Trinity." Even though at the request of ELL teachers he offered to add more groups, school administrators refused, with the excuse that they needed more evidence-based assessments of his program in Lewiston.

The reason why no comprehensive approach emerged to support refugees struggling to adjust to school is the spotty and competitive approach to providing assistance for refugee support and the school administration's priorities. The extra funds made available by the federal government to support the ELL program are minimal, and funding for anything additional like extended day, special tutoring, or special parental outreach either comes from the overall budget or has to be sought elsewhere. The school administrators were unwilling to prioritize the needs of ELL students over others in the allocation of internal funds for programs, and they were also unwilling, on principle, to go in search of extra grant funding that would exclusively target ELL students. By the end of the decade, several teachers had left the school system for other schools that offered an approach to ELL students that more closely reflected their own values, and the elementary school with the highest enrollment of ELL students was reorganized under the federal government's "failed schools" program because so many of the ELL children had failed to make adequate progress. If schools offer a window into community politics, many of Lewiston's ELL teachers tried hard to model an inclusive school community where ELL students are full members rather than outsiders, problems to be managed, or failures who compromise school quality.

A second reason why no comprehensive approach emerged was the piecemeal approach to refugee assistance adopted by each small nonprofit. Each nonprofit that attempted to engage with refugee families had a specific area of focus: preparing preschool children for school, monitoring lead levels in children, offering grief counseling for children who had lost a parent. Catholic Charities offered very limited programs that reflected priorities for the federal government, such as basic job skills training. Catholic Charities' tiny staff of caseworkers and the few caseworkers employed by Trinity attempted to stitch together a set of services to help people manage on a daily basis, but no single entity had the funding or the vision to build a comprehensive, wraparound system for supporting refugees in an economic environment characterized by austere funding for education, job skills, employer training, and basic family support. After attending meetings of the collaborative for two years, I realized that, for all its good intentions, the group could make little progress because of concerns about partnering across different agencies, reluctance to share resources and information, and, as described previously, fears about angering school or city authorities by overtly challenging exclusionary practices. For these and other reasons, the collaborative struggled to attract regular participation by members of the Somali and Somali Bantu communities, who were working on a different set of initiatives to support their communities. I turn to their initiatives in chapter 7.

Conclusion

The people described in this chapter are trying to push back against the insidious myths presented in chapter 5, myths that equate poverty with irresponsibility and turn attention away from economic policies that produce insecurity and impoverishment and cause harm to the people with whom they work. As neoliberal assessments of human value and the dismantling of the welfare state make poor people a target of public derision and moral disparagement, poor immigrants come under particular scrutiny as unworthy foreigners who impose even more illegitimate burdens on public resources. Those who work in the neoliberal borderlands to help both the native and foreign-born poor are finding it increasingly difficult to promote a philosophy that values diversity and public support for the poor in the midst of popular discourses that conjoin inequality, economic insecurity, and xenophobia and blame the poor for their failures.[22] They join anthropologist David Haines, who asks why "the most common measure of progress in resettlement is employment" and economic self-sufficiency rather than education, the ability of parents to stay home with their kids while raising them, or ensuring resettled refugees are healthy and emotionally stable.

The creation of the welfare state in the United States and Europe offered the hope of an expanded definition of the commons and a broadened sense of community. Tracking its dismantlement through neoliberal reforms that prioritize privatization, the merits of competition, the narrative of self-help and individual responsibility, autonomy, individualism, and self-sufficiency, scholars catalog emergent discourses that scapegoat foreigners and the poor as economically unproductive and dependent, exacerbating xenophobia and narrowing the boundaries of who qualifies as worthy citizens. Upset and surprised by the racist and xenophobic turn in multicultural advanced capitalist countries, progressive scholars struggle to explain a resurgent biopolitics that brackets rather than dissolves categories of people, targeting some—the poor, the racialized, the foreign—for exclusionary intervention. Although the myths in chapter 5 make the visibly different foreigner a convenient target as the source of insecurity and economic disintegration, fostering nationalist sentiments that obscure the policy engines of inequality and consolidate loyalty for regimes of exclusion, the people featured in this chapter are quick to note that those targeted by xenophobic myths are not alone in their exclusion. The hostile treatment of refugees reveals much about the hostile treatment of others in the neoliberal borderlands who struggle with idealized requirements for economic self-sufficiency and identities marked by cultural or racial difference. "It often seems as if everyone hates the poor," write political philosophers Michael Hardt and Antonio Negri, who suggest that the poor and the racialized are often viewed as one and the same: "One should also remember how often hatred of the poor serves as a mask for racism. . . . Everywhere there is hatred for the poor there is likely to be racial fear and hatred lurking somewhere nearby."[23] The people profiled here would agree: one of their consistent observations was that the treatment of newly arrived refugees mirrored the treatment of the poor more generally. Grasping the relationship between xenophobia and racism and hierarchies of legitimacy, Lewiston activist Ismail Ahmed tells me, "We can no longer talk about refugees in Lewiston but rather must talk about the marginalized poor."

We saw in part I that the humanitarianism of the international refugee regime is about containment and that containment is about sovereignty, nativism, and racism. It is about the question of who can legally cross borders, who belongs, who is worthy, who fits in, and who gets to make choices about their future. The nativism and racism lodged within humanitarianism are visible in the technology of refugee camps in the form of border controls, authoritarian camp management, and expectations of refugee docility and apolitical innocence. This and chapter 5 explored how the nativism and racism lodged within humanitarianism emerge again when refugees who are allowed to cross borders become unwanted neighbors. The specter of unwanted refugees moving in next door has provoked city protests against VOLAG-based refugee resettlement in several U.S. cities and a call by city administrators across the country for the right of cities to reject refugees contracted to VOLAGS for resettlement.

In Lewiston, antirefugee racist and nativist sentiments emerged in public forums (such as open public meetings run by city officials and the Center for the Prevention of Hate Violence, Mayor Macdonald's anti-immigrant rhetoric, people yelling "Go Home!" and "Dress like an American!" in the street), in private conversation (in stories repeated among friends and family about chickens in the kitchen, government-provided cars, welfare support, and more), and in vitriolic commentary (both signed and anonymous) in the local newspapers. Does humanitarianism only "work" when it is carried out far away, on anonymous people who can easily be portrayed as helpless, docile, and grateful? When the objects of humanitarianism show up next door and begin receiving public assistance, driving cars, expressing opinions, and agitating for their rights, humanitarianism is confronted with its internal nativism and racism, especially in a context of economic insecurity and neoliberal rhetoric.

Racism uses neoliberalism as a rhetorical smokescreen, turning xenophobia and fear of foreignness or difference into an economic argument. Neoliberalism also makes use of racism: colonizing it for its own purposes, namely, stripping poor people of assistance and support. By utilizing the slippage between poor people and people of color, neoliberalism taps into racist fears to push economic reforms that hurt all of the poor in the name of worthiness.

While much has been written about the surge in popular and political rhetoric that vilifies the poor, anthropologists have begun paying attention to "a new structure of feeling that privileges empathy, care, and compassion" within neoliberal economies of inequality.[24] Calling attention to such forms of "affective labor" as forms of productive citizenship, Andrea Muehlenbach notes, "Affective labor remedies not material poverty, but collective relational crisis. It restores not economic wealth but the foundations of public morality."[25] Taking affective labor seriously as productive of social relations and moral communities, as holding "an enormous potential for autonomous circuits of valorization, and perhaps for liberation" means validating the work of people like those profiled here as symbolically greater than their modest accomplishments might suggest.[26] When anthropologist Elizabeth Povinelli suggests, "Rather than argue with neoliberals that social welfare was or was not a failure, we might ask what the conditions of failure were such that welfare and multiculturalism failed," she urges her readers to reject the neoliberal calculus "that bodies and values are stakes in individual games of chance and that any collective agency (other than the corporation) is an impediment to the production of value."[27] Rather, she asks, in tandem with those profiled here, why not emphasize instead how welfare alleviates suffering and enhances life, even if it has not produced financial independence or self-sufficiency?

The reaction to the arrival of refugees by some citizens and officials in Lewiston demonstrates how the rhetoric of economics trumps all other concerns and eviscerates arguments about the extension of care and the benefits of diversity. Even though the facts show that the presence of refugees has brought economic resources and vitality into the area (including, for example, at least $9 million in grant funding from 2001 to 2010 and about eighteen new stores downtown owned and operated by Somalis),[28] concern about how much the refugees cost the city continues to dominate public discourse. Talking about money allows people who are unhappy about black refugees in their city to avoid accusations of racism and silences dissenting voices as out-of-touch softies and tax-and-spend liberals.

Musing about the polarizing perspective in neoliberalist attacks on the welfare state, in which people are either economically self-sufficient through waged employment (and thus responsible) or social leeches, Povinelli asks,

> Why did welfare suddenly seem not to work? Here would be one answer: because within a neoliberal state, any social investment that does not have a clear end—a projectable moment when input values (money, services, care) can be replaced by output value—fails economically and morally. And a social investment is an economic and moral failure *whether or not the investment is life enhancing.* Even if one could demonstrate that social welfare enhanced the lives of the poor, if one could not also show that social welfare moved people from dependency to independence, as narrowly defined, welfare would be deemed a failure. Again, this is not some general condition of failure but the specific condition of failure in a world where social dependency has been cast as the moral opposite of individual responsibility.[29]

Those profiled here are deeply involved in fighting for a different calculus of success and human value. When Cheryl Hamilton says, "Refugee resettlement is about life," she means it is about creating a healthy community where people feel safe, hopeful, and capable. Everyone profiled here brings an affective disposition to their work that privileges empathy, care, compassion, and mutuality. Through the everyday struggles of teaching children to read, addressing depression caused by war-related trauma and the loss of family members, challenging recalcitrant landlords, attending court hearings for kids caught shoplifting, and ensuring refugees receive welfare assistance that will enable them to eat, pay rent, and cover their utility bills, a fight is being waged in the neoliberal borderlands. Those whose work to provide services is based in an ethic of professional pride at providing help to those who need it and expanding the boundaries of community to all residents regardless of income, culture, language, origin, or ability to be self-sufficient are challenging the policies that shrink the provision of support to those in precarity. They may be losing the current battle, but not without offering alternative under-standings to predominant discourses that chastise the poor and insist that economic self-sufficiency is the definition of worthiness. It is in these spaces that the affect of community building and mutuality pushes back against neo-liberalism, where solidarity predicated on sharing life in a particular place together produces efforts to build a better version of the city.

In conclusion, those profiled here are working in the neoliberal border-lands to model inclusive community and compassion, while avoiding local ac-tivism because activism perceived as confrontational might disrupt the public funding that pays their salaries and modest grants.[30] They are engaged in the sort of affective work that attempts to buffer the blows of racism, xenophobia, and neoliberal demands for economic independence, self-sufficiency, auton-omy, and self-help, and through their work they are modeling a professionalism shot through with compassion, mutuality, and love for an inclusive vision of community. They see their work helping Somali immigrants as saving and renewing the city. The cost of loving one's way to social change is that change is incredibly incremental, more often personal than public, and emotionally costly as well as fulfilling. But many of those profiled here do not see any other way toward a future they want to live in.

PART III Refuge

A Visit, 2011

Jama and I arrive for a visit at Abdiya's new apartment in the public housing complex on the edge of town, where she has recently relocated from her horrible downtown tenement, with its screaming tenants in the apartment above her, domestic violence incidents next door, and racist hostilities from other neighbors. Abdiya couldn't wait to qualify for the public housing complex.

At her front door we are met by one, no, two, no, three, no . . . four little kids running into the entry from the adjacent room. No adults in sight. As we call for Abdiya, we hear footsteps on the second floor, then the stairs, and finally thirteen-year-old Nur appears. He has been left home with all the little kids, who we can now see number seven. Abdiya is on her way home from running errands with her husband and grown daughter, Nunnay, so while we wait I ask Nur about school. He tells me he loves English and has been working on expository writing and persuasive essays, and track, admitting, with a sheepish smile, "I'm slow." "Well, you're only a freshman," I offer. "Yes," he grins. I tell him I'll look for him next year at the track and maybe he'll even recognize me, referencing our interaction this past spring at a track meet when he was flustered by my greeting, unable to recognize me in the unexpected context.

Nur is one of the most soft-spoken boys I know. I recall his reaction when I gave him photographs of his father, whom he does not remember, and grandfather, whom he never knew. As he studied the photographs, he gently ran his fingers over his ears, forehead, eyes, nose, and chin, tracing his facial contours while comparing his features with theirs. His grandfather died in 1988 during our stay in the village; his father went crazy in the refugee camp and never made it to America.

Nur's middle school years were punctuated by suspensions for a variety of supposed infractions, some so unlikely that at one point an exasperated social worker intervened with school authorities on his behalf. Abdiya had returned over and over again to the school to advocate for her son, finally throwing up her hands and telling me, "I can't wait to get him out of there!" I noted with relief that he seemed to be adjusting well to high school.

Abdiya and her crew arrive in two vans, emerging with another baby, more little kids, her husband, and her adult daughter Nunnay. Because polygyny (marriage between one man and more than one woman) is illegal in the United States, Abdiya was initially resettled separately from her husband and cowife until they all relocated to live near each other again in Lewiston, where Abdiya babysits her cowife's kids while the cowife attends school. Abdiya and Nunnay settle onto the rug, which is covered in potato scraps and lots of small broken pieces of plastic, while Abdiya's husband makes himself comfortable on the huge U-shaped velour couch, as do Jama and I. The kids, who now number perhaps a dozen, play between the two rooms that together constitute the apartment's first floor, cuddling in laps and then dashing off, giggling and reaching for the photos Abdiya wants to share with me.

Abdiya and Jama have just come back from their first return visit to the Kenyan refugee camp, where Abdiya's son, Abdullahi, the baby she had when we knew her in Banta as a young divorcée, still lives since being rejected for resettlement. She had to leave him behind when she came to the United States with her younger children. The photos show a handsome young man standing in front of the small shop and tailor operation that he runs with the money she sends to support him. She recounts the wonderful visit they had, but also her shock at how much money she spent because everyone there is so desperate for help. Nearly frantic to find a way to make more money so she can send more to her son, Abdiya attends every job-training program she can find and applies for jobs everywhere but has not been able to find steady work. Her English is spotty; she lacks formal education; and she cannot replace the front teeth she lost in a car accident because she has no money for a dentist. I suspect employers reject her for these reasons, without bothering to recognize her intelligence and competence.

Jama tells me that something is terribly wrong with Nunnay. When Jama and Abdiya were in Kenya, Nunnay, who was home taking care of all the kids, had a breakdown. The older kids and other relatives repeatedly phoned them to report Nunnay's problems: she couldn't take care of the kids, was unable to control herself, was constantly breaking down in crying fits, leaving the apartment, wandering off, running away. "How many kids does Nunnay have?" I ask. This is the first time I've met her because she moved to Lewiston shortly before Abdiya left for her visit to Kenya. She looks so young—she can't be more than twenty-four, twenty-five at the most. "She has seven kids and a husband but he's not . . . supportive," Jama delicately chooses the word. "He's a bad husband?" I ask, bluntly. Yes, Jama nods, he's a bad husband. Keeping things together for a bad husband, five little brothers and sisters, and seven little kids of her own was just too much.

It quickly becomes apparent that Nunnay is really a mess. She was hospitalized for a month after Abdiya's return while mental health professionals tried to stabilize her. Many refugees are uncertain about whether Western therapy can help with Somali problems, like jinn and possessing spirits, but some try anyhow when things get really desperate. As we look through Abdiya's photographs from her trip, a photo appears of Abdiya shaking the hand of an older man. It is the father of Abdullahi and Nunnay, whom Abdiya encountered in the refugee camp for the first time in almost two decades. Abdiya starts laughing, describing his formality at shaking her hand, but Nunnay bursts into tears. Jama says this happens all the time now, and they cannot figure out how to make her better. Abdiya had told me that after her husband in the camps went crazy, he beat her so badly that as a consequence she is partially blind in one eye, and I cannot help but wonder about Nunnay's childhood in the camps, living with a brute. As Nunnay sobs, life continues around her. Abdiya tends to the little kids, who are now hungry, settling a few of them into sleeping positions in the middle of the rug for an afternoon nap after their snack. A few won't quiet down, and she silences them with a rapid, threatening hand motion. Jama says quietly to me, "She is managing a lot. She takes care of everyone—all her kids, all her daughter's kids, her mentally ill daughter, her cowife's kids, her husband." On top of her stressful life in Lewiston, she scrapes together money from occasional jobs and babysitting to support her son and his family in the camps. The burden seems unmanageable.

Once all the kids are more or less quietly resting, our conversation shifts to Abdiya's citizenship test. She spent months studying. When I dropped by her apartment several months earlier to quiz her, I saw how carefully she was preparing by writing out all the answers over and over again in scrawling longhand to commit them to memory. To gain citizenship, refugees must be able to answer all the questions in English, which means that to prepare for the test Abdiya learned how to write in English and memorize all one hundred possible questions in English. I know that her desire for a job and to be able to visit her son fueled her determined approach to gaining citizenship. Resettled refugees are not allowed to leave the United States until they pass their citizenship test, which they can attempt only after living here for five years. Everyone I know is studying to gain citizenship so they can travel to the camps to visit relatives left behind.

Abdiya reports that the citizenship interviewer asked her six questions, which she gleefully and robotically repeats: "The Louisiana Purchase!" I have no idea what that means, but Jama intervenes to explain: "It's the answer to the question: what did the U.S. buy from France?" Abdiya continues to list the other questions, still committed to memory months after she passed the test:

"Who is the current president? What is the ocean to the east of the U.S.? John Roberts!," which Jama translates as, "Who is the justice of the Supreme Court?" The final question is "Who is the father of our nation?," which I ask her to repeat, astonished at the patriarchal framing.

Abdiya and Jama report that life in Kenya and Somalia is now worse than ever because of the terrorist group Al-Shabaab, which has taken control of southern Somalia.[1] Al-Shabaab soldiers do not want anyone to leave Somalia and threaten those they catch on the road from the Jubba Valley to Kenya with beheadings. "They are cutting off people's heads, like animals!" Jama says, in outrage. "Cutting off hands, legs, cutting out eyeballs. Why? It isn't the religion. I know I'm not a mullah, but I know it's not the religion." A few days previously, when I was visiting Sadiq, his brother phoned to say he was recently arrested and briefly incarcerated by an Al-Shabaab member who disliked his cell phone's ringtone. He was trying to figure out how to flee, as was Sadiq's mother. She had tried to escape to Kenya but was caught and held by an Al-Shabaab member for three days. Her captor told her that if she tried to escape again he would behead her. Al-Shabaab is trying to use the local civilian population as shields and threatens everyone with beheadings if they try to escape.

Jama says those trying to escape now have to go north, nearly to the Ethiopian border, before heading west to get to Kenya since Al-Shabaab men started to heavily patrol the route from Banta. "I can't understand why the rest of the world just lets this happen!" he says. "Somalia has so few people, just a few million. So many women and children are being hurt. Why doesn't the rest of the world just step in and stop the madness?" Abdiya nods her head emphatically. I try to give a serious answer, mumbling something about the lesson from Black Hawk Down and how the United States does not want to intervene anymore. But, he protests, there were united opposition forces fighting then. There were armies then. Now it is just a bunch of kids with guns. They could stop it, easily. As the napping kids start to stir and we gather our things to leave, Nunnay is still sobbing.

The visit captures several dimensions of the lives of Somali Bantu refugees in Lewiston: the difficulty finding a job; the enormous challenges for women struggling to care for many children and husbands who do not contribute to domestic chores; the worries about children repeatedly suspended from school; the debilitating burden of traumatic memories; the overwhelming need to come up with enough money to support large families in Lewiston and beloved family members in the camps; the desire for citizenship in order to be mobile; the ongoing worry about relatives in the land of Al-Shabaab kids with guns; the great care and effort that people exert to support each other, such as Jama for his relative and close friend Abdiya, Abdiya for her married daughter's mental health and her son's financial health in the camps, Nunnay for Abdiya's desire to spend a month with her son in Kenya, Abdiya for her cowife so she can attend school. Worry pervades home life and distracts already distracted parents, some of whom retreat into depression and withdraw from their children. Parental distraction means some boys gain greater freedom to slip out of the house and lose themselves in the street, and some daughters become over-burdened with the domestic chores abandoned by their exhausted mothers. Marriages fray under the pressures of new chores, new expectations for gender roles, poverty, and new structures of family life. For someone like Abdiya, what do self-sufficiency and integration look like? How do Somali Bantu refugees in Lewiston define these two tenets of the U.S. refugee resettlement program?

Making Refuge

The Somali and Somali Bantu refugees appear in the previous three chapters as either unexpected, needy problems to be managed and accommodated with as little disruption to the host community as possible (chapter 4), as illegitimate welfare beneficiaries and security threats who do not belong (chapter 5), or as fellow community members to be supported as the face of Lewiston's future (chapter 6). A central question weaving through these different versions is whether their presence is welcome or detrimental. During my interviews and fieldwork, I was struck by how rarely those whose voices are recorded in part II acknowledged the ways in which the refugees themselves were orga-nizing community-based initiatives, advocating for themselves, and defining what self-sufficiency and integration should look like. This is not a critique of those who worked to assist resettlement or in the helping professions; rather, it is a suggestion that non-Somalis and Somalis remained distinct groups, al-though internally divided, with very narrow points of engagement during the first decade of resettlement.

In 2009, a city administrator told me, "It's about time one of the refugee groups stepped up and started helping people. . . . It's really needed." Somali immigrants had in fact established several NGOs in the early years of the de-cade, mostly focused on business interests and professional networking. But the Somali Bantus, because of their greater rates of illiteracy and lower rates of English competency and education, desired different forms of advocacy during their first years in Lewiston. This section shifts our focus to the ways in which Somali Bantus (like the Somalis before them) worked to make their own refuge. In their version of Lewiston's story, Somali Bantus challenged rac-ism and discrimination, learned to advocate for things they wanted, and figured out how to gain a foothold in American civic life while attempting to protect community values and cultural integrity.

Alongside efforts to take charge of their own affairs and narrate their own story, the Somali Bantu community in Lewiston is wrestling with internal debates about new cultural values and practices made accessible by the move to America, especially regarding family dynamics. When I ask friends from Banta what they most remember from their cultural orientation classes in Kakuma refugee camp, they quickly list a common set of lessons, startling in their focus on reconfigured family relationships and responsibilities: No polygyny. No arranged marriages. No marriage before age sixteen. No hitting your spouse. No swatting your kids for discipline. No female circumcision. No traditional healing practices (which often rely on the involvement of family members to cure the ill). There is a reason why these were the lessons most seared into people's consciousness: they were learning that many of their normal practices for managing marriage, family, and domestic life would be wrong and illegal in their new country.

Village life in prewar Somalia was based largely on relationships within families and kin groups and with neighbors, governed by clear lines of authority that assigned more power to elders than youths, made parental authority unquestionable, and gave older men power over community politics and married women power in the realms of domestic life, parenting, and some forms of spiritual healing. People's identities were constituted through their relationships to other people in their extended family and kin group: as mothers, sisters, wives, husbands, fathers, daughters, sons, and so forth. Each role carried particular collectively understood responsibilities, expectations, and obligations, and village life afforded little room for contesting the parameters of expectations for people whose subjectivities were defined by their social embeddedness.

Extended families often lived together in compounds of several huts encircling an open space for eating, working, and relaxing, and family life was quite public because most people spent the majority of time outdoors, either in their fields or in the open areas of their compounds. I remember retreating into my tiny hut on occasions when I felt ill or overwhelmed, and within the hour my door would fly open to admit neighbors who settled onto the floor mats to chat, concerned that I was alone inside, suffering. In a rural village like Banta, neighbors overheard your conversations and commented on your cooking, your children's antics, your appearance, your heaps of stored corn or containers of sesame oil, your treatment of your spouse, and much more. Overheard conversations were repeated from compound to compound, and anyone who wished could see where everyone else was and what they were doing. Villages held communal rituals for healing and worship and treated marriage and raising children as a collective responsibility. Privacy, individual autonomy, and individualism were not popular concepts.

In Banta, children played freely throughout the entire village during their early childhood, supervised if necessary by any nearby adults, before taking greater responsibilities on family farms and with domestic chores as they grew up. Parents expected obedience to their commands, but otherwise demanded little of their children. Childhood in Somali Bantu families was not an orchestrated, structured experience with intimate parental involvement; to the contrary, children were often left to play on their own with little to no parental attention. Visiting Somali Bantu friends in their apartments in Lewiston or hosting them at my house, I see how the open approach to childhood that Somali Bantu parents held in prewar Somalia has persisted. One day when Idris and his family were coming to lunch at my house, he phoned in the morning to say that another cousin and his family wanted to come too. When the vans pulled up in our driveway, fifteen people poured out, including ten children under the age of five who occupied themselves during lunch playing our musical instruments, drawing pictures, doing puzzles, dancing, and running while the five adults ate and talked. During lunch, Idris mentioned the high volume as the kids banged, squealed, giggled, shrieked, played video games, and ran from room to room. When I asked if it was too noisy for them, they all laughed at the absurd question, responding, "Not for us! We were worried about you!" Lots of children energetically playing, occupying themselves as parents attend to other matters, is a staple feature of Somali Bantu home life.

In Banta, boys were circumcised at birth; girls at the age of eight or nine, when they began to take on the domestic tasks expected of women. Arranged marriages negotiated through extended family networks married girls at the age of fourteen and boys before they turned twenty. Newlyweds often lived with one of the couple's parents, ensuring lots of child care as grandmothers took over child-rearing responsibilities. As a family grew in size and gained greater access to farmland, a man might marry another wife or two. Jealousy and antagonism sometimes erupted between cowives who chose to live separately, but often cowives lived together, sharing child care and domestic responsibilities, sometimes having closer relationships with each other than with their husband. A swift slap on the bottom with an open hand or a thin stick constituted the most extensive sort of physical parental discipline I witnessed during my residence in Banta, and over the course of that year I knew of three incidents of spousal violence—two by husbands against wives and one by a wife against her husband. Neighbors quickly intervened in all three cases, which were mediated by local religious authorities who levied fines against the perpetrators. Local midwives, healers, and religious specialists handled illnesses, using a range of techniques that included burning small holes in the skin to cure pain, cupping, medicinal herbs, amulets, prayer, and spirit possession and exorcism ceremonies.

But in America, many basic dimensions of Somali Bantu family life and rituals of cohesion, community, solidarity, and support are defined as pathologies that are either criminal (female circumcision, arranged early marriages, polygyny, healing practices like burning, socially controlled physical violence to maintain discipline and authority); negligent (low parental supervision of children, curing through prayer or exorcism); or unhealthy (eating from communal bowls, eating with hands rather than utensils, sleeping and sitting on the floor rather than on furniture). As Somali Bantu families whose lives were upended in the war attempt to rebuild their fractured community in Lewiston, they face the enormous challenge of doing so according to totally new and barely understood rules for social life.

The following chapters show how they are attempting to navigate the twin expectations of self-sufficiency and integration in their new home. For people who prioritize community life and social networks over individualism, self-sufficiency means community independence rather than individual economic autonomy, and integration does not mean abandoning their values in a bid to become American. Their first decade in Lewiston brought massive challenges as Somali Bantu refugees tried to prioritize mutual social responsibility and strong diasporic connections to loved ones left behind in Africa while living in the land of individual autonomy and making a home in the particular locality of Lewiston, all while adjusting to living in extreme poverty in the land of plenty and as black people in a white society.

They began by contesting the presumption that they were objects of policy rather than architects and that their integration was to be effected through the efforts of local institutions and the helpers who managed their engagements with mainstream society. Instead, Somali Bantu refugees created their own bodies of political and civic activity to manage internal community matters and relationships between community members and other city residents, bodies through which refugee immigrants sought to define new collective norms and internal support structures relevant in the United States. It has been a fraught, painful, challenging process as gender roles, parental authority, and youth culture opened for debate under the influence of American values, popular culture, and the pressures of racism. Their story, of course, is still unfolding, but their experiences during their first decade in Lewiston show

how indigent refugees work to make their own refuge with spare assistance, how assimilation goes both ways by changing not only immigrants but also the cities to which they move, and how transnational and diasporic connections intersect with the particular places where resettled refugees make new homes.

CHAPTER 7

Making Refuge

We expected more democracy in America.
—Refugee immigrant in Lewiston

After arriving in Lewiston, Somali Bantu community elders faced the immediate task of figuring out how to insert their perspectives and viewpoints into
local political and civic arenas, which initially only enabled their participation
in highly orchestrated and contained ways such as through focus groups and
meetings called by authorities with agendas defined by them. In addition to
claiming the right to speak out about issues of concern to their community,
Somali Bantu leaders also wished to distinguish themselves from the Somali
community that had preceded them to Lewiston by, in particular, denouncing
the racism they experienced from Somalis in Somalia and the Kenyan refugee
camps. They faced barriers in both arenas because local bureaucratic authorities did not always view them as competent decision makers, and fellow Somalis resisted their allegations of historic discrimination. Many of their early
initiatives pushed back against their bureaucratic containment and silencing.

Somali Bantu political culture is profoundly democratic, which was formerly
possible in small villages where everyone worked on the same time schedule.
Villagers discussed matters of mutual concern in large meetings in open out-
door gathering spots where everyone had the right to speak and share their

views, and women, normally occupied with domestic chores and child care, were able to participate as children played together within view just beyond the meeting grounds. Inequalities existed, of course: men had more power than women, and their occasional use of violence to maintain authority was carefully policed and mediated by elders and family members; elders (men and women) had more power than youths and expected respect and compliance with their wishes. Authority was vested in certain elders, who made decisions for the community after listening to all sides, and whose decisions were (usually, in my experience) respected because of their seniority and publicly acknowledged wisdom.

In the transition to life in Lewiston, Somali Bantu expectations of democratic, transparent, and vetted decision-making processes ran aground on the reality that local institutions and authorities viewed them not as decision makers but rather as unschooled objects of policy (echoing their experience in the refugee camps). Refugee elders tried to respond appropriately in the new context, learning bureaucratic languages, attending workshops, and transforming their style of political practice and decision making to match American expectations for clear leaders who speak on behalf of a community and hierarchical organizational structures that ascribe more power and public recognition to some than to others. This proved to be a challenging adjustment, as the former practice of deliberative decision making regarding internal community issues ran up against the challenges of time constraints due to dramatically different work schedules and transportation barriers, the inability of women to participate because of their child care responsibilities in isolated apartments, the demand by outsiders for quick decisions in some contexts, the expectation by city leaders or institutions for one representative to speak on behalf of the community, and struggles over authority as the elders lost power to members of the English-speaking and literate younger generation.

Somali Bantus learned early on that democracy works differently in U.S. bureaucratic culture, where the institutions with which they engage most intensely—schools, hospitals, social services authorities—do not need to be responsive to their concerns or desires despite their expectation to be involved through translators of their choice. The ire about schools in particular ran deep, as Somali Bantu parents told me over and over how they experienced the ELL program as a paramount example of top-down administration and exclusion even though the program consisted largely of their children. The Department of Justice memorandum said nothing about mandating parental involvement in the ELL program, and school administrators were thus free to limit parental involvement to annual parent-teacher conferences while refusing teacher efforts to create parent-teacher groups or a regular ELL parent advisory committee during the first decade (see chapter 6). In one meeting I attended about parental concerns with the ELL program, a refugee father complained to a school administrator that the school made policy and called parents to a meeting to inform them about policies affecting their children but never asked parents for their views or responses. Other parents in the conversation nodded their agreement, and one noted that the way the school system treats refugee parents is just like the way Americans intervene in African villages, such as when a humanitarian group shows up and announces, "We are bringing you a well!" when what the village really wants is a school. There is no discussion—just the Americans telling the villagers what they are doing with the expectation that the villagers should accept it and be happy about it. Pointedly, he emphasized that this does not make for a successful relationship.

That particular meeting concluded peacefully, although the parents left without having achieved any of their objectives (employment for refugee parents as groundskeepers, demarcated prayer time in school, extended-day ELL classes, and extra tutoring for ELL students to allow their children to catch up more quickly to their American peers). But the meeting demonstrated what I heard over and over from Somali Bantu parents: "We expected more democracy in America," as one man put it, summarizing collective frustration about constantly being told what they could and could not talk about in meetings, feeling silenced about how schools handled their children, and realizing that school, city, and hospital administrators did not feel compelled to respect their priorities and objectives about education, health care, translation services, or other forms of social engagement. What Somali Bantus understood as democratic practice—namely, their right to speak out about matters that concerned them—American administrators saw as the refugees' bureaucratic incompetence. A few more examples reveal why.

"We Can't Invite People and Then Cut Them Off Before They Are Finished"

A few organizations tried to engage with the refugee population through the use of focus groups, a popular form of contained data production for organizational use, arranged through Somali and Somali Bantu cultural brokers who are put in charge of gathering community members to talk about issues of interest to the convening agency. (One refugee caseworker joked that the experience of Somali immigrants in Lewiston is "Move to Lewiston! Join a focus group!") A significant component of the cultural broker job is to ensure that agency goals govern focus group outreach, placing cultural brokers between the expectations of the agencies that employ them and the community members they are employed to attract to meetings. Whereas in Somali political culture, meetings are open to anyone who wishes to attend and those who attend expect to be able to speak about any issue of concern to them and for as long as they wish, agencies conducting focus groups predetermine the specific topics to be discussed, the length of the meeting, and the participants. Time and again, agencies felt focus group discussions veered too far from the topic; focus group participants felt their concerns went unheard; and refugee cultural brokers got caught in between.[1] For example, the expectation by NGOs that the same participants will come to each meeting for qualitative and statistical continuity is an impossible expectation because Somali and Somali Bantu community members view participation in focus groups and other programs as something to be shared. If one group of people hoards the opportunity to participate in a focus group or program training, especially when they are compensated for attendance, or if the cultural broker bars the door to community members in the interest of consistent participation, other community members accuse them of selfishly hogging an opportunity. Exclusivity is a sure route to tension and accusations, and everyone in the refugee community understands that it is far more democratic to ensure that everyone who wishes can participate.

The theme of control permeated many meetings I attended at social services agencies that were discussing how to reach out to New Mainers, leaving cultural brokers to explain how difficult it is to invite people to a meeting and then tell them what they can and cannot talk about. "We can't invite people and then cut them off before they are finished," cautioned refugee cultural brokers over and over again at planning meetings. After a meeting organized by a housing authority where women began screaming at each other as the convener tried to intervene to force them to talk about the topic selected by the organizers rather than the issue about which the women were upset, a cultural broker familiar with such scenes told me, "Sometimes service providers invite parents and want them to talk about a specific thing, but the parents want to talk about something else. The service providers try to make the parents only talk about the thing they want to focus on, but the parents have to be able to address the thing they want to address too."

The unruliness that Somali and Somali Bantu parents sometimes exhibit about obeying the rules for theme and time in focus group discussions orchestrated by service providers is easily interpreted as bureaucratic incompetence, which can be challenging for even the most well-meaning service providers. Service providers do not know what to do when immigrant participants talk for too long at meetings, talk about things unrelated to the meeting agenda, do not follow rules for participation, and then get frustrated that they are invited to participate in a meeting where their concerns are being ignored. The inability to control the conversation is precisely why schools do not want to have parent committees and wish to bar teachers from meeting autonomously with parents. Focus groups constrain refugee voices and focus refugee involvement on only those topics of concern to the agencies, whether or not the refugees share those concerns. When a mental health agency calls a focus group to learn about mental health concerns from parents, and all parents want to talk about is their experience of exclusion from the local schools, or when the housing authority convenes a group to talk about creating a community self-help group and the participants want to talk about their anger at each other's misbehaving children, the convening agencies are frustrated that participants do not stay on topic, and refugees are frustrated that what they see as their premier concern—worry about their children—is unheard.

Adventures in Capacity Building

One way host communities can try to avoid the intercultural challenges posed by troublesome refugees is to encourage refugee self-help organizations to take over the responsibilities of acculturation and community support. The federal refugee resettlement program promotes refugee self-sufficiency in part through the creation of ethnic-based community organizations (EBCOs) to undertake self-help projects that, in theory, will take primary responsibility for caring for refugee community members. Such associations must adhere to the bureaucratic logic of American nonprofits, obligating community members to participate in capacity-building and leadership development initiatives (often followed by grant-writing workshops) to prepare them to run their own ethnic-based nonprofits.

The Somali Bantu community was among the groups selected for training when the state of Maine received a half-million-dollar ORR grant to develop leadership and organizational capacity in its refugee communities to enable them to create EBCOs.[2] Several representatives from the Somali Bantu community attended the first of the four required workshops but failed to return to the second, which prompted the annoyed project administrator to phone me to complain and ask me to pressure them to attend the third meeting. After I dutifully made some phone calls, I learned that the location of the second meeting had been changed from Lewiston to Portland at the last minute, making transportation impossible for some of the participants, and that those who had provided child care for the participants in the first meeting had not received the promised compensation from the project. Even though I thought their absence justified under the circumstances, I offered to join them for the third workshop, located in Portland, partly to make sure they returned to the program to salvage their reputation with the project administrator, who held an important position in the state.

The leaders for the workshop were two well-meaning middle-aged white women with a long history of professional leadership development and capacity building but with little apparent experience with refugees or non-native English speakers. We began about an hour late, with an introduction by the lead facilitator who provided a complicated explanation about the importance of setting goals, prefacing her remarks with comments about the wonderful new diversity that the refugees had brought to Maine: "It's wonderful," she told them, "to see different skin colors and clothing styles in Maine!" As she talked, her associate handed out colored cards that participants could hold up when they heard an unfamiliar word. Cards immediately started going up: anthropology (in response to my introduction), solid, homogeneous. The facilitator carried on with a technical discussion of goal achievement that included so many difficult words that we could not progress through the flurry of cards. "Framework." She drew a tree on the board and said, "This tree is like your framework, your structure." Another card. Then she drew things hanging off the tree and said, "These are your objectives"—another card—"your goals, but that's also part of the mission statement, so we'll get to objectives and goals tomorrow. The tree is a metaphor," she explained, provoking another card to go up.

By now I was pretty confused as well. Goals and objectives are different, or the same? Since the facilitators provided no examples by way of illustration and solicited no responses from the participants, it was impossible to gauge what the audience was grasping. The second facilitator took over and talked for another twenty minutes, the use of cards flagging as the lecture went on. Finally the participants reanimated as the introductory section concluded with a lengthy discussion about when to stop for the day, since there was a competing multicultural event that many of the participants planned to attend. We agreed to end at lunchtime.

After an orienting activity involving postcards of art by European masters, we were broken into small groups and sent to separate rooms to write a practice mission statement and a practice vision statement. Our group included representatives from a Somali and a Somali Bantu organization along with the project administrator for the grant. In response to directions to choose a facilitator, a scribe, and a reporter, we chose a young Somali Bantu man to facilitate, but the project administrator intervened to say that since he had not attended the last meeting he could not facilitate. The role went to a woman from the other Somali organization. The scribe was also a woman from the Somali organization, who tried valiantly to record the comments despite limited literacy skills. By the end of our session, our statement reflected the comments from the Somali group about children's needs but somehow none of the suggestions offered by the Somali Bantu participants—housing, adult literacy, jobs, intercommunity trust—were incorporated. I couldn't help pointing this out, so the administrator added the word "adults" to our pretend mission statement. After reconvening with the other groups to share our final statements with each other, the day concluded with an exercise called plus/minus, where participants listed positive and negative aspects of the day's experience. Positives included the flexibility to end at noon, rather than 4 PM. Negatives were more numerous: the lateness of some participants, to which one of the Somali Bantu women responded, calmly, "You don't know the situation some people faced in trying to get here. Some people came from far away and had some troubles getting here." The project administrator intervened to reprimand her, stating that no one is supposed to respond to plus/minus comments; all are just supposed to listen. Another participant offered as a minus the fact that the workshop was scheduled at the same time as another major multicultural event in the city, to which the administrator, ignoring the previous directive, responded with frustration that everyone in the room should have been aware of the competing events and thus the scheduling mishap was their fault.

I knew that the Somali Bantu man who had coordinated his community's participation had worked an eleven-hour night shift—from 4 PM until 3 AM the previous night—as a janitor in a fast-food restaurant. After three hours of sleep, he began assembling other community members to get them down to Portland for the early meeting, which required finding an available car and circling the city to pick everyone up before the hour-long drive south. The group was chastised for arriving late, told they could not take an active role because of their absence from the previous meeting, ignored when they did try to contribute, silenced when they explained the reasons for their late arrival, and told they were lucky to be allowed to participate. After their hour-long drive home, the man who organized the Somali Bantu participation returned directly to work for his next eleven-hour shift. They did not return for the next meeting, nor did I intervene again to encourage them.

But such failures by Somali Bantu participants to meet the expectations set for them by institutional administrators are damaging, as agencies attempting to make a connection become frustrated that Somali Bantus are not playing their parts correctly. Their roles are scripted as focus group participants who respond to questions but do not make demands, as new residents who should be grateful to be invited to meetings, as objects of policy who do not contribute to making policy, and as political neophytes who need to be taught about leadership, capacity building, and decision making. Talking about the frustration with Catholic Charities that many local agencies felt, a social worker told me, "We all suffer from high expectations. We want the best for the newcomers so we want the providers to do everything to the best of their ability." But then she added, "And we expect the best behavior from our clients," noting how hard it is when the refugees do not behave in ways desired or expected by providers. In the incidents described above, refugees were "the problem" because of their failure to follow the rules and do what they were told. For the refugees, the only solution was to take control of their public presence in formats they controlled, to learn how to make their desires clearly understood by policy makers, and to organize their own programs to meet needs they defined for themselves.

"Learning How Things Work Here"

While Lewiston's civic organizations were cautiously figuring out how to extend themselves toward the refugee community through focus group meetings and discussions in the collaborative, Somali Bantus had taken note that the EBCO model would allow them to create a public presence, manage their internal affairs, and compete for grants to offer caseworker assistance, translation, conflict mediation, and so forth. Several Somali Bantu community members worked diligently throughout 2006 to create a Somali Bantu community association EBCO (hereafter called "the association"), seeking help from service providers, anthropologist allies, lawyers, the IRS, and a professional website designer. As instructed, they held community meetings to elect a board, write a mission statement and bylaws, and begin planning the projects for which they hoped to receive grant support.

Things started well. The community identified several priorities, beginning with a soccer program for young adults and a summer program for their elementary school children in response to parental worries that their older children had no activities and their younger children were not progressing out of ELL classes fast enough. Alongside these efforts, board members also embarked on a public education campaign with schools, service providers, hospitals, and city leaders to teach their American neighbors about why they are called Somali Bantus rather than simply Somalis and to convince their audiences of the need for Somali Bantu (rather than Somali) caseworkers and translators to ensure adequate and trustworthy representation. Sadiq, the community spokesperson, accepted invitations all over southern Maine to talk about Somali Bantu identity and history, a task he undertook with remarkable commitment. On one occasion, for example, Sadiq and I were invited to give an early morning breakfast presentation to the Waterville Rotary club about the refugee community in Lewiston. Unusually, he was a bit late arriving, whispering an apology as he slipped into a seat next to me at the breakfast table, saying that he was late because he had just come from Syracuse. Isha and some other women were driving from Lewiston to Syracuse the previous afternoon for a wedding and their van broke down on the highway in Massachusetts. They phoned him for help, so he drove to Massachusetts, picked them up, took them to Syracuse, and then immediately turned around to return to Maine so he could be in time for our presentation. In other words, he had just driven fifteen hours straight and had not slept in two days. "You should have phoned me to cancel!" I whispered, horrified. "Why would I do that?" he asked, surprised.

Sadiq proved to be a whiz at information management. As we sat together at the 2009 Lewiston High School graduation, I noticed he was filling his program with notes and asked what he was doing. "I'm gathering information!" he responded. As part of his quest for useful knowledge to pass on to community members and because, as he once explained to me, "I don't know how things work here," he always attended graduation ceremonies, whether or not he knew any of the graduates, to gather information about scholarship opportunities, awards, donors, and college destinations of local graduates. Gathering information also motivated him to publicize his community's achievements by asking the local newspaper to cover things like his college graduation, when he became the first Somali Bantu to gain a college degree in Maine, the 2009 high school graduation of the first four Somali Bantus to graduate in Maine, the soccer program and summer camp, clothing distributions at the association's office, and other community initiatives. He promoted refugee success and achievement rather than sending thank-you letters to the newspaper.

Demanding Self-Representation

The point of all the public outreach and information gathering by the Somali Bantu community association leadership was to insert themselves into spaces of opportunity and to explain why their identity differed from the city's Somali population in order to demand separate representation through Somali Bantu (rather than Somali) caseworkers and translators. When first arriving in the United States, many Somali Bantus felt uncomfortable allowing Somalis to translate for them partly because they feared mistranslation caused by differences in language and dialect, but also because many did not trust Somalis with information about their health, income, children, and other intimate details.[3] But retelling stories about their marginalization and discrimination in Somalia in order to make their case met animated opposition from some members of Lewiston's Somali community, who protested that the Somali Bantu label is little more than a strategic marketing campaign based in fictional renditions of history and entrepreneurial motivations. The ensuing fights over Somali Bantu self-representation occupied many Somali Bantu community leaders during their first years in Lewiston.

Sadiq was furious that some Somalis brought their racism with them to Lewiston, wielding it against Somali Bantus by trying to deny their memories of injustice while simultaneously humiliating them with racist epithets. Somali Bantu friends recount story after story about the racist incidents they experienced in Lewiston from fellow Somalis: a Somali man at a barber shop insisting that the barber change the razor after clipping the hair of Somali Bantu customers before using it on a Somali; a Somali man urinating on a photograph in the newspaper of a Somali Bantu teenage soccer star; high school students who regularly hear the saying, "Jareer are the same whether in Chicago or Jilib" (the Somali version of "You can take them out of the bush but you can't take the bush out of them"); local community college students whose Somali classmates tease them about their inability to function in class before noon in reference to another common saying that the brains of jareer only work in the afternoon; Somali women taunting Somali Bantu women that Somali Bantu men want to marry Somali women but no Somali men would want Somali Bantu women.

Sadiq will never forgive racism. As a young man, he watched armed Somalis invade his town to demand food, girls, and the belongings of others. He witnessed the massacred men from Duqiyow in their death embrace, roped together around the trunk of the largest mango tree in the area. He fled to Banta to escape the militias who had taken over his hometown of Bu'aale, eventually fleeing Banta for Kenya with the girl who later became his wife, leaving behind their families. In the refugee camp, he became the second Somali Bantu to graduate from high school, enduring the taunts of his Somali schoolmates who refused to sit near him or study with him. He encouraged younger Somali Bantus to stay in school, eventually becoming their teacher after the move to Kakuma. His sense of self was forged by the cruelty and racism directed against villagers by Somali pastoralists and in the camps where Somali classmates angry about his intelligence and academic success called him derogatory and mocking names. Although one normally empathetic service provider argues that in Lewiston, "Somali Bantus will simply have to get over" their memories of past discrimination, Sadiq is certain that he will never lose his rage against racism.[4]

After becoming the spokesperson of the Somali Bantu community association, Sadiq represented the community in a multitude of public events with a relentless message: "We will not accept discrimination. In Somalia we experienced discrimination because of our ancestry, and our communities were destroyed and families killed because of it. Here, in the U.S., we are free and we will never come under Somalis again."[5] Whereas the Somali leaders who had arrived before him in Lewiston wanted to present a united community voice, arguing that in America no one cares about internal Somali differences and that all Somalis are perceived as just black, Sadiq refused to comply with the message of unity, insisting on narrating the Somali Bantu story of poverty, marginalization, and discrimination in order to ensure that Somali Bantus could represent themselves to city officials, service providers, and funders. "Somalis were trying to colonize us and that is what I was trying to avoid," he explained about his determined advocacy of Somali Bantu rights to self-representation and resources, including competing for translation contracts at hospitals rather than working for the already established Somali-owned agencies.

Somali Bantus' persistence led to reprisals from some Somalis who viewed their efforts as an attempt to wield the Somali Bantu moniker solely to access resources by relentlessly promoting an old narrative no longer relevant in Lewiston's context.[6] The desire to claim a united face for the entire Somali community is understandable. After all, when Somalis first started moving to Lewiston, city administrators told them that they would only listen to one leader to represent the community because it was too confusing to hear different sides from different Somali networks and factions. Somali friends laugh when they recount how several city administrators upset about the Letter told Somalis that the mayor doesn't speak for the city, leading some to wonder why the city government can be internally divided but not Somalis.

But in addition to forging legibility through singular representation, the Somali backlash against Somali Bantu claims is, sadly, also about racism and ignorance. Somalis from northern Somalia may have never encountered jareer Somalis or heard about Somalia's history of slavery, and some may simply have been unaware of the impact on jareer Somalis of their constant experiences of racist discrimination. One Somali man who works in the Lewiston public schools took me aside one day to tell me, privately, that he has learned so much about his country from hearing about the experiences of his Somali Bantu colleagues in the United States. He said that although he hears his Somali peers denounce the claims of Somali Bantus, he now understands that the claims of racism and discrimination are valid. Other Somalis are angry that Somali Bantu claims appear to construct a hierarchy of victimization that overvalorizes the suffering of Somali Bantus, arguing, instead, that all who came to the United States fled for their lives.

But, of course, struggles over limited resources and the perception of a zero-sum game in the world of social services play an important role in the denial of a separate Somali Bantu identity by other Somalis. When they arrived in Lewiston, many Somali Bantu adults were completely dependent on interpreters and cultural brokers for assistance with medical care, the schools, social services providers, and government offices. At that time, educated

Somalis with several years of residence in the city held all the translator and cultural broker positions. While some of these translators worked very hard on behalf of newly arrived Somali Bantu refugees, Somali Bantus were also working hard to develop skills as cultural brokers and translators in order to represent themselves. The desire by Somali Bantus to be represented by those Somali Bantus with competent English meant that Somalis would lose control over coveted cultural brokerage and translation jobs.

"We Paid You to Dig Our Toilets!"

Since the entire refugee resettlement program is based on competing for scarce federal, state, and private resources in the form of grants to fund critically important social support work, the system is set up to promote competition. In Lewiston the unavoidable result was rivalry within and between EBCOs to obtain grants, in part because for many refugees they offered the best opportunities for employment. Thus the emphasis on self-help as a route to refugee self-sufficiency and integration also had the effect of promoting ethnic differences as a form of competition.[7]

Lewiston's service providers struggled with a response to the demand for separate representation by the Somali Bantu leadership, which some interpreted as unappreciative whininess. One hospital administrator in charge of translation policy organized a panel presentation in 2007 for Somali Bantus to make their case about separate translation to physicians and hospital staff. At the conclusion of the presentation, a doctor in the audience stood up, bright red in the face and shaking with emotion, to shout that his parents came from Canada with nothing and no one helped them, they were poor, they suffered, they didn't speak English, and they neither asked for nor received special assistance. Furthermore, he continued, stories of Somali history and victimization were not relevant to his work as a doctor and he objected to this use of his time. As soon as he finished speaking, Sadiq jumped to his feet applauding loudly, thanking the doctor for making such an important point. When I asked Sadiq afterward about his reaction—I had thought the doctor was chastising the group for asking for special treatment—he responded that it was obvious the doctor was extremely upset and Sadiq agreed with his argument that translation issues should not be his concern as a doctor, but rather should be effectively handled by the hospital administration.

The association leadership organized another panel for a large conference of social service providers in 2007 about cultural and linguistic competency, where they spoke to a packed auditorium about their background and need for separate translators, emphasizing their distrust of the people who discriminated against them back in Somalia. They took turns describing things that they experienced in Somalia and in the camps to justify their claims. Sadiq mentioned that even in the refugee camps, Somali Bantus still did all the menial tasks like digging latrines. By talking in such a public place about their grievances, the Somali Bantu panel at the conference set off an explosion among translators, caseworkers, and the broader Somali and Somali Bantu communities. After the panel discussion, a Somali caseworker for one of the social services agencies accosted Sadiq, yelling: "We *paid* you to dig our toilets!" He responded, furiously, "Yes, sometimes, but why were Somali Bantus the *only* people doing those horrible jobs?" A Somali activist friend who thinks that everyone in the broader Somali community should be working toward unity and togetherness, not division and difference, identifies this panel presentation as the start of the major fights in Lewiston about Somali Bantu identity claims and self-help efforts. But then, without irony, he says that he tells the Somali children who call Somali Bantu children ooji (slave) on the playground that they should not do that because it is bad and hurtful. It was precisely to confront the everyday normalness of such racist acts that the association leadership chose to talk in public about their historic experiences and to make a case for independent representation.

While fighting for its community members to be hired as translators, the association began applying for grants, eventually renting an office on Lisbon Street staffed by community members to help people with everything from rides to negotiating with utility companies about service suspensions, organizing community collections for family emergencies, translating for medical appointments, and mediating marital disputes. They initially targeted small grants in the range of a few thousand dollars for short-term projects and basic office support. Some years they received no funding; in other years they were more successful, gaining $10,000 or more. But although the launch of the association seemed like a wonderful culmination of collective hard work, community unity, and self-help, before long the competitive model for meeting community needs through grant-driven "self-empowerment" undertaken by an exclusive board of leaders challenged Somali Bantu understandings of normal political practice in ways that fractured the fragile community.

"In Africa We Have Time"

Within a year of its creation, tensions emerged between board members about the allocation of the organization's paltry funds and the structure of decision making, and community members began expressing their suspicions that board members were inaccurately representing the community to outsiders or were pocketing grants intended for the whole community. Making the rocky transition from a village context where wealth and access to resources were publicly assessed and mediated to one where board members could deal privately in cash, checks, and bank accounts enabled accusations against community leaders of operating in the name of the community but for personal gain: making deals and getting kickbacks, engaging in secret conversations with authorities and funders and attending conferences where their actions and words were unknown to community members, or involving community members in public appearances (like panel discussions) while keeping (usually only imagined) stipends for themselves. As one angry (non-English-speaking) community member told me, "We want to go to conferences too!" By 2009, every invitation for a (normally pro bono) public presentation or dance performance caused organizers to discuss how to handle suspicions that they had been paid, while other community members gossiped that payments had been secretly negotiated and pocketed by the organizers. When we were planning the dance performance for the opening of the Museum LA exhibition, one of the women involved said, sighing, "It doesn't matter that we don't get paid, but everyone will believe that we did."[8] The jealousies and suspicions that emerged in Lewiston reflected just how few members of the community had points of engagement with other organizations and institutions in Lewiston and how dependent community members were on the few adults who spoke English and could participate in the world of grant makers and other local authorities.

"The community is broken," Sadiq told me in 2008, lamenting the dissolution of community bonds into accusations and allegations of corruption as different factions split and realigned over and over along lines of language, village membership back in Somalia, or even Somali clan affiliation. In Somalia, such community breakdowns would have occasioned days of lengthy discussions, an approach to problem solving impossible in the American context of unpredictable and nonaligned work schedules, poor public transportation, and so many more responsibilities that everyone has to attend to that get in the way of attending lengthy community meetings. Somali Bantus understand that the fast and simple "majority rules" solution fails as a practice of democratic decision making because the losers get nothing, which usually means ongoing dissatisfaction. "In Africa we have time," says Congolese musician Lokua Kanza, a claim echoed by one of the Somali Bantu interpreters, who says, "In Somalia we would stay until everyone has had the chance to speak, even if it takes all night" to mend a community rift.[9] But in the United States, organizational bylaws give more weight to some (board members) than others (community members) and contrasting work schedules make perfect collective attendance at meetings impossible, which means people end up feeling left out. The requirement for a spokesperson or identifiable leader for grants and for interaction with institutions is an impossible challenge in a community that expects everyone to have a say. Spokespeople and leaders, who have full-time jobs, school careers, and large families, simply cannot canvass the community each time they must make a statement or represent the community to a city official or prospective donor.

The profound restructuring of daily life in the United States has made old patterns of decision making obsolete or unworkable, and the transition to paid employment has ruptured the universal daily schedule of a community dependent on farming. "Now if you try to schedule a community meeting at 4 PM, for example, half the adults are at their jobs, the others are at appointments, at school, and in class, at interviews," one man tells me. "No one has time to come together anymore. In the U.S. everything is about money. You need money for everything! In Africa you didn't really need money—rent, utilities, car, car insurance. Everyone is running after money, and it goes out as soon as it comes in! Plus we have to send money home." A system that relies on competition to access money, as the grant structure for EBCOs requires, means that the community becomes infected with an understanding of resources as things to be fought over rather than shared, resulting in jealousy and rumors.

As factions broke off and then negotiated a peaceful reunion, only to break off again a few months later, other frustrations with the services provided by the organization grew. During the days I spent in the office on Lisbon Street, I witnessed the limitless array of requests from community members for rides, help with utility bills, complaints about family disputes that needed mediation, help with translation at the hospital or the court, questions about green card or driver's license applications, and more. The English speakers in the organization were trying to fulfill the demands placed on them by the claims of community leaders that Somali Bantus only wanted translation services and assistance from other Somali Bantus and not from Somalis. But the tiny number of English speakers, every single one of whom was also attending school, working, and parenting, could not possibly meet the vast, pressing, and constant needs of hundreds of non-English-speaking community members for translation and other services. When translators began missing appointments, double-booking translation jobs, keeping poor accounting records, or rushing through client appointments, a few Somali Bantus began using Somali translators again because of ongoing frustrations with their own community's inability to meet everyone's needs. As the self-help systems broke down and it became apparent that the few Somali Bantu translators could not meet the high demand for help, one of the community leaders who had forcefully advocated on behalf of community-selected translators told me about their "failure": "I am so embarrassed. I have never been so embarrassed in my entire life."

"Our problem is that we lack management skills," Sadiq told me, in disappointment about the association's inability to meet the huge demand for translation services while simultaneously operating as informal caseworkers, community volunteers, students, and parents. He may be right, but it is also true that the task they set for themselves and, indeed, the expectation of community self-sufficiency through self-help initiatives, was simply impossible to achieve. "We are tying the rope at one end, but it is unraveling from behind," he lamented, reflecting on how the association followed all the bureaucratic steps to create their organization, gain recognition, negotiate translation contracts, and open their own office, only to have things unravel because of poor time management, overwork, and infighting. By 2009 I had become worried about the health of people like Sadiq and Idris, two of the most active translators and caseworkers, who were expected to fulfill every role imaginable by their own community members and by social services agencies who depended on them as cultural brokers, while each attended school full time, worked nearly full time, raised their families, and constantly attempted to mediate intercommunity disputes over leadership and representation.

The neoliberal model of austere support, available through competition, to refugee communities facing widespread poverty, illiteracy, racism, communication barriers, and trauma expects them to solve their problems through "self-help initiatives." When they fail, which seems inevitable given the reality of their situation in the United States as indigent non-English-speaking illiterate newcomers, the systemic structure implies failure is their fault. It is hard to find a better example of bad faith assistance. There is also something oddly awry in a system that awards millions of dollars in ORR grants to organizations like VOLAGs that offer short-term, basic, occasional services to refugees while absorbing part of the grants as administrative overhead. For instance, in 2008, ORR provided half a million dollars in grant funding to the local VOLAG and the State of Maine Multicultural Affairs Office for refugee assistance, while Trinity's total 2008 annual budget was about $150,000 and the Somali Bantu association's budget was under $10,000.

"The Elders Are So Lost"

Frustrated and upset by the constant bickering of their elders, a group of Somali Bantu young adults led by Idris decided to split from the association to create their own organization in 2008. Many Somali Bantu women expressed their disgust at the infighting as well (while also wondering aloud whether the male board members were secretly hoarding community money), in part because the fighting among the men sometimes spilled over into the domestic arena as one weapon became rumor-mongering about each other's wives. In

2010, the board tried to strengthen its integrity by ejecting several members who were failing to fulfill their duties as defined in the bylaws (attending meetings and volunteering), prompting those dismissed to try to form another separate breakaway organization, to file a court case contesting the terms of their dismissal, and to send a letter signed by ten people to all the relevant funding agencies, including ORR, accusing the association of nepotism, corruption, and fraud. Sadiq bore the brunt of the accusations because of his role as spokesperson for the organization. Someone broke through the wall of his apartment with knives, forcing him to take out a restraining order against one of his accusers.

The accusers faced consistent setbacks because none could match Sadiq's level of organizational, cultural, and linguistic competency as well as community commitment. The court threw out the charge against Sadiq for the dismissal of board members with a reprimand about filing "frivolous charges," and the police offered protection to Sadiq's family. When the letter was investigated, it turned out that half of those who signed could not read and did not fully understand what they were signing. Accusations flew about who was to blame for the misunderstanding, as counteraccusations were made that the letter writers were colluding with Somali spoilers motivated by a desire to destroy the Somali Bantu community association, although the leaders of other Somali self-help organizations were furious at those who wrote the letter because it compromised the reputation of all Somali organizations in the city. In the fallout from the scandal, Somali Bantu community leaders from other cities, including Sheikh Axmed Nur's son from Syracuse, came to Lewiston weekend after weekend, trying to mend the breach, and even I was asked to try to act as a neutral broker for reconciliation.

The intercommunity fractures reveal all the complexity that lies behind but is elided by the neat label "Somali Bantu." In the new context of identity politics in Lewiston predicated on ethnic competition for scarce resources and centralized leadership, the salience of Somali Bantu identity comes in and out of focus depending, in part, on whether people think they will get better services and more resources from claiming that identity or from allying with Somalis. When identity negotiations intersect with the inadequate fit between, on the one hand, the hierarchical model of institutional structure and decision making in America and, on the other, long-held understandings of democratic practice from Somalia, fighting erupts.

Some of the Somali Bantu elders in the breakaway faction were clearly upset about their loss of authority and status, feeling relegated to the margins rather than occupying positions of leadership. In one of the meetings I mediated, one of the oldest men in the breakaway faction explained, "*It must be the elders* who should decide things. The youth can't do it because they don't know anything. The elders will always check the chair to make sure it's not broken before sitting; youth will just sit without checking." He was frustrated that the "youth," by which he meant Sadiq and other English-speaking board members in their thirties and forties who are the backbone of the association, were failing to attend to those issues he saw as the preeminent community problems: "Our children are out of control; our wives are out of control; and we need a new leadership to deal with it." The elders are men who should be assuming the position of leadership in their communities, but their lack of English means they cannot represent themselves or the community; they have lost their land and thus their control over family resources; their wives often control more resources than they do because of TANF and women's rotating credit associations; they feel their wives and children no longer respect their authority; they are making scant progress in limited English classes; and if they have jobs at all, they are degrading, minimum wage jobs with no hope of improvement. All they have left to claim are paltry resources from modest grants and the insistence that they, not the English-speaking younger adults, should be making decisions and representing the community. Instead, they are aware that they have become the least rather than the most capable.[10] "The elders are so lost," a community member observed to me about the failure of the community's elders to cope with life in America. Gesturing in frustration to the young English-speaking man from his home village in Somalia who accompanies him to meetings, one of the elders involved in the internal conflicts over representation and resources grumbled, "I am an elder, but I have to take this young man with me everywhere I go. I cannot speak for myself."

Domestic Disharmony

The struggles for control of the emerging hierarchical political structures of community representation and decision making recounted here occurred alongside the dissolution of hierarchies of another sort. Life in America introduced dramatic transformations to the domestic realm, laying siege to the old family order predicated on hierarchies of age and gender. Women began contesting male power; children resisted parental authority; parents felt undermined by government intervention in their lives; and the enormous challenges of poverty, language, loss, racism, and trauma burdened men and women who had been holding things together over two decades of displacement. During their first years in Maine, family dramas shook the refugee community as men and women began fighting over things like chores, affairs, divorces, domestic violence accusations, and money. The Somali Bantu association leaders tried to offer traditional counseling to solve these new problems while also running interference with authorities like police and lawyers who operate according to a different set of rules. As women made more demands on men for help with domestic chores, and men tried to figure out how to translate their authority from former models based on the threat of violence and the practice of polygyny to the new context, marital relations shuddered and cracked.

A male friend tells me, "In Somalia, men lead the family, but here women do." Women raise the children, run the household, and manage the money that they obtain through TANF, food stamps, and women's rotating credit associations, all of which undermine men's understandings of their roles as household heads.[11] Women in polygynous marriages register paternity with the state, ensuring that the government rather than the father determines and ensures child support payments.[12] One young man explains, "Women are so liberated here. They are growing so much. But for men there's hardly anything to embrace here." Perhaps the loss of the right to use violence, even if they only did so rarely, has been devastating to their sense of power, control, pride, responsibility, and obligations, he suggests.

During a visit with Garad and his wife Halima, the talk turned, as it often did in the early years, to their efforts to adjust to a culture where men and women are "the same." "Sometimes we struggle with our wives because the wives here are totally different," Garad tells me, as his wife sits next to him nodding. "The women here watch American wives. Here men serve themselves and have to cook. In Somalia men did the outside jobs, but here everyone helps each other [in the home]. Here I come home from work [as a cart pusher at Walmart] and my wife tells me to change the baby's diaper or to make her tea. I never had to mop the floor before! We've lived together for fifteen years, and we've never had the struggles we have now about this. I want to help my wife, but I want to do the man's jobs, not the woman's jobs." His wife is laughing as she listens. "But can't you work together?" I ask. "We *do* do things together," he responds. "If she wants me to cook tea for her, I do. If she feels sick and wants me to wash the dishes, I do it. But I'm always hearing about these struggles in the families now. Some men won't change diapers or wash dishes."

Our conversation made me realize how many more domestic chores there are in the United States. There never used to be diapers to change, dishes to wash, floors to mop. Couples farmed and brought home food from their fields to prepare. Women hauled water, ground corn, and cooked porridge, sharing the labor among cowives, mothers, and daughters, or with neighbors. Now, living in isolated separate apartments rather than extended family compounds, women face shopping, garbage hauling, cleaning, washing dishes, laundry, watching children, and more in a lonely social environment. There is a vast array of things women have to do outside the home as well to take care of their large families: interacting with doctors, schools, caseworkers, social workers, landlords, and utility companies. There is a ton of paper—identity documents, bills, school forms, medical records, paychecks, car insurance, benefits forms, citizenship paperwork—to manage and save. Husbands and wives are struggling over how to divide all these new tasks, all of which come under the general category of domestic labor and thus should be considered women's work.

Life in Lewiston can feel utterly isolating for women stuck inside small apartments with six, seven, eight kids, next to neighbors who are fighting or who have blaring TVs. Heading outside in winter is an exhausting affair, with all the layers for the kids, the long walk downstairs to the street, the lack of public transportation, the misery of the freezing air, slippery sidewalks, and long gray shadows. Some women become overwhelmed, their children lingering late after school to avoid having to go home to chores or babysitting. When some wives began making demands on their husbands for more help with child care, diaper changing, shopping, and cleaning, astonished men who had never participated in these chores before and lack the skills conferred about what to do. Some of "the helpers," like Beth, intervened to try to convince the husbands of their clients to help out more around the house. Some husbands, like Garad, obliged. Others, aghast, refused.[13]

Frustrated women began circulating rumors about what men were doing all day long while women were stuck at home with the kids. Unlike Banta, where life was publicly lived, Lewiston offers plenty of opportunity for secrecy, and women became increasingly upset about how much time their husbands spent away from home, either working or mired in the community politics described above. To reinforce their demands for more of their husbands' time, some women began trying to bar the door against their husbands' departure, jumping on their backs to force them to stay home or throwing lamps and cooking pots to block their passage to the door. Husbands responded in fury at their wives' efforts to control their movements. When women called 911 and husbands were arrested, wives scored points but then did not want to press charges because they had already demonstrated their power. During their first few years in Lewiston, the whole community was talking about the fighting and 911 calls. "The women are crazy!" one young unmarried male friend told me, "and the police are crazy too because they take the side of the wife."

While many of the fights started because women felt abandoned by husbands who were gone for hours, several friends acknowledged that men were beginning to marry second wives in secret, provoking some of the first wives to act out aggressively against their husbands. In the best cases, cowives live near each other, depend on each other for child care, cooking, shopping, and other chores, and enjoy each other's company. This is particularly the case for women who were cowives in Kenya and relocated to Lewiston to live near each other again after being separated in the resettlement process. Some wives, like Abdiya, will take on child care duties so the cowife can pursue a job, or the wives will watch each other's children while they take turns attending English classes. Many cowives spend every day together, maintaining the built-in support system that characterized many polygynous marriages in Somalia. But when a cowife joins a marriage in secret or against the first wife's will, trouble brews.

Angry wives know their husbands will not call 911 when they get violent, one man tells me, "because the husbands know their wives will be arrested and they don't want that! They don't want to be left to care for all the kids, and their wives will never trust them again and will leave them." The rumor mill augments the fighting, and the large number of single mothers makes secret marriage an easy possibility for men. One woman, a mother of six, broke her husband's car windshield, slashed his tires, and was arrested twice for trying to throw her husband out of their apartment because she suspected him of infidelity. When she got the divorce she was demanding, men lined up to offer marriage, and she chose the youngest unmarried man of the bunch, whom she does not intend to share with another wife.

Men tried to justify their reluctant use of violence against their wives as necessary to assert their right to leave the apartment or to marry a second wife. At a wedding feast, one of the younger adults broke into a conversation about changing expectations for marriage to propose his theory about polygyny. He currently had one wife but was eager to figure out a way to have another while still adhering to American law. "Here in the U.S. it's common for American men to have a wife and a girlfriend on the side," he reasoned, suggesting that since Somali Bantus are allowed to have four wives according to Islam, they should be allowed to have one wife and other girlfriends to adhere to American law while still "practicing their traditions." "Isn't this what many Americans do anyhow?" he asked. I explained that while adultery in the United States might in fact be common, it is still considered wrong and grounds for divorce. He responded that he thought it would be a workable solution for Somali Bantu men who want to marry according to U.S. law but also practice polygyny, and that women would be in agreement because such an arrangement would be in accordance with Islam and cultural tradition. Everyone wins! "I think you should ask the women in the room what they think," I suggested. When asked, all the assembled women responded, emphatically, "Absolutely not."

As fights to redefine the rules of marriage and domestic life raged within the community, I had many long conversations with friends about alternatives to violence when husbands and wives are furious with each other. Community leaders were upset that some of the helpers became involved with domestic violence incidents, bringing in lawyers and official mediators, because they felt their community elders should be the ones doing the mediating. As John Holtzman has described for Sudanese refugees, domestic violence within a Somali Bantu marriage can sometimes be a call for community involvement to mediate a resolution to maintain the marriage and not an indication that the marriage is broken, which is often the American response.[14] Whereas American authorities pressure accusers to pursue their claims in court or with lawyers, community mediators intervene to listen to the problems, negotiate a solution, and levy a fine on the misbehaving spouse. The Somali Bantu association mediators spent a lot of time during the early years of resettlement interceding in accusations of infidelity, abandonment, loss of trust, and lack of support while trying to explain to American lawyers and police that their traditional counseling practices of mediation and levying fines would solve domestic problems better than the court system.

It took several years for the marital fighting and secret marriages to settle down, for some men to take on new domestic chores, and for women to assume more control of their lives within and outside the home. Men recognize they will never regain the kind of automatic authority they once held, and many are fully supportive of the association's new women's empowerment programs that teach women to drive, provide assistance for job applications, support a basket-weaving cooperative, and offer women a space they control to mediate conflicts among themselves. The association recognized that women need collectively acknowledged time and space to come together to talk about their concerns, solve their problems, and share their worries. Women have kept alive the critically important rotating credit associations, through which members each receive periodic infusions of cash, the funerary association that ensures help for funeral costs, and cooperative shopping, which enables families to pool their resources to buy in bulk. These healthy structures of mutual support and solidarity counterbalance the tensions between women over men and between women and men, while also providing an alternative economic model to non-Somalis in Lewiston.

The Value of Wage Work

In today's world of security concerns and the ascendance of a neoliberal definition of personhood (where one's worth is measured by one's wages), we have seen how humanitarianism and charity are subject to a moral economy that assesses worthiness on the basis of quiescent apolitical victimhood or citizenship claims based on a history of economic productivity. In this logic, the only worthy recipients are those defined by abject innocent victimization in refugee camps or American community members defined by citizenship and economic productivity. We have seen how those in refugee camps try to conform to the former image, whereas in the ideology that informs the U.S. refugee resettlement program, new arrivals must immediately get to work to become economically self-sufficient. The implication is that community membership is gained only through economic productivity, conformity, and gratitude.

But Somali Bantus bring a different understanding to the world of paid employment, pushing back against the expectations in a neoliberal economy that one's value is determined by one's economic productivity and that paid employment takes precedence over all other aspects of life. When Sadiq's refugee resettlement assistance ended and he realized that he would have to sacrifice his dream of education for an hourly job, he quit his job to be able to pursue a college degree, and his family applied for welfare assistance instead. He could not accept the American insistence that monotonous, demeaning, dead-end wage work is more important than a college education for very poor people. He eagerly returned to a job after finishing his degree but, like many other Somali Bantu friends, struggled against a logic that placed work ahead of family. Because Somali Bantus have large families, it is not unusual for parents to have to make time to take a child to a doctor's appointment or to address a problem at school. But surprised Somali Bantu friends realized that employers may be reluctant to grant time off to attend to a sick family member, which to them seemed utterly inhumane. One friend who received a phone call at work that his child was admitted to the emergency room left his job in a rush after informing his immediate supervisor, but returned to work the next day to a reprimand from his boss for leaving work early. His boss explained that he should have waited until the end of the workday to go to the hospital. My friend was so distressed by such logic that he quit his job on the spot, incensed that an employer would put a few hours at a job ahead of a sick child. Although this particular employer is a social services agency trying to make connections with the Somali community, every single Somali hired by the agency over the past decade has quit because of such microsupervising.

In addition to family, many Somali employees refuse to relinquish faith practices to conform to work schedules. In one incident, a group of Somali employees at a local factory had negotiated with their supervisor to coordinate break times with appropriate prayer times, but when that supervisor left for a new job, his replacement refused to honor the agreement, insisting instead on a different break schedule that was not in accordance with Muslim prayer times. Indignant, the Somali employees quit. As the story was recounted to me by an involved official, state mediators intervened to resynchronize break and prayer times because the employees had written on their job applications that they needed to be able to pray at work, which obligated an accommodation from the employer. Everyone returned to work, having demonstrated a public point about the relative importance of faith and wage work.

Other Somali values, like loyalty and dignity, sometimes clash with workplace hierarchies. When a local business fired a white supervisor whom all the Somali employees admired and trusted, they quit en masse, explaining to the local newspapers that their loyalty to her superseded their loyalty to the job. The Somalis all returned to work after the embarrassed employer rehired the supervisor, having provided a demonstration of loyalty that was approvingly covered in local newspapers. A friend quit his cashier job at a local big-box store when his supervisor assigned him the additional task of cleaning the bathrooms. Protesting that he was hired for a job that required a professional appearance (and a new wardrobe), my friend chose dignity over a minimum wage.[15] Somali Bantus and Somalis want jobs and explain with pride their strong work ethic and eagerness to work, but they do not subscribe to a perspective that insists that human worth is measured by income, that economic self-sufficiency is the highest value, or that minimum wage jobs trump family, loyalty, faith, and dignity. These first experiences with work in America show their resistance to an all-encompassing definition of belonging and personhood that reduces people to their earning power.

Conclusion

Despite the fractures of factionalization, the struggles within the association over self-representation, leadership status, and internal decision making practices are evidence, for many community members, of their success at creating a new life in America. Their identity assertions gained traction, their leaders gained recognition and invitations to conferences, and (very modest) grants flowed into the association, which became the first Somali Bantu EBCO in the country to have its own office. In this version of Lewiston's story, the refugees made claims about their rights, built a public presence, and commandeered resources for the benefit of their community, which sustained itself through self-help initiatives and a resounding spirit of volunteerism. The fighting is about how to transform internal community politics from a Somali-style model of broad, inclusive democracy to an American-style model of hierarchical democracy. The fighting is about who gets to be on top of the new hierarchy.

Through their efforts to build their own organization and maintain their own structures of support and solidarity, Somali Bantu leaders were defining self-sufficiency and integration for themselves. To them, self-sufficiency means competing for grants to provide programs and casework for community members rather than depending on the helpers, and shielding community members from interventions of local authorities by trying to solve problems through traditional counseling rather than the courts. Self-sufficiency thus means cultural autonomy to handle matters within their own community, but not necessarily economic autonomy, which is a strange concept in a community that insists that resources are things to be shared rather than individually acquired (and where, in any event, resources are scarcely available). I was reminded of the pervasive ethic of sharing one night when I went out to dinner with Idris and Abdirisak. When I asked for the check, Abdirisak said he had already paid, and when I got out my wallet to cover my portion, they both started laughing at my breach of Somali cultural etiquette. "We don't ever do that!" Abdirisak chided me, recounting his astonishment during his first meal at Denny's the previous week, when he watched in amazement as the four white people at the table next to him tallied up their portions of the bill using their cell phone calculators, counting down to the penny. Shaking their heads at such bean counting, they reminded me that whoever has money pays for the whole group, which they find to be a very equitable and fair way to handle money. Like sharing cars, offering to house friends and relatives dislocated by moving or fires, contributing constantly toward each other's wedding, funeral, and other expenses, pooling money to buy food in bulk, and knowing that one income will support entire extended families in Lewiston, Kenya, and Somalia, pooling and sharing resources remains a fundamentally important Somali Bantu cultural value and one that does not mandate constant expressions of gratitude.

Integration, to Somali Bantu refugees, means equality, not assimilation. It means the ability to speak for themselves, have their opinions heard, participate in decisions that affect them, assert their desires, and participate in public presentations as equal community members with a right to voice their views. It means participating in American political, civic, and economic arenas on their own terms, with their cultural values of family, faith, and dignity intact.

Since refugee communities like the Somali Bantus have a history of independent self-management and a strong ethic of intracommunity support, the model of competitive funding for refugee self-sufficiency seems, at first glance, like a good one, allowing refugees to manage their own lives, handle their problems and challenges, and resuture their community ties. There are many indications that this is happening—despite the persistent flare-ups, in 2014 the association office was still an important base for the community, mediating family disputes and providing caseworker support on a shoestring budget. When the

FIGURE 7.1 "Lewiston Is Better Than This," protesters marching down Lisbon Street against Mayor Macdonald's remarks to the BBC, 2012. Photograph by Russ Dillingham / *Sun Journal*.

pregnant wife of a man involved in challenges to the association was tragically killed in an automobile accident, the association led the fund-raising efforts to support the nine children she left behind. When the younger community members broke from the association to form their own youth-focused organization (see chapter 8), Sadiq helped them acquire nonprofit status. Some of those who signed the letter denouncing the association now volunteer in the association's office.

And yet a reliance on EBCOs enhances community isolation and shifts the responsibility for self-sufficiency and integration onto the shoulders of refugee communities, who have the least access to resources, further burdening the structures of community support that are already groaning under the weight of adjusting to life in America. As certain people are empowered as leaders who receive training in leadership capacity and public recognition, one paradoxical result is increased insularity and isolation, as community members value intracommunity communication over intercommunity communication. Those who emerge as leaders because of their positions as cultural brokers or EBCO board members must constantly balance their positions as the public face of their community to granting agencies, local authorities, and the media against the desire by other, usually older, community members who wish to retain pre-resettlement forms of authority and decision making as time-proven structures of community solidarity and mutual support.[16]

Thus for many Somali Bantus, the story of their first decade of resettlement is bound up with struggles to retain some political and cultural autonomy while adjusting to structures of decision making and hierarchy in their new context. Seen from this perspective, refuge is something that Somali Bantu refugees believe they actively fought for, fought over, and forged through struggle and debate. Refuge is an ongoing process of political and cultural negotiation and not a geographical state given to refugees lacking agency.

By the end of their first decade in Lewiston, Somali Bantus had won the right to self-representation and independent translation, gained the respect and recognition of city authorities, had their first community member join the city's school board, and founded their own mosque. Their insistent refusal to tolerate Somali racism shifted intercommunity discourse in the city toward greater collaboration between equals and, currently, Somali and Somali Bantu EBCOs are working toward more collaboration on projects of mutual interest. When Mayor Macdonald condemned Somali immigrants to the BBC in racist, derogatory language, Somalis and Somali Bantus marched together down Lisbon Street to protest his remarks. Holding hand-lettered signs that read, "LEWISTON IS BETTER THAN THIS," "Carpetbaggers: That's White Supremacist-Speak! Translation: Anti-Racist," "Lewiston Welcomes Culture and Diversity," and, most significantly, "IT'S OUR CITY TOO!!! ALL-AMERICAN CITY," Somali and Somali Bantu immigrants are making claims to participatory citizenship on the basis of residence and forging a collective vision of a future city they are (re)making, through constant struggle, together.

CHAPTER 8

These Are Our Kids

We moved here to save our lives. We didn't choose
to come to America. We are refugees. We came
here to find safety, so we could save the lives of
our children, so our children could be safe. But our
children are not safe here. We are terribly worried
about them.
—Somali Bantu father in Lewiston

After one meeting where some of the younger community members and I
attempted, unsuccessfully, to mediate with the breakaway faction responsible for the letter accusing the association of corruption, the young adults
emerged frustrated and angry. One announced that he wanted nothing more
to do with internal community politics, saying that the elders were behaving badly, incapable of good leadership, wasting everyone's time, and tearing
things apart. He was walking away for good. But Idris responded, "There are
so many people who really need help! We can't just leave it like this. We have
to try to make it better and find a solution."

While the community association waged its campaign for self-representation
and traditional counseling to mediate marital disputes, the English speakers
in Idris's generation who worked as translators in the local schools and at

Trinity had a front-row seat to the challenges faced by children arriving from Kakuma and entering public schools in Lewiston. They saw firsthand their trajectories of adjusting to life in America—fashioning new identities relevant to the American context and traversing the vast cultural territory between their home lives and their school lives. They saw that the community elders utterly lacked the capacity to help their children navigate this new world.

Realizing that they were in the best position to work with youth, Idris and his peers created a new EBCO, the Somali Bantu Youth Association of Maine (SBYAM), to focus on youth development. As the Somali Bantu community association did previously, they started with a soccer program for young teens as well as a homework help program for older students, trying to fill afternoons and weekends with activities for Somali-speaking kids shut out of other options. One of their earliest objectives was to encourage a commitment to education, especially for girls. Concerned that not a single Somali Bantu student had graduated from high school by 2008 and that girls were routinely dropping out of high school to get married, SBYAM began in 2008–9 with meetings to encourage youths to focus on their studies and develop a life plan. One of their earliest meetings brought two dozen Somali Bantu teenage girls together for a discussion about the importance of setting career goals, delaying marriage until after high school, and resisting the allure of social media for connecting with boys. The board members all spoke earnestly about their willingness to intervene with parents who might be pressuring the girls to marry before graduating from high school. The meeting was both serious and hilarious, as the young male SBYAM presenter humorously warned about the ways in which boys try to get girls' attention through Myspace, Facebook, and texting: "He'll say, 'I love you, you are my everything!' So much sweet talk! 'Oooh, my sweetheart.' . . . He'll promise you everything!" The assembled girls dissolved into giggles while sharing their experiences with precisely that sort of teenage seduction. Turning serious, the presenter implored them to understand the dangers of social media and the longer-term consequences of ignoring schoolwork in favor of flirting on Myspace and Facebook. Everyone started laughing all over again when one of the young male board members interjected to say he knew the girls spent all their time on social media because that was how he contacted them to invite them to this meeting.

As the straddling generation of their community, acknowledging the wisdom of their elders while recognizing the challenges to their leadership in the new context of life in America, SBYAM board members were walking a very fine line between respecting their elders while subverting their authority by resisting early marriage, insisting that girls finish school, taking on public positions of leadership in the community, and refusing to be drawn into petty skirmishes over identity politics. In 2009–10, as SBYAM members began brokering the yawning cultural gap between non-English-speaking parents and their school-age children, refugee parents asked them for help with their children's behavior; other youth-oriented organizations sought them out for collaboration; and Somali and Somali Bantu adults alike began turning to them for help with gaining competency in American society. This chapter traces the terrain of parenting challenges, children's identity struggles, encounters between children and the juvenile justice system, racism, and culture change that the young adults who formed SBYAM attempted to mediate from 2009 to 2014.

"These Are Our Kids"

One June day in 2009, a group of seven SBYAM board members drove up to my house to work on a grant proposal. We sat around my dining room table for hours to hammer out a proposal to fund their soccer program and start a dance program. Trying to maintain their popular soccer program even when they were denied access to playing fields in Lewiston (because the fields had to rest or were claimed by other city sports leagues who received priority), they had rented an indoor soccer space at a facility near Portland the previous weekend at a cost of $300 per hour, which they paid for themselves. They hoped a grant might bring in funds to offset the personal contributions they were each making to keep their programs afloat. We discussed the budget at length, with some board members wanting to ask for the maximum while others insisted that as a young organization with no track record, they should ask for the minimum and then prove themselves. As we debated the appropriate language, the board members spoke with ease about leveraging their programs, maximizing their impact, developing cultural competency, and following standard protocols for accounting, assessment, and outcomes. Noticing the photograph on my dining room wall of several young children clad in raggedy shorts dashing through the center of Banta in 1988, Abdirisak interrupted our discussion to exclaim, "Look at Banta!" As we all studied the photograph, he asked, "Is one of those little children Idris?" Several of the young men and women at the table, including Idris, were small children in Banta when I lived there, and we interrupted our work to reflect on the trajectory that brought them to my dining room table to talk in bureaucratic language about assessment, accountability, and outcomes.

A month later they learned they did not get the grant, a decision that was reversed in response to protests that the Lewiston-based organization had not funded any grant proposals submitted by local refugee EBCOs. The grant augmented other small amounts they had received for the homework help program and an outreach program about H1N1. As we reviewed SBYAM's growing track record with grants and program development later that year, I noticed Idris's obvious exhaustion and asked about his schedule. He was still working full time as a translator at a local public school, taking four courses toward his degree in social work at the local community college, doing the internship required by his degree program, directing SBYAM, and running the weekend SBYAM soccer and homework help programs, all while raising his three children and mentoring his two younger siblings. He was sleeping about five hours a night. Concerned about his deteriorating health, I suggested he take fewer courses or cut back his work hours, but learned that his job at the school was on an hourly wage, not a salary, which meant he was not paid for snow days, vacation days, or during the summer months. Supporting his siblings back in the refugee camp as well as his family in Lewiston and feeling the pressure to finish school quickly to get a full-time salaried job, he felt he had to be working every minute to keep his goals on track.

But he also felt growing anxiety about how to keep Somali Bantu kids on track in school and in life. As I watched SBYAM develop its programs from 2009 to 2014, I was repeatedly struck by the leaders' sense of having no time to lose. When the accusations about "GANGS" exploded, when suspension rates skyrocketed, when police began apprehending small children shoplifting in local stores, and, after 2012, when Somali Bantu kids ended up in the juvenile detention center, SBYAM leaders felt increasing pressure to develop more youth programs because, as Idris gravely explained, "These are our kids." They were simultaneously working against the demonization of Somali Bantu kids as troublemakers and facing the reality that some Somali Bantu kids were beginning to misbehave because of their repeated failure in school and their parents' confusion about how to parent in America.

Knowing that they were the best-qualified people in town to translate the norms of U.S. society to confounded refugee parents and act as role models for youth, SBYAM began organizing discussions and workshops in response to concerns about youth misbehavior. Parents and youths alike trusted them because of their work history as translators and caseworkers in schools and at Trinity. These jobs gave them the firmest footholds in American society of anyone in the Somali Bantu community and enabled them to arrange meetings where parents and children could talk with police officers, social workers, and juvenile justice authorities in a safe space organized by people they trusted.

Parenting in America

The refugee resettlement program resettled individual families, not communities, so when Somali Bantus from the Banta area relocated to live with each other again in Lewiston, they were trying to resuscitate the structures of mutual support that had allowed them to survive a decade of war and displacement in refugee camps. But parents expecting peace and autonomy found they had few defenses against American values and norms that penetrated and desta-bilized their families. Those families who received welfare assistance, partici-pated in home visit programs, or lived in public housing learned that they had to submit to the surveillance of caseworkers and housing inspectors who monitored household residents, changes in income, parenting practices, and cleanliness. Somali cultural brokers bemoaned the erosion of parental author-ity that accompanied such monitoring because parents are so afraid of making a mistake that might lead to deportation or losing their children to the state.

In addition to the perception that government (including school) authori-ties usurp the power of refugee parents by scrutinizing their behavior, many young adults also point to the novel dimensions of American popular cul-ture that parents have never before encountered. To be sure, many American parents struggle with the impact of popular culture's glorification of sex and violence, youth autonomy and independence, and consumption, but Somali Bantu parents arrived with far fewer tools for confronting and deflecting these cultural influences. As their children quickly became proficient in new technology like TV and the Internet, non-English-speaking parents remained ignorant of what their kids were doing and watching. With no idea how to navigate the new technological and cultural terrain, parents did not know how to intervene, explain, contextualize, or denounce the grotesque aspects of popular culture being consumed by kids fascinated with violent or sexualized video games and music videos or how to help their children define themselves in relation to it, an especially fraught situation in a community recovering from a decade of violence and endemic rape.

One day I took Abdiya's seven-year-old daughter shopping to buy a toy promised in return for a short essay, an experience that revealed to me what mainstream American popular culture aimed at children might feel like to refugee parents. We arrived at Walmart and excitedly headed for the girls' toy aisle. I knew that she really wanted a Hannah Montana doll, but the only dolls on display were rock star models in skimpy clothing: one in a bikini, another sporting a midriff top, miniskirt, and go-go boots. Looking in disappointment over the options, we agreed that these dolls were not what she was looking for. Her eyes wandered to the play makeup—eye shadow, rouge, and lipstick in various colors—but I knew I could not take her home with makeup. Moving on to the jewelry aisle, she spotted huge silver hoop earrings that said "Han-nah" in fancy script and pulled them off the rack hopefully, but, knowing her mother would be unhappy about their enormous size, I gently coaxed her keep looking. At last, an hour later, we chose a Hannah Montana watch and small hoop earrings, and I left the store appalled at how difficult it was to find a toy of a young female teenage popular culture icon appropriate for a modest young girl.

Somali Bantu parents had little experience with navigating the American culture of consumption, where you are what you buy. Their children were subjected to a constant barrage of things to desire, reasons to desire those things, and assurances that they needed those things to be relevant, modern, and American. One school principal whose population is over half Somali Bantu emphasized to me that, more than anything, the Somali Bantu students desperately wanted to be just like everyone else. They quickly abandoned their plastic sandals from Kenya for high-tops and platform wedges and, for boys, the baggy pants and baseball caps of their American peers. Some children began lying to their parents to get consumer items, claiming that their teachers required them to have an iPod or Nike shoes. In their early years in Lewiston, mystified parents pooled and borrowed money to provide these supposed necessities until Somali caseworkers intervened to dispel the deceptions.

Thus, SBYAM is trying to teach parents how to differentiate among consumption demands, how to be relevant in their kids' lives when they do not understand American culture, how to interact with school authorities, how to adopt American approaches to parental discipline, and how to embrace positive aspects of American culture while rejecting the rest. It has been a hard job.

"We Have Freedom Here and You Don't Have to Listen to Your Parents!"

Abdirisak recounted a conversation he overheard between two children at the elementary school when he was dropping off his child. A Somali Bantu boy was describing to a white classmate how much fun he had running around the neighborhood until late at night. The white boy responded that his parents would never let him do that because it was not safe and his parents wanted him home at night so they knew where he was. Abdirisak said the Somali Bantu child explained, "We are living in America! We have freedom here, and you don't have to listen to your parents! That means we can do whatever we want and go wherever we want. Just tell your parents that!" The interchange made a big impression on Abdirisak, leaving him to wonder why Somali Bantu parents were failing to have the kind of control over their children that white parents seemed to have. "Is it because Somali Bantu parents don't know about things like kids getting stolen and that it can be dangerous at night?" he wondered. He, like many other young adults with young children of their own, watched with alarm the waning authority over their children of older refugee parents, trying to piece together the factors that chipped away at family integrity for many Somali Bantu families in Lewiston over their first decade.

Somali Bantu parents arriving in America heard over and over again that physical discipline would be punishable by arrest or deportation and that their children had the right to call 911 to report abuse. Even though parents seldom employed harsh forms of physical discipline in prewar Somalia, newly arrived parents quickly became terrified to exert any form of discipline at all over children who threatened to call 911 if their parents asserted authority against their wishes. Holding the threat of violence in the background even if it was rarely employed meant, in Somalia and Kenya, full parental control. Losing that right without having any suitable replacement, in a context where children gained linguistic and cultural skills much more rapidly than their parents, meant a lot of confused parents and a lot of freewheeling kids.

The stakes were different for girls and boys. When the relaxed approach to parenting young children translated to city life in Lewiston, boys gained greater freedom to run around unsupervised while girls came under increasing scrutiny to behave respectably as parents attempted to protect them from America's public sexual culture in the only way they knew how: early arranged marriage and lots of responsibilities for domestic tasks. During their first decade in Lewiston, as some boys headed toward criminal mischief and some girls chafed at parental control, both genders defined the lessons they learned in school about American freedom and individualism as freedom from parental authority. Living in a culture that celebrates youth and disparages age, where children are given constant lessons that "to be an individual is good," "to make choices for yourself is good," how can parents who utterly lack American linguistic and cultural competency possibly compete with these narratives for respect and parental authority?

Chores formerly assigned to boys—farm work, weeding, watching for birds, and harvesting—no longer exist in Lewiston, but girls are expected to contribute more to household chores than ever before. "Here the girls still do all the household chores, but the boys don't have any farm work so they are totally free to run around," Idris explained to a group of social workers who were interested in providing support to refugee parents. In a different conversation, Sadiq told me, in frustration, "Parents don't require their sons to do anything! They don't help at home, and the parents don't set rules for them." He described the common experience of visiting friends when a teenage son returns late at night, "and the mom just says, 'There's food in the kitchen if you're hungry.' The son doesn't talk to her and she doesn't ask where he's been or what he's been doing."

By 2010, as boys began getting in trouble in the streets at night and as parents unable to control their sons became increasingly alarmed by their misbehavior, SBYAM, the community association, parents, police, and social workers opened discussions about how to engage boys who have no after-school programs or home responsibilities. At a meeting organized by Idris with social workers and community resource police officers to ask for advice about parenting strategies for boys, a female Somali caseworker asked about the kinds of chores American boys do in Lewiston. When the assembled non-Somali social workers suggested cooking, babysitting, sweeping, vacuuming, or cleaning the bathroom, the Somali caseworker and Idris looked at each other dubiously before the woman responded, "Somali culture is so traditional and women and men have such different roles. Men do absolutely no housework or work with the kids. Never." She acknowledged that she has noticed that Somali Bantu men do more household chores than Somali men, especially when the wife is sick or has a new baby, but also emphasized that women and girls are as intent on maintaining distinct gender roles as men: "Girls want to be seen as competent in the household. They want to prove they can do all the household chores. Nothing is expected of boys until they're eighteen, when they're supposed to get a job." Managing all the housework is important to a girl's self-identity and self-worth, and overwhelmed mothers rely heavily on their daughters to keep their households running. While Somali Bantu boys are released from household responsibilities and some begin to become unmoored, some girls begin to chafe at the roles assigned to them. The following two sections offer short vignettes to describe what is at issue for girls and boys adjusting to life with refugee parents in Lewiston.

Raising Girls

"THE WORST THING I HAVE SEEN IN MY WHOLE LIFE"

During a visit to the apartment of Garad and his wife, Halima, the conversation turns, as it often did during 2008–12, to parenting girls. With the ever-popular World Wrestling Entertainment channel on mute in the background and their kids leaping off the couch and wrestling with each other on the floor to imitate the wrestlers, Garad tells me, "If my daughter was in Somalia now at age fourteen, she would be married, but here she has to be eighteen. Here girls watch American girls and behave outside of their religion. In Somalia this would never happen. American girls have boyfriends. They are hugging and kissing in public. This would never happen in Somalia." His wife, who has been playing with their youngest daughter while we talk, interjects, "Our culture is being challenged in America. The worst possible thing is when people see a girl walking with a boy who is not related to her, talking closely. It's very shameful. That's what made us [have early marriage] in Somalia because we couldn't watch our daughters being with boys. It's just so shameful! Here in the U.S., when people see girls on the street talking with boys, they will call the mother and tell on them, and it's awful. Here everyone is very, very worried about their daughters but they are also very scared to confront and control their daughters because the daughters can call the police." I ask, "So . . . how do you control your daughters?" She throws up her hands and says, "We don't!"

Her husband agrees. "That's the worst thing I have seen in my whole life. Parents can't control their kids." He tells me that he understands that his children will grow up in a different culture than his culture and will decide for themselves how they will live, but for the moment he and his wife, among the most loving couples and parents I know, worry about protecting their daughters while trying to guide them toward a life path in a radically different cultural environment.

"DO YOU THINK YOU'LL SEE A SOMALI BANTU GIRL GOING TO COLLEGE?"

Roqiya and Sacadiya, both fourteen, were debating the merits of having a baby during a homework help session. Roqiya proclaimed her disinterest in babies because they require too much work and keep you up all night, to which Sacadiya responded with incredulity, "But you have to have a baby! How can you not have a baby?" A non-Somali tutor who overheard their conversation broke in to suggest that girls don't have to have babies, and in any event can wait until they finish high school to have babies, but Roqiya explained that her parents were insisting that she get married soon rather than attend high school. "My father is very old and he wants to see my babies before he dies, and my mother says I can't go to high school because I have to get married," she explained. She knew it would likely be only a few years before she was up all night with her first baby.

The pressure on young Somali Bantu girls to get married early was intense during their first decade in the United States. Iman, one of the first four Somali Bantus to graduate from high school, watched most of his female peers drop out to get married. "All the daughters hear is that their mothers married at their age and had babies a year later. That's what they know. Do you think you'll see a Somali Bantu girl going to college in the next eight years?" he asked me. "Sure," I responded, but he emphatically disagreed. "No! All they know is their moms were married at fourteen, their sisters married early, and they will be married early. It's not like the Somalis—most of those girls go to college. We don't." Iman considered dropping out of high school himself when a female friend left school for an arranged marriage, but Idris convinced him to graduate and pursue college. Somali Bantu boys know that parents looking for good mates for their daughters do not choose students, so the pressure to marry girls early to young men with jobs also compels young men to leave school in search of work.

To be a good parent means ensuring that your daughter is married to someone you choose or approve of, fulfilling your responsibility to provide her with a spouse. The pressure from relatives in Somalia and in the Kenyan refugee camps to marry daughters early is powerful, and parents in Lewiston find themselves stuck between the insistence by distant relatives to arrange a daughter's marriage and the daughter's desire to stay in school. "They are trying to control the culture from Kenya!" one father tells me, about his attempts by his mother, still living in Somalia, to arrange the marriage for his fourteen-year-old daughter in Lewiston. His daughter now refuses to talk on the phone when his mother calls from Somalia because she is so upset about her grandmother's focus on planning her engagement. Phone calls zip back and forth between Lewiston, Kenya, Somalia, and other American cities as families negotiate potential partners, terms, and dates. For many parents, early marriage is the key to safety, stability, and security for their daughters, but it is also a public demonstration and confirmation of community life. Marriage sits at the intersection of two moral ideologies and support structures: family responsibility and the moral circulation of money through extended family networks that link people across time and space. When arranged marriages are negotiated between family networks that extend across the United States and into Kenya and Somalia, the monetary exchanges that accompany marriage make their way along these networks to implicate a broad range of people in the success of the match. And weddings themselves are community affairs; people routinely travel hundreds or thousands of miles to attend weddings, which last for days and are open to anyone who wishes to attend. When Idris got married in Portland, Oregon, his entire family from Lewiston, most of the SBYAM board members, and the SBYAM soccer team flew to Oregon to support him and join the festivities, which included a soccer tournament with teams from Portland and Seattle and multiple feasts. Weddings are so important to community life that some people, like Sadiq, have started to wonder if they are a problem because people drop everything—their homework, a good night of sleep for the next day's soccer game, jobs, volunteer responsibilities—to attend weddings. But many parents fear that if weddings become individualized affairs arranged between the young couple for guests only of their choice, a linchpin of community life will be lost.

"Snitches!" say the group of Somali Bantu high school girls at an SBYAM meeting when I ask about the worst parts of life in Lewiston. All the girls talk at once, describing the barrage of phone calls that fly between parents reporting to each other on the perceived misdeeds of each other's daughters. "The cell phone is the rumor line!" Xawo complains. Fatuma tells a story about a man who phoned her mother to report that she had left a school event with a group of fellow students and did not go where she was supposed to. She got in terrible trouble with her mother when she returned home, and in a rage she went to the police station the next day to report the man for spying on her. The other girls all tell similar tales about people calling their parents with stories about their behavior and how completely watched and policed they feel. "We are a very snitching community!" Xawo concludes, sadly.

In addition to its importance for community cohesion and transnational connection, early marriage is also about sex. Marrying girls as soon as they can be sexually active ensures that pregnancy happens only in a sanctioned relationship. But as the value of education gains traction, parents are stuck between protecting their daughters from the possibility of out-of-wedlock births and the desire to allow their daughters to finish high school. Girls are trying to balance their new life possibilities in Lewiston and the pressures from diasporic networks and parental concerns about the possibility of sexual impropriety.

It is obvious that girls are under significant stress. Everyone is watching and monitoring and gossiping about their behavior, and Somali Bantu girls are chafing at the burden. "They are carrying the weight of their culture," an ELL teacher observes. When I talk with Somali Bantu high school girls about marriage, I hear the same thing over and over: "I want to be a good daughter." "I want to follow my parent's wishes." "I want to make my parents happy." Some girls are very worried about their overburdened mothers' precarious mental health and do not wish to cause them any more stress. But many of the same girls are also working maniacally in school to demonstrate to their parents the value of their education in order to offer a stronger case against leaving school to get married. Some girls came up with a strategy to promise themselves to a boy of their choosing, approved by their parents, if their parents would let them finish school. Thus their parents feel assured that a good match has been made and that they can monitor their daughter's behavior with the chosen boy until marriage after high school. They want the respect, family honor, and social status that comes with being a good daughter, but it is clear that they also want to have fun in high school without being constantly monitored, reported on, and yelled at by worried parents anxious to protect them.

"It's now well accepted that girls should marry after high school," Sadiq tells me, acknowledging that when girls marry in high school they are unlikely to continue their education because of the demands of family life. But then he acknowledges that nevertheless some parents still feel compelled to arrange marriages for daughters in high school because of fears of out-of-wedlock pregnancy, "the worst possible thing that can happen to a family." Families face social ostracism if a daughter becomes pregnant before marriage, even to the point where people would cross the street to avoid having to greet the father of a pregnant, unmarried girl. "It's not fair that there are no repercussions for the boy," Sadiq acknowledges, but unmarried pregnant girls usually refuse to name the father anyhow.

As if to fulfill their parents' greatest fears, young teenagers were indeed beginning to become sexually active, and by 2012 several girls were pregnant before getting married. A social worker who interacts daily with many young teens and carries a great deal of anger about the ways in which Somali Bantu youths were shut out of programs at school that might have helped them when they first arrived in Lewiston, reflected, "Teenage pregnancy is not about sex. It's about having no hope, no plan for the future." Some parents are even starting to talk about abortion, as news of unexpected pregnancies shoots through the community like lightning. No one knows what to do, and parents start having the same debates one hears in other American communities about providing birth control to unmarried teenagers: will accessible birth control effectively control pregnancy at the cost of encouraging even more teenagers to have sex before marriage? In confusion, some parents begin pulling away from well-meaning social workers who provide information about birth control to unmarried girls, while other parents promote the idea that making birth control available is the only reasonable thing to do.

Families try to work out the lines of responsibility for children born to unmarried girls: Should the couple be forced to marry? Should the father, if the girl reveals his name, be registered with DHHS to ensure child support payments? Should the parents of the boy pay some sort of compensation? Iman tells me, "In the U.S. you don't need a father to have a baby. In American culture, they don't care if the baby has a father. I see [non-Somali] girls all the time getting pregnant and there is no father, and no one cares. We think there *has* to be a father. A father has to pay money if you have a baby. In America they don't mind. They're on their own. But you have to have a father! You have to get help from the father. You can't do everything on your own." Just that morning, the newspaper had reported that over 40 percent of the babies born in the United States in 2007 were born to single women. Iman's insistence thus carried the fear of what might happen if Somali Bantu girls started behaving like American girls, and fathers became dispensable.

"WE ARE REALLY FIGHTING ABOUT THIS IN THE COMMUNITY"

In addition to the desire to protect their daughters and ensure that pregnancy happens only within marriage, everyone recognizes that marriages are also about money exchanges. Marriages occasion donations from friends and neighbors and the transfer of wealth from the groom's family to the bride's. In a context of economic deprivation, the temptation to find a match for one's daughter before she can elope or become pregnant is great because the latter would likely mean forgoing the customary marriage payment. By ensuring the flow of money throughout the community, marriage provides an important economy of support, but when the urgency to marry a daughter runs up against her desire to finish high school, the result can be incredibly stressful for young women who are trying to be good daughters while also achieving academically.

Some girls try to escape altogether by hurriedly eloping with boys of their choice earlier than they would have had to get married, just to ensure they marry someone of their choice rather than someone chosen by their parents they may not like. Several girls have fled the state to avoid arranged marriages, seeking help from other family members or "boyfriends" in other cities. Some girls call 911 to threaten suicide in protest against their parents' plans for their arranged marriage. Parents talk constantly about what to do in cases like these and how to stay within the law while still pursuing arranged marriages as a form of protection for their daughters and economic exchange. Girls know that fleeing or calling 911 might mean an irreparable break from their family support structure. It is an option of desperation.

At a wedding feast in Lewiston in 2007 for one of Sheikh Axmed Nur's grandsons, as the assembled guests sat on mats and pillows eating from platters of roasted goat, corn cakes, cardamom rice, salad, and the bananas present at every meal, a teenage boy arrived home and dutifully circled the room greeting his elders and shaking hands before disappearing into a back bedroom. While many of the elder men wore sarongs and prayer caps, the teenager sported a huge sagging backpack, enormous baggy pants that exposed almost all of his underwear, an oversized sports jersey, gold chains, a sideways baseball cap, and earbuds snaking from his neck to his backpack. Greeting his elders with appropriate Somali phrases, he switched to English when he got to me, asking, "How's it going?" In response I asked how he was, which earned me a grin and the popular rejoinder, "Just chillin." As I watched him leave, thinking about the relationship between his home life and his school life, the conversation turned to concerns about the changes that were infiltrating family life and the new seductions available to the youths. Sheikh Axmed Nur's daughter mentioned that young Somali Bantu men in Syracuse were starting to drink alcohol: they would gather in someone's apartment and drink beer and wine and get very drunk. Lots of discussion ensued about how to handle living in a country where people routinely drink. Then someone turned the conversation toward the ubiquitous theme of marriage. A recent case provided the fodder: a young couple fell in love and went to a sheikh to be secretly engaged in the presence of a witness. The girl's parents had promised her to a different boy, from whom they had received money, and were furious about the deception. They relentlessly pressured her to rescind her promise and agree to marry the boy of their choice, which she eventually did. The wedding guests debated this sequence of events at length: Should the couple have secretly engaged? Should the witness have informed the mother? Should the sheikh have sanctioned the secret engagement? Should the mother have tried to intervene, since the engagement already happened in the presence of the sheikh? Should the girl be allowed to change her mind after promising to marry the boy of her choice? Everyone in the room had a different opinion about the conduct of all the parties, arguing about what tradition and Islam do and do not allow, about the extent to which girls should have the freedom to choose their marriage partners, and about the ongoing propriety of arranged marriages in America. Everyone is confused about the moral course of action for protecting daughters, following the rules of customary economic exchanges that cement marital ties, and recognizing the new cultural context of extended educational opportunities for girls.

Some Somali cultural brokers have adamant feelings about culture change. A Somali caseworker told me that she tells her friends who phone her to come celebrate a young daughter's wedding, "No! I cannot come celebrate this!" She cautions her friends about their daughters, "When you marry and have a baby you are set back five years," trying to convince her community that early marriage is destructive rather than protective of girls. "We are really fighting about this in the community," she tells me. Although SBYAM tries to disrupt the practice by encouraging girls to resist the pressures from their parents to marry before finishing high school, they realize that it can be very hard for a girl to go against parental wishes and that standing between girls and their parents might undermine the efforts they are making in other areas to strengthen waning parental authority. They are stuck between helping girls pursue education and convincing parents whose authority they are working to bolster to refrain from using that authority to arrange early marriages.[1]

Reflecting on the new strategies girls are pursuing to avoid arranged marriages, Sadiq tells me, "We must stop doing this. We cannot make girls marry against their will, and they cannot keep marrying so young. The problem is that as soon as a parent sees their daughter talking to a boy they assume the worst and arrange the marriage. But talking to a boy doesn't mean anything!" While SBYAM is working to offer support to girls to finish high school before marriage, Sadiq hopes the community association's women's empowerment program can finally open a space for women to address their concerns about their daughters in ways that allow for outcomes other than early marriage.

A Somali politician and activist known for her anti-Islam pronouncements, Ayaan Hirsi Ali, writes in her autobiography about the patriarchal abuses of Muslim Somali culture, posing the Somali confrontation with the West as dichotomous and Manichean.[2] But SBYAM advocates schooling for girls, cautions parents against early marriage, and helps girls to negotiate around unwanted arranged marriages. The young adults involved in SBYAM are trying to teach against an American orientation of instant gratification, immodesty, and children who order their parents around while demonstrating respect for some American values, like education for girls, alongside Somali and Muslim values, like respect for adults, modesty, and an orientation toward family. The efforts by SBYAM and other Somali and Somali Bantu leaders to promote girls' education and stop early marriage show that Islam and Somali culture in Lewiston is not the Islam and Somali culture of Hirsi Ali's memory. They are trying to show how Somali culture is adaptable to rather than replaceable by life in America.

Raising Boys
"THEY'RE FAILING EVERY MINUTE OF EVERY DAY"

The first thefts by Somali Bantu boys occurred in 2009, when young kids stole a few things from visitors at Trinity that Kim easily recovered. When the panic about "GANGS" hit the news, it was apparent to Idris and many others that kids becoming disarticulated from parental authority and emotionally battered at school were going to be in trouble. "We are sitting on a time bomb," a worried social worker observed to me about the dual impact of waning parental authority and school alienation. Sadiq warned, "Some parents are raising their children here just like they did in Africa. They just run around, play freely, coming home to eat when they feel like it. But here there are so many dangers. The parents don't really even grasp the dangers."

But what are the dangers? In a conversation with a social worker friend one day, she predicted dire difficulties ahead for Somali Bantu boys who take to the streets because they are bored at home and ignored by parents who are busy with so many other children, work, classes, and appointments. In response I played devil's advocate, telling her that I always ran around my neighborhood as a kid and my parents never knew where I was or what I was doing. It wasn't a problem, just an old-fashioned American childhood. Why was it a problem for these kids? She hesitated, then said, "I don't want this to come out wrong, but the issue is, they're black. They are black kids in America. They are perceived as a problem in public and they're labeled that way." I think about the panic precipitated by the GANG memo, how quick the newspaper was to promote the image of "Somali youths attacking vulnerable white people," the demand that the police target Somali kids walking home from school as troublemakers, the high suspension rates, and agree that she is right.[3] The social worker believes that black children running around the downtown provoke fears and insecurities in authorities who treat those children like criminals, which the boys then internalize as part of their emerging Americanized identities.

A Somali activist explains another consequence: "Our kids have no defenses and our parents don't understand what's at stake, what their kids are being exposed to. We are seeing it and learning about it all at once, and our kids are so vulnerable to getting sucked in." She wants to be clear that there are many good things about American culture—she names technology, women's reproductive health, education—but that the bad things, such as consumerism, youthful disrespect and misogyny in popular culture, the valorization of exaggerated "ghetto" performance in music videos, explicit images of sex and violence on the Internet, are all new things for them with which parents have no experience.

Her point is affirmed by ELL teachers, who notice the power of popular culture's black urban ghetto aesthetic for Somali Bantu boys, although not for the girls, who seem more invested in their parents' culture. "I see it in the register," one teacher says. "Some want to be American so badly they adopt the register of black rap talk." She describes how she intervenes to require them to use "classroom language," because she believes some young people still learning English really do not understand the difference in registers and need her to tell them. Many teachers and social workers affirm that Somali boys do not really identify with African American culture as portrayed in the media, but Somali Bantu boys do. In contrast to Somali boys, Somali Bantu boys "*know* they're black," the social worker says. "They were the lower caste in Somalia and they are here in America too. They adopt the look, the attitude, the swagger, the swearing." It's a pose, like trying on an identity. Teachers and police concerned about escalating aggressive behavior of some of their Somali Bantu male students attribute it to the violence they absorb from video games, music videos, the Internet, and which surrounds them in downtown life. One frustrated teacher remarks that dealing with aggressive behavior through suspensions and expulsions rather than positive school interventions solves no problems and only produces a self-perpetuating cycle.

Another worried teacher tells me, "Kids [from refugee families] are getting extremely frustrated with their rate of failure. They're failing every minute of every day." The girls can still find validation in their household skills, but the boys, most especially those who cannot participate in sports because they are still in ELL classes, have nothing. Sports make a huge difference for Somali Bantu boys, many teachers tell me, because it provides one arena in which they are not failing and where they are equal with their peers. An ELL teacher explains, "They know they're not good in the classroom. They know they're not equal, but they can be equal on the soccer field. They can excel on the soccer field." That so many ELL students cannot join sports teams is one more experience of alienation.

"UNIVERSAL SHIT STORM"

By 2009, parents, and especially single mothers, were beginning to grasp the dangers and turned to Idris for advice about how to control their boys who were staying out all night. Parents tried to keep their sons safely at home by buying things like computers, TVs, DVD players, Xbox games, and cell phones, but some were still disappearing for hours or even days with their phones turned off. A sympathetic community resource police officer told me, "The parents are just breaking down. They don't know what to do."

Mothers overwhelmed by many children and not enough help who were losing touch with their children became a constant topic of discussion among social workers in the collaborative, who worried that the emotional and physical history of trauma carried by many refugee women interfered with their ability to feel connected to their children. As some of the mothers lost control of their sons, their expectations that life would be better here evaporated into the reality of living "a worrisome life," as one Somali Bantu father put it. While maintaining confidentiality, mental health counselors in the collaborative who worked with refugee women reported that their overwhelming topic of concern was their children. A Somali Bantu caseworker told me, "Women do not want to talk about their rapes and the violence they experienced in the camps. Instead they want things to go well for their children. That is what will make them feel better." A mental health counselor said her worried refugee clients were navigating a "universal shit storm" of life in America, assaulted by one thing after another: poverty, sickness, trauma, many kids, exhaustion, confusion, illiteracy, demands for home visits by social workers, and, of course, the weather. Having a child suspended or arrested pushes them right to the edge.[4]

In response to appeals from parents caught in the universal shit storm and afraid of losing their children, Idris began organizing confidential meetings between parents, community police resource officers, community worker Janet Saliba, and social workers from the collaborative to create a safe space where parents could ask questions, get help, and feel supported. Unlike the focus groups or school meetings where parents were supposed to respond to agendas set by the organizers, these meetings belonged to the parents. Idris, Janet, the officers, and the social workers offered simply to listen to the parents and brainstorm about ideas for helping them regain their authority as they figured out how to parent in America.

"OUR CHILDREN ARE NOT SAFE HERE"

The first meeting Idris organized (in 2010) included ten parents whose children were in the most trouble at school and with the law. Unsurprisingly, suspensions topped the list of concerns articulated by stressed parents. One after another, the parents asked, "Why are our kids the ones in trouble?" "When you see kids in trouble, it's always Somali, Somali Bantu, Somali, Somali Bantu. Why is that?" "Why have we come here to have our children always in trouble? Does the school hate our children? Do they want us to leave?" One father asked, pointedly, "Is it because we're black?" The parents shared example after example of suspensions and their failed efforts to communicate with the schools. As different parents broke down, crying and clearly in great distress, other parents comforted them as Idris and the others affirmed their stories and listened, quietly, to story after story. One woman started sobbing as she explained her confusion about why her sons were always suspended even though she could not understand why. "What is happening?" she asked. "Why is this happening to us?"

After social workers offered to go to the schools with the parents to ask about suspensions, several parents wanted to talk about the GANG allegations against their children. "Gangs are something new!" one parent explained. "We don't know what they are. We don't know if our children are involved." One parent begged the police to talk to the parents of children who were involved because "no one knows anything about this." The assembled parents nodded their agreement when one parent explained, in the passage quoted in this chapter's epigraph: "We moved here to save our lives. We didn't choose to come to America. We are refugees. We came here to find safety, so we could save the lives of our children, so our children could be safe. But our children are not safe here. We are terribly worried about them."

The police calmed the parents by explaining that despite the newspaper reports, their children were not forming gangs. A few older kids had collared a few younger kids to do their bidding—stealing small things, taunting other children, and so forth—but the police had identified the older instigators and were working with them, assuring the assembled parents that their children could be "redirected to more positive activities." The officers, Janet, and social workers offered the parents lots of suggestions about precisely the amount of physical force a parent can wield with a misbehaving child and described strategies used by American parents to exert discipline by taking away privileges or offering small rewards for good behavior. The mood lightened a bit when one parent asked the police to make sure her son wasn't kissing girls in the park, which elicited approval from the parents, laughter from the policeman, and a lengthy discussion about the limits of police authority and the worrisome turn to public romance by teenagers. For parents who have never witnessed young people kissing in public, it is hard to differentiate between appropriate and inappropriate displays of affection according to American standards. All public kissing is shocking.

In a later conversation, one of the resource officers reflected, "The parents have bought their kids all these American things that the kids demand: cell phones, Xboxes, electronics, and the parents don't know they can take these things away. There's a certain dynamic that the parents just don't know about, that you have the right as a parent to take away stuff and privileges. That if your child takes off out of anger, it's not a bad reflection on you, and you should call the police for help. We're educating the parents to talk to each other and give each other support. The kids are irritated about it, but the parents are starting to regain control now. We're seeing a difference. The kids are behaving better and now there's more fear of getting in trouble and getting caught."

A few weeks later, the first Somali Bantu children were arrested and sent to the juvenile detention facility on a charge of assault, and the news flew through the community like a shock wave. Then another child stole money from his parents that he distributed to his friends, many of whom promptly went shopping. Idris, Janet, and Kim tracked down the story, pulled all the implicated boys and their parents into a meeting with the police, and remained in the room together until the boys accounted for every penny. The items were gathered and returned and the money reimbursed. For many of the boys involved and their parents, this meeting was a turning point because the children saw their parents as competently allied with the police and other adults in monitoring their behavior and holding them accountable. Everyone agreed that the following summer was one of the quietest yet as the community resource officers, SBYAM members, and parents worked together to better supervise and monitor the children's behavior. Through Idris's meetings, parents learned they could ask the officers for help without being labeled bad parents, and the kids learned they could not pull the wool over their parents' eyes any longer with threats of calling 911 or claims about their freedoms in America.

"The Youth Are in a Different Culture"

And yet intergenerational gaps grew wider. In 2010, Idris asked me to help organize a history project for Somali Bantu teenagers, who were asking him about why they were in America and why they were called Somali Bantus. I thought back to a conversation with Abdiya's nine-year-old son the previous year. Looking at photographs I had brought to the family's apartment of Abdiya as a young woman in Banta and of his late grandfather, the little boy asked, "Why did we come here?" I told him there was a war and his mother had to leave her village to keep her family safe. "Why was there a war?" he persisted. "Did white people come and attack us?" Idris was concerned that young people had no idea about their history and suggested that a project for youths to interview their parents and grandparents about their lives in Somalia before the war and about the war itself might be a wonderful opportunity to teach Somali Bantu teenagers about their history while fostering intergenerational communication. We secured a small grant to cover expenses and held meetings with interested teenagers to develop a basic set of questions. The teenagers set out to begin their interviews, but we quickly discovered that the young people could not understand their parents' stories recounted in Somali or Maay Maay. The language was too hard, the cadence unfamiliar, the vocabulary too complex. Surprised, we regrouped and decided that SBYAM board members would participate as translators in each interview, assisting the parents and their children to talk with each other. The extent of the intergenerational communication breakdown was a revelation.

By 2013, SBYAM leaders were trying different kinds of projects to help parents and children learn to talk to each other. At one meeting, Ahmed taught elementary school children to tell their parents about school when they got home before going out to play. "Tell your parents something about your school day every single day," he suggested. "Show them your report card and what it means. Bring your parents to school and introduce them to your teacher. Try hard to communicate with your parents by telling them when you are leaving the house, where you are going, and who you will be with. Tell them, 'I'm going to the park! I'm going to Abdi's house!'" He reminded them that because their parents didn't speak English, they had to put in the effort to keep communication open. "Make little private jokes with your mom so you can laugh and have fun together," he advised.

While encouraging kids to be more conversant with their parents, SBYAM leaders were also teaching parents what questions to ask their kids. When

Ahmed suggested to one parent that she could ask her child about school when he got home, the mom responded in confusion, "But what is there to ask?" Having never been to school, she had no conception of what she might talk about. The sad result, noticed by SBYAM leaders and social workers alike, is that some Somali Bantu children think their parents do not care about them. They see their parents consumed by the demands of managing life in Lewiston with very large families, and when they get home from school, parents rarely have time to sit and talk. Girls arrive home from school to be put in charge of babysitting younger siblings or cooking dinner; boys drop off their backpacks and immediately dash back outside again. The communication gap widens as the children become increasingly fluent in English and abandon Somali. One mother tells me that her two youngest children only speak English, not Somali, and since she cannot speak English, they never communicate.

One young friend described overhearing how some white parents talk to their kids when they drop them off at school, saying loving things, hugging them, and telling them, "Have a nice day, honey." He tells me that he wants his mom to talk to him like that too, but, instead, "She yells at me like I'm a two-year-old." A white social worker who works closely with Somali Bantu children says, "These kids think they don't need their parents. They take care of themselves. They don't think their parents love them. I can't tell you the number of kids who say their parents don't care about them. The girls say their moms want them to get married so they don't cause shame, not because they care about whether or not they are happy. Parents don't talk to their kids, never pay attention to them, never ask them anything. They don't know how."

But SBYAM leaders know parents are trying to show their love. Arranging a safe marriage is a form of love; cooking and ensuring food is available whenever your child comes home is love; overcoming your fear to talk with police about how to parent in America is love; attending parent meetings to rage about suspension practices is love; buying electronics in an effort to keep your children playing at home rather than in the street is love. I think back to village life in prewar Somalia, when parents and kids worked together during the day and relaxed together in the evenings, telling stories and jokes. I don't remember parents ever asking, "What did you do today?" or "How are you feeling today?" Kids played and helped in the fields and listened to parents' stories and advice, but no one ever asked children to explain what they were doing or feeling. But here, in America, young people live in totally different worlds than their parents. "There is no family life," a Somali caseworker laments. "There is no connection. In America everyone is busy on different time schedules. Parents and older siblings are working different hours. Everyone comes and goes independently. No one talks to each other." One parent tells me about the intergenerational breakdown in communication: "The youth are in a different culture."

Drug Dealers in the Park

In 2013, a Somali Bantu friend whose office window overlooked the downtown park began to realize that drug dealers from other cities were coming to Lewiston, using the park as a distribution center, and roping in young children from the refugee community as runners. Shocked about this recent turn of events, my friend began calling parents to come get their children. But the drug dealers were so intimidating that the moms who came to collect their children ended up going home alone. My friend said, "The men are telling the women to control their children, and the women are yelling at the men, 'What do you know? You just sit out there under a tree all day long and don't know anything about the kids.'" I asked my friend, "Well, why aren't the men taking responsibility for the kids and keeping them away from the drug dealers?" He looked at me like I was clueless and said, "What can the men do? Their kids don't even know them. They try to call their kid over and the kid ignores them like they don't even know them. The kids don't have anything to do with their dads. The dads can't stand up to the drug dealers, besides." A social worker tells me that she thinks Lewiston will become the next major drug distribution center in the state because the drug dealers are beginning to figure out that they can control the children of refugee parents. This disturbing story resonates with many other stories I was hearing about the severed connection between fathers and their children, as older refugee men's authority waned both with their children and their wives.

Men's relationships with their children are one dimension of their overall loss of authority, as described in chapter 7. Attempting to maintain disciplinary control in an environment where children claim freedom and autonomy from parents has forced some men into inflexible and authoritarian expressions of parental authority that are increasingly simply ignored by their children. "The relationship is broken because the dads don't know how to talk to their kids," a Somali Bantu social worker tells me. He recounts an example of working with a father whose son was struggling with behavioral problems. The father was attempting to parent by issuing demands and orders, setting rigid boundaries for the child. My friend suggested that the father should try talking with his child rather than setting strict rules: "If there is something big to discuss, like moving apartments, taking a trip, or another family decision, talk it over with your child and involve him in your decision making." The father was mystified about what it might mean to involve his child in his decision making, a totally foreign concept to him. Listening to this story, I thought of a recent conversation with Sadiq, who told me in astonishment, "The other day I was discussing with my wife our plans for a vacation this summer, and my daughter came into the conversation telling us what we should and shouldn't do for vacation!" His daughter had overheard friends at school talking about Hawaii, so she was insisting that the family should visit Hawaii for their vacation. "I've never even heard of Hawaii!" Sadiq says, laughing. He is proud of his daughter for developing into an assertive young woman, but nonetheless finds the attitude challenging, telling me, "In Somalia, the home was like a dictatorship, but here it's a democracy." Children who have been taught never to look an adult in the eye while talking to them learn at school always to look adults in the eye, disturbing parents who experience direct eye contact as disrespectful. Like direct eye contact, involving one's children in one's decision making is something completely new. While Somali Bantu community members struggle to replace their participatory and democratic political decision-making practices with a more exclusive, representative, and hierarchical American model, they are similarly challenged to replace their model of hierarchical family structure based on absolute parental authority with a more democratic approach to parenting that grants children far more power in the household than ever before. It is this style of American parenting, involving negotiation, dialogue, collaborative decision making, and the management of privileges that SBYAM is attempting to make available to parents.

Somali Bantu American Youth Identity

One day when Somali and Somali Bantu high school students were looking over my photographs from Somalia, a few began debating whether the photographs depicted Somali life or only Somali Bantu life. When one of the young Somali Bantu boys asked, "What's the difference?" a Somali girl said, "You are different. You have bigger noses and different dances," a statement that several other Somali Bantu students challenged as incorrect. Such questions and confusions prompted Idris's desire to create the oral history project for young teenagers who were asking him, "Why are we called Somali Bantu?" In our first meeting with the teenagers, they spoke heatedly about the ways in which their Somali peers used the term "jareer" to distinguish and denigrate them. Fatuma complained that her Somali classmates used the term all the time, but only in a derogatory way, which so enraged her that she actually fought the girls who taunted her with it. She and the other girls described how Somali girls sometimes snatched off their headscarves in the school bathrooms to get a look at jareer hair, provoking physical fights. Everyone in the meeting agreed that whereas "jileec" is used to describe all kinds of soft things such as fabric and paper, "jareer" is only used to describe people and only in a bad way.

Some of the SBYAM board members at the meeting brought up a Bollywood film dubbed in Somali that they had watched together the previous weekend: "We were really enjoying it—it was such a nice love story. But then the bad guy was described as jareer! We couldn't believe it! We rewound the sound to listen over and over and yes, it was true, the Somali translation used the word 'jareer' to describe the bad guy. The movie was ruined." The teenagers all agreed that, as one girl put it, "Whenever you hear 'jareer,' it's only in a bad way." Fatuma shared her dismay that when she phones the Line of Seduction, a Somali social networking phone line that people can call to join any one of a number of simultaneous conversations about a wide variety of topics, someone always asks her whether she is jareer or jileec. She knows and resents the fact that identifying herself as jareer puts her in an inferior category. While their older siblings and the young adults in the community express pride in their identity as Somali Bantus, finding it personally meaningful and instrumentally useful, teenagers are much more interested in tossing out the Somali Bantu label altogether because they experience it in youth culture as uniformly pejorative.

Idris opened one of the history project meetings by asking the teenagers, "Why did we come to America?" No one knew. "People died so we could come here. Do you know about that?" he asked. Everyone shook their heads. One teenager responded with a question: "Why were we selected to come here, and why are we called minorities?" This prompted an outpouring of other questions: "Where did the word 'Somali Bantu' come from?" "Why do Somali Bantus speak three different languages?" "Why isn't there a Somali Bantu language if there is a Somali Bantu group?" "What's the relationship of Somali Bantus to Reer Shabelles? To Mushungulis? To Bantus?" "What's the difference between jareer and ooji?" The questions expanded as Fatuma asked, "What's the relationship between *qabil* [clan] and village?" Xawo added, "And what is qabil anyway? I am so confused!" It became apparent that while the teenagers were interested to learn about these parts of their history, they did not expect the names would be significant to them in America. And it was particularly clear that they had no interest in maintaining an identity as Somali Bantus.

Some of the English-speaking young adults worry about what will replace Somali Bantu identity, as they watch their younger siblings adopting the stereotypes of black identity presented in popular culture, which is the predominant experience Somali Bantu children have with African Americans. Young adults who remember life in Kakuma and who arrived in the United States with enough English to graduate from high school try to model values based in Somali culture and Muslim faith while seeking success through education, American style, by trying to replace exaggerated popular iconography of ghetto culture with alternative models of how to be black, Muslim Somali Americans.

One college student who graduated from Lewiston's high school, Abdi, says, "When we got to Kakuma, we saw that our people who were well educated got jobs. They were our teachers. They could buy bicycles. They worked hard and got jobs because of it. We knew about the limitations in Somalia because our parents talked about it, so we began to understand the importance of education." Their self-confidence and self-worth were forged, in part, by seeing people in the older generation, like Sadiq, achieve success as teachers and leaders. But they fear that because their younger siblings growing up in America do not have the experience they had in Kakuma, they are not as directed and are more susceptible to the derailing threats of consumerism, sex, drugs, crime, and negative representations of blackness in the media. Ahmed, the eldest of five brothers with a single mother, interjects, "We feel really responsible for our younger brothers. It is only me to help my brothers make good decisions. Here there are so many choices and you have to always make sure you are making good decisions." Abdi and Ahmed call their younger brothers and sisters "the in-between generation," not fully American but also not Somali. Like Garad and Halima, they are uncomfortable seeing younger teens kissing and holding hands in public, changing their dress styles to mimic ghetto aesthetics, and becoming detached from Muslim practice. Ahmed talks about the experience of living in a Muslim soundscape in the refugee camp, where days were punctuated by the call to prayer over loudspeakers and sheikhs in the street paused to give children advice or blessings. Alienated from parents and school, lacking an enveloping sensory Muslim environment, losing the Somali language, learning to kiss and hold hands in public, adopting an aesthetic of street toughs, being viewed as problems in school and on the streets: these are the things that really worry Ahmed, Abdi, Idris, and the other young SBYAM leaders as they try to provide alternative role models for how to be black and Muslim in America.

Assimilation?

Ideas about immigrant assimilation based on the experiences of European immigrants to the United States that predict that each generation will be more assimilated (to mainstream, white American society) than their parents ignore the very different terrain of incorporation and integration navigated by immigrants of color. Studies in the 1990s offered more nuanced models of integration that attended to factors like racism, discrimination, poverty, social capital, family support, class status, and spatial geography.[5] These studies suggested that immigrants of color who experience poverty, racism and discrimination in schools and the job market, a breakdown in intergenerational communication, the loss of parental authority, and demographic ghettoization may experience downward mobility, "dissonant acculturation" in which children and their parents are acculturating at different rates, or "segmented assimilation" in which the second generation assimilates to minority, "adversarial," or "oppositional" American culture.[6] "Children of immigrants experiencing the most difficult economic and social conditions are more prone to see themselves as part of undifferentiated American minorities," write two scholars who conducted much of the early work on race and acculturation.[7] In her 1994 review of the new research of these and other scholars on the significance of race for integration, sociologist Mary Waters summarized, "The second generation that casts their lot with America's minority groups will most likely be at risk of downward social mobility."[8]

A decade later, scholars again nuanced these models of downward mobility and assimilation to oppositional American culture. Sociologist Philip Kasinitz noted that those who believe assimilation is harmful to immigrants of color because assimilation will mean downward mobility "point to the destructive effects of racialization into 'ghetto' or 'underclass' culture. But the aspects of culture they point to—individualism, nihilism, materialism, the high rate of marital breakup, the low rate of saving, the low value it places on education, the high degree of penetration by mass media—are hardly unique to any real or imagined 'culture of poverty.' They are precisely the supposed aspects of 'ghetto' life that most closely approximate, albeit in extreme form, the ways of the broader society."[9]

Kasinitz and other scholars warn against assuming that the adoption of any of these cultural practices is by definition an indication of downward mobility or oppositional acculturation: "ghetto" style may be sartorial and not substantive; "ghettoized" ethnic enclaves may provide a structure of social buffering that nurtures community networks, support structures, and entrepreneurial initiatives; the second generation may develop a much more fluid identity that embraces some aspects of American culture alongside values inherited from their parents; assimilation might mean embracing civil rights projects of social transformation rather than simply negatively expressed oppositional culture; and ongoing transnational and diasporic networks might counter racism and provide, instead, globalized networks of belonging and affirmation.[10]

The small but growing literature on Somali youth in the diaspora expresses concerns about the challenges Somali American youth face from racism and discrimination and the likelihood that they will experience dissonant acculturation because of poor intergenerational communication, loss of parental authority, family fragmentation, and identity crises, leading them to "adopt the mantle of [North American] blackness" and oppositional culture.[11] Acknowledging the newness of Somali immigration to the United States, Kapteijns and Arman suggest dissonant acculturation is already "rampant" in Somali refugee communities but express hope that a strong sense of ethnic pride, enduring cultural values, and a coherent community identity (which together constitute "Soomaalinimo" or "Somaliness") can provide a buffer for Somali American youth to maintain connections to their parents and Islam while also forming relationships with people in mainstream society.[12] Other scholars note the importance of participation in diasporic networks for Somali youth in the diaspora, maintained through phone calls, the Internet, the circulation of DVDs and videos, phone chat rooms, and so forth, through which youths simultaneously forge "three or more different kinds of identity" (transnational Somali, transnational Muslim, and localized).[13] One study of Somali American youth in Boston suggests that youths are playing with American popular culture hip-hop swagger without losing their connection to Somali cultural identity and values, noting that, for the youths in the study, "acting like an American was not equated with becoming an American" because of Somali resistance to racism, strong Muslim identification, and an "internal moral compass as Somalis."[14]

But Somali Bantu children are in a slightly different position than Somali children because they experience racism as black people in America but also from their Somali peers. The emerging response of Somali Bantu youths in Lewiston embraces their sense of "Somaliness" while rejecting the racism that accompanies the Somali Bantu moniker and adapts, perhaps with more enthusiasm than their Somali peers, aspects of American hip-hop sartorial culture. I am wary of arguing that this means Somali Bantu youths are "in between" cultures or culturally fragmented because fragmentation or inbetweenness implies another state that is "whole," which is never the case. Somali Bantu American kids are used to having identities or subjectivities that emerge from their many social relations because of fluid family structures and extended kinship networks. Their subjective orientation to the world is not as distinct individuals passing through, negotiating different cultural realms, but as people constituted by their associations and relations in all these realms simultaneously.[15] "Wholeness" is a presumption that Henrietta Moore calls a "pretheoretical commitment," a state that is assumed as normal when in fact it is imagined, but which then becomes the norm in contrast to which some people are imagined as fragmented.[16] But there is no whole Lewiston culture, no whole African American culture, and no whole Somali Bantu culture. The first encompasses the xenophobes and the helpers, racism and welcome, nasty and compelling values promoted in popular culture. The second includes mainstream role models like Barack Obama and gangsta rap stars. The third is constituted through debates about the historical legacy of difference, a full embrace of Somaliness, Islam, and changing cultural practices.

The Somali Bantu youths I know are drawing on attachments to teachers, parents, extended family members, sheikhs, popular culture icons, young adult role models, white and Somali peers, and those with whom they interact on international Muslim websites and phone chat rooms.[17]

While the experiences of Somali Bantu youths fashioning lives in Lewiston may be more extreme, many youths behave differently in school and in public than at home, and all kids creatively make youth culture with their peer group that draws on a selected popular culture styles, bodily and sartorial practices, technology, language, and more. Somali Bantu youths may have more disparate possibilities from which to choose, but they are constituting themselves across an array of possibilities and choices, which is different than saying they are fragmented and thus confused. Because they are in their first decade of playing with and making meaningful the values and performances that constitute their identity, they are not yet finished (and, of course, will never be). What matters is which associations and performances receive positive validation and which get them into trouble. The leaders of SBYAM are trying to make sure that they, as role models, are part of the conversation, inserting positive values of parental engagement, adherence to Islam, respect for authority, service to the community, prioritizing education, maintaining transnational family and cultural connections, and being proud of their identity as Africans. They offer soccer programs and African dance sessions, homework help and prayer as part of their open house events. Through videos, DVDs, and YouTube they follow and practice the latest dance moves from Kenya, and through Islamic Internet sites they address questions of romance, dating, love, interpersonal relationships, and making ethical Muslim choices in a Christian context. They bolster parental authority while also helping parents embrace new cultural outlooks and practices. They recognize that the real challenges for Somali Bantu American kids are poverty and racism, so they fight racist stereotypes about GANGS while also strengthening the community bonds that give Somali Bantu refugees resilience and offering points of contact with mainstream society to help youths craft successful life trajectories of their own design.

In this way, SBYAM is trying to ensure that Somali values of sharing, mutuality, faith, family, and parental authority remain strong, that personal identities constituted through the social rather than the material remain in place, and that destructive popular-culture caricatures of blackness do not gain hegemony, trying, instead, to construct blackness as rooted in a Somali and Muslim value system and a cultural diasporic consciousness. Idris explains that a central part of SBYAM's mission is to show kids how to live in the face of racism without letting it define them and provoke a constantly reactionary stance. "Words like the 'n' word and 'adoon' are words and they aren't going away," he says. Thus, SBYAM focuses its efforts on teaching young people to live as black Somali Bantus in a world where such words exist.

Like immigrants before them, Somali Bantu refugees face economic penury in a context of assumptions about the moral imperatives of self-help initiatives, xenophobia and racism, exclusion, and tolerance as the highest form of acceptance. Like immigrants before them, they rely on support from kin and ethnic enclaves. Like immigrants before them, their family structures and cultural practices morph under the protective and invasive intervention of legal authorities and social services providers. Like immigrants before them, they face intergenerational chasms, arguments about the morality of culture change, and language loss. Like immigrants before them, they are building their own civic institutions, demanding civil rights, and exerting their own forms of political engagement. Among the many things that are particular to their experience is their blackness in a country of dichotomous race, their religion in a country that fears Islam, their strong and technologically enhanced diasporic ties, their minority status within the broader Somali diaspora, and their cultural comfort with mobility. How these dimensions of their identities will unfold as they start their second decade in the United States is unclear. Will they be able to blur the race line and confound the categories? Will they be able to normalize Islam as another mainstream American religion? Will their diasporic belongings and mobilities shape youth culture in novel ways in the future?

Toward Advocacy

When a few Somali Bantu children started getting arrested after 2010, SBYAM added workshops on the juvenile justice system to their roster of activities, hoping to teach children and their parents about what happens when you break the law and have to go to court. For these workshops, SBYAM gathered a panel of authorities including police officers, a judge, a court-appointed advocate, and others who work with youths in the justice system to help kids and their parents understand the consequences of arrest. These meetings were fascinating moments of engagement between the white Lewiston establishment and Somali Bantu kids and parents, where everyone had to work to overcome language barriers and learn how to communicate effectively. A description of one of the juvenile justice panels shows why.

Each panelist was asked to speak for five minutes about his or her role in the juvenile justice system, after which parents and children in the audience could ask questions. It was immediately apparent which panelists were accustomed to speaking through translators and which were having a brand-new experience. The community resource police officer, who had worked with SBYAM in the parent meetings described above, knew just how long to talk before pausing for the interpreter to translate, producing a seamless, balanced pattern of English, Somali translation, English, Somali translation. Those who had never spoken through translators failed to pause for translation, forcing the translator to interrupt when the flow of English stretched beyond the boundaries of adequate translation and then cutting back in to begin talking in English again before the translator finished speaking.

Once the panelists and their translators were finished, parents and children in the audience were invited to ask questions, and new communication difficulties became clear as the metaphors used by speakers sounded outrageous in translation. In response to the query of one child who asked, "How do you become a police officer?" the chief of police answered, "Stay in school [several kids chimed in, dutifully, 'Yes, we know, stay in school!'] and keep your nose clean." The kids all looked at the translator and grabbed their noses in confusion as he explained, after clarifying with the police chief the significance of a clean nose.

The discussion continued with questions from parents about the long-term implications of having a police record and how to force their children to obey the law, and from kids about what the FBI is for and what defines a misdemeanor. A shy boy raised his hand, timidly asking, "Judge, can you explain that thing hanging over our head?" Earlier in the program, the judge, straight-faced, somber, and intimidating, had explained that juveniles do not always go to jail for every crime, but for minor offenses like curfew infractions, tobacco use, and alcohol use they might be sentenced to parole without any jail time. "But you'll still have this hanging over your head," he had cautioned, sternly, "and if you screw up you might have to go to jail." The shy boy asked his question holding his hand parallel to the crown of his head as other audience members nodded their agreement with the question. As the judge grasped the literal interpretation, he finally cracked a smile before explaining what it means to have something hanging over your head.

These sorts of meetings were carefully coordinated moments of engagement, where SBYAM board members distributed themselves throughout the audience to maintain order while ensuring all those who had questions had the opportunity to ask them. As their success with such meetings grew, they continued to expand their programming by adding citizenship classes for adults and, eventually, literacy classes as well. Having established themselves as knowledgeable, trustworthy, capable, and fluent in American society, many Somali speakers who avoided such classes run by white people finally felt able to take on these new challenges of life in America. The SBYAM citizenship classes boasted a 100 percent passing rate. Board members taught all the classes with

FIGURE 8.1 Celebrating after a U.S. citizenship ceremony, Portland, Maine, 2012.
Photograph by Jorge Acero.

curricula they designed themselves, and relied on volunteers from the refugee community and Bates College for additional help.

By 2010 their roster was consistently packed with activities. At one SBYAM board meeting I attended in March of that year, the six members present organized their plans for the upcoming weekend: Jama was participating in weekly young police officer training on Thursday; all board members were obligated to participate in training on race and violence with CPHV on Friday; over the weekend four Somali Bantu high school students and one board member chaperone were supposed to attend a youth leadership conference in Washington, DC, which Abdirisak agreed to chaperone since Jama had chaperoned a youth trip to Boston the previous weekend; Ahmed was supposed to join the Washington trip but could not because he was also invited to a democracy workshop for young leaders in Maine the same weekend; Jama and Khadija agreed to attend leadership training led by a local organization scheduled for all day Saturday and Sunday in Portland; Nur would be working with a group of high school students all day Saturday and Sunday on an SBYAM-supported video project; and Idris, Rahima, and another board member were being interviewed on Saturday by a possible donor. That left the citizenship classes on Saturday and Sunday unstaffed. Ibrahim volunteered to take over the citizenship program for the weekend, and Idris would join him as soon as the interview concluded. Then they began looking ahead to the following weekend, which included a conference presentation at Harvard, among other commitments.

In its first five years, SBYAM had managed to free itself of intracommunity tensions and build strong links to city institutions that engage with refugees. During those years, SBYAM established itself as a capable organization in the eyes of funders and as offering a safe place for community members to ask questions about living in America in meetings between white authorities and Somali Bantu community members, where Somali Bantu community members rather than white authorities set the agenda. Their workshops were helping parents regain disciplinary control over their kids, and fewer girls were dropping out of high school to get married. Several Somali Bantu high school graduates were attending college; many board members had completed community college degrees; a few were enrolled in BA and MA programs; and, in an exciting first, Jama joined the Lewiston school board in 2014.

But the effort it took to achieve so much cannot be underestimated: board members devoted countless hours over many years to planning, volunteering, and working incredibly hard to turn small grants into meaningful programs that would make a difference for their community. Their newest program, adult literacy classes, included almost a hundred adult Somali students. The urgency Idris and his cohort felt for kids a few years ago is now directed at their parents.

While orchestrating literacy and citizenship classes for adults, SBYAM pursued another strategy to bridge the world of white institutions and refugee community members. With the help of a local white social worker, SBYAM became a state-recognized caseworker agency that could receive payment through MaineCare (Maine's public medical care program) for working with clients who were referred for casework assistance because they were receiving mental health services or involved in the juvenile justice system. Several board members became certified as caseworkers, and the agency hired a white caseworker and Somali caseworkers, the first time in the city that a white person or a Somali worked for a Somali Bantu employer.

The addition of formal caseworker services meant that the organization's staff became legally empowered as advocates for their clients rather than simply cultural brokers and information mediators. As caseworkers, they are in a position to establish requirements for schools to follow when one of their clients is suspended or expelled, and they can make demands of agencies that are supposed to be providing services to their clients but whose treatment of their clients is culturally incompetent, inadequate, or racist. Because many of SBYAM's caseworkers had previously worked for mental health agencies and in the hospitals and schools, they understand how those systems work, what services are available, and how to work their way up through the management to demand services for their clients. Rather than throwing a child with behavioral problems right back into ELL classes after a suspension and brush with the law, for example, an SBYAM caseworker can require that the child receive special education services, which obligates different (and better) forms of engagement with the child and the family than are available through only the ELL program.

As it dawned on me what the addition of caseworker services meant, I realized the long road that Idris had taken to position himself and his organization as advocates for their community. Watching kids get suspended over and over and be disciplined without the benefit of cross-cultural counseling competencies or special education services for children who might qualify, watching parents emotionally withdraw under the mounting pressures of life in Lewiston, and feeling increasing urgency to learn how to advocate, Idris got a BA in social work, entered an MA program, got training through his jobs in the hospitals, schools, and a mental health agency, registered as a 501c3 nonprofit organization, learned the bureaucracy to become certified as a MaineCare-supported agency, hired a staff, and took on clients. It took him a less than decade to figure all of this out, and now he and his staff are in a strong position to advocate for their clients because they have a complete understanding of how the systems work that intervene in and interrupt the lives of Somali Bantu community members and they have the authority to demand changes. They are in a position not only to encourage Somali Bantu youths to stay in school but also to push for changes in school culture that will more effectively mitigate harm.

But of course, the catch is that Idris and his agency can only do casework for those people who have a mental health diagnosis (primarily PTSD, depression, and anxiety disorders) or for children who get arrested. And here we confront the greatest irony of all. A sink-or-swim definition of refuge means that the best opportunity for help for some impoverished, exhausted refugees only comes if they receive a diagnosis of mental illness or commit a criminal act. Turning refugees into the sick and the criminal is, for those so labeled, a catastrophic form of refuge.

Conclusion

The Way Life Should Be

Migrations are acts of settlement and of habitation
in a world where the divide between origin and
destination is no longer a divide of Otherness, a world
in which borders no longer separate human realities.
—Saskia Sassen, *Guests and Aliens*

In his June 2012 Enough Is Enough column in the *Twin City Times*, Lewiston mayor Robert Macdonald railed against the "rude behavior of teenagers, immigrants, and unproductive parents" for talking on their cell phones at the high school's recent graduation ceremony in the huge Lewiston Colisée. His complaints quickly narrowed to only the immigrant attendees, those "from oppressive refugee camps, which harbor crime, disease, and hunger" to whom "Lewiston residents have opened our city." While acknowledging that some immigrants are properly appreciative, he chastised those who "take advantage of our generosity and act like we owe them," concluding his article with these words:

> During the singing of our National Anthem, these ingrates chose to sit talking to each other or talking on the phone. They need to be reminded that when the "Star Spangled Banner" is played, they are expected to show it the same respect and courtesy that U.S. citizens show it.

They are guests here, and they are expected to adapt to our culture. If this is too much to ask, then perhaps it's time [for them] to leave.[1]

The online responses to this article included forty comments. Twenty-two agreed, some emphatically so, with the mayor, many employing the same sort of rhetoric described in chapter 5 (calling the immigrants "bottom-dwellers," "greedy and inconsiderate," "rude and unappreciative," who "stink up the place," "need to learn our language so we can FUCKING UNDERSTAND THEM" and are "reward[ed] . . . for their barbaric behavior"). But fifteen of the comments, many from self-identified local teachers, chastised the mayor and the negative commenters for their racist, ignorant, bigoted comments, suggesting that they might wish to compare their anti-immigrant allegations with those wielded in earlier generations by the KKK against their French Canadian and Irish immigrant ancestors and asking why the rude behavior of white people was so quickly overlooked in favor of blaming immigrants as a category.

Barbara McManus, a Lewiston ELL teacher, wrote, "The exuberance demonstrated by our new citizens is due in part, to the realization that miraculously, someone in that family has attained a level of education that seemed impossible. They too, are proud parents, relatives, of some of the graduates. Some call Africa so that the entire family can hear the ceremony, right here and over there. Imagine for a moment, a dozen or two people gathered around a cell phone in Africa, trying to hear what is going on in America, and the tearful and meager celebration that follows." Others wrote, "Somalis are among my most appreciative parents," whose presence in Lewiston "has softened the impact of the recession, the housing bust, and school budget cutbacks," reminding the mayor that as an elected official, he is supposed to represent all of the city's residents. One commenter asked, "Seriously, what kind of Mayor would write something like this?"

These comments capture in stark form the ongoing debates among Lewiston's residents about civic belonging. Although some, like Mayor Macdonald, continue to champion the view that Somali immigrants are guests who are expected to demonstrate gratitude and appreciation while self-consciously striving to assimilate, others challenge such boundary making by emphasizing residence rather than citizenship as the meaningful measure of belonging, advocating for the right of immigrants to demonstrate their sense of belonging by, among other things, exuberantly phoning relatives in Africa during a high school graduation ceremony. Although many Somalis are gaining citizenship and, of course, children born in the United States are automatically citizens, it is residence rather than citizenship that stimulates people like Kim Wettlaufer, Mayor Gilbert, Lt. Robitaille, Barbara McManus, and other non-Somali residents of Lewiston to speak out in support of the civic rights of Somalis who share their city to be viewed as neighbors rather than guests.

"Welcome to Maine: The Way Life Should Be" reads the sign at Maine's state border. Somali and Somali Bantu immigrants heartily embraced this message of promise and possibility to make their refuge in Lewiston through dedicating themselves to creating their own structures of solidarity and mutual support, networking with social workers, teachers, police, and other professionals to establish points of contact with the mainstream community, defining for themselves what self-sufficiency and integration should look like, demanding accommodations and respect for their values and practices, and engaging in vigorous internal debates about how to repair ruptured cultural understandings of marriage, gender norms, authority, discipline, and parenting in ways relevant to their new context and reflective of community values. Their efforts to create the way life should be have been fraught, contested, hard, and sometimes damaging, but throughout their process of adjustment they are insistent on their own agency to make decisions for themselves.

The rhetoric of assimilation posits that change works in only one direction—through the self-transformation of the immigrant who strives to join the mainstream host society. In 2008, the federal Office of Refugee Resettlement funded a national conference for representatives from Somali Bantu communities from throughout the country to come together in Lexington, Kentucky, for a day of workshops and discussions about their first years in America. In his formal presentation, one of the speakers from the ORR office lectured his Somali Bantu audience about the importance of change and assimilation, emphasizing that they will have to leave tribalism and the steady Africa-centric grip of tradition behind and embrace change in order to adapt to American life. As he spoke, I looked out over his audience of young men and women whose lives had been utterly transformed, shattered and rebuilt; people who moved from small farming villages in Africa where lions and hippos are daily threats to cities in America where they face threats of an entirely different sort, from mud and grass huts where life is public and cooperative to isolated apartments in American cities where they are assaulted by their neighbors, from cooking with charcoal and bathing in rivers to using electricity and running water, from farming with short-handled hoes with a hope for rain to working the night shift as cleaners at Dunkin' Donuts. I wondered how many people in his audience, on their journeys from Somalia to Kenya and Dadaab to Kakuma, witnessed the deaths of family members from militia attacks, starvation, and dehydration, how many experienced rape, how many made the terrible choice to leave behind family members who could not make the trip to America. Many in the audience learned Swahili in the refugee camps and English in America, and all the men were wearing suits rather than sa-rongs or *qamis*. Throughout the day, attendees shared e-mail contacts and cell phone numbers during breaks and posted photographs of the conference from their cell phones on Facebook. Nothing about their lives has been stable, unchanging, or resistant to change; their very presence in that auditorium meant they had embraced change every chance they got.

The speaker's emphasis on the need of those in his audience to change and assimilate echoes, of course, the autobiographical American story about im-migrant integration noted in chapter 8 and evidenced in the words of Mayor Macdonald and his supporters and the ubiquitous insistence on conformity by the bloggers and other Lewiston residents introduced in chapter 5. But such a flat view of assimilation rests on two faulty assumptions. The first is that assimilation and integration are about wholeness and assimilating to some other, already existing culture. The second is that assimilation only works in one direction: the immigrant assimilates to the host society and not the other way around.

The story of Somali and Somali Bantu refugee immigrants in Lewiston challenges both assumptions. Chapter 8 noted the problem of a "pretheoreti-cal commitment" to the idea of wholeness, which implies Somalis in the grip of cultural change are somehow in between or fragmented while they recon-stitute a new whole through culture change and gaining citizenship. But their devotion to diasporic connections suggests that wholeness for Somali Ameri-cans includes both the experience of emplacement in Lewiston and ongoing transnational connections, an embrace of many aspects of American culture (education, cars and other forms of technology, Western medicine, changing gender roles, and more) and subjective membership in a global Somali Is-lamic community (and a value system that prioritizes faith, mobility, family, a particular aesthetic, and resource sharing as a normal expectation rather than a commendable act). Presumptions of wholeness obscure not only emergent Somali American cultural formations but also the ways in which many do-mains of social life in Lewiston are changing for the city's non-Somali residents as well because of the presence of Somali American residents. Lewiston's story shows that assimilation goes both ways: immigrants change, adapt, and hybrid-ize, but also transform the host community.

Citizenship, Mobility, and Diaspora

At the annual 2011 SBYAM soccer tournament, parents gathered along the sidelines for the final match as the two best teams in the league faced off. The talk continually turned to everyone's worry about their relatives in East Africa because yet another upsurge in violence in southern Somalia sent people fleeing across the border into Dadaab to seek safety from Al-Shabaab atrocities and famine. Several Somali Bantu men from Lewiston visiting Kenya for the first time since their resettlement phoned to report that life in the camps was worse than ever and they planned to return early to Lewiston. People were starving to death.

A constant experience during my years of conversations, meals, and meetings with Somali Bantus in Lewiston is the incessant ringing of cell phones with calls from the Kenyan refugee camps and Somalia. People talk daily with their distant relatives, checking in about news, safety, movements, threats, and health. One day in the back office of Aliyow's store when I was looking at the Somali Bantu Experience website with a group of Somali Bantu acquaintances, there appeared a photo of Khalar, who was the youth community health worker and our frequent companion during our residence in Banta. Khalar stayed behind in Somalia when others fled the second time, living off his farms and, now, remittances from friends and relatives in Lewiston. Abkow pulled out his cell phone and said, "Let's call him!" Within a few minutes he reached someone in Banta with a cell phone, who located Khalar, and suddenly his still-familiar voice was on the line asking about Jorge and the baby I was carrying when I lived in Banta. I asked about his news and learned that his family of seven was barely surviving because of drought and insecurity due to robberies by Al-Shabaab militia. There was no food and his children were starving. I knew Abkow was sending him money every month, and I promised to send additional money that afternoon.

As Khalar and I talked, Sadiq's phone rang. It was his brother from Somalia calling to ask for money. That morning when I was visiting Iman, his phone rang with a call from his older brother in Somalia, asking for money. The brother was fleeing Mogadishu because of the upsurge in violence between government forces and Al-Shabaab and was not yet sure where he would end up. He was phoning to ask Iman's family to be prepared to send him additional money when he found someplace safe. Isha, Idris, and Idris's older brother were supporting Ciise, Rabaca's family, and now Ambiya's family as well. The combination of Al-Shabaab threats and drought sent Ambiya from Somalia to Dadaab with her husband—the man who abducted her at gunpoint in Banta—and their children, from where she was able to reconnect by phone with Isha. In one of war's many ironies, the man who stole Ambiya is now surviving on the remittances sent by his wife's family to support them.

In 2011–12, everyone was anxiously worried about their relatives in Somalia trying to live through or escape from the predations of Al-Shabaab. Debates about escape routes and deteriorating life in the refugee camps dominated conversation. People returning from visiting Dadaab reported that the most recent wave of refugees from Somalia's ongoing violence included young men who grew up in a lawless country, and, intimately familiar with murder and robbery, were now wielding violence in the camps to steal and rape. Abkow reported that thugs burned down the markets in two of the camps and life there is "totally horrible. The extremists are trying to use the camps as a battleground." And perils of a different nature have emerged as well: some of my Somali Bantu friends are receiving death threats if they return to Kenya because of their prominence and activism on behalf of Somali Bantus in the United States. Somali Internet sites keep readers well apprised of people's political activities in the United States, Europe, and Africa.

Everyone has dozens of close relatives who are desperate for help. The owner of Aliyow's store, who travels back and forth to East Africa for his business, asks me, in distress, "Who do you choose to help?" Everyone I know agrees: their resources are spread so thin between covering their expenses in Lewiston and sending as much money as they possibly can to extended families in Dadaab, Kakuma, and Somalia, and they know that relatives who receive remittances are surrounded by starving and desperate people who do not. Concerned that the millions of dollars in remittances sent to East Africa every month might be redirected to support Al-Shabaab, the U.S. government announced its intent to shut down the money transfer operations used by Somalis, provoking panic in Lewiston as everyone tried to send as much money as possible before the network closed to hold their relatives over until a new channel opened.[2]

And yet, despite the danger and fear, as soon as Somali Bantu refugees became eligible to apply for citizenship after the mandatory five-year waiting period, SBYAM's citizenship classes filled with students avidly memorizing the questions in English so they could gain U.S. citizenship in order to visit their relatives in Kenya. Citizenship brings greater security against deportation, but the primary draw is the right to travel across international borders, which is prohibited during the probationary five years after resettlement.[3] Tutors in SBYAM's citizenship classes pose as citizenship test interviewers, asking questions from the list of official test questions, which people learn to answer by rote memorization. A joke circulates in the community: one person asks another, pretending to be the citizenship interviewer, "Why do you want to become an American citizen?" The applicant answers, "So I can travel to Africa!" At that everyone cracks up and yells, "Wrong answer!" While applicants recognize the need to claim nationalist patriotism as part of their citizenship interview, for many people citizenship is about transnational mobility and diasporic linkages.

Citizenship deepens diasporic identity and participation through enabling mobility, even if emotional connections to Somalia remain conflicted for Somali Bantu refugee immigrants. Some, like Jama, renounce any attachment to Somalia. After gaining citizenship, he proudly showed me that his passport card listed his nationality as United States, although he is irked that the card also indicates Somalia as his country of birth because he feels no allegiance to Somalia and, to the contrary, says he is ashamed to be from such a destructive place. Although he was born there, he fled with his family at the age of six, returning during the repatriation in 1995, when life in the Jubba Valley was terrible, before fleeing again. When I ask about his memories from the second short stay, his grave face says more than his words. He recounts a few instances from his memory of that year—his uncle attempting to guard his mature crops from Somali invaders who aimed their guns at him and told him they would blow him away if he took one more step. "And we knew they would," Jama said. "They were killing anyone who tried to protect their farm. It was the same shit." He refuses to talk about his memories from the second flight across the desert to Dadaab. He wishes his passport card listed his country of origin as Kenya, where he came of age, began attending school, and learned English, and from where he departed to the United States.

Like Jama, many young people in Lewiston claim stronger personal attachments to Kenya than Somalia, naming Kenya as their place of origin and ongoing cultural connection through their ties to family and friends there as well as their consumption of Kenyan music and dance styles. Ahmed, who is often called to speak at city and state events as a Somali Bantu youth leader, talks about wanting to find a way to help his country of birth, but other young adults disagree, saying they will help their relatives but have given up on Somalia. Ahmed is not so sure, explaining, "The U.S. gave me an intellectual life, but Somalia gave me life. I was born there; my ancestors are from there; my relatives still live there." He struggles with the implication that becoming a U.S. citizen would obligate him to renounce his attachments to Kenya and Somalia, explaining that for him, being Somali and being American are intimately connected: "If I wasn't Somali I wouldn't be here. I'm here in America *because* I'm Somali." Ahmed holds a complex approach to describing an identity forged through mobility. Another student, already a U.S. citizen, says, "It's just adding something. I want citizenship so I can check on job applications that I'm a citizen, but I didn't renounce anything. It's just an addition. It's a resource for me. I don't deny where I'm from, but really I don't know anything about Somalia. . . . Citizenship is just a document." It is a document that he needs to return to the camps to visit his mother, who was not included in the resettlement program.

Many immigrants to the United States in earlier generations maintained transnational linkages, identities, and relationships despite the emphasis on assimilation in American nationalist lore, but Somalis and Somali Bantus may be distinguished as among the most transnational. Mobility is at the heart of Somali culture and experience, an expectation and norm shared by Somali Bantus despite their more sedentary background. Citizenship status, for the Somali Bantus I know, means the legal right to mobility as a physical dimension of diasporic belonging and global networks maintained through technology. Citizenship enables enhanced diasporic connections, through allowing travel and the hope for greater access to resources in the United States (through employment) that can be used to support relatives abroad. But if citizenship for many is about mobility, diasporic participation, and belonging, what is the relationship between diaspora and locality? What does living in Lewiston actually mean to the Somali Bantu refugee immigrants who live there?

Somali Bantu diasporic self-consciousness is based in a sense of cultural integrity rooted in Islam, a shared place of origin and historic experience, and persistent global networks, but also is shaped in constant dialogues about how to live Somali Muslim values in the United States. It is not a barricaded diaspora identity, holding onto traditional practice; rather, it is a constantly evolving identity that morphs and shifts in dialogue with encounters with other practices and beliefs. As we have seen, young people debate the significance of clan, racialized difference, status, tribalism, gender norms, religious fundamentalism, history, and Islamic practice in a Western context, in person and on vibrant and lively Internet sites, Facebook pages, and phone chat lines. My young Somali Bantu friends regularly post quotes from the Quran on Facebook (as well as words of wisdom remembered from Cali Osman), engage in debates about identity and Islam on Somali Bantu websites and Facebook pages, share homemade videos about changing cultural practices in the diaspora (youth romance, parent-child relations, making good choices), and consume videos about youth culture in Africa.[4] Diaspora scholarship has challenged the focus on immigrant assimilation by introducing important perspectives on hybridity, creativity, and creolization, but how does the experience and imagination of diaspora also intersect with emplacement, with the physical reality of living in a particular place?[5]

For good reasons, Somalis (and, by association, Somali Bantus) are often described as quintessential models of flexible mobility whose home is located in kinship networks and social groups rather than physical locations. "Transnational nomads" is one apt description.[6] But even the globally mobile, like Somali and Somali Bantu refugee immigrants, inhabit particular places and must face the ideological and physical constructions of "home" required of all human beings. In his book *Insiders and Outsiders: Citizenship and Xenophobia in Contemporary South Africa*, anthropologist Francis Nyamnjoh criticizes the fascination with deterritorialization in the literature on mobility and identity: "No amount of questioning by scholars, human rights advocates and immigrants immersed in the reality of flexible mobility seems adequate to de-essentialise the growing global fixation with an 'authentic' place called home. Thus trapped in cosmopolitan spaces in a context where states and their hierarchy of 'privileged' citizens believe in the coercive illusion of fixed and bounded locations, immigrants, diasporas, ethnic minorities and others who straddle borders are bound to feel like travelers in permanent transit."[7] When Somali Bantus in Lewiston give public presentations about their experiences of mobility and immigration, even when their presentations stress their experiences of discrimination and violence, there are inevitably two questions from the audience: Do you want to go home? Would you return home if you had the chance? The presumption, of course, is that Somalia is home. Somali Bantus respond by stressing that Lewiston is their future, while acknowledging their ongoing emotional connections to the people—parents, children, siblings, and grandchildren—still living in East Africa. (At one such event, one Somali Bantu friend answered the persistent question with a proverb, "When you look at a pile of ashes take care because it might still produce fire," before explaining that he would return only to visit his mother, whom he has not seen in a decade.) Somali Bantus are trying to explain that while their diasporic belongings and transnational connections are fundamental dimensions of their being-in-the-world, Lewiston is now home. And Lewiston, in turn, is transformed by the dynamic presence of diasporic Somali and Somali Bantu immigrants.

Mutual Transformation

"Is there a universal orientation within liberalism that allows an open engagement with the difference in other cultures, or does its method of incorporating otherness revolve around its particularistic viewpoint so that the relationship with difference is always a form of blurred domestication?" asks Nikos Papasterdiadis.[8] But some forms of "domestication" are essential, because immigrants have to learn to navigate a new society, which means understanding laws, attending school, knowing "how things work here," and so forth. The interesting question is how those being domesticated respond by both seeking help and shaping new subjectivities through adapting while simultaneously encouraging their new neighbors to adapt to them. While Somali Bantu immigrants are changing gender roles, finding new approaches to arranged marriages, learning new parenting strategies, navigating new political bureaucracies, trying new forms of medical intervention, and crafting new subjectivities as U.S. citizens and diaspora members, other residents in Lewiston cannot help but be changed as well by their presence and engagement in the local arena. In short, everyone is adapting. Some adaptations are small and quotidian: a judge learns how to talk through a translator; an "old French woman" learns how to buy spices in a Somali-owned shop; a Franco-American museum director learns to love sambusas; white kids on the playground begin speaking to their friends in Somali; Somali girls at a high school track meet pray in Arabic for the success of the white high jumper who is in their math class; white locals wish they had elders.

But other changes are far-reaching. The "boo-hoo white do-gooders and their carpetbagger friends" know that city institutions, schools, workplaces, and local culture must change to adapt to Somali immigrants. They are among the architects of change, from Cheryl Hamilton and CareerCenter director Mary LaFontaine, who want to train employers to work with New Mainers; to the ELL teachers fighting to change school culture; to Kim Wettlaufer, who helps his clients come to recognize their similarities and form solidarities; to the police department that creates a special community resource substation to engage with Somali immigrants. Their efforts are augmented by those of Somali and Somali Bantu cultural brokers who work in social services agencies and medical facilities teaching non-Somalis about Somali perspectives on faith, family, and more, translating Somali practices and beliefs along with words to non-Somalis.

In its second decade of Somali immigration, Lewiston now has two mosques, and Fridays bring hundreds of men and boys to the street in qamis on their way to pray. Thousands of women and girls in hijab move through public spaces daily, and hardly anyone yells, "Go home!" or "Dress like an American!" any longer. People praying at appropriate times is now normal in schools and in some of the larger workplaces. Mental health professionals are meeting with imams and traditional healers to learn more about Somali conceptions of sanity and possession. Somali and Somali Bantu community organizations are intervening more in the civic life of the city, by, as we have seen, marching down Lisbon Street proclaiming "LEWISTON IS OUR CITY TOO," arguing with school authorities, writing op-eds and letters to the editor, and running for the school board. The situation in the refugee camps penetrates Lewiston as those returning from distressing visits alert the local newspaper and provide interviews about the dire situation in Dadaab and Somalia. Prompted by the worry that their students carry into school from distracted parents, local ELL teachers spearhead fund-raising initiatives for grassroots organizations in the camps. Despite the xenophobes and racists, Lewiston is a success story because ideas about mutual responsibility, cultural values, political practice, and civic engagement jostle and bump and are transformed in the arenas of public discourse and personal reflection. It is precisely in small locales like Lewiston where new versions of "America" are being forged as mobile immigrants and long-term locals create new forms of sociality, understanding, and collaboration.

The helpers are pushing back, alongside the immigrants, against local discourses fed by popular national rhetoric that distinguish between the "deserving poor" (white citizens who worked in the mills and feel abandoned by their city's economic downturn) and the "undeserving poor" ("unproductive parents" and black refugees who came to the United States as objects of humanitarian charity). They reject the hierarchies of legitimacy that define some people but not others as acceptable beneficiaries of assistance by insisting on a society that offers care to those who need it on the basis of coresidence, regardless of race, origin, citizenship status, or religion. The ELL teachers, some of the police, former mayor Gilbert, and many others see the immigrant refugees as part of their community and thus part of their responsibility as human beings living together in a particular place. While their definitions of success may eventually include economic self-sufficiency, their more immediate definition of success prioritizes health, security, education, safe housing, and other quality-of-life factors rather than economic productivity. Integration, for the helpers and immigrants alike, is about feeling safe and taking care of each other, not about neoliberal conceptions of personal responsibility or conformity to mainstream American norms and values (of individualism, consumption, a monetary assessment of personal value). To the contrary, many of the helpers express their admiration for Somali values that they see as desirable and waning in American life: strong community bonds, nonmaterialist values, sharing and cooperation, humor in the face of hardship.

Progressive scholars theorize about how to create a sense of the commons (by which they mean the public good, the social community) that is inclusive, border crossing, and nonhierarchical, offering portraits of political action that confront biopolitical exclusions (based on socially constructed categories like race, foreignness, citizenship status, and so forth) in particular localities and that forge connections and networks that transcend particular localities.[9] Bonnie Honig sees the potential to repurpose immigrant activism to forge a new democratic cosmopolitanism that crosses borders. If immigrants make democracy through fighting for their rights and insisting on being heard, then, she says, "We have a story here of illegitimate demands made by people with no standing to make them, a story of people so far outside the circle of who 'counts' that they cannot make claims within the existing frames of claim making. They make room for themselves by staging nonexistent rights, and by way of such stagings, sometimes, new rights, powers, and visions come into being."[10] Immigrants can stretch political practice into a form of democratic practice that works across borders, not just in the interest of the nation, she theorizes, thus raising the question of whether the transborder networks and commitments held by Somali and Somali Bantu refugee immigrants might redefine the commons in Lewiston to also include others outside the local community. Michael Hardt and Antonio Negri offer an argument about the forms of resistance they call "altermodernities," which are created through a process of people coming together to imagine and enact alternative futures based on emerging understandings of historic practice and tradition across time and space.[11] They offer as examples the Zapatistas in Chiapas and Bolivian resisters to the privatization of water access. These sorts of resistances do not produce reified identities based in claims to authenticity or resistances based on assimilationist trajectories, but rather entirely new forms of sociality in which people are constantly remaking their world in dialogues with resistances, ruptures, novelties, and the imagination. This vision of altermodernity captures the efforts of the Somali Bantu community association and SBYAM to experiment thoughtfully with new forms of subjectivity in conjunction with rethinking and transforming more traditional forms of practice and subjectivity (of community representation, political hierarchy, gender expectations, youth identities, and so forth). They are in the process of shaping and becoming not assimilated Americans, but something new, and they are doing so by forging solidarities and networks with a wide range of collaborators who themselves are transforming their understanding of community through these engagements.

Suzanne Hall raises the question of how to "re-orientate the politics of diversity and belonging when there is a large and affective apparatus that contrives and maintains prejudice."[12] How will people in Lewiston confront racism and xenophobia? Hall points to the importance of the welfare state for protecting the vulnerable (although the shrinking welfare state is creating vulnerabilities as well), moving beyond assimilation "towards an acknowledgement of allegiances as a multiple rather than a singular coherence" (as is the case with the simultaneous experience of emplacement and diasporic belonging), collaboration on common projects in which contributions and participation of diverse populations are made visible (such as with the Museum LA exhibition and SBYAM's citizenship classes), and new forms of empowerment (such as SBYAM's development as a caseworker organization).[13] These stories and possibilities begin a second decade of transformation, and we do not yet know how the story will unfold.

The Way Life Should Be

While anthropologists and others have been fascinated over the past few decades with the speedy movement of people, money, and ideas through globalization, with globe-spanning diasporic connections and transnational networks, with theories about cosmopolitanism as a future alternative to contemporary regimes of multiculturalism and the xenophobia they confront, this story has placed us at the intersection of mobility and emplacement, diaspora and locality. Such intersections are where border crossings of a specific sort take place, where slow globalization shifts and blurs boundaries as ideas, cultural practices, relationships, and demographics morph, grow, and slowly become transformative.[14] The slow globalization of refugees and migrants whose movement is relentless even when temporarily constrained means local worlds will be constantly changing as mobility intersects with emplacement and migrants transform local places through their presence. Often (mis)characterized as sites of clashes and crashes, such intersections are more often sites of negotiation, learning, self-reflection, and social change.

Anthropologists have long since abandoned the bounded conception of culture that undergirds images of clashing and crashing, replacing it with a fascination with emergence and becoming, constructions of lived experience that emphasize the imagination, creativity, and dynamism of human life. Subjectivities that are emergent and becoming, rather than fully formed and bounded, are an attractive way to think about the dynamic intersection of mobility and emplacement, about what happens in particular localities when immigrants move in. And yet, anthropologists must also be mindful to see and record the cultural value systems, beliefs, and practices that those who pass through that intersection bring to it. Locality and emplacement are the other side of emergence and becoming, and we should not avoid trying to document the cultural terrain of particular places in our desire to showcase mobility and emergence.

Pundits and popular discourse continue to use the culture concept, although in ways that make anthropologists suspicious and unhappy: as deterministic, essentializing, and exotic.[15] Anthropologists must mind the gap here. How do those of us who continue to find value in the culture concept talk about it in ways that redirect its definition from the popular, essentialized version while still recognizing the sedimentation of meaning and practice that enables groups to recognize and cohere around collectively held values? We do so by describing how such groups debate their values in dialogue with those who hold different values and shift their practice through such engagements, but as groups and not just individuals. Difference is constantly emergent, constantly renegotiated, constantly revalued, but continues to contain group-ness over time. Groupness is maintained by socially constructed racial differ-ence, racism, linguistic repertoires, diaspora identifications, and the diasporic networks within which people, ideas, talk, and money flow. The dialogues, debates, and negotiations in Lewiston cohere around the question of the way life should be.

For the past two decades, Lewiston's immigrants have been refuting the humanitarian presumption that people displaced by war should be forced to abide by paternalistic and neocolonial rules and borders that constrain their ability to seek safety. That is not the way life should be. They have been refut-ing the presumption that immigrants must assimilate by leaving their culture at the door in their new places of residence. That is not the way life should be. They and their advocates malign a government that abandons resettled refugees upon arrival by refusing substantive and meaningful assistance for education, job skills, and other support while they adjust, promoting instead a starkly neoliberal understanding of human worth as equal to a paycheck. That is not the way life should be.

During a conversation with Ahmed and Abdi about their simultaneous connections to the transnational and the local, Abdi recounted a recent ex-perience at a local gas station. As he was filling his car, he overheard the loud conversation of two white men in another vehicle. One of the men told the other, gesturing to Abdi, "And now they're 50 percent of the population!" Abdi chuckled to himself, thinking, "No, we're not." But one can imagine that they will be. And Sadiq, Idris, Abdiya, Ahmed, Abdi, and their peers, alongside Kim, Beth, Larry Gilbert, the ELL teachers, and their colleagues, will continue working to create the best version of Lewiston that they can imagine, striving to find the way life should be.

Introduction

1. Besteman 1999b; Besteman and Cassanelli 2000.
2. Here and throughout the book I use pseudonyms for those who are not public figures.
3. Anderson 2009; BBC News 2008; *Foreign Policy* 2008, 2009; Menkhaus 2008; Refugees International 2011. See also Fergusson 2013; Garvelink and Tahir 2011.
4. See Besteman 1994, 1996a, 1996b, 1999b and Besteman and Cassanelli 2000, where Banta is called Loc.
5. Van Lehman and Eno 2002.
6. Huisman 2011: n.p.
7. Hudson 2006.
8. Nadeau 2005.
9. Nadeau 2011.
10. Nyers 2006.
11. The UNHCR put the number of forcibly displaced people at 43 million in 2014, 27 million of whom were displaced by conflict or catastrophe within their home countries.
12. Fassin and Rechtman 2009: 253.
13. Bauman 2004; see also Agamben 1995; Horst 2006; Malkki 1995b, 2002; Nyers 2006.
14. Huntington 1993, 2004; Kaplan 1994. Thanks to Kristin Koptiuch for this insight.

I. Becoming Refugees

1. An audio clip of Cali reciting one of his poems is accessible at "Historical Audio Links," The Somali Bantu Experience, http://web.colby.edu/somali-bantu/images -and-audio/audio/.

2. The meticulous portraits of communities sundered by civil wars provided by Beatriz Manz (2004) on Guatemala, Tone Bringe on Bosnia (Bringe and Christie 1993), and ethnographic historian Jan Gross (2001), who uncovered the secret of the July day in 1941 when half of the villagers of Jedwabne, Poland, murdered the other half, demonstrate how an intimate knowledge of localities and comprehensive knowledge of the global forces that impact localities combine to tell war stories of profound depth and complexity.

3. See Cassanelli 1982; Lewis 1988.

4. For detailed accounts of this history that draw on Italian and British colonial documents and oral histories, see Besteman 1999b; Cassanelli 1982; Declich 1987; and Menkhaus 1989.

5. Somali Bantus believe *ooji* comes from the Italian word for day, a reference to the stereotype that riverine farmers couldn't think beyond the time frame of a day. *Adoon* means slave.

6. Mohamed Eno (2008) offers a comprehensive overview of jareer status. See also Besteman 1999b.

7. See Lewis 1961.

8. Although the structure of Somalia's clan-based kinship system suggests rigidly defined patrilineal identities, in reality adoption by a clan different from that of one's birth was relatively common. For example, Bernhard Helander (1996) estimated that the majority of the members of the clan where he did his ethnographic fieldwork in the Baay region, adjacent to the Jubba Valley, started life in a different clan. People sought out adoption for a wide variety of reasons: to access land, for protection, to relocate to a new community.

9. Cali Osman and Sheikh Axmed Nur were both Ajuraan, a subclan with a distinguished history that became part of the Hawiye clan centuries ago. Caliyow Isaaq claimed membership in the Laysan branch of the Rahanweyn clan, although he had a Hawiye wife, and Sheikh Axmed Nur's eldest wife was Rahanweyn; their children Xawo and Mohamed married during my stay in Banta (the occasion of the wedding music recording that I played at the slide show reunion in Lewiston).

10. They were affiliated with the Bartire clan.

11. Rawson 1994.

12. Anthropological disagreements about the relative importance of kinship, class, inequality, and foreign aid in contributing to Somalia's civil war are outlined most clearly in my published debate with I. M. Lewis (Besteman 1996a, 1998; Lewis 1998). See also Besteman 1996b, 1999a.

13. Besteman 1994 analyzes land tenure reform in the valley.

14. The Jubba Valley farmers were certainly not the only group to suffer horribly during the civil war. See Kapteijns 2012 for a detailed account of the targeted "clan cleansing" violence in the greater Mogadishu area following the collapse of Siad Barre's government.

15. Menkhaus 1992.

16. As an account based on the recollections of dozens of people, the story of Banta told here reflects my efforts to cross-check every claim with numerous witnesses

to each incident. I reviewed the story many times in individual and group meetings in Lewiston, Syracuse, and Hartford in 2006–7, and two friends from Banta read and offered further corrections to my written narrative. But as a compilation of memories recounted in the wake of trauma and displacement, it is entirely possible that details are fuzzy, misremembered, or transformed over many years of discussion by those who experienced these events.

17. Reports on the circumstances of Somalia's minorities during the war include Danish Immigration Service 2000; Eno 2008; Eno, Eno, and Van Lehman 2010; Hill 2010.

18. The international intervention included Operation Restore Hope, launched in 1992 with the U.S.-led, UN-backed United Task Force, which concluded in 1993 and was followed by UNOSOM, another U.S.-led, UN-backed security effort that ended in 1995.

19. Mbembe 2011: 117.

2. The Humanitarian Condition

1. Agier 2005: 3.

2. Agier 2005: 15, emphasis in original.

3. Agamben 1998. For a recent critique, see Magnus Fiskejö (2012), who suggests that the posited relationship between state sovereignty and homo sacer may be "a fictional reconstruction" (173) since prestate and nonstate societies practiced expulsion as well as the granting of refuge.

4. Malkki 1992, 1995a, 1995b, 1996, 2002.

5. Daniel and Knudsen 1996; Nyers 2006; Verdirame and Harrell-Bond 2005.

6. See Malkki 1995b.

7. There is a vast literature, some of which is cited here, outlining the moral implications for humanitarian action toward refugees emerging from the Enlightenment view of a "shared humanity." Fiona Terry's (2002: 19) succinct statement that "humanitarian action posits a universal ethic founded on the conviction that all people have equal dignity by virtue of their membership in humanity" captures the basic argument.

8. Fassin 2005: 366.

9. See Agier 2010; Fadlalla 2009; Finnström 2008; Gatrell 2013; Hyndman 2000; Nyers 2006; Verdirame and Harrell-Bond 2005.

10. Gatrell 2013: 242. Gatrell is also critiquing assumptions about the dependency of African refugees on humanitarian organizations.

11. I did not conduct ethnographic fieldwork in the refugee camps. This chapter and chapter 3 are based on oral history interviews with refugees, former UNHCR staff, ethnographic studies, reports by humanitarian agencies, and news accounts.

12. Gatrell 2013; Sassen 1999 (also Nyers 2006). Sassen writes, "The first change appeared in the Third Edition of the *Encyclopedia Britannica* issued in 1796: 'refugee' was extended beyond that particular case of Protestants to anyone leaving his or her country in times of distress, a general term also covering specific cases like the word 'émigré,' applied to aristocrats who left France during the French Revolution" (1999: 35).

13. Gerstle and Mollenkopf 2001.
14. Bohmer and Shuman 2008; Churgin 1996.
15. Sassen 1999: 83.
16. Gatrell 2013. See also Torpey 2000.
17. Arendt (1951) 1966: 267, 269.
18. See Haines 2010; Loescher and Scanlan 1986.
19. Brettell 2007; De Genova 2005; King 2001; Sanchez 2000.
20. Gatrell (2013: 88) notes that the International Refugee Organization focus on assisting those fleeing communism overlooked the concerns of the large number of refugees in South Asia, East Asia, and the Middle East during this era.
21. Loescher and Scanlan 1986.
22. Einolf 2001; Loescher and Scanlan 1986; Malkki 1995b. An initial bill signed by Truman in 1948 limited the number of Jews to be accepted by the United States, although this concern was later softened as a greater concern with communism overtook the refugee debate.
23. Feldman 2007.
24. Loescher and Scanlan 1986.
25. Gatrell 2013: 109; Malkki 1995b: 499.
26. See Kennedy 2004 for a discussion of the legal debates around this issue.
27. Khosravi 2010: 70.
28. The phrase "murderous humanitarianism" comes from Robin D. G. Kelley (2000: 19). In their article on "methodological nationalism," Andreas Wimmer and Nina Glick Schiller (2002) note how social scientists began to accept the normativity of the nation-state structure by problematizing migrants as policy concerns during and after World War II.
29. Gatrell 2013: 241.
30. The UNHCR annual Global Trends report (see, for example, UNHCR 2012) shows the pattern of housing refugees in poorer countries in the global south.
31. Hyndman 2000: 17. See also Verdirame and Harrell-Bond 2005. On the charge that policies and practices of the global north prompt refugee flows in the global south, see, in addition to my argument in chapter 1, Bohmer and Schuman 2008 on Central American refugees; Shemak 2010 on Caribbean refugees; Agier 2010; and Bauman 2004.
32. Ethnographic discussions of these points are available in Agier 2005, 2010; Bauman 2004; Bohmer and Schuman 2008; Edkins 2000; Fadlalla 2009; Fassin 2005, 2007; Hyndman 2000; Nyers 2006; Turner 2010; Verdirame and Harrell-Bond 2005.
33. Aleinikoff 1995: 263. See also Gorlick 2003; Hyndman 2000; Loescher 2003; White and Marsella 2007.
34. Edkins 2000: 15.
35. Verdirame and Harrell-Bond 2005. Prior to the massive influx of Somali refugees in 1991, Kenya had not previously required its tiny number of resident refugees to live in confined camps.
36. Nyers 2006: 85; Verdirame and Harrell-Bond 2005: 271; Agier and Bouchet-Saulnier 2004: 302.

37. Agier 2005: 45.

38. Agier 2010; see also Turner 2004 on Tanzanian camps.

39. Horst 2006: 112.

40. Verdirame and Harrell-Bond 2005.

41. Gourevitch 2010: 109; Verdirame and Harrell-Bond 2005: 334, emphasis in original. See also Agier 2005.

42. Crisp 1999; Horst 2006: 91.

43. The processes of refugee resettlement and asylum differ in one critical respect. An asylum application is made after the applicant has already managed to cross the border into the country in which he or she wishes to request asylum. In contrast, refugee resettlement applications are negotiated only from afar, usually from the country to which a refugee has fled, for entry into a third country, and only under the auspices of UNHCR. The contemporary process of managing refugee admittance to the United States is based on minimizing the opportunity for asylum claims by ensuring that refugees are kept far away from American borders.

44. Bohmer and Shuman 2008; Loescher and Scanlan 1986.

45. Loescher and Scanlan 1986.

46. Peter Schrag (2011) reviews the long-standing tension in America between the need for immigrant labor to power economic development and the hostility toward immigrants as undesirable, diseased, and culturally dangerous.

47. Gil Loescher and John A. Scanlan (1986) report that 800,000 immigrants arrived in the United States in 1980.

48. Haines 2010.

49. Boas 2007.

50. Boas 2007.

51. In 2004, when the first Somali Bantus began arriving in the United States, the P2 designation also included Cubans, religious minorities from Iran and the former Soviet Union, Baku Armenians, and American-associated Vietnamese (U.S. Senate Judiciary Committee Hearing 2004).

52. UNHCR 2002: 14.

53. UNHCR 2002: 2.

54. UNHCR 2002: 7.

55. Boas 2007: 438.

56. Boas 2007: 463, 455.

57. Barnett 2003.

58. Lacey 2001; UNHCR 2002; Finkel 2002.

59. Goffe 2004; Manning 2004; UNHCR 2002.

60. Swarns 2003a; Lovgren 2003.

61. Lacey 2001; Harman 2001; Lorch 2002.

62. Lorch 2002; UNHCR 2002; Swarns 2003a.

63. UNHCR 2002; Swarns 2003b; Barnett 2003: 12.

64. UNHCR 2002: 7; Lorch 2002.

65. U.S. Senate Judiciary Committee Hearing 2004. See *Economist* 2003; Lacey 2001; Lorch 2002; UNHCR 2002.

66. U.S. Department of State 1999.

67. Frelick 2007: 34.

68. Frelick 2007: 47.

69. U.S. Senate Judiciary Committee Hearing, Immigration Subcommittee 2002.

70. U.S. Senate Judiciary Committee Hearing, Immigration Subcommittee 2002.

71. U.S. Senate Judiciary Committee Hearing, Immigration Subcommittee 2002.

72. U.S. Department of State n.d.

73. U.S. Department of State 2004.

74. The report comments that lengthy processing delays "allowed for misunderstanding and resistance to grow in some of the U.S. destination communities, among people who were uncertain of what to expect and who sometimes gave public voice to fearful worst-case scenarios that were widely off the mark." Antirefugee activists in several cities selected for resettlement, including Hadley, Massachusetts, and Cayce, South Carolina, successfully blocked the resettlement of Somali Bantu refugees in their communities.

75. Haines 2010: 170; Bohmer and Shuman 2008; Kennedy 2004; Loescher and Scanlan 1986; Schrag 2011.

76. For example, Gibney 2004.

77. For example, Bauman 2004.

78. For example, Fassin 2005; Ticktin 2006.

79. Albeit, certainly, with a dimension of care.

3. Becoming Somali Bantus

1. In the sense, of course, of James Scott (1999).

2. Much of this chapter is based on oral histories recounted by my former Banta neighbors and others from the Jubba Valley as well as interviews with former UNHCR staff who worked in Dadaab and scholars who visited or conducted fieldwork in Dadaab. Thus, as with chapter 1, this chapter captures how those with whom I spoke narrate their memories of their experiences in Dadaab.

3. Other studies that explore refugee agency include Steven Robins's (2009) description of a coalition created in South Africa by an HIV/AIDS activist group, NGOs, and refugees to use South Africa's progressive constitution to promote a notion of transnational citizenship that would offer greater protections to refugees; Simon Turner's (2010) and Liisa Malkki's (2002) attention to the political activism of refugees in, respectively, Lukole and Mishamo refugee camps; Cindy Horst's (2006) and Jennifer Hyndman's (2000) descriptions of the forms of mobility and transnational networks maintained by Somali refugees in Dadaab to access resources; Fiona Terry's (2002) and Peter Nyers's (2006) reviews of the challenge to humanitarian visions posed by "warrior refugees"; Ilana Feldman's (2012) work on how Palestinian refugees appropriate the language of humanitarianism to demand civil rights as refugees; Nell Gabiam's (2012) analysis of how Palestinian refugees in Syria reject development schemes intended to reduce their suffering, a subjectivity they believe is important for maintaining claims to their right to return home; Rahul Chandrashekhar Oka's (2014) argument that refugees in Kakuma

insist on consumption and marketing activities that camp administrators oppose because such practices offer a sense of dignity and normalcy; and Shahram Khosravi's (2010) autoethnography of his own experience as a refugee.

4. Menkhaus 2010: 93.

5. Declich 2000: 31.

6. See Besteman 1999b; Declich 1987; Menkhaus 1989.

7. Menkhaus notes that Somali militias targeted food aid directed toward Bantus in Somalia during the early years of the civil war: "Now that they were dispossessed of all they had, the Bantu's destitution itself became a commodity to exploit" (2010: 98).

8. Menkhaus 2010: 99.

9. Menkhaus 2010: 99.

10. Kenneth Menkhaus says this was Zimbabwean Leonard Kapungo, the UNOSOM director of the Department of Political Affairs from 1992 to 1995 (personal communication, March 20, 2011), as does Dan Van Lehman (personal communication, September 7, 2012).

11. Omar Eno, interview, Portland, Oregon, July 18, 2007.

12. Francesca Declich (2000), an anthropologist who worked in the Kenyan refugee camps, reported that jareer refugees arriving at the camps were expected to provide information about their lineage, ethnic group, village of origin, tribe, clan, and/or subclan on the UNHCR camp registration form, a form that provided new arrivals with an identity as refugees and camp residents. Declich noted that arriving refugees unable to offer a clear tribe or clan identity were designated "Bantu," whether or not they spoke a Bantu language or used the term to define themselves.

13. Dan Van Lehman, interview, Portland, Oregon, July 18, 2007. See also Eno and Eno 2007.

14. Dan Van Lehman, personal communication, November 18, 2012.

15. Dan Van Lehman, personal communication, November 25, 2012.

16. Tanzania eventually granted citizenship to about 3,000 Somali Bantu refugees.

17. Van Lehman 1999.

18. Several of my informants suggested the four major jareer groups that ultimately became the Somali Bantus were Mushunguli (Zigua speakers from the lower Jubba), Maxaway (Af-Maay speakers from the lower Jubba), Reer Shabelle (Af-Maxaa speakers from around the Bu'aale area), and Elye/Rahanweyn (Af-Maay speakers from Saakow-Baay region). In Somalia, the last considered themselves somewhat superior to the first three groups, a distinction my informants claim disappeared after the consolidation of Somali Bantu identity in the camps and the diaspora.

19. Abdulle, interview, Hartford, March 25, 2007.

20. U.S. Department of State 1999.

21. *Economist* 2003. See also the description of the three-day bus journey in Chanoff 2002.

22. See, for example, Bohmer and Shuman 2007, 2008; Khosravi 2010; Malkki 2007; Ordoñez 2008.

23. Bohmer and Shuman 2007: 609. See also Fassin 2013.

24. Writing about an applicant who was denied asylum because his life trajectory meant he did not speak the language his interviewer believed he should, Jan Blommaert notes, "The dominant reflex to increases of hybridity and deterritorialization, unfortunately, too often appears to be a reinforced homogeneity and territorialization" (2009: 425).

25. Fassin and Rechtman 2009: 281–82. Malkki adds, "We should be ready to consider the possibility, at least, that contemporary asylum seekers and immigrants are de facto being forced to convert the psychic trauma of impoverishment and hopelessness into a performed psychic trauma of formulaic political violence" (2007: 341).

26. In apartheid South Africa, state authorities pushed a pencil through a person's hair to confirm African ancestry for identity documents. "African" hair was thought to offer greater resistance to the pencil.

27. I learned that other countries with refugee resettlement programs besides the United States also subscribed to a racialized understanding of Somali Bantu identity as verifiable through physical characteristics when a representative of the Australian government asked me to analyze photographs of Somali Bantus applying for asylum and provide an authoritative statement about whether or not they were Somali Bantu based on their physical appearance. Instead I sent him a copy of "American Anthropological Association Statement on 'Race,'" (May 17, 1998, http://www.aaanet.org/stmts/racepp.htm).

28. Van Lehman and Eno 2003.

29. Dan Van Lehman, personal communication, March 1, 2007.

30. Reported in Briggs 2005. According to the article, after the mother arrived in Burlington, Vermont, she was able to pursue the case through DNA testing, which proved the family relationship.

31. Sanders and Zucchino 2006.

32. Peter Nyers (2006) and Peter Gatrell (2013) analyze the use of images of nameless refugees to depict destitution and dependency by humanitarian agencies, insights that could be enhanced by research on the public audiences to whom these images appeal.

II. Introduction

1. Images of Somalis uneasily confronting an escalator have become a meme. The scene in the film *Rain in a Dry Land* showing a Somali Bantu family arrayed at the base of the escalator in the airport after arriving for the first time in the United States makes a dramatic impression on viewers. At one large meeting of social services providers I attended in Portland, Maine, participants described this scene as the most impactful moment in the film for them. A YouTube video made in Sweden of two Somali women poised at the top of an escalator in a shopping mall, unable to screw up the courage to step onto the stairs as other shoppers pass by them, has been reposted on Facebook and Somali and racist websites, generating hundreds of comments from people either sympathetic to the women's

uncertainty, making fun of their own parents for their fear of escalators, or nastily castigating Somalis as intellectually and culturally inferior and unfit to live in modern society.

2. Stated in "2012/13 State of Maine ORR Funded Programs," Office of Refugee Resettlement, November 28, 2012, http://www.acf.hhs.gov/programs/orr/resource /ffy-2012-13-state-of-maine-orr-funded-programs.

3. Sudanese "lost boy" Valentino Achek Deng, in his autobiography written with the assistance of David Eggers, poignantly recollects his dashed hopes for education under the burden of working in the back room of a furniture showroom: "The job kept me in the back of the store, among the fabric samples. I should not feel shame about this, but somehow I do: my job was to retrieve fabric samples for the designers, and then file them again when they were returned. I did this for almost two years. The thought of all that time wasted, so much time sitting on that wooden stool, cataloguing, smiling, thanking, filing—all while I should have been in school—is still too much for me to contemplate" (Eggers 2007: 20).

4. U.S. Senate Committee on Foreign Relations 2010.

5. Haines 2010: 163. Haines notes that the reductions in refugee assistance that began in the 1980s in response to concerns about "refugee dependence" resulted in "limited overall improvement in the economic situation of Southeast Asian refugees" during 1982–85 (2010: 162). The extension of direct assistance to refugees has continued to decline since then.

6. In 2000, Mary Waters wrote that immigration scholars had been slow to draw on scholarship about race in their analyses of immigrant experience, reflect- ing an uncertainty about how to analyze the sometimes tense relations between native-born and immigrant people of color. Philip Kasinitz (2004) and Nancy Foner (2005) are among the scholars now investigating the relationship between immigrants of color and native-born African Americans.

7. Nadeau 2011.

8. From 2006 to 2010 I spent one to four days a week (and in 2011–12 several days a month) in Lewiston doing participant observation, conducting interviews, volun- teering in schools and social services agencies, attending committee meetings for local NGOs and community organizations, and engaging in advocacy and public education projects with local activists and refugee community members. In addi- tion to traditional participant observation (afternoons visiting refugee friends in their apartments, sharing tea with friends in the Somali café or in their commu- nity offices), my research in Lewiston included oral history interviews with refu- gees (chapters 1 and 3); formal interviews with officials and staff in city and state government, local schools, NGOs, medical offices, and other agencies charged with assisting and building programs for refugees from 2001 to 2006 (chapter 4); infor- mal conversations with a wide spectrum of Lewiston's non-Somali residents in fo- rums ranging from stores to office waiting rooms to community meetings where residents shared their concerns about changes in their city (chapter 5); advocacy work with activist and community networks and NGO boards from 2006 to 2011 (chapters 4 and 6); and participation in public outreach projects in collaboration

with Somali and Somali Bantu community leaders and local organizations (such as public panel discussions and an exhibit at Museum LA) (part III). Besteman 2010 provides additional information about my field research, methodology, and advocacy activities.

9. Macdonald 2012a.

4. We Have Responded Valiantly

1. I often use "refugee" and "immigrant" interchangeably in this chapter and the next because as secondary migrants Somalis were both refugees and immigrants. Many of the professional leaders of the Somali community preferred the term "immigrants," which they felt more accurately captured their social status in Lewiston.

2. Unlike many other states, Maine has allowed people, including noncitizen refugee immigrants and asylum seekers, to request GA help the day they arrive. This form of welfare support is under attack by Governor LePage, who claims it attracts welfare dependents.

3. A new concern with immigrant integration is reflected in the production of policy documents and how-to manuals, such as GCIR 2006.

4. Phil Nadeau, interview, January 14, 2010. Also see Nadeau 2005, 2011.

5. Nadeau 2005: 120.

6. "A Letter to the Somali Community," ImmigrationsHumanCost.org, October 1, 2002, http://www.immigrationshumancost.org/text/raymond.html. The Letter is also the subject of a documentary film called *The Letter* (Hamzeh 2003).

7. These stories and others are collected in Somalis in Maine Archive, Scholarly Communication and Research at Bates, http://scarab.bates.edu/somalis_in _maine/.

8. See interviews in the film *The Letter* (Hamzeh 2003). Nadeau (2005) shows that the percentage of the local share of property taxes that went to support immigrant and refugee programs was .97 percent in 2003 and the total cost to the city of GA for immigrants and refugees was $145, 979.

9. Phil Nadeau, interview, January 14, 2010.

10. Nadeau credits Mark Grey (2000) for inspiring this phrase.

11. These estimates are from an informal census conducted in 2010 by the Somali Bantu Community Mutual Assistance Association.

12. Another particularly notable exception to the business-as-usual attitude was the New American Sustainable Agriculture Project created after the arrival of Somali Bantus by a local nonprofit, Coastal Enterprises. Through this project, dozens of Somali Bantu men and women began cultivating small plots, selling their produce to farmers' markets and local restaurants. The project was later absorbed by a local nonprofit called Cultivating Community (accessed February 26, 2014, http:// www.cultivatingcommunity.org).

13. Nadeau 2007: appendix D.

14. News articles reported similar complaints in Boston (Vaznis 2009), Pittsburgh (Smydo 2006), and Springfield, MA (Glater 2006).

15. Interview, May 6, 2010.

16. According to Nadeau's 2007 report to Maine's congressional delegation, "NCLB [No Child Left Behind] states that students must be tested and held to the same standards in math as their English speaking peers as soon as they enter the county. In reading there is a one year grace period. Thus, if a 12 year old, comes to us from another country with no prior schooling, after one year, he/she is expected to meet the same standards as English speaking peers in reading, writing and science" (2007: 18). The report also notes that because of Maine's comparatively high standards, many ELL students are "failing" who would be passing in other states.

17. The high school principal weathered complaints that some students washed their feet in the lavatory basins at prayer time, informing concerned parents that according to the school nurse, foot washing is not a health hazard. Several teachers laughed in conversations with me at their recollection that he told them, privately, that he wished more students would wash their feet.

18. Pollock 2004.

19. Brown 2006: 13.

20. Brown 2006: 46.

21. Ellison 2009.

22. See Gilbert 2011; Jones-Correa 2011.

23. On the history of refuge, see Rabben 2011.

24. Jacklet 2004. See also Manning 2004; Wagner 2003.

25. Povinelli 2011.

26. For example, Govenor LePage introduced in his 2012 budget a sixty-month cap on benefits, identifying immigrants dependent on benefits as one of his targets. People who reach the sixty-month cutoff but still need help could seek it through the GA programs in their local cities, but in 2014 Governor LePage instituted a new rule that GA staff could no longer provide assistance to immigrants who had not yet achieved citizenship (including asylum seekers). The governor also attempted to scale back the amount of state aid provided to cities for GA. Some cities, such as Portland, refused to obey the new rule, and community action groups throughout the state protested it. As of this writing the rule is being reviewed in court. Lewiston's Mayor Macdonald staunchly supported the governor's actions.

5. Strangers in Our Midst

1. Since the myths encompass both Somali and Somali Bantu immigrants, in this chapter I use "Somali" to include both groups.

2. Meyer 2010.

3. Ellison 2009; Jones 2004.

4. See Ellison 2009.

5. The CPHV prepared a myth-busting memo to use in their community dialogues and school programs that challenged claims that local schools provided Somalis with a separate prayer room, removed pork from school lunches out of deference to Islam, and distributed money to Somali families. The superintendent of schools told me that he had also written a myth-busting letter in response to parental complaints about unfair special privileges for refugees.

6. In an article about resurgent public expressions of racism in Britain and their iterative presence in the online arena, Paul Gilroy (2012) addresses the importance of social media—blogs, Facebook, YouTube videos—as a space of public commentary and interpretation for which researchers have yet to fully develop adequate interpretive tools. He is particularly interested in the resonance between such expressions and the public statements about multiculturalism and race by British politicians. In Lewiston, I was struck by how often people critical of the immigrant Somali population cited online comments posted in response to news articles about Somalis as the basis for their "facts."

7. This chapter departs from the more chronological structure of the previous chapters to capture the reigning sentiments of confusion, insecurity, and racism that characterized some conversations, editorials, and blogs in Lewiston from 2006 to 2011. My discussion is not intended to stereotype residents who are hostile to the presence of refugees—all of whom remain anonymous here with the exception of public figures and those who identified themselves by name in their published comments in the newspaper—but rather aims to highlight resonances between localized concerns in Lewiston and broader concerns in American popular and political culture about insecurities introduced by immigrants. The story I tell here shows how the current American mythology of dangerous immigrants gains particular footholds in Lewiston's cultural and economic context.

8. Ahmed, Besteman, and Osman 2010; Besteman and Ahmed 2010.

9. Staff Sergeant Thomas Field was from neighboring Lisbon, Maine. Master Sergeant Gary Gordon, of Lincoln, Maine, was also killed in the battle.

10. Macdonald 2012a. This sentiment appears regularly in local editorials. A few random selections from editorials in spring 2010 include the following: Roland Morin wrote, "As a Franco, I find the comparison insulting! The people from Quebec came here to work—not to live off welfare!" (*Twin City Times*, March 18, 2010); Jacqueline Smith wrote, "The only comparison between the French-Canadians and the Somali is that neither is native to this country. Don't try to excuse one by down-grading the other" (*Twin City Times*, April 8, 2010).

11. Rachel Desgrosseilliers and Karla Rider, interview, June 17, 2010.

12. Besteman and Ahmed 2010; Cullen 2011; Goad 2002.

13. Because I used the DHHS category "noncitizen residents," the number could include some non-Somalis as well. The figures would not include Somalis who have naturalized, although the process of applying for citizenship in the Somali population was just beginning in 2009. I am grateful to David Maclean in Lewiston's DHHS office for his kind assistance.

14. Since Governor LePage assumed office, the link to "The Real Facts" on the DHHS website has been removed.

15. Rector 2008.

16. Nadeau 2008.

17. Mary LaFontaine, interview, May 20, 2010.

18. After providing seasonal employment in Lewiston for several years, in 2009 the wreath-making company failed to return because it lost its contract

with L.L.Bean, although 150 Somalis put their names on the sign-up sheet just in case they decided to hire again.

19. Mamgain with Collins 2003.

20. Bates College Department of Anthropology 2008.

21. L.L.Bean accommodates non-English-speaking immigrants to meet the company's need for seasonal labor. Workers can pray during break time, use the bathroom sinks to wash their feet before prayers, and wear whatever clothing they prefer so long as it is safe, according to refugees who have worked there; see Toner and Hough 2011.

22. Work Ready job training programs require an eighth-grade diploma, which prohibits most adult Somalis even though local teachers tell me off the record that they suspect many white Lewistonians in the Work Ready program cannot read at an eighth-grade level.

23. In May 2012, the RefugeeWorks website announced a transition to a new organization called Higher, which would focus on "supporting businesses in developing workforce solutions and by creating welcoming workplaces through on-site cultural competence training." See RefugeeWorks, May 17, 2012, http://refugeeworks .blogspot.it.

24. Seele 2009: 3.

25. Meyer 2010.

26. Supervisors at the social services agencies with whom I spoke about this problem complained that the local schools and community colleges were failing to ensure that Somali refugees graduated with writing skills adequate for independent report writing. They noted that their slim budgets made it difficult to support extra training.

27. *Twin City Times* 2011.

28. Taylor 2011.

29. Because Mayor Macdonald won his first term by the slimmest of margins against a man who died days before the election, friends in Lewiston unhappy about Macdonald's policies cheer each other up by saying, "Remember, he barely beat a dead man!"

30. Jim Dowling, interview, June 7, 2010.

31. Shortly after moving to Lewiston, Isha and her youngest son were chased through the city park by a dog whose owner stood laughing and urging the dog on as, panicked, they tried to outrun it. Later, the police arrested four Somali boys after they fought back against a white man whose unleashed dog chased them in the park. Kim Wettlaufer, who witnessed both incidents, was furious, wondering why the men with the illegally unleashed dog were not arrested.

32. Personal communication, December 18, 2009.

33. Gilbert 2009.

34. But the price of citizenship is nearly prohibitive. In one of his many op-eds designed to rebut pernicious myths, Mayor Larry Gilbert wrote about the rising cost of citizenship to help Lewiston residents realize just how expensive the process is. In 2010, the cost of a green card was $985; the naturalization test cost $675; and the fingerprinting and biometric data tests cost $85.

35. *BBC News* 2012.
36. Macdonald 2012a.
37. One conversation I overheard in the courtyard of Trinity's day shelter offered a slightly different angle from non-Somalis on Somali gender norms. As I walked past a small group, a woman gesturing furiously exclaimed to her interlocutors, "That shit's illegal here!" A man in the group responded, "Yeah, four wives to one man! Four hens in the kitchen! Who needs that?"
38. Seele 2010.
39. Lauren Gilbert (2009) reports the refusal of the city council to allow Ismail Ahmed to serve on the Downtown Task Force after the mayor appointed him because he was not a citizen, an account confirmed by Ismail.
40. Honig 2001: 76.
41. Echoing the desire for gratitude as a response to the (perceived) extension of charity, Achille Mbembe mimics a popular view of immigrants in France in a passage from which this chapter's epigraph is taken: "These people are in France for personal gain; they treat the French state like one 'big insurance company.' The republic undertakes enormous sacrifices and receives in return only hatred and jeers. Herein lies their radical difference, the demonstration that they have never been, and never will be, a part of us" (2011: 109).
42. Derrida and Dufourmantelle 2000; see also Khosravi 2010; Nyers 2006.
43. Herzfeld 1993: 171.
44. Katerina Rozakou (2012) describes an interesting case of a group of activists in Greece who attempted to assist refugees squatting in urban areas by positioning themselves as guests, thus making the refugees into hosts as a form of political activism and refugee empowerment.
45. About the extension of hospitality to the refugee foreigner, a practice that "has existed since the beginning of civilization," Paul Ricouer says the refugee "assumes the role of 'beggar' in relation to the host society" (2010: 44, 41).
46. Lidwien Kapteijns and Abukar Arman (2004: 19) note that Somalis' "distinctly assertive culture" can be challenging to host communities who expect quiescence and conformity.
47. Macdonald 2012a.
48. Jonathan Xavier Inda (2006) analyzes the popular and political representations of illegal immigrants as ethically irresponsible, criminals, job takers, and consumers of public resources not meant for them. See also Ho and Loucky 2012.
49. A scene in the documentary film *Rain in a Dry Land* (Makepeace 2006) shows several Somali Bantu families dividing their food purchases in the driveway of their Springfield, Massachusetts, apartment building while other residents watch and comment that they would like to be able to share and work together like the Somali Bantus do.
50. Honig 2001: 102.

6. Helpers in the Neoliberal Borderlands

1. None of this work took the form of fieldwork oriented toward the production of an ethnography of schools or social services agencies, but rather followed the tradition of action anthropology in which volunteer and advocacy work is a logical extension of ethnographic participant observation, especially with marginalized or vulnerable communities. Although this is not the place to discuss action anthropology, some of my works discuss my engagement as a researcher-advocate (Besteman 2010, 2014). My volunteer work also meant close involvement with the development and activities of the Somali Bantu community association, SBYAM, and Somali activists, about whom I write in chapter 7.

2. The neoliberal borderlands, of course, are also, in a way, the neoliberal front lines. In this chapter I employ the term "borderlands" because of my focus on the collaborative struggles shared by those who provide assistance and those who seek assistance. Those studies that illuminate the antagonistic struggles include Luhrmann 2010 and Kingfisher 2007 on homeless shelters; Collins and Mayer 2010 on welfare reform and workfare programs; Kingfisher and Goldsmith 2001 and Kingfisher 1998 on welfare officers; and Ong 1996 and 2003 on social workers who work with refugees; also Vertovec 2011; Brodwin 2013.

3. Halfway through his first term he lambasted state workers, calling them "about as corrupt as can be" for withholding enthusiastic support for his reforms (Canfield 2012).

4. The people profiled here are quick to promote the hard work and accomplishments of their staff and colleagues and resist any suggestion that they are somehow more devoted than others doing the same work.

5. Interview, February 26, 2010.

6. Cawo M. Abdi (2012: 98) reports that Somalis in the United States have the highest poverty rates of all newcomers, at 51 percent, which is four times that of the United States and twice that of African Americans.

7. Available at http://larrygilbert.typepad.com (accessed May 26, 2015).

8. Larry Gilbert, interview, May 20, 2010.

9. Malone 2010.

10. See, for comparison, Andrea Muehlenbach (2013a) on what she calls "the moral style" of neoliberalism in Lombardy, where a Catholic philosophy shapes local action by emphasizing the importance of mutual love, compassion, and ethical behavior within the neoliberal economy.

11. Marc Robitaille, interview, May 20, 2010.

12. Federal agents raided a Somali-owned butcher and grocer in February 2010 without first informing the local police and without publicly revealing the reason for the raid.

13. Lead levels among Somali Bantu children living downtown were extremely high, prompting a public health investigation into the causes (see Lindkvist 2003a). By 2013, several tenements were razed because of excessive lead.

14. A note on methodology: in 2009–10 I spent time in two local schools as a volunteer (and not a researcher). Descriptions of classroom activities are based

on my experiences as a volunteer and were not part of a school-based research project. Most of this section is based on the many interviews I conducted outside of school with ELL teachers, school staff, community members, and other social services providers who engaged with schools and agreed to be interviewed for this project.

15. When presented with these statistics, a school official protested that the numbers reflected number of incidents rather than number of students, presenting a skewed picture by failing to reflect that some students were repeatedly suspended. Their alternative data show that in the middle school that year, Somali students were 35 percent of students suspended.

16. Bus suspensions also often led to school absences, because someone with a car must be located to drive to and from school each day. No one was able to provide statistics for bus suspensions, information that is not collected by the state.

17. Noguera 2008: 132.

18. Pollock 2008. At a meeting organized by community advocates about the high suspension rates of Somali students, the teachers, social workers, and counselors noted that what appears to be an effort to assert a zero-tolerance policy regarding behavior and the desire to be seen as applying the same disciplinary expectations and punishments for Somalis as non-Somalis rejects an acknowledgment that background issues might be relevant to children's behavior. A woman from Maine's parent advocacy organization pointed out that the language of "no special treatment" and "conformity by all" sounds similar to things she heard back in the 1970s about special needs students and the refusal by many schools to alter their normal way of doing things to accommodate difference. "If they fail it's their fault!" she mimics.

19. For example, the model that presents the background of refugee children as one of deficiency (see Foley 2008; Roy and Roxas 2011).

20. The point was made that the school already partners with the local Adult Education program to review grades with parents and teach them about the online system, and that a school official had just formed the first ELL parent advisory committee, with handpicked participants. Hopeful about this news, I asked at Adult Education about their program and learned that there was, in fact, no organized school-sponsored information session. When I located participants in the school-sponsored parent advisory group, I learned that it was discontinued for the year after only one meeting.

21. From Caroline Sample's private blog, April 15, 2010, quoted with permission.

22. See, for example, Amin 2013; Besteman and Gusterson 2009; Khosravi 2010; Papasterdiadis 2012; Thomas 2009; Weston 2005.

23. Hardt and Negri 2009: 45, 49.

24. Muehlenbach 2013b.

25. Muehlenbach 2011: 67. Her argument echoes an earlier argument by Hardt that affective labor produces "social networks, forms of community, biopower" (1999: 96).

26. Hardt 1999: 100.

27. Povinelli 2009: 98, 97.

28. Ahmed, Besteman, and Osman 2010; Cullen 2011.

29. Povinelli 2009: 98.

30. Such tempered advocacy reveals the limits of the welfare state as well, of course. But while those profiled here are reluctant to act locally in ways that might blow back on their ability to raise money for their organizations or that might get them fired for insubordination, they do exercise the option to lobby the government for policy changes. Legislative hearings in January 2014 about proposed changes to welfare eligibility that would deny new immigrants access to General Assistance, for example, provided an opportunity for about a hundred people to protest the proposed reductions (see Billings 2014).

III. Introduction

1. Al-Shabaab formed from the remnants of the Islamic Courts Union government that was ousted by the U.S.-supported Ethiopian invasion of Somalia in 2006. The group's initial mandate was to contest foreign intervention.

7. Making Refuge

1. An example from a local agency with the mission to make local mental health services more accessible to poor and marginalized residents is instructive of the task faced by Somali and Somali Bantu cultural brokers. At a meeting where the agency decided to hold focus groups with New Mainers to learn about their mental health concerns, someone brought up the possibility of also conducting focus groups with service providers to hear about their experiences of working with New Mainers. The project director suggested this would be problematic because service providers are busy and would expect a concrete result from their participation, provoking the Somali Bantu caseworker to gently suggest that Somali Bantu focus group participants also want concrete results from their participation. The project director had the good sense to be chagrined about her assumption that immigrants are objects of study whose participation does not merit action.

2. Ironically, the selection process modeled administrative disorder rather than precision. A meeting in Lewiston to explain the grant and invite applications was announced via e-mail to only a few people a few days beforehand, followed by frantic phone calls the morning of the meeting to collect refugee representatives. Two hours after the appointed starting time, the project administrator had assembled an audience of about a dozen bewildered people from Lewiston's refugee population, to whom he explained that the program would offer "comprehensive capacity building within communities," "leadership development," "strategic planning and mission development," "networking opportunities," and training about "the development of organizational structure to leverage support." At the conclusion of the meeting, the administrator announced that the applications, which consisted of five essay questions on organizational goals, projects, successes, and failures, and five organizational profile questions, would be due immediately, that very afternoon. Not an auspicious beginning for a project that purported to offer bureaucratic and administrative capacity building.

3. Over time, many Somali translators and caseworkers developed excellent relationships with their clients. Some Somali translators from Kenya and Ethiopia earned special trust from Somali Bantus because, as I was told, "They are innocent." Innocent of what? I asked. "Of crimes. Of abuses. Of killings. They stand with their tribe, but they weren't there during the war and that makes a big difference. The others—we don't know what they did during the war."

4. I asked many friends from Banta about the possibility for a rapprochement between Somali Bantus and Somalis in resettlement and was often told that while the two groups may live together in the United States, trust will always be an issue for Somali Bantus. One man responded, "We cannot forget what happened to us. I just look at my hands, where I was stabbed, at the scars from the beatings and stabbings, from when I was tied up, and I can't forget that. We are different people [he put the backs of his hands together and pushed them apart to demonstrate]. We can't forget what Somalis did to us."

5. The extraordinarily busy Somali cyberspace, anchored by several major online forums, offers a heartbreaking display of ongoing anti-Bantu racism, where discussions about the significance of Somali Bantu identity regularly invoke ugly and degrading racist language and stereotypes. Sadiq has been the subject of several racist diatribes in these forums, and my use of a pseudonym for him and other community leaders is in recognition of the threats that they have received through diaspora networks.

6. Because I worked with Somali Bantu community members on projects of self-representation (through creating an informational flyer, a website, museum exhibitions, and panel presentations), I was also pilloried for supporting divisiveness. A prominent businessman wrote a letter to the CEO of a local hospital denouncing the request for Somali Bantu translators and attacking me for my involvement, and I received threats because of my collaboration with Somali Bantu leaders.

7. See McCabe 2010.

8. A refugee friend suggested to me that such pervasive petty suspicions about money started in Kakuma, where English speakers got paid jobs translating, teaching, or working in the health care sector and everyone else was jealous that the new world of interacting with officials and outsiders meant cultural mediators could get resources that they could keep hidden.

9. Lokua Kanza, remarking ruefully on the thirty-five-minute time slot for his portion of the Africa Now! concert at the Apollo Theater, New York, March 16, 2013.

10. Drawing on fieldwork in Copenhagen and London, Nauja Kleist (2010) notes that Somali men in the diaspora feel their authority has been superseded by the welfare state while women have become more empowered, a loss they attempt to overcome through deeper engagements in Islam, return visits to Somaliland, and community associations.

11. See also Abdi 2014.

12. Since polygyny is illegal in the United States, only one wife is recognized as the legal wife, and the other will have her children's paternity registered with the state as her assurance of legal recognition.

13. One task many women are reluctant to cede is their control over the kitchen. Although some men began to take on responsibility for cleaning tasks, nearly everyone agrees that men cannot get involved in the kitchen. One man tells me, diplomatically, "If I try to do something in the kitchen it will only be a big argument. I avoid that." His wife nods emphatically, indicating that he has learned the limits of his contribution to domestic life. Even high school students agree: one of my most spirited conversations with a group of high school students involved rules for men and women in the kitchen. The boys insisted that the Quran says men should help their wives, but the girls uniformly dismissed their claims, insisting that men have no business in the kitchen.

14. Holtzman 2000.

15. Somali understandings of how money should intersect with morality received additional public attention when Museum LA offered a public program on Islamic banking to accompany the *Rivers of Immigration* exhibition. In the presentation by a representative from a local bank about the research on Islamic banking she undertook with Bates College anthropology students, the assembled non-Somali audience members and even the bank representative herself remarked that a banking structure with transparent fees rather than interest would be widely embraced beyond just the Muslim community.

16. See Ahmed 2011; Gilbert 2009. Ihotu Ali (2009) expresses concern that Somali community associations in Minnesota are oriented toward internal support structures and promoting cultural and religious accommodation in schools and workplaces rather than integration with the host community, wondering if self-isolation will be harmful in the long run.

8. These Are Our Kids

1. One day Idris told me about a new program called Safe Children, inaugurated by the humanitarian agencies that run the Kenyan refugee camps that everyone was talking about. The program's mandate is to stop early marriage and arranged marriage. I was amazed to learn that the agencies in charge of the camps were attempting this sort of social reform on displaced refugees and asked Idris what he thought about it. He responded without hesitation, "I think it's about time."

2. Ali 2007.

3. LaFlamme 2009.

4. Some women struggling with the universal shit storm participate in home visit programs from public health or social workers that are intended to provide support for overwhelmed parents, but even these programs can introduce stress because mothers do not want to appear incompetent in front of authorities. If a social worker observes a parent in an unguarded moment slapping a child, the social worker is obligated to report it as child abuse, and the news whips around the community because so many parents feel so vulnerable in the face of the possibility of losing their children to the government. At one collaborative meeting, Somali and Somali Bantu caseworkers explained to white social workers the challenges experienced by Somali and Somali Bantu parents involved in home

visit programs. The parents want to model good parenting and demonstrate that they are capable by cleaning and preparing for the home visit, but sometimes the effort is too great, and a parent cannot pull it together to feel presentable for the social worker and cancels the visit at the last minute. Everyone present knew what happens next: those who cancel get labeled "treatment resistant" or "noncompliant," earning another blot on their parenting record.

5. See Brettell 2007; Foner 2005; Foner and Fredrickson 2004; Foner, Rumbaut, and Gold 2000; Itzigsohn 2009; Portes and Rumbaut 1996; Suárez-Orozco et al. 2010; Waters 1994; Zhou 1997.

6. Zhou 1997; Portes and Zhou 1993; Foner 2005.

7. Portes and Rumbaut 1996.

8. Waters 1994: 801.

9. Kasinitz 2004: 287.

10. See Foner 2005; Itzigsohn 2009.

11. Forman 2005: 51; Kapteijns and Arman 2004; Samatar 2004.

12. Kapteijns and Arman 2004: 24; see also Al-Sharmani 2007.

13. Hammond 2011: n.p.

14. Shepard 2008: 236, 231.

15. While this is not the place for a discussion of African conceptions of personhood, anthropologists have demonstrated that the Western model of the individual contrasts in fundamental ways with the understandings held in many non-Western cultures that people are constituted through their relations with others. People, as individuals, are thus composites of their social relations. See Besteman 2014; Pina-Cabral 2013; Sahlins 2011a, 2011b.

16. Moore 2004.

17. See also Kleist 2010.

Conclusion

1. Macdonald 2012b.

2. The growing literature on Somali remittances estimates that Somalis remit $1–2 billion per year (Hammond et al. 2011; Sheikh and Healy 2009), probably making Somalia the largest per capita recipient of remittances (Hammond 2010). See also Lindley 2010.

3. Abdirisak experienced this prohibition firsthand. When he drove up to visit Idris during the year Idris was in Job Corps in northern Maine, he somehow missed the turnoff to the school and drove over the bridge into Canada by mistake. He immediately turned around and tried to reenter the United States, but since his accidental border crossing violated his probationary status, he was jailed for three days while Immigration and Customs Enforcement sorted out his story. "I hate jail!" he told me vehemently after he was freed. But three days of jail was certainly better than the other possible outcome, which was deportation.

4. Idris uses a recording of his father's flute music that I made in 1988 as his cell phone's ringtone.

5. Anna Amelina and Thomas Faist (2012), Nicolas De Genova (2005), Peggy Levitt (2012), and Nina Glick Schiller (2012), among others, discuss how scholars must move beyond the binaries of stranger/member, foreigner/citizen, immigrant/resident, and so forth, to investigate instead spheres of belonging and engagement, phenomenologies of emplacement, and special localities as constituted by social relations.

6. Horst 2006.

7. Nyamnjoh 2006: 230–31.

8. Papasterdiadis 2012: 402.

9. Amin 2013; Hall 2013; Hardt and Negri 2009; Honig 2001.

10. Honig 2001: 101.

11. Hardt and Negri 2009.

12. Hall 2013: 51 is discussing Amin 2013.

13. Hall 2013: 52.

14. Thanks to Britt Halvorson for this insight.

15. Besteman and Gusterson 2005.

REFERENCES

Abdi, Cawo M. 2012. "The Newest African-Americans? Somali Struggles for Belonging." *Bildhaan* 11: 90–107.

Abdi, Cawo. 2014. "Threatened Identities and Gendered Opportunities: Somali Migration to America." *Signs* 39 (21): 459–83.

Agamben, Giorgio. 1995. "We Refugees." Translated by Michael Rocke. *Symposium* 49 (2): 114–19.

Agamben, Giorgio. 1998. *Homo Sacer: Sovereign Power and Bare Life*. Translated by Daniel Heller-Roazen. Palo Alto, CA: Stanford University Press.

Agier, Michel. 2005. *On the Margins of the World: The Refugee Experience Today*. Cambridge: Polity.

Agier, Michel. 2010. "Humanity as an Identity and Its Political Effects (A Note on Camps and Humanitarian Government)." *Humanity* 1 (1): 29–45.

Agier, Michel, and Françoise Bouchet-Saulnier. 2004. "Humanitarian Spaces: Spaces of Exception." In *In the Shadows of "Just Wars": Violence, Politics and Humanitarian Action*, edited by Fabrice Weissman, translated by Vincent Homolka, Roger Leverdier, and Fiona Terry, 297–313. Ithaca, NY: Cornell University Press.

Ahmed, Ismail. 2011. "Fragmented and Collaborative Leadership in a Changing Somali Community." In *Somalis in Maine: Crossing Cultural Currents*, edited by Kimberly A. Huisman, Kristin M. Langellier, Mazie Hough, and Carol Nordstrom Toner. Berkeley, CA: North Atlantic.

Ahmed, Ismail, Catherine Besteman, and Rilwan Osman. 2010. "The Top Ten Myths about Somalis and Why They Are Wrong." *Twin City Times*, July 1.

Aleinikoff, T. Alexander. 1995. "State-Centered Refugee Law: From Resettlement to Containment." In *Mistrusting Refugees*, edited by E. Valentine Daniel and John C. Knudsen, 257–78. Berkeley: University of California Press.

Ali, Ayaan Hirsi. 2007. *Infidel*. New York: Atria.

Ali, Ihotu. 2009. "Staying off the Bottom of the Melting Pot: Somali Refugees Respond to a Changing U.S. Immigration Climate." *Bildhaan* 9: 82–114.

Al-Sharmani, Mulki. 2007. "Diasporic Somalis in Cairo: The Poetics and Practices of Soomaalinimo." In *From Mogadishu to Dixon: The Somali Diaspora in a Global Context*, edited by Abdi M. Kusow and Stephanie R. Bjork, 71–94. Trenton, NJ: Red Sea.

Amelina, Anna, and Thomas Faist. 2012. "De-naturalizing the National in Research Methodologies: Key Concepts of Transnational Studies in Migration." *Ethnic and Racial Studies* 35 (10): 1707–24.

Amin, Ash. 2013. "Land of Strangers." *Identities* 20 (1): 1–8.

Anderson, John Lee. 2009. "The Most Failed State." *New Yorker*, December 14.

Arendt, Hannah. (1951) 1966. *The Origins of Totalitarianism*. New York: Harcourt, Brace and World.

Barnett, Don. 2003. "Out of Africa: Somali Bantu and the Paradigm Shift in Refugee Resettlement." Center for Immigration Studies. http://cis.org /SomaliBantuRefugees.

Bates College Department of Anthropology. 2008. "Perceived Barriers to Somali Immigrant Employment in Lewiston: A Supplement to Maine's Department of Labor Report." http://abacus.bates.edu/pix/PerceivedBarriers09Jan20.pdf.

Bauman, Zygmunt. 2004. *Wasted Lives: Modernity and Its Outcasts*. Cambridge: Polity.

BBC News. 2008. "Somalia Is 'Most Ignored Tragedy.'" October 6. http://news.bbc.co .uk/2/hi/africa/7653928.stm.

BBC News. 2012. "African Migrants Who Call America's Whitest State Home." September 12. http://www.bbc.com/news/magazine-19548520.

Besteman, Catherine. 1994. "Individualisation and the Assault on Customary Tenure in Africa: Land Registration Programmes and the Case of Somalia." *Africa* 64 (4): 484–515.

Besteman, Catherine. 1996a. "Representing Violence and 'Othering' Somalia." *Cultural Anthropology* 11 (1): 120–33.

Besteman, Catherine. 1996b. "Violent Politics and the Politics of Violence: The Dissolution of the Somali Nation-State." *American Ethnologist* 23 (3): 579–96.

Besteman, Catherine. 1998. "Primordialist Blinders: A Reply to I. M. Lewis." *Cultural Anthropology* 13 (1): 109–20.

Besteman, Catherine. 1999a. "A Reply to Bernhard Helander." *American Ethnologist* 26 (4): 981–83.

Besteman, Catherine. 1999b. *Unraveling Somalia*. Philadelphia: University of Pennsylvania Press.

Besteman, Catherine. 2010. "In and Out of the Academy: The Case for a Strategic Anthropology." *Human Organization* 69 (4): 407–17.

Besteman, Catherine. 2014. "On Ethnographic Love." In *Mutuality*, edited by Roger Sanjek, 259–84. Philadelphia: University of Pennsylvania Press.

Besteman, Catherine, and Ismail Ahmed. 2010. "Refugee Economic Impact Study." Available as a link from Andrew Cullen, "Somalis: A Decade in Lewiston," *Lewiston Sun Journal*, December 18, 2011.

Besteman, Catherine, and Lee V. Cassanelli, eds. 2000. *The Struggle for Land in Southern Somalia: The War behind the War*. Reprint, London: Haan.

Besteman, Catherine, and Hugh Gusterson, eds. 2005. *Why America's Top Pundits Are Wrong*. Berkeley: University of California Press.

Besteman, Catherine, and Hugh Gusterson. 2009. "Introduction." In *The Insecure American*, edited by Hugh Gusterson and Catherine Besteman, 1–23. Berkeley: University of California Press.

Billings, Randy. 2014. "Asylum Seekers, Maine Advocates, Protest Change in Aid Rules." *Portland Press Herald*, January 11. http://www.pressherald.com/politics /Protesters_rally_against_curtailing_public_aid_for_new_asylum_seekers.html.

Blommaert, Jan. 2009. "Language, Asylum, and the National Order." *Current Anthropology* 50 (4): 415–41.

Boas, Heidi. 2007. "The New Face of America's Refugees: African Refugee Resettlement to the United States." *Georgetown Immigration Law Journal* 21 (3): 431–68.

Bohmer, Carol, and Amy Shuman. 2007. "Producing Epistemologies of Ignorance in the Political Asylum Process." *Identities* 14: 603–29.

Bohmer, Carol, and Amy Shuman. 2008. *Rejecting Refugees: Political Asylum in the 21st Century*. London: Routledge.

Bornstein, Erica. 2012. *Disquieting Gifts: Humanitarianism in New Delhi*. Palo Alto, CA: Stanford University Press.

Brettell, Caroline. 2007. "Introduction: Race, Ethnicity, and the Construction of Immigrant Identities." In *Constructing Borders / Crossing Boundaries: Race, Ethnicity, and Immigration*, edited by Caroline Brettell, 1–23. New York: Lexington.

Briggs, John. 2005. "Bantu Refugee Family Together Again." *Burlington Free Press*, January 8.

Bringe, Tone, and Debbie Christie. 1993. "We Are All Neighbours." *Disappearing World*, Granada Television.

Brodwin, Paul E. 2013. *Everyday Ethics: Voices from the Front Line of Community Psychiatry*. Berkeley: University of California Press.

Brown, Wendy. 2006. *Regulating Aversion: Tolerance in the Age of Identity and Empire*. Princeton, NJ: Princeton University Press.

Canfield, Clark. 2012. "Paul LePage, Republican Governor of Maine, Calls State Workers 'Corrupt.'" *Huffington Post*, April 27. http://www.huffingtonpost.com/2012 /04/27/lepage-corrupt-state-workers_n_1460871.html.

Cassanelli, Lee V. 1982. *The Shaping of Somali Society*. Philadelphia: University of Pennsylvania Press.

Castles, Stephen, and Mark J. Miller. 1993. *The Age of Migration*. New York: Guilford.

Chanoff, Sasha. 2002. "After Three Years: Somali Bantus Prepare to Come to America." *Refugee Reports* 23 (8): 1–11.

Churgin, Michael. 1996. "Mass Exodus: The Response of the United States." *International Migration Review* 30 (1): 310–44.

Collins, Jane, and Victoria Mayer. 2010. *Both Hands Tied: Welfare Reform and the Race to the Bottom in the Low-Wage Labor Market*. Chicago: University of Chicago Press.

Crisp, Jeff. 1999. "A State of Insecurity: The Political Economy of Violence in Refugee-Populated Areas of Kenya." Working Paper No. 16. Geneva: UNHCR.

Cullen, Andrew. 2011. "A Decade Later: The City, Somalis, and Spending." *Lewiston Sun Journal*, December 18.

Daniel, E. Valentine, and John C. Knudsen, eds. 1996. *Mistrusting Refugees*. Berkeley: University of California Press.

Danish Immigration Service. 2000. *Report on Minority Groups in Somalia*. Joint British, Danish, and Dutch Fact-Finding Mission to Nairobi, Kenya, September 17–24. http://www.nyidanmark.dk/NR/rdonlyres/0317E0EF-BB21-493F-A41C-1E0BD6D49EE5/0/FactfindingmissiontoKenyaSomalia2000tildanskhjemmeside.pdf.

Declich, Francesca. 1987. "I Goscia della regione del medio Giuba nella Somalia meridionale: Un gruppo etnico di origine Bantu." *Africa* (Rome) 42 (2): 570–99.

Declich, Francesca. 2000. "Fostering Ethnic Reinvention: Gender Impact of Forced Migration on Bantu Somali Refugees in Kenya." *Cahiers d'Etudes Africaines* 40 (157): 25–63.

De Genova, Nicolas. 2005. *Working the Boundaries: Race, Space, and "Illegality" in Mexican Chicago*. Durham, NC: Duke University Press.

Derrida, Jacques, and Anne Dufourmantelle. 2000. *Of Hospitality*. Translated by Rachel Bowlby. Palo Alto, CA: Stanford University Press.

Economist. 2003. "A Home at Last, but Not for Many." May 31, 29–32.

Edkins, Jenny. 2000. "Sovereign Power, Zones of Indistinction, and the Camp." *Alternatives: Global, Local, Political* 25 (1): 3–26.

Eggers, Dave. 2007. *What Is the What: The Autobiography of Valentino Achak Deng*. New York: Vintage.

Einolf, Christopher. 2001. *The Mercy Factory: Refugees and the American Asylum System*. Chicago: Ivan R. Dee.

Ellison, Jesse. 2009. "The Refugees Who Saved Lewiston." *Newsweek*, January 26, 69.

Eno, Mohamed. 2008. *The Bantu-Jareer Somalis: Unearthing Apartheid in the Horn of Africa*. London: Adonis and Abbey.

Eno, Omar A., and Mohamed A. Eno. 2007. "The Journey Back to the Ancestral Homeland: The Return of the Somali Bantu (Wazigwa) to Modern Tanzania." In *From Mogadishu to Dixon: The Somali Diaspora in a Global Context*, edited by Abdi M. Kusow and Stephanie R. Bjork, 13–43. Trenton, NJ: Red Sea.

Eno, Omar, Mohamed Eno, and Dan Van Lehman. 2010. "Defining the Problem in Somalia: Perspectives from the Southern Minorities." *Journal of Somali-Anglo Society*, no. 47: 19.

Fadlalla, Amal Hassan. 2009. "Contested Borders of (In)humanity: Sudanese Refugees and the Mediation of Suffering and Subaltern Visibilities." *Urban Anthropology* 38 (1): 22–41.

Fassin, Didier. 2005. "Compassion and Repression: The Moral Economy of Immigration Policies in France." *Cultural Anthropology* 20 (3): 362–87.

Fassin, Didier. 2007. "Humanitarianism as a Politics of Life." *Public Culture* 19 (3): 499–520.

Fassin, Didier. 2013. "The Precarious Truth of Asylum." *Public Culture* 25 (1): 39–63.

Fassin, Didier, and Richard Rechtman. 2009. *Empire of Trauma: An Inquiry into the Condition of Victimhood.* Princeton, NJ: Princeton University Press.

Feldman, Ilana. 2007. "Difficult Distinctions: Refugee Law, Humanitarian Practice, and Political Identification in Gaza." *Cultural Anthropology* 22 (1): 129–69.

Feldman, Ilana. 2012. "The Humanitarian Condition: Palestinian Refugees and the Politics of Living." *Humanity* 1 (1): 155–72.

Fergusson, James. 2013. *The World's Most Dangerous Place: Inside the Outlaw State of Somalia.* Boston: Da Capo.

Finkel, David. 2002. "For Chosen Few, First Steps to a New Life: Somali Refugees Delayed by Post-9/11 Security Worries Begin Journey to America." *Washington Post*, August 18, A1.

Finnström, Sverker. 2008. *Living with Bad Surroundings: War, History, and Everyday Moments in Northern Uganda.* Durham, NC: Duke University Press.

Fiskejö, Magnus. 2012. "Outlaws, Barbarians, Slaves: Critical Reflections on Agamben's *Homo Sacer.*" *HAU: Journal of Ethnographic Theory* 2 (1): 161–80.

Foley, Doug. 2008. "Questioning 'Cultural' Explanations of Classroom Behaviors." In *Everyday Antiracism: Getting Real about Race in School*, edited by Mica Pollock, 222–25. New York: New Press.

Foner, Nancy. 2005. *In a New Land: A Comparative View of Immigration.* New York: NYU Press.

Foner, Nancy, and George M. Fredrickson. 2004. "Introduction: Immigration, Race, and Ethnicity in the United States: Social Constructions and Social Relations in Historical and Contemporary Perspectives." In *Not Just Black and White: Historical and Contemporary Perspectives on Immigration, Race, and Ethnicity in the United States*, edited by Nancy Foner and George M. Fredrickson, 1–19. New York: Russell Sage Foundation.

Foner, Nancy, Ruben G. Rumbaut, and Steven J. Gold, eds. 2000. *Immigration Research for a New Century.* New York: Russell Sage Foundation.

Foreign Policy. 2008. "The 2008 Failed States Index." June 23. http://www.foreign policy.com. Accessed November 19, 2012.

Foreign Policy. 2009. "The 2009 Failed States Index." June 22. http://www.foreign policy.com/articles/2009/06/22/the_2009_failed_states_index.

Forman, Murray. 2005. "Straight Outta Mogadishu: Prescribed Identities and Performative Practices among Somali Youth in North American High Schools." In *Youthscapes: The Popular, the National, the Global*, edited by Sunaina Maira and Elisabeth Soep, 3–22. Philadelphia: University of Pennsylvania Press.

Frelick, Bill. 2007. "Paradigm Shifts in the International Responses to Refugees." In *Fear of Persecution: Global Human Rights, International Law, and Human Well-Being*, edited by James D. White and Anthony J. Marsella, 32–56. Lanham, MD: Lexington.

Gabiam, Nell. 2012. "When 'Humanitarianism' Becomes 'Development': The Politics of International Aid in Syria's Palestinian Refugee Camps." *American Anthropologist* 114 (1): 95–107.

Garvelink, William, and Farha Tahir. 2011. "Somalia Remains the Worst Humanitarian Crisis in the World." Center for Strategic and International Studies, December 16. http://csis.org/publication/somalia-remains-worst-humanitarian-crisis-world.

Gatrell, Peter. 2013. *The Making of the Modern Refugee.* Oxford: Oxford University Press.

GCIR (Grantmakers Concerned with Immigrants and Refugees). 2006. "Immigrant Integration Toolkit." Sebastopol, California. https://www.gcir.org/publications/toolkit.

Gerstle, Gary, and John Mollenkopf, eds. 2001. *E Pluribus Unum? Contemporary and Historical Perspectives on Immigrant Political Incorporation.* New York: Russell Sage Foundation.

Gibney, Matthew J. 2004. *The Ethics and Politics of Asylum: Liberal Democracy and the Response to Refugees.* Cambridge: Cambridge University Press.

Gilbert, Larry. 2011. Written testimony of Mayor Larry Gilbert Sr., Mayor, City of Lewiston, Maine, before the U.S. Senate Committee on the Judiciary, Subcommittee on Immigration, Refugees and Border Security, July 26.

Gilbert, Lauren. 2009. "Citizenship, Civic Virtue, and Immigrant Integration: The Enduring Power of Community-Based Norms." *Yale Law and Policy Review* 27: 335–97.

Gilroy, Paul. 2012. "'My Britain Is Fuck All': Zombie Multiculturalism and the Race Politics of Citizenship." *Identities* 19 (4): 380–97.

Glater, Jonathan. 2006. "Agreement Is Reached for Students from Somalia." *New York Times*, March 2.

Goad, Meredith. 2002. "Somalis Use Few Benefits: Municipal Officials Say Rumors of Abuse Untrue." *Waterville Morning Sentinel.*

Goffe, Leslie. 2004. "New Life in US for Somali Bantus." *BBC News*, August 13.

Gorlick, Brian. 2003. "Refugee Protection in Troubled Times: Reflections on Institutional and Legal Developments at the Crossroads." In *Problems of Protection: The UNHCR, Refugees, and Human Rights*, edited by Niklaus Steiner, Mark Gibney, and Gil Loescher, 79–99. New York: Routledge.

Gourevitch, Philip. 2010. "The Alms Dealers: Can You Provide Humanitarian Aid without Facilitating Conflicts?" *New Yorker*, October 11, 102–9.

Grey, Mark. 2000. "New Immigrants in Old Iowa." *Anthropology News* 41 (8): 9.

Gross, Jan. 2001. *Neighbors: The Destruction of the Jewish Community in Jedwabne, Poland.* Princeton, NJ: Princeton University Press.

Haines, David. 2010. *Safe Haven? A History of Refugees in America.* Sterling, VA: Kumarian.

Hall, Suzanne M. 2013. "The Politics of Belonging." *Identities* 20 (1): 46–53.

Hammond, Laura. 2010. "Obliged to Give: Remittances and the Maintenance of Transnational Networks between Somalis at Home and Abroad." *Bildhaan* 9: 125–51.

Hammond, Laura. 2011. "Defying Conventional Wisdom? Diaspora Youth and Participation in Somalia." *Horn of Africa Journal* 2. http://afrikansarvi.fi/issue2/25-artikkeli/56-defying-conventional-wisdom.

Hammond, Laura, Mustafa Awad, Ali Ibrahim Dagane, Peter Hansen, Cindy Horst, Ken Menkhaus, and Lynette Obare. 2011. "Cash and Compassion: The Role of the Somali Diaspora in Relief, Development and Peace-Building." United Nations Development Program. http://www.refworld.org/pdfid/4f61b12d2.pdf.

Hamzeh, Ziad. 2003. *The Letter: An American Town and the "Somali Invasion."* Hamzeh Mystique Films.

Hardt, Michael. 1999. "Affective Labor." *boundary 2* 26 (2): 89–99.

Hardt, Michael, and Antonio Negri. 2009. *Commonwealth.* Cambridge, MA: Harvard University Press.

Harman, Danna. 2001. "US Opens Arms to Bantu Somalis." *Christian Science Monitor* 94 (14): 6.

Helander, Bernhard. 1996. "The Hubeer in the Land of Plenty: Land, Labor, and Vulnerability among a Southern Somali Clan." In *The Struggle for Land in Southern Somalia: The War behind the War,* edited by Catherine Besteman and Lee V. Cassanelli, 47–72. Boulder, CO: Westview.

Herzfeld, Michael. 1993. *The Social Production of Indifference: Exploring the Symbolic Roots of Western Bureaucracy.* Chicago: University of Chicago Press.

Hill, Martin. 2010. *No Redress: Somalia's Forgotten Minorities.* London: Minority Rights Group.

Ho, Christine G. T., and James Loucky. 2012. *Humane Migration: Establishing Legitimacy and Rights for Displaced People.* Sterling, VA: Kumarian.

Holtzman, Jon D. 2000. "Dialing 911 in Nuer: Gender Transformations and Domestic Violence in a Midwestern Sudanese Refugee Community." In *Immigration Research for a New Century,* edited by Nancy Foner, Rubén G. Rumbaut, and Steven J. Gold, 390–408. New York: Russell Sage Foundation.

Honig, Bonnie. 2001. *Democracy and the Foreigner.* Princeton, NJ: Princeton University Press.

Horst, Cindy. 2006. *Transnational Nomads: How Somalis Cope with Refugee Life in the Dadaab Camps of Kenya.* Oxford: Berghahn.

Hudson, Susan. 2006. *The Quiet Revolutionaries: How the Grey Nuns Changed the Social Welfare Paradigm of Lewiston, Maine.* New York: Taylor and Francis.

Huisman, Kimberly A. 2011. "Why Maine? An Examination of the Secondary Migration Decisions of Somali Refugees." In *Somalis in Maine: Crossing Cultural Currents,* edited by Kimberly A. Huisman, Kristin M. Langellier, Mazie Hough, and Carol Nordstrom Toner. Berkeley, CA: North Atlantic.

Huntington, Samuel. 1993. "The Clash of Civilizations?" *Foreign Affairs* 72 (3): 22–49.

Huntington, Samuel. 2004. *Who Are We? The Challenges to America's National Identity.* New York: Simon and Schuster.

Hyndman, Jennifer. 2000. *Managing Displacement: Refugees and the Politics of Humanitarianism.* Minneapolis: University of Minnesota Press.

Inda, Jonathan Xavier. 2006. *Targeting Immigrants: Government, Technology, and Ethics.* Malden, MA: Blackwell.

Itzigsohn, José. 2009. *Encountering American Faultlines: Race, Class, and the Dominican Experience in Providence.* New York: Russell Sage Foundation.

Jacklet, Ben. 2004. "Refugees Find Freedom Isn't Free: Life Is Confusing and Expensive for Portland's Somali Bantus." *Portland Tribune,* August 31.

Jones, Maggie. 2004. "The New Yankees." *Mother Jones,* March–April.

Jones-Correa, Michael. 2011. "All Immigration Is Local: Receiving Communities and Their Role in Successful Immigrant Integration." Washington, DC: Center for American Progress.

Kaplan, Robert. 1994. "The Coming Anarchy." *Atlantic*, February.

Kapteijns, Lidwien. 2012. *Clan Cleansing in Somalia: The Ruinous Legacy of 1991.* Philadelphia: University of Pennsylvania Press.

Kapteijns, Lidwien, and Abukar Arman. 2004. "Educating Immigrant Youth in the United States: An Exploration of the Somali Case." *Bildhaan* 4: 18–43.

Kasinitz, Philip. 2004. "Race, Assimilation and 'Second Generations,' Past and Present." In *Not Just Black and White: Historical and Contemporary Perspectives on Immigration, Race, and Ethnicity in the United States*, edited by Nancy Foner and George M. Fredrickson, 278–98. New York: Russell Sage Foundation.

Kelley, Robin D. G. 2000. "Introduction: A Poetics of Anticolonialism." In Aimé Césaire, *Discourse on Colonialism* (1955). New York: Monthly Review Press.

Kennedy, David. 2004. *The Dark Sides of Virtue: Reassessing International Humanitarianism.* Princeton, NJ: Princeton University Press.

Khosravi, Shahram. 2010. *"Illegal" Traveller: An Auto-ethnography of Borders.* New York: Palgrave Macmillan.

King, Desmond. 2001. "Making Americans: Immigration Meets Race." In *E Pluribus Unum? Contemporary and Historical Perspectives on Immigrant Political Incorporation*, edited by Gary Gerstle and John Mollenkopf, 143–72. New York: Russell Sage Foundation.

Kingfisher, Catherine. 1998. "How Providers Make Policy: An Analysis of Everyday Conversation in a Welfare Office." *Journal of Community and Applied Social Psychology* 8: 119–36.

Kingfisher, Catherine. 2006. "The Dialectic of Insecurity." *Insecurities* 13: 173–85.

Kingfisher, Catherine. 2007. "Discursive Constructions of Homelessness in a Small City in the Canadian Prairies: Notes on Destructuration, Individualization, and the Production of (Raced and Gendered) Unmarked Categories." *American Ethnologist* 34 (1): 91–107.

Kingfisher, Catherine, and Michael Goldsmith. 2001. "Reforming Women in the United States and Aotearoa / New Zealand: A Comparative Ethnography of Welfare Reform in Global Context." *American Anthropologist* 103 (3): 714–32.

Kleist, Nauja. 2010. "Negotiating Respectable Masculinity: Gender and Recognition in the Somali Diaspora." *African Diaspora* 3: 185–206.

Lacey, Marc. 2001. "Somali Bantu, Trapped in Kenya, Seek a Home." *New York Times*, December 9, 1A.

LaFlamme, Mark. 2009. "Police Investigate Somali Attacks." *Lewiston Sun Journal*, December 17.

Levitt, Peggy. 2012. "What's Wrong with Migration Scholarship? A Critique and a Way Forward." *Identities* 19 (4): 493–500.

Lewis, I. M. 1961. *A Pastoral Democracy.* London: Oxford University Press.

Lewis, I. M. 1988. *A Modern History of Somalia.* Boulder, CO: Westview.

Lewis, I. M. 1998. "Doing Violence to Ethnography: A Response to Catherine Besteman's 'Representing Violence and "Othering" Somalia.'" *Cultural Anthropology* 13 (1): 100–108.

Lindkvist, Heather. 2003. "Lead Hazard Awareness in Lewiston, ME." Auburn/Lewiston Lead Hazard Control Program. http://www.bates.edu/Prebuilt/leadrep.pdf.

Lindley, Anna. 2010. *The Early Morning Phone Call: Somali Refugees' Remittances.* New York: Berghahn.

Loescher, Gil. 2003. "UNHCR at Fifty: Refugee Protection and World Politics." In *Problems of Protection: The UNHCR, Refugees, and Human Rights,* edited by Niklaus Steiner, Mark Gibney, and Gil Loescher, 1–18. New York: Routledge.

Loescher, Gil, and John A. Scanlan. 1986. *Calculated Kindness: Refugees and America's Half-Open Door, 1945 to the Present.* New York: Free Press.

Lorch, Donatella. 2002. "Following Freedom's Trail." *Newsweek,* September 2.

Lovgren, Stefan. 2003. "Refugees in the US: One Family's Story." *National Geographic News,* June 20.

Luhrmann, T. M. 2010. "Uneasy Street." In *The Insecure American: How We Got Here and What We Should Do about It,* edited by Hugh Gusterson and Catherine Besteman, 207–23. Berkeley: University of California Press.

Macdonald, Robert E. 2012a. "Enough Is Enough: Extremist Liberals Widen the Divide with Somalis." *Twin City Times,* September 6.

Macdonald, Robert E. 2012b. "Enough Is Enough: LHS Graduation Marred by Teens' Rude Behavior." *Twin City Times,* June 9.

Makepeace, Anne. 2006. *Rain in a Dry Land.* Makepeace Productions. Distributed by Bullfrog Films.

Malkki, Liisa. 1992. "National Geographic: The Rooting of People and the Territorialization of National Identity among Scholars and Refugees." *Cultural Anthropology* 7 (21): 24–44.

Malkki, Liisa. 1995a. *Purity and Exile: Violence, Memory, and National Cosmology among Hutu Refugees in Tanzania.* Chicago: University of Chicago Press.

Malkki, Liisa. 1995b. "Refugees and Exile: From 'Refugee Studies' to the National Order of Things." *Annual Review of Anthropology* 24: 495–523.

Malkki, Liisa. 1996. "Speechless Emissaries: Refugees, Humanitarianism, and Dehistoricization." *Cultural Anthropology* 11 (3): 377–404.

Malkki, Liisa. 2002. "News from Nowhere: Mass Displacement and Globalized 'Problems' of Organization." *Ethnography* 3 (3): 351–60.

Malkki, Liisa. 2007. "Commentary: The Politics of Trauma and Asylum: Universals and Their Effects." *Ethos* 35 (3): 336–43.

Malone, Richard J. 2010. "Bishop Malone Objects to TCT Editorials." *Twin City Times,* April 8.

Mamgain, Vaishali, and Karen Collins. 2003. "Off the Boat, Now Off to Work: Refugees in the Labour Market in Portland, Maine." *Journal of Refugee Studies* 16 (2): 113–46.

Manning, Rob. 2004. "Somali Bantus Find a Home in Oregon." Oregon Public Broadcasting, June 23.

Manz, Beatriz. 2004. *Paradise in Ashes: A Guatemalan Journey of Courage, Terror, and Hope*. Berkeley: University of California Press.

Mbembe, Achille. 2011. "Provincializing France?" *Public Culture* 23 (1): 85–119.

McCabe, Carolyn. 2010. "Bridging the Gap? An Exploratory Study of the Role of Ethnic Community-Based Organizations in Refugee Integration in the United States." Institute for Social and Economic Development Applied Innovations Working Paper.

Menkhaus, Kenneth. 1989. "Rural Transformation and the Roots of Underdevelopment in Somalia's Lower Jubba Valley." PhD diss., University of South Carolina.

Menkhaus, Kenneth. 1992. *Report on an Emergency Needs Assessment of the Lower Jubba Region (Kismaayo, Jamaame, and Jilib Districts), Somalia*. Seattle: World Concern.

Menkhaus, Kenneth. 2008. "Somalia: A Country in Peril, a Policy Nightmare." Enough, September 3. http://www.enoughproject.org/publications/somalia -country-peril-policy-nightmare.

Menkhaus, Kenneth. 2010. "The Question of Ethnicity in Somali Studies: The Case of Somali Bantu Identity." In *Milk and Peace, Drought and War: Somali Culture, Society and Politics*, edited by Markus V. Hoehne and Virginia Luling, 87–104. London: Hurst.

Meyer, Judith. 2010. "Advice for America." *Lewiston Sun Journal*, February 7.

Moore, Henrietta. 2004. "Global Anxieties: Concept-Metaphors and Pre-theoretical Commitments in Anthropology." *Anthropological Theory* 4 (1): 71–88.

Muehlenbach, Andrea. 2011. "Affective Labor in Post-Fordist Italy." *Cultural Anthropology* 26 (1): 59–82.

Muehlenbach, Andrea. 2013a. "The Catholicization of Neoliberalism: On Love and Welfare in Lombardy, Italy." *American Anthropologist* 115 (3): 452–65.

Muehlenbach, Andrea. 2013b. "On Precariousness and the Ethical Imagination: The Year 2012 in Sociocultural Anthropology." *American Anthropologist* 115 (2): 295–311.

Nadeau, Phil. 2005. "The Somalis of Lewiston: Effects of Rapid Immigration to a Homogenous Maine City." *Southern Maine Review*, April, 104–46.

Nadeau, Phil. 2007. City of Lewiston Report to Maine's Congressional Delegation: Federal Funding Deficiencies for Refugee and Secondary Migrant Services and Programming. October 17.

Nadeau, Phil. 2008. "The Flawed U.S. Refugee Workforce Development Strategy for Somali Economic Self Sufficiency in Lewiston." Paper presented at Race, Ethnicity and Place Conference IV, Miami, Florida.

Nadeau, Phil. 2011. "A Work in Progress: Lewiston Responds to the Rapid Migration of Somali Refugees." In *Somalis in Maine: Crossing Cultural Currents*, edited by Kimberly A. Huisman, Kristin M. Langellier, Mazie Hough, and Carol Nordstrom Toner, 53–72. Berkeley, CA: North Atlantic.

Noguera, Pedro. 2008. "What Discipline Is For: Connecting Students to the Benefits of Learning." In *Everyday Antiracism: Getting Real about Race in School*, edited by Mica Pollock, 132–37. New York: New Press.

Nyamnjoh, Francis B. 2006. *Insiders and Outsiders: Citizenship and Xenophobia in Contemporary South Africa*. Dakar: CODESRIA.

Nyers, Peter. 2006. *Rethinking Refugees: Beyond States of Emergency*. New York: Routledge.

Oka, Rahul Chandrashekhar. 2014. "Coping with the Refugee Wait: The Role of Consumption, Normalcy, and Dignity in Refugee Lives at Kakuma Refugee Camp, Kenya." *American Anthropologist* 116 (1): 23–37.

Ong, Aihwa. 1996. "Cultural Citizenship as Subject-Making: Immigrants Negotiate Racial and Cultural Boundaries in the United States." *Current Anthropology* 37 (5): 737–62.

Ong, Aihwa. 2003. *Buddha Is Hiding: Refugees, Citizenship, the New America*. Berkeley: University of California Press.

Ordoñez, J. Thomas. 2008. "The State of Confusion: Reflections on Central American Asylum Seekers in the Bay Area." *Ethnography* 9 (1): 35–60.

Papasterdiadis, Nikos. 2012. "Seeing through Multicultural Perspectives." *Identities* 19 (4): 398–410.

Pina-Cabral, João de. 2013. "The Two Faces of Mutuality: Contemporary Themes in Anthropology." *Anthropological Quarterly* 86 (1): 257–76.

Pollock, Mica. 2004. *Colormute: Race Talk Dilemmas in an American School*. Princeton, NJ: Princeton University Press.

Pollock, Mica, ed. 2008. *Everyday Antiracism: Getting Real about Race in School*. New York: New Press.

Portes, Alejandro, and Rubén G. Rumbaut. 1996. *Immigrant America: A Portrait*. Berkeley: University of California Press.

Portes, Alejandro, and Min Zhou. 1993. "The New Second Generation: Segmented Assimilation and Its Variants." *Annals of the American Academy of Political and Social Science* 530 (1): 74–96.

Povinelli, Elizabeth. 2009. "Beyond Good and Evil: Whither Liberal Sacrificial Love?" *Public Culture* 21 (1): 77–100.

Povinelli, Elizabeth. 2011. *Economies of Abandonment*. Durham, NC: Duke University Press.

Rabben, Linda. 2011. *Give Refuge to the Stranger: The Past, Present, and Future of Sanctuary*. Walnut Creek, CA: Left Coast.

Rawson, David. 1994. "Dealing with Disintegration: U.S. Assistance and the Somali State." In *The Somali Challenge: From Catastrophe to Renewal?*, edited by Ahmed I. Samatar, 147–87. Boulder, CO: Lynne Reinner.

Rector, Amanda K. 2008. "An Analysis of the Employment Patterns of Somali Immigrants to Lewiston from 2001 through 2006." Center for Workforce Research and Information, Maine Department of Labor, Maine State Planning Office.

Refugees International. 2011. "Somalia." http://refugeesinternational.org/where-we -work/africa/somalia.

Richards, Paul. 1996. *Fighting for the Rain Forest: War, Youth, and Resources in Sierra Leone*. Oxford: Heinemann.

Ricouer, Paul. 2010. "Being a Stranger." Translated by Alison Scott-Baumann. *Theory, Culture and Society* 27 (5): 37–48.

Robins, Steven. 2009. "Humanitarian Aid beyond 'Bare Survival': Social Movement Responses to Xenophobic Violence in South Africa." *American Ethnologist* 36 (4): 637–50.

Roy, Laura A., and Kevin C. Roxas. 2011. "Whose Deficit Is This Anyhow? Exploring Counter-Stories of Somali Bantu Refugees' Experiences in 'Doing School.'" *Harvard Educational Review* 81 (3): 521–41.

Rozakou, Katerina. 2012. "The Biopolitics of Hospitality in Greece: Humanitarianism and the Management of Refugees." *American Ethnologist* 39 (3): 562–77.

Sahlins, Marshall. 2011a. "What Kinship Is (Part One)." *Journal of the Royal Anthropological Institute* 17: 2–19.

Sahlins, Marshall. 2011b. "What Kinship Is (Part Two)." *Journal of the Royal Anthropological Institute* 17: 227–42.

Salazar, Noel B., and Alan Smart. 2011. "Anthropological Takes on '(Im)Mobility.'" *Identities: Global Studies in Culture and Power* 18 (6): i–ix.

Samatar, Ahmed I. 2004. "Beginning Again: From Refugee to Citizen." *Bildhaan* 4: 1–17.

Sanchez, George J. 2000. "Race and Immigration History." In *Immigration Research for a New Century*, edited by Nancy Foner, Rubén G. Rumbaut, and Steven J. Gold, 54–59. New York: Russell Sage Foundation.

Sanders, Edmund, and David Zucchino. 2006. "Left Behind as His Family Flees: Bantu Refugees Heading to US Often Split Up." *Los Angeles Times*, January 15.

Sassen, Saskia. 1999. *Guests and Aliens*. New York: New Press.

Schiller, Nina Glick. 2012. "Situating Identities: Towards an Identities Studies without Binaries of Difference." *Identities* 19 (4): 520–32.

Schrag, Peter. 2011. *Not Fit for Our Society: Immigration and Nativism in America*. Berkeley: University of California Press.

Scott, James. 1999. *Seeing Like a State*. New Haven, CT: Yale University Press.

Seele, Peter. 2009. "Report: Employers Should Relax Standards to Hire Somalis." *Twin City Times*, January 22.

Seele, Peter. 2010. "L-A Needs Gentrification, Not Ghetto-fication." *Twin City Times*, March 18.

Sheikh, Hassan, and Sally Healy. 2009. "Somalia's Missing Million: The Somali Diaspora and Its Role in Development." New York: United Nations Development Programme.

Shemak, April. 2010. *Asylum Speakers: Caribbean Refugees and Testimonial Discourse*. New York: Fordham University Press.

Shepard, Raynel M. 2008. *Cultural Adaptation of Somali Refugee Youth*. New York: LFB Scholarly Publishing.

Smydo, Joe. 2006. "City Schools Settle Complaint Filed for Somali Refugees." *Pittsburgh Post-Gazette*, May 23.

Suárez-Orozco, Carola, Hee Jin Bang, Erin O'Connor, Francisco X. Gaytán, Juliana Pakes, and Jean Rhodes. 2010. "Academic Trajectories of Newcomer Immigrant Youth." *Developmental Psychology* 46 (3): 602–18.

Swarns, Rachel L. 2003a. "Africa's Lost Tribe Discovers American Way." *New York Times*, March 10.

Swarns, Rachel L. 2003b. "U.S. a Place of Miracles for Somali Refugees." *New York Times*, July 20, 1.1.

Taylor, Scott. 2011. "Lewiston Mayoral Candidates Want More Development." *Lewiston Sun Journal*, October 6.

Terry, Fiona. 2002. *Condemned to Repeat? The Paradox of Humanitarian Action.* Ithaca, NY: Cornell University Press.

Thomas, Deborah A. 2009. "The Violence of Diaspora: Governmentality, Class Culture, and Circulations." *Radical History Review* 103: 83–104.

Ticktin, Miriam. 2006. "Where Ethics and Politics Meet: The Violence of Humanitarianism in France." *American Ethnologist* 33 (1): 33–49.

Toner, Carol Nordstrom, and Mazie Hough. 2011. "L.L. Bean, Community Gardens, and *Biil*: Somalis Working in Maine." In *Somalis in Maine: Crossing Cultural Currents*, edited by Kimberly A. Huisman, Kristin M. Langellier, Mazie Hough, and Carol Nordstrom Toner, 169–89. Berkeley, CA: North Atlantic.

Torpey, John. 2000. *The Invention of the Passport: Surveillance, Citizenship and the State.* Cambridge: Cambridge University Press.

Turner, Simon. 2004. "Under the Gaze of the 'Big Nations': Refugees, Rumours and the International Community in Tanzania." *African Affairs* 103: 227–47.

Turner, Simon. 2010. *Politics of Innocence: Hutu Identity, Conflict, and Camp Life.* Oxford: Berghahn.

Twin City Times. 2011. "Macdonald to Run for Mayor of Lewiston." September 15.

UNHCR (United Nations High Commissioner for Refugees). 2002. "America Here We Come." *Refugees* 3 (128). http://www.unhcr.org/3d9ac1502.html.

UNHCR. 2012. "Global Trends Report: 800,000 New Refugees in 2011, Highest This Century." June 18. www.unhcr.org.

U.S. Committee for Refugees and Immigrants. 2009. "World Refugee Survey: 2009." http://www.refugees.org/resources/uscri_reports/archived-world-refugee-surveys/2009-world-refugee-survey.html.

U.S. Department of State. n.d. Office of Refugee Resettlement Report from the 2003 National Consultation Somali Bantu Planning Workshop.

U.S. Department of State. 1999. Unclassified State 239014 cable from PRM on Designation of Somali Bantu Refugee Group in Kenya for Resettlement Processing, sent from Secretary of State in Washington, DC, to all African diplomatic posts. December 19.

U.S. Department of State. 2004. "Annex to Chapter 1, Resettlement of the Somali Bantu: A Case Study of Processing Complexity and Unforeseen Delays." In *The United States Refugee Admissions Program: Reforms for a New Era of Refugee Resettlement*. April 20. Washington, DC: U.S. Department of State. http://2001-2009.state.gov/g/prm/refadm/rls/rpts/36057.htm.

U.S. Senate Committee on Foreign Relations. 2010. "Abandoned upon Arrival: Implications for Refugees and Local Communities Burdened by a U.S. Resettlement System That Is Not Working." July 21. Washington, DC: U.S. Government Printing Office.

U.S. Senate Judiciary Committee Hearing. 2004. "Global Refugee Problem." Testimony by Mr. Charles Kuck, Managing Partner, Weathersby, Howard and Kuck, LLC. September 21.

U.S. Senate Judiciary Committee Hearing, Immigration Subcommittee. 2002. Testimony by Gene Dewey, Assistant Secretary of State, Bureau of Refugees, Population, and Migration, Leonard Glickman, President of Hebrew Immigrant Aid Society, and Bill Frelick, Director of Policy, U.S. Committee on Refugees. February 12.

Van Lehman, Daniel James. 1999. "Expanding Protection for Marginalized Refugee Minorities: Resettling Somali Mushungulis to Southeast Africa." Master's thesis, Cornell University.

Van Lehman, Daniel, and Omar Eno. 2002. "The Somali Bantu: Their History and Culture." Washington, DC: Center for Applied Linguistics. http://www .hartfordinfo.org/issues/wsd/immigrants/somali_bantu.pdf.

Van Lehman, Dan, and Omar Eno. 2003. "Objectives, Itinerary and Outcomes of the Mission to Kakuma." March 14. Unpublished report.

Vaznis, James. 2009. "US Inspects Boston's Language Instruction: Schools Neglected English Learners." *Boston Globe*, August 26.

Verdirame, Guglielmo, and Barbara Harrell-Bond. 2005. *Rights in Exile: Janus-Faced Humanitarianism*. New York: Berghahn.

Vertovec, Steven. 2011. "The Cultural Politics of Nation and Migration." *Annual Review of Anthropology* 40: 241–56.

Wagner, Angie. 2003. "The New Land: A Somali Bantu Clan Readjusts in America." *Seattle Times*, August 10, A3.

Waters, Mary. 1994. "Ethnic and Racial Identities of Second-Generation Black Immigrants in New York City." *International Migration Review* 28 (4): 795–820.

Waters, Mary. 2000. "The Sociological Roots and Multidisciplinary Future of Immigration Research." In *Immigration Research for a New Century*, edited by Nancy Foner, Rubén G. Rumbaut, and Steven J. Gold, 44–48. New York: Russell Sage Foundation.

Weston, Kath. 2005. "Class Politics and Scavenger Anthropology in Dinesh D'Souza's *Virtue of Prosperity*." In *Why America's Top Pundits Are Wrong: Anthropologists Talk Back*, edited by Catherine Besteman and Hugh Gusterson, 154–179. Berkeley: University of California Press.

White, James D., and Anthony J. Marsella. 2007. *Fear of Persecution: Global Human Rights, International Law, and Human Well-Being*. Lanham, MD: Lexington.

Wimmer, Andreas, and Nina Glick Schiller. 2002. "Methodological Nationalism and Beyond: Nation-State Building, Migration and the Social Sciences." *Global Networks* 2 (4): 301–34.

Zhou, Min. 1997. "Growing Up American: The Challenge of Confronting Immigrant Children and Children of Immigrants." *Annual Review of Sociology* 23: 63–95.

Banta, Somalia: clan families in, 40–42; early research in, 1–3; impact of war on, 10, 42–54, 292n16; life and social structure in, *3*, 5–11, *6*, *8–9*, 19–28, 35–37; postwar history of, 26–28; refugees from, 4, 50–54

Barre, Siad, 4, 41–42, 44

Bates College, 11, 122, 150–51

Bauman, Zygmunt, 29–31

behavioral programs, Somali students and, 191–97

Binti Caliyow Isaaq, 20–21, *23*

Black Hawk Down (film), 191

Black Hawk Down debacle, 5, 142, 208

Boas, Heidi, 70

business-as-usual paradigm, Lewiston Somali refugee influx and, 115–21

Cabdulkadir Osman, 49–50, 103, 109

Cabdullahi Nur, 48

Cabdulle Cabdi Osman, 2, 19

Cali Osman, 2–4, 12, 19, 26, 35–37, *36*, 54; ancestry of, 37–42, 292n9; civil war and, 48–49; death of, 54; as refugee, 50–54; Somali politics and, 43

Caliyow Isaaq, 2–3, 19–20, *25*, 35–37, 85; ancestry of, 38–42; civil war and, 47–48; death of, 51; refugee trek by, 50–54; Somali politics and, 43

capacity building initiatives, 219–22, 307n2

CARE, 65, 84–85

CareerCenter (Lewiston), 147–50, 155, 286

Caribbean refugees, African Americans and, 108

car ownership by Somali refugees, 155–56

caseworkers, Somali refugees as, 152–54; SBYAM and, 274–75

Catholic Charities, 104, 117, 123, 142, 197

Catholic Church, immigrant communities and, 181–82, 305n10

cell phones: parenting and use of, 253–57; Somali use of, 155–56, 281–85

Center for Immigration Studies, 70–71

Center for Strategic and International Studies, 5

Center for the Prevention of Hate Violence, 126–28, 135, 139–41, 301n5

Chandrashekhar Oka, Rahul, 296n3

Charron, Sue, 115, 117–21, 155

children of Somali Bantus: challenges in Lewiston for, 244–46; cultural norms concerning, 210–13. *See also* family structure; parenting by Somali Bantus

Chinese Exclusion Act, 60

Ciise Osman, 45, *46*, 53, 93, 99–100, 281

citizenship: advocacy by Somali Bantu refugees for, 272–75; driving and car ownership linked to, 155–56; mobility and, 280–85; myths concerning Somali refugees' refusal of, 159–60, 303n34; for Somali refugees, 98–100, 207–8, 278–79, 282–85, 302n13

civic life: Lewiston refugees' participation in, 219–22, 272–75, 277–79; myths concerning Somali refugees' participation in, 160–63

civil war: global politics and, 44–50, 55–56, 292n2; race and ancestry and, 37–42; Somali Bantu identity and, 80–89

clan families: civil war and, 44–50; "clan cleansing" violence and, 292n14; race and ancestry and, 39–42, 292n8; Somali politics and, 42–43

"Clash of Civilizations, The" (Huntington), 30–31

class inequalities, Somali clan system and, 40–43, 292n12

Coastal Enterprises, 300n12

Colby College Museum of Art, 142–44, 148

Cold War: Somali politics and, 42–43; U.S. resettlement policies and, 68–71, 74, 294n22

collaborative projects with Somali refugees, 29; immigration history in Lewiston and, 142–43; social services and, 157–59, 180–82, 187; Somali students and, 129–30, 191–97

colonization: civil war and, 55–56; Cold War and, 42–43; labor practices under, 80; race and ancestry and, 38–42; Somali Bantus and, *37*, 75–76

"Coming Anarchy, The" (Kaplan), 31

commons, sense of, 287–88

Haitian refugees, U.S. resettlement policies and, 68–71

Haji Adan, *88*

Hall, Suzanne, 288

Hamilton, Cheryl, 118–21, 135, 151, 176, 200, 286

Hardt, Michael, 288

Harrell-Bond, Barbara, 66, 72

Hawiye clan family, 39–42, 292n9; civil war and, 45–50

health services for Somali refugees, 124–28, 177–80, 274–75, 305n13

Hebrew Immigrant Aid Society, 73, 104

Helander, Bernhard, 292n8

helping professions, neoliberalism's impact on, 171–76

Herzfeld, Michael, 164, 169

Higher (refugee organization), 303n23

hijab, public harassment over wearing of, 160–61

Hmong refugees, 104

Holocaust, 61

Holtzman, John, 236

homo sacer, refugees as, 58, 293n3

Honig, Bonnie, 163–66

Hopkins, Andrew, 89, 92

Horst, Cindy, 66, 296n3

hospitality, humanitarianism and, 164–67, 304n45

"hostipitality," Derrida's concept of, 164

housing for Somali refugees, myths in Lewiston concerning, 154–55

Huguenots, 60

humanitarianism: community building and, 182; debate over rights and, 143–44; ethnic identity in Somalia and, 80–89; hospitality and, 164–67; Lewiston refugee experience and, 135–37; moral implications of, 293n7; nativisim and racism in, 198–201; refugee regime and, 64; resettlement policies and, 69–71, 74–76; security concerns vs., 71–74; Somali Bantu view of, 79–89, 96–100

Human Rights Watch, 5, 51

Huntington, Samuel, 30–31

Hyndman, Jennifer, 63, 65, 296n3

Idow Roble, 3

Idris Osman, 12, 19, 49, 53–54; in Lewiston, 109, 211, 230–31, 243, 281, 310n3; in refugee camp, 99; SBYAM and, 244–46, 260–62, 275; on Somali youth, 262–64

Iman Osman, 19, 22, 67, 103, 105, 108, 281

Immigrant Legal Advocacy Project, 118, 125

immigrants and immigration policy: democracy and role of, 163–67; immigrant integration paradigm and, 30–31, 110–13; impact in Lewiston of, 110–11; refugee regime and, 63–64, 300n1; U.S. resettlement policies and, 68–71, 295n46

imperialism, framing of Somali refugee crisis and, 143–44

integration and immigration: agency of Somali refugees and, 238–41; assimilation ideology and, 267–71; barriers to, 30–31, 110–13, 209–13; myths concerning, 140–67. *See also* assimilation

intercommunity factionalization of Lewiston Somali Bantus, 230–32

International Clinic (Lewiston), 125–28, 177–80

International Committee of the Red Cross (ICRC), 50–54

International Office of Migration (IOM), 89

International Refugee Organization, 61, 294n20

Internet, Somali communication on, 282–85

interview strategies, Somali Bantu reverification and, 90–96

Isaaq clan family, 39–42

Isha Iman, 12, 20, 45, *46*, 51, 53–54, 153; in refugee camp, 85, 93; resettlement in Lewiston and, 103, 105, 281

Islamic banking, 309n15

Ismail Ahmed, 141–42, 144, 150–54, 304n39

Italian colonialization, Somali Bantu identity and, 80

Jama Mahmood, 176

jareer ancestry, 39–42, 52, 67; Italian colonial labor practices and, 80; reverification process and, 89–96, 297n12; Somali Bantu identity and, 78–89, 98–100, 266–67, 297n18; Somali racism concerning, 81, 223–26 jileec ancestry, 39–42, 67; Italian colonial labor practices and, 80; Somali Bantu identity and, 78

jobs. *See* employment

job training programs in Lewiston, Somali enrollment in, 148–54

Kahiye Nur, 48

Kakuma refugee camp: agency of refugees in, 96, 296n3; reverification process and, 90–96; support from U.S. refugees in, 282–85

Kanza, Lokua, 308n9

Kaplan, Robert, 31

Kapungo, Leonard, 297n10

Kasinitz, Philip, 268, 299n6

Kemper, Anne, 19

Kenya, Somali youth and attachment to, 283–85

Khosravi, Shahram, 62

kidnapping, civil war and proliferation of, 45–50

kinship structures: American criteria for, 93–94; race and ancestry and, 39–42, 292n8, 292n12; Somali Bantu identity and, 79, 210–13

Kleist, Nauja, 308n10

Ku Klux Klan, 181

labor statistics on Somali refugees, 147–54

LaFontaine, Mary, 147–48, 150, 155, 286

land reforms, Somali politics and, 42–43

LePage, Paul, 15, 144, 159, 173, 300n2, 301n26

Letter, The (documentary), 300nn7–8

Letter incident, 121–23, 135, 160, 162

Lewis, I. M., 42–43

Lewiston, Maine: accommodation and containment policies in, 131–34; assimilation of Somalis in, 269–71; business and community life in, 160–62; crime rates in, 156–58; diversity management in, 129–31; economy and demographics of, 13–19, 17–18, 110–13, 139–40, 144–47; history of immigration in, 142–44; housing policies in, 154–55; institutional response to refu-

gees in, 124–28; job and labor conditions in, 148–54; legacy of refugee resettlement in, 134–35, 286–88; mutual transformation of refugees and citizens in, 285–88; myths concerning refugees in, 139–67; police force in, 147, 158, 183–85; politics and resistance to Somalis in, 121–23, 180–82; racism and nativism in, 198–201; Somali refugees' impact on, 4, 10–13, 108–13, 115–21, 123–24; xenophobia in, 139–40

Lewiston Sun Journal, 141, 144, 151–52, 156

literacy skills: advocacy by Somali Bantus for, 273–75; job opportunities and access to, 149–54; refugees' lack of, 12–13, 71, 78, 107, 118, 124

L.L.Bean, Somali employees at, 109, 148–50, 302n18, 303n21

Los Angeles Times, 97

Lost Boys of Sudan, 69, 74, 299n3

Lutheran Immigration and Refugee Services, 104

Macdonald, Robert (Mayor), 113, 143–44, 154, 160–62, 164, 173, 180, 240–41, 277–78, 280, 301n26, 303n29

MaineCare, SBYAM and, 274–75

Maliya Cali Osman, 51, 52

Malkki, Liisa, 58, 63, 296n3

Malone, Bishop Richard, 182

Many and One Rally, 122

Marian Cabdi Dhaqane, 26

marriage in Somali Bantu culture: civil war and, 47–50; parenting Somali girls and, 250–57, 309n1, 309n4; resettlement and, 210–13, 232–36, 243–44

Maxamed Gedi, 41, 45, 47–48, 53

Mbembe, Achille, 56, 139, 304n41

Mberwa Haji, 83–84

McManus, Barbara, 278

Médécins Sans Frontières, 65

media coverage: of Lewiston resettlement, 121–23, 127–28, 130, 140–41; of Somali Bantus, 14–19, 29–31, 70–71, 74–76, 298n1. *See also* online media, blog comments about Somalis on; social media

Menkhaus, Kenneth, 5, 79, 80–81

mental health issues for Somali refugees, 205–9, 259–62, 307n1

mobility: citizenship and, 280–85; downward, with immigration, 267–71

Mohamed Caliyow Isaaq, 51, 95, 107

Mohamed Eno, 81

money: marital cultural norms and, 255–57; remittances to Somali refugee camps and, 281–85, 310n2; Somali refugees' attitude toward, 229–30, 281–85, 308n8, 309n15

Moore, Henrietta, 269–70

Mother Jones magazine, 5, 14, 140

Mozambique, Somali Bantu ties with, 70, 84–85, 88–89

MUKI political organization, 81

multiculturalism in Lewiston, Somali resettlement and, 129–34

Museum LA, 142–44, 159, 165, 309n15

Mushunguli group, 82–89

myths about Somali refugees in Lewiston, 139–67, 178–80, 302n7

Nadeau, Phil, 120, 122–28, 134–35, 200n8

National Geographic magazine, 71

nationalist ideology in Somalia, Cold War and, 42–43

Negri, Antonio, 288

neoliberalism: community building by Somali refugees and, 169–98, 230, 305n2; racism and, 198–201; refugee regime and, 64, 115–16

neo-Nazi groups, presence in Lewiston of, 122–23

New American Sustainable Agriculture Project, 300n12

Newsweek magazine, 14, 71, 140

New Yorker magazine, 5, 14, 66

New York Times, 70–71

No Child Left Behind, Somali students and, 187–97, 301n16

Noguera, Pedro, 189

nongovernmental organizations (NGOs): refugee camps and, 65–67; Somali refugees' formation of, 209–13

nonprofit agencies, services for Somali students from, 196–97

nonrefoulement, principle of, 62

Nur Libah, *149*

Office of Refugee Resettlement (ORR), 104, 107–8, 118, 135, 279; leadership grants from, 219–22, 230

Office of U.S. Coordinator of Refugee Affairs, 68

"official refugee" category, 57

Omar Eno, 11, 81, 85, 92

online media, blog comments about Somalis on, 140–41, 144–45, 155–57, 160–61. *See also* social media

ooji ancestral classification, 38–42, 227, 292n5

oral history interviews, research on Somali Bantus and, 299n8

Pakistan, refugees in, 63

Palestinian refugees, 296n3

Papasterdiadis, Nikos, 285

parenting by Somali Bantus: intergenerational gaps and, 262–64; resettlement impact on, 210–13, 246–50; Somali boys and, 257–62; Somali girls and, 250–57

parent-teacher support groups, resistance to proposals for, 193–97, 217–19, 306n20

participation observation, research on Somali Bantus and, 299n8

patrimonial politics, Somali clan system and, 42–43

pencil test, reverification process and, 92–96, 298n26

personhood, African conceptions of, 310n15

poetry, political power in Somalia of, 48–50

police force in Lewiston: Somali boys and, 259–62; Somali refugees and, 147, 158, 183–85

politics: clan structure and, 39–42; in Lewiston, 180–82; social services and, 180, 306n30; in Somali Bantu culture, 105–10, 215–17; U.S. resettlement policies and, 68–71

Pollock, Mica, 128

polygynous families: disruption among Lewiston refugees of, 233–36; resettlement and problems with, 94–96, 206, 210–13, 308n12

Portland, Maine, Somali refugees in, 116–18, 132–34
postcolonialism, refugee camps as continuation of, 62–64
poverty of Somali Bantu refugees, 103–8, 147–54, 305n6
Povinelli, Elizabeth, 137, 199–200
pretheoretical commitment, assimilation and, 269, 280
primitivism, characterization of Somali Bantus and, 71
Protocol Relating to the Status of Refugees, 61
P3 family reunification process, 99–100

Rabaca Osman, 48, 53, 85, 92–93, 99, 281
racism: antirefugee activism and, 198–201; framing of Somali refugees and, 143–44, 166–67; myths of crime and, 156–57; social media and, 302n6; against Somali Bantus, 80–96, 110, 223–26, 298n27, 308n5; Somali boys and, 258–62; in Somali culture, 37–42, 66–67; U.S. resettlement policies and, 68–71, 299n6
Rahanweyn clan family, 39–42, 292n9
Rain in a Dry Land (film), 298n1, 304n49
ransom and kidnapping, civil war and proliferation of, 45–50
rape: civil war and, 47–50; in refugee camps, 52; Somali experiences with, 253–57
Raymond, Laurier (Mayor), 113, 121–23, 180
Reagan, Ronald, 68
reciprocal disorientation, 56
Refugee Act of 1980 (U.S.), 68, 72
refugee camps: administration and structure of, 58–59, 65–67, 79, 81–89; Al-Shabaab terrorists and, 208; conditions in, 51–54, 279–80; ethnographic studies of, 65–67, 81–89; hierarchy and administration of, 65–67; jareer groups in, 81–89; nativisim and racism in, 198–201; refugees' visits to, 206, 282–85; remittances from Somali refugees to, 281–85, 310n2; security concerns in, 71–74; Somali refugees in, 29, 281–85, 294n35, 307n3; statistics on, 63; as warehouses, 62–64. See also specific camps, e.g., Dadaab Refugee Camp

Refugee Cash Assistance Program, 104
refugee regime, contemporary research on, 60–64
refugees (generally): agency of, 96–100, 296n3; civil war and creation of, 44–50; classification of, 57–59, 293n12; in Dadaab Refugee Camp, 65–67; international refugee regime, 60–64; mutuality in Lewiston among, 178–80; myths in Lewiston concerning, 140–67; political agency of, 77, 96–100; research sources and statistics on, 29–31, 291n11, 292n2
Refugees International, 5
Refugees magazine, 69–71
RefugeeWorks, 151, 303n23
religious issues: faith practices in workplace and, 237–38; Somali refugees and, 126–28
research advocacy, 305n1
resettlement of Somali refugees, 10–11, 30, 59, 68–71; asylum and, 74–76, 295n43; barriers and challenges in, 103–8, 298n1; citizenship and, 98–100; competition for resources among, 226–27; federal management of, 103–5; fraudulent practices during, 92–96; government surveillance and, 171–76; Lewiston's early experience with, 115–21; resistance in U.S. communities to, 296n74; reverification procedures and, 87–89; security concerns and, 71–74
reverification process, Somali Bantu resettlement and, 87–96
Richards, Paul, 35, 55–56
Ricoeur, Paul, 304n45
Rilwan Osman, 141–42, 158–59
Rivers of Immigration: From the Jubba to the Androscoggin (museum exhibit), 142–44, 165, 309n15
Robins, Steven, 296n3
Robitaille, Marc, 183–85, 278
Rousseau, Bill, 147

Safe Children program, 309n1
Sahara Mahamad, 26–27
Salazar, Noel, 57
Saliba, Janet, 157, 176–78, 260
Sassen, Saskia, 60, 277, 293n12

Schrag, Peter, 295n46
scientific socialism, Barre's concept of, 41–42
seasonal jobs, Somali refugees' access to, 148–50, 303n18
secondary migrations by Somali refugees, 116–17
Section 8 housing subsidies, myths concerning Somali refugees and, 154–55
security concerns, resettlement policies and, 71–74
self-essentialization of Somali Bantus, 89–100
self-representation, refugees' demand for, 223–26, 308n6
self-sufficiency: agency of Somali refugees and, 238–41; barriers for refugees in achieving, 104–8, 209–13; capacity building initiatives and, 219–22, 227–30; myths in Lewiston concerning, 140–67
sexuality, Somali cultural norms and, 253–57
"shared humanity," Enlightenment concept of, 293n7
sharing, Somali cultural practice of, 239–42
Sheikh Axmed Nur, 3, 8, 19, 35–37; ancestry of, 37–42, 292n9; civil war and, 48; death of, 99; as refugee, 51–52, 85; resettlement for children of, 95–96, 99; Somali politics and, 43
slave trade: civil war and, 55–56; race and ancestry and, 38–42; Somali Bantus and, 37, 69, 75, 79–80, 83–84
small business ownership by Somali refugees, 152–54, 161–62
Smart, Alan, 57
social media: blog comments about Somalis on, 140–41, 144–45, 155–57, 160–61; expressions of racism on, 302n6; Somali youth and, 244–46. See also online media, blog comments about Somalis on
social service providers: competition for services of, 226–27; interaction with Somali refugees, 185–87; neoliberalism and, 171–72, 185–201; SBYAM and, 274–75
social structures in Somalia: clan families and, 39–42; impact of war on, 5–11
Somalia: Cold War and, 42–43; humanitarian disaster in, 5–11; race and ancestry in, 37–42

Somali Bantu Experience: From East Africa to Maine, The (museum exhibit), 142–44, 148
Somali Bantus: assimilation and, 267–71; creation of term, 11, 79–80, 98–100; discrimination in refugee camps against, 66–67; ethnic identity of, 77–89, 222–27, 265–67, 308n4; in Kenyan refugee camps, 29–30, 59–60; in Lewiston, Maine, 11–12, 17–19, 27–28, 56, 110–13, 123–24; myths in Lewiston concerning, 139–67; repatriation to Somalia of, 52; resettlement experiences of, 29–30, 105–10, 215–17; security concerns about, 71–74; self-essentialization by, 89–100; U.S. resettlement policies and, 10–11, 30, 68–71, 74–76, 87–89, 295n51
Somali Bantu Youth Association of Maine (SBYAM), 153, 159, 176, 180; advocacy by, 271–75; assimilation and, 267–71; creation of, 244–46; ethnic identity issues and, 266–67; intergenerational gaps and efforts of, 262–64; marital cultural norms and, 255–57; Somali parenting and, 247–48
sovereignty, refugees and, 62, 293n3
standardized testing, burden for Somali students of, 193–97
state structures: impact on Somali refugees of, 171–76; in refugee camps, 79; refugees and, 58–59, 294n28
stereotypes of Somali refugees: myths in Lewiston based on, 140–67; teachers' management of, 190–97
strategies of containment, refugee regime and, 63
subsistence farming, research on, 6–11
Sudanese refugees, 65–67; "Lost Boys," 69, 74
support networks, Somali refugees' creation of, 165–67
suspension rates for Somali students, 187–91, 260–62, 306nn15–17

Tanzania, Somali Bantu ties with, 70, 83–84
teachers, Somali refugees and, 187–97
technology, refugee unfamiliarity with, 105
Temporary Assistance for Needy Families (TANF), 104, 117, 144–47
Terry, Fiona, 293n7